Second Edition

Classroom Assessment *for* Student Learning

DOING IT RIGHT - USING IT WELL

Jan Chappuis

Rick Stiggins

Steve Chappuis

Judith Arter

PEARSON

Boston Columbus Indianapolis New York San Francisco Upper Saddle River
Amsterdam Cape Town Dubai London Madrid Milan Munich Paris Montreal Toronto
Delhi Mexico City São Paulo Sydney Hong Kong Seoul Singapore Taipei Tokyo

Vice President and Editorial Director: Jeffery W. Johnston
Vice President and Publisher: Kevin Davis
Editorial Assistant: Lauren Carlson
Vice President, Director of Marketing: Margaret Waples
Senior Marketing Manager: Joanna Sabella
Senior Managing Editor: Pamela Bennett
Senior Project Manager: Mary M. Irvin
Senior Operations Supervisor: Matt Ottenweller
Senior Art Director: Diane Lorenzo
Cover Designer: Steven Davidson
Cover Art: SuperStock
Project Coordination: Element/Thomson North America
Composition: S4Carlisle Publishing Services
Copy Editor: Robert L. Marcum
Printer/Binder: Edwards Brothers Malloy
Cover Printer: Lehigh-Phoenix Color Corp.
Text Font: Palatino LT Std

Every effort has been made to provide accurate and current Internet information in this book. However, the Internet and information posted on it are constantly changing, so it is inevitable that some of the Internet addresses listed in this textbook will change.

Library of Congress Cataloging-in-Publication Data
Classroom assessment for student learning / Jan Chappuis . . . [et al.]. — 2nd ed.
p. cm.
Includes bibliographical references and index.
ISBN 978-0-13-268588-7
1. Educational tests and measurements—United States. 2. Motivation in education—United States.
3. Students—Rating of.
LB3051.C555 2012
370.15'40973—dc23
2011031746

10 9 8

ISBN 10: 0-13-268588-4
ISBN 13: 978-0-13-268588-7

ACKNOWLEDGMENTS

This book and CD are the result of a team effort, and that team extends far beyond us four authors. First and foremost, we wish to acknowledge colleagues from whom we have learned over the years: Carol Commodore of Oconomowoc, Wisconsin; Anne Davies of British Columbia; Cassandra Erkens of Lakeville, Minnesota; Janet Malone of Encinitas, California; Ken O'Connor of Toronto, Ontario; Donna Snodgrass of Cleveland State University; Vicki Spandel of Sisters, Oregon; and Ruth Sutton of Manchester, United Kingdom. Each has made unique and important contributions to our collective understanding of sound classroom assessment practice. In this same sense, we wish to express appreciation to the Assessment Reform Group of the United Kingdom, and particularly to professors Paul Black and Dylan Wiliam for their work in bringing to the forefront a world of exciting ideas about assessment *for* learning.

Many teachers and administrators graciously responded to our request for explanations of how classroom practice has changed as a result of their study of the first edition of this book. In sharing their reflections, each has contributed to the specificity and practicality of this second edition. We are grateful for their stories illustrating that changes in assessment practice can change the classroom environment and students' approach to learning.

We are in debt to the Kentucky Department of Education, especially to Karen Kidwell and the teams of educators who have worked over the past year to deconstruct the Common Core State Standards using our learning targets framework. The many lengthy discussions we have had together have enriched the content of Chapter 3. We are indebted also to Kim Zeidler-Watters, Director of the P–12 Math and Science Outreach Unit of PIMSER at the University of Kentucky, and Diane Johnson of Lewis County Schools in Kentucky for their deep knowledge of implementation of classroom assessment, their examples, and their valuable feedback.

On the production side, special thanks to Jennifer Cavanagh, our events coordinator, who beyond being able to find anything on the Internet, has an extraordinary eye for detail and quality. Also, our deepest gratitude for outstanding editorial work, insightful advice, and humor goes to our freelance editor, Robert L. Marcum. (As a side note, this is his final project. He is retiring after more than two and a half decades of service to the language he loves so well, and to the noble cause of enriching the lives and achievement potential of students everywhere. We sincerely wish him well.)

Finally, over the years, we have shared our ideas with many thousands of teachers across the country. We have benefited as you have shaped the concepts to fit your own classrooms and shared your applications with us. We have learned much about improving assessment practices from you, and for this we thank you all.

Jan Chappuis

Rick Stiggins

Steve Chappuis

Judy Arter

Portland, Oregon, May 2011

INTRODUCTION TO THE SECOND EDITION

Much has changed in the education landscape since the first edition of *Classroom Assessment* for *Student Learning* went to press in 2004, but the principles of assessment quality have remained the same. The second edition of this book remains deeply rooted in those principles, but you will find a number of significant changes in this edition, including the following:

- We have updated the context and the examples to address the current challenges you face and to refine our explanations of (1) the design considerations that will lead to accurate assessment and (2) the classroom applications that represent current thinking about most effective use.
- Our revisions are designed to help the book function as a teacher. Each chapter begins with its learning targets—what that chapter is designed to teach you—and ends with a selection of activities intended to help you master the chapter's learning targets. The activities are designed to deepen your understanding of the chapter content, provide discussion topics for learning-team meetings, and guide implementation of the practices taught in the chapter. The CD bundled at the back of the book includes all of the forms necessary for completing each activity.
- Teaching with the first edition of *Classroom Assessment* for *Student Learning* since 2004, we have encountered a multitude of great questions. We address them in the revised text, but some stand out as sufficiently important to deserve special attention, especially those representing common misconceptions. You will find these questions and answers, including advice on avoiding typical problems, in a feature called "FAQs" (Frequently Asked Questions") in the relevant chapters.
- Woven throughout the book are anecdotes from classroom teachers who have worked with our materials to implement sound classroom assessment practices. The anecdotes describe a key change in how they use assessment and subsequent effects on students, following the frame of "I used to. . . . Now I. . . . As a result. . . . " These stories illustrate how the assessment practices taught in this book can significantly change students' attitudes and approach to learning.
- We have included an expanded array of examples to illustrate the concepts presented in each chapter. All of the mathematics and English language arts examples are based on the Common Core State Standards. All other subject-specific examples derive from commonly found content standards in that subject.
- The new examples also offer a better balance between elementary and secondary applications.
- You may be approaching the study of classroom assessment as an individual, with a partner, or as a part of a team. All materials have been created to accommodate each of those three different learning contexts. For those who are working with a team, we have included information on the CD that explains how to set up a learning team, offers suggestions for planning and pacing the work, and gives advice on facilitating team meetings. In addition, we have included tips for success and suggestions for actions that district and building leadership can take to support your learning.

CONTENTS

Chapter 1 Classroom Assessment: Every Student a Learner 1

Chapter 1 Learning Targets 2
Classroom Assessment Literacy 2
Keys to Quality Classroom Assessment 3
  Key 1: Clear Purpose 4
  Key 2: Clear Targets 6
  Key 3: Sound Assessment Design 7
  Key 4: Effective Communication 8
  Key 5: Student Involvement 8
Classroom Assessment Competencies 10
Summary 12
Chapter 1 Activities 13
Activity 1.1 Keep a Reflective Journal 14
Activity 1.2 Connect Your Own Experiences to the Keys to Quality 14
Activity 1.3 Complete the Assessment Practices Inventory 15
Activity 1.4 Survey Students 16
Activity 1.5 Collect Samples of Student Work 16
Activity 1.6 Reflect on Your Own Learning 17
Activity 1.7 Set up a Growth Portfolio 18

Chapter 2 Clear Purpose: Assessment *for* and *of* Learning 19

Chapter 2 Learning Targets 19
A Balanced Assessment System 20
Impact of Formative Assessment on Achievement 22
  Distinguishing Between Formative and Summative Assessment 24
  Why the Distinction Is Important 26
  What This Has to Do with Clear Purpose 26
Seven Strategies of Assessment *for* Learning 27
  Where Am I Going? 28
  Where Am I Now? 30
  How Can I Close the Gap? 32
The Seven Strategies as a Progression 35
Summary 35
Chapter 2 Activities 36
Activity 2.1 Keep a Reflective Journal 37
Activity 2.2 Audit Your Assessments for Balance 37
Activity 2.3 Conduct a Team Self-evaluation 38

Activity 2.4 Assess Your Feedback Practices 39
Activity 2.5 Assess Prerequisites for Self-assessment and Goal Setting 40
Activity 2.6 Reflect on Your Own Learning 40
Activity 2.7 Select Portfolio Artifacts 41

Chapter 3 Clear Targets 42

Chapter 3 Learning Targets 43
Types of Learning Targets 44
Knowledge Targets 44
Reasoning Targets 47
Skill Targets 54
Product Targets 55
Disposition Targets 57
We Need Good Curriculum Guides 59
Deconstructing Complex Content Standards 60
1. Determine the Target Type 61
2. Identify the Prerequisite or Underlying Knowledge, Reasoning, and/or Skills 61
3. Check Your Work for Alignment and Reasonableness 66
Communicating Learning Targets to Students 68
Converting Knowledge and Reasoning Learning Targets to Student-friendly Language 69
When the Written Curriculum Is Not the Taught Curriculum 72
Using the Textbook in Place of the Curriculum 72
Using Units, Activities, or Projects in Place of the Curriculum 73
The Benefits of Clear Learning Targets 74
Benefits to Teachers 74
Benefits to Students 77
Benefits to Parents 78
Concluding Thoughts 80
Summary 81
Chapter 3 Activities 82
Activity 3.1 Keep a Reflective Journal 83
Activity 3.2 Connect Clear Targets to Assessment Quality 83
Activity 3.3 Classify Learning Targets 83
Activity 3.4 Identify Clear Learning Targets 84
Activity 3.5 Deconstruct a Content Standard 84
Activity 3.6 Create Student-friendly Learning Targets 85
Activity 3.7 Reflect on Your Own Learning 85
Activity 3.8 Select Portfolio Artifacts 86

Chapter 4 Sound Design 87

Chapter 4 Learning Targets 87
Assessment Methods—A Set of Four Options 88
Selected Response 89
Written Response 90
Performance Assessment 90
Personal Communication 91
Matching Assessment Methods to Learning Targets 93
Assessing Knowledge Targets 93
Assessing Reasoning Targets 96
Assessing Skill Targets 99
Assessing Product Targets 100
Assessment Development Cycle 102
Step 1: Determining Users and Uses 104
Step 2: Specifying the Intended Learning Targets 106
Step 3: Selecting the Appropriate Assessment Method(s) 107
Step 4: Determining the Appropriate Sample Size 107
The Steps in Test Development 112
Use and Refinement 113
Assessment *for* Learning Using Assessment Blueprints 115
Summary 115
Chapter 4 Activities 116
Activity 4.1 Keep a Reflective Journal 117
Activity 4.2 Practice with Target-method Match 117
Activity 4.3 Audit an Assessment for Clear Purpose 118
Activity 4.4 Audit an Assessment for Clear Learning Targets 119
Activity 4.5 Make a Test Blueprint 120
Activity 4.6 Try an Assessment *for* Learning Application 120
Activity 4.7 Reflect on Your Own Learning 121
Activity 4.8 Select Portfolio Artifacts 121

Chapter 5 Selected Response Assessment 122

Chapter 5 Learning Targets 123
When to Use Selected Response Assessment 124
Developing a Selected Response Test 125
Planning Steps 125
Step 1: Determine Users and Uses 125
Step 2: Identify Learning Targets 126
Step 3: Select Assessment Method(s) 126
Step 4: Determine Sample Size 126

Development and Use Steps 128
Step 5: Develop or Select Items, Exercises, Tasks, and Scoring Procedures 128
Step 6: Review and Critique the Overall Assessment for Quality Before Use 144
Step 7: Conduct and Score the Assessment and Step 8: Revise as Needed for Future Use 147
Selected Response Assessment *for* Learning 148
Where Am I Going? 148
Where Am I Now? 150
How Can I Close the Gap? 153
Summary 157
Notes 158
Chapter 5 Activities 159
Activity 5.1 Keep a Reflective Journal 160
Activity 5.2 Audit Items for Quality 161
Activity 5.3 Create a Test 163
Activity 5.4 Develop an Assessment *for* Learning Activity 164
Activity 5.5 Prepare Quiz or Test for Formative Use 165
Activity 5.6 Reflect on Your Own Learning 167
Activity 5.7 Select Portfolio Artifacts 168

Chapter 6 Written Response Assessment 169
Chapter 6 Learning Targets 170
When to Use Written Response Assessment 171
The Planning Stage for a Written Response Assessment 171
Determining Users and Uses 172
Identifying Learning Targets 172
Selecting Assessment Method(s) 172
Determining Sample Size 172
The Development Stage for a Written Response Assessment 174
Developing the Items 174
Short Answer or Extended Response? 175
Devising Short Answer Items 175
Devising Extended Written Response Items 177
Offering Choices 180
Preparing the Scoring Guides 181
Scoring Guide Options 181
Creating Task-Specific Rubrics 186
Creating General Rubrics 189
Critiquing the Overall Assessment for Quality 192

The Use Stage 192
Conducting and Scoring the Assessment 192
Revising for Future Use 193
Written Response as Assessment *for* Learning 194
Summary 197
Chapter 6 Activities 198
Activity 6.1 Keep a Reflective Journal 199
Activity 6.2 Evaluate a Written Response Assessment for Quality 199
Activity 6.3 Create a Short Answer Item and Scoring Guide 200
Activity 6.4 Create an Extended Written Response Item and Scoring Guide 201
Activity 6.5 Apply an Assessment *for* Learning Strategy 202
Activity 6.6 Reflect on Your Own Learning 202
Activity 6.7 Select Portfolio Artifacts 203

Chapter 7 Performance Assessment 204

Chapter 7 Learning Targets 205
When to Use Performance Assessment 205
Assessment Development Cycle for a Performance Assessment 207
Determining Users and Uses 207
Identifying Learning Targets 208
Selecting Assessment Method(s) 208
Determining Sample Size 208
Selecting, Revising, or Developing the Task 210
The Content of the Task 211
Structure of the Task 213
Sampling 216
Creating Tasks to Elicit Good Writing 218
Evaluating the Task for Quality 221
Selecting, Revising, or Developing Rubrics 226
Rubric Terminology 226
Content of the Rubric 227
Structure of the Rubric 231
Descriptors in the Rubric 232
Process for Developing Rubrics 235
Evaluating the Rubric for Quality 240
Use Stage 240
Seven Strategies for Using Rubrics as Instructional Tools in the Classroom 245
Where Am I Going? 245
Where Am I Now? 246
How Can I Close the Gap? 247

Using a Performance Task as an Assessment *for* Learning 250
Summary 252
Notes 253
Chapter 7 Activities 254
Activity 7.1 Keep a Reflective Journal 255
Activity 7.2 Evaluate a Performance Task for Quality 255
Activity 7.3 Create a Performance Task 256
Activity 7.4 Create a Writing Task Using the RAFTS Format 257
Activity 7.5 Evaluate a Rubric for Quality 258
Activity 7.6 Create a Rubric 259
Activity 7.7 Create a Student-friendly Version of a Rubric 260
Activity 7.8 Use Rubrics as Assessment *for* Learning 261
Activity 7.9 Structure a Task for Formative Use 262
Activity 7.10 Reflect on Your Own Learning 262
Activity 7.11 Select Portfolio Artifacts 263

Chapter 8 Personal Communication as Classroom Assessment 264

Chapter 8 Learning Objectives 266
When to Use Personal Communication Assessment 266
  Sampling 267
  Wait Time 269
Personal Communication Options: Instructional Questions and Answers 270
  Developing Questions to Assess Knowledge and Understanding 270
  Developing Questions to Assess Reasoning 270
  Suggestions for Effective Formative Use of Instructional Questions 271
  Summative Use of Instructional Questions 275
Personal Communication Options: Class Discussions 275
  Developing Class Discussion Topics and Questions 276
  Suggestions for Effective Use of Class Discussions 276
Personal Communication Options: Conferences and Interviews 279
  Developing Questions and Topics for Conferences and Interviews 279
  Suggestions for Effective Use of Conferences and Interviews 279
Personal Communication Options: Oral Examinations 280
  Developing Questions for Oral Examinations 280
  Suggestions for Effective Use of Oral Examinations 281

Personal Communication Options: Journals and Logs 281
Response Journals 282
Dialogue Journals 283
Personal Journals 283
Learning Logs 284
Possible Sources of Bias That Can Distort Results 284
Reminder of Problems and Solutions 285
Summary 286
Chapter 8 Activities 288
Activity 8.1 Keep a Reflective Journal 289
Activity 8.2 Frame Diagnostic Questions 289
Activity 8.3 Use Questioning Strategies to Deepen Understanding 290
Activity 8.4 Develop and Use a Class Discussion Rubric 291
Activity 8.5 Conduct a Line-up Discussion 292
Activity 8.6 Develop Oral Examination Questions 294
Activity 8.7 Use Journals or Logs in the Classroom 295
Activity 8.8 Reflect on Your Own Learning 296
Activity 8.9 Select Portfolio Artifacts 296

Chapter 9 **Record Keeping: Tracking Student Learning 297**
Chapter 9 Learning Targets 299
Preliminary Decisions 299
Differentiating Information for Formative or Summative Use 299
Deciding Where You Will Keep the Information 306
Record-keeping Guidelines 311
Guideline 1: Organize Entries by Learning Represented 311
Guideline 2: Track Information about Work Habits and Social Skills Separately 314
Guideline 3: Record Achievement Information by Raw Score, if Practical 316
Options for Student Record Keeping 318
Summary 323
Chapter 9 Activities 325
Activity 9.1 Keep a Reflective Journal 326
Activity 9.2 Plan Formative and Summative Assessment Events 327
Activity 9.3 Organize Your Recording System 328
Activity 9.4 Track Work Habits and Social Skills 329
Activity 9.5 Develop Student Record-keeping Forms 330
Activity 9.6 Reflect on Your Own Learning 331
Activity 9.7 Select Portfolio Artifacts 331

Chapter 10 Converting Summative Assessment Information into Grades 332

Chapter 10 Learning Targets 334
The Challenges of Report Card Grading 334
Three Grading Guidelines 336
Guideline 1: Use Grades to Communicate, Not to Motivate 336
Guideline 2: Report Achievement and Other Factors Separately 340
Guideline 3: Reflect Only Current Level of Achievement in the Academic Grade 341
Summarizing Information 342
Verify Accuracy of Data 342
Convert Entries to a Common Scale 343
Weight Information as Needed 343
Combine Information Thoughtfully 343
Converting Rubric Scores to Grades 345
Average Ratings 346
Pattern of Ratings 347
Combining Rubric Ratings with Other Assessment Information to Get a Final Grade 348
Reporting the Final Grade 350
Keep the Link to Learning Targets 350
Make Modifications with Care for Special Needs Students 352
Decide Borderline Cases with Extra Evidence 352
Involve Students 353
Six Steps to Accurate, Fair, and Defensible Report Card Grades 354
Rubric to Evaluate Grading Practices 354
Summary 358
Chapter 10 Activities 359
Activity 10.1 Keep a Reflective Journal 360
Activity 10.2 Develop Solutions Other than Grades 360
Activity 10.3 Analyze Steps in Your Grading Process 361
Activity 10.4 Revisit How You Convert Rubric Scores to Grades 362
Activity 10.5 Evaluate Your Grading Practices 362
Activity 10.6 Reflect on Your Own Learning 363
Activity 10.7 Select Portfolio Artifacts 363

Chapter 11 Portfolios 364

Chapter 11 Learning Targets 365
Kinds of Portfolios—Focus on *Purpose* 366
Growth Portfolios 366

Project Portfolios 367
Achievement Portfolios 367
Competence Portfolios 367
Celebration Portfolios 367
Working Folders 368
Portfolio Contents—Focus on *Learning Targets* 368
Artifact Selection 369
Work Sample Annotations 371
Student Self-reflection 372
Goal Setting 375
Sharing Options 375
Keys to Successful Use 376
1. Ensure Accuracy of the Evidence 376
2. Keep Track of the Evidence 376
3. Invest Time up Front 377
4. Make the Experience Safe 377
Summary 377
Chapter 11 Activities 379
Activity 11.1 Keep a Reflective Journal 380
Activity 11.2 Try a New Portfolio Option with Students 380
Activity 11.3 Revise an Existing Student Portfolio System 381
Activity 11.4 Start a Personal Portfolio 382
Activity 11.5 Review Your Own Classroom Assessment Portfolio 383
Activity 11.6 Reflect on Your Own Learning 383
Activity 11.7 Select Portfolio Artifacts 384
Activity 11.8 Reflect on Your Learning over Time 384

Chapter 12 Conferences About and with Students 385

Chapter 12 Learning Targets 386
The Feedback Conference 388
Keys to Success 388
The Goal-Setting Conference 390
Keys to Success 391
The Progress Conference 394
Focusing on Growth over Time 394
Focusing on Achievement Status 394
Identifying Participants 394
Preparing the Students 395
Preparing the Parents or Other Adults 395
Conducting a Two-Way Conference 396
Conducting a Three-Way Conference 396

Followup 396
The Showcase Conference 397
Preparing the Students 397
Conducting a Showcase Conference 397
Followup 398
The Intervention Conference 398
Summary 398
Chapter 12 Activities 400
Activity 12.1 Keep a Reflective Journal 401
Activity 12.2 Conduct and Debrief a Feedback Conference 402
Activity 12.3 Conduct and Debrief a Goal-setting Conference 403
Activity 12.4 Organize a Student-led Conference 404
Activity 12.5 Reflect on Your Own Learning 404
Activity 12.6 Select Portfolio Artifacts 405
Activity 12.7 Stage a Share Fair 406

Appendix: CD Table of Contents 408
References 411
Index 414

CHAPTER

1

Classroom Assessment: Every Student a Learner

Used with skill, assessment can motivate the reluctant, revive the discouraged, and thereby increase, not simply measure, achievement.

For many of us, *assessment* is probably not at the top of the list of topics when we think about what we want to spend time learning. But we would guess that, in the last few years, you may have been called upon to do one or more of the following things, each of which may have left you wishing for a stronger understanding of why it is important to do or of how to do it well.

- Develop common assessments with other teachers in your subject area or grade level.
- Work with a team to "deconstruct" the new Common Core State Standards to help identify what should be the content of daily instruction and assessment.
- Attend a Response to Intervention (RTI) training and then make a presentation to the rest of the faculty on the benefits for students.
- Focus on differentiated instruction this year as a strategy to help more students master content standards.
- Use more formative assessment in the classroom because the research says it will work.
- Move to a grading system that centers more on communicating what students know and can achieve and removes from grades such nonachievement variables as attendance, effort, and behavior.

All of these actions, along with many other currently popular school improvement initiatives involving assessment, are aimed at raising student achievement in an era of high-pressure accountability testing. Each action requires classroom teachers to have classroom-level assessment expertise to carry them out effectively. And yet the opportunity to develop that expertise may not have been available to you through preservice or inservice offerings.

Without a foundation of what we call *classroom assessment literacy*, few if any of these initiatives will lead to the improvements we want for our students. Assessment-literate educators understand that assessments can serve a variety of important *users* and fulfill *purposes* in both supporting and verifying learning. They know that quality assessments arise from *crystal-clear achievement targets* and are designed and built to satisfy specific *assessment quality control* criteria. Those steeped in the principles of sound assessment understand that assessment results must be *delivered into the hands of the intended user* in a timely and understandable form. Finally, they are keenly aware of the fact that assessment can no longer be seen merely as something adults do to students. Rather, students are constantly assessing their own achievement and acting on the inferences they draw about themselves. Assessment-literate educators know how to *engage students in productive self-assessments* that will support their learning success.

We have framed these components of assessment literacy, derived from the expertise of the measurement community, in terms of five keys to assessment quality. Each chapter will focus on one or more of these keys to quality. Each chapter includes activities you can complete individually, with a partner, or with a team to put the principles of assessment literacy into action in your classroom. By the end of your study, you will have the expertise needed to handle any classroom assessment challenge.

Chapter 1 Learning Targets

At the end of this chapter, you will know the following:

- What the five keys to classroom assessment quality are
- Why they are important to assessment accuracy and effective use of assessment information

CLASSROOM ASSESSMENT LITERACY

We define *classroom assessment literacy* as the knowledge and skills needed to do two things: (1) gather *accurate* information about student achievement, and (2) use the assessment process and its results *effectively* to improve achievement (Figure 1.1).

FIGURE 1.1 Definition of *Classroom Assessment Literacy*

The knowledge and skills needed to

1. Gather accurate information about student achievement.
2. Use the assessment process and its results effectively to improve achievement.

When people think about assessment quality, they often focus on the accuracy of the instrument itself—the extent to which the assessment items, tasks, and scoring rubrics produce accurate information. This is a key feature of assessment quality, but it gives a far from complete picture of what we have to understand to use assessment well in the classroom.

You may be surprised to know that teachers can spend up to 30 percent or more of their classroom time in assessment-related functions. No wonder—consider all of the things that go into and make up the classroom assessment process:

- Planning and managing both formative and summative assessments in the classroom
- Identifying, clarifying, and teaching to valued learning targets
- Designing or selecting high-quality assessment items and tasks
- Devising high-quality scoring keys, guides, and rubrics
- Using assessment results to plan further instruction
- Offering descriptive feedback during learning
- Designing assessments so that students can self-assess and set goals
- Tracking student achievement along with other relevant data
- Setting up a system so students can track and share their progress
- Calculating grades that accurately represent student achievement at the time they are assigned

When viewed as a larger picture, we see that the accuracy of assessment items, tasks, and scoring rubrics is only one slice of the pie. Prerequisites must be in place to ensure accuracy of results. In addition, classroom assessment quality requires that we use the assessment process and its results effectively. If our assessment practices don't result in higher achievement, we would say a component of quality is missing. And, because accurate assessment skillfully used benefits learning, this expanded definition of classroom assessment literacy must become part of our understanding of what it means to teach well. Figure 1.2 shows the expanded definition as an "Assessment Literacy Pie."

KEYS TO QUALITY CLASSROOM ASSESSMENT

All of the pieces contributing to sound classroom assessment instruments and practices are built on a foundation of the following five keys to quality:

1. They are designed to serve the *specific information needs of intended user(s)*.
2. They are based on clearly articulated and appropriate *achievement targets*.
3. They *accurately measure* student achievement.
4. They yield results that are *effectively communicated* to their intended users.
5. They *involve students* in self-assessment, goal setting, tracking, reflecting on, and sharing their learning.

FIGURE 1.2 Components of Classroom Assessment Literacy

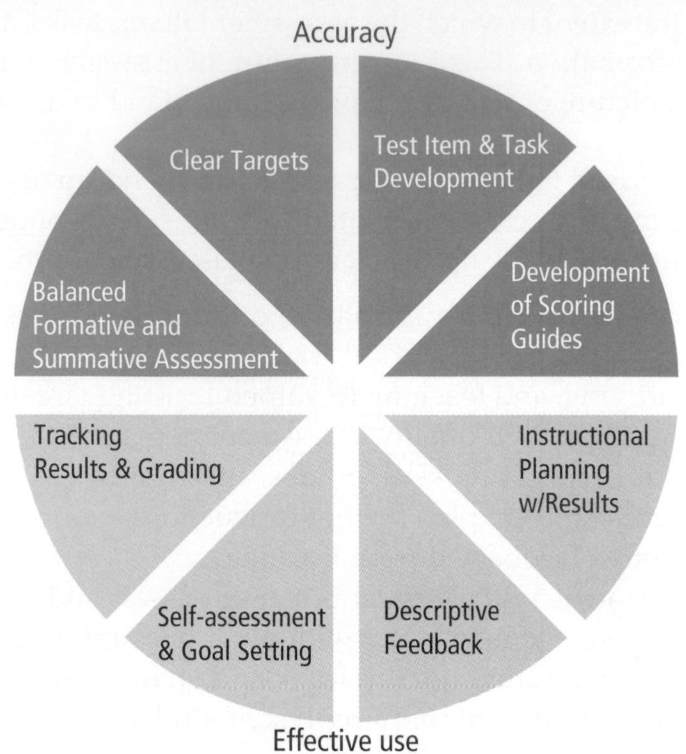

Figure 1.3 shows a graphic representation of the five keys to quality. We will use this figure as our "mall map" throughout the book to indicate which key or keys to quality each chapter addresses.

Key 1: Clear Purpose

We assess, in part, to gather information about student learning that will inform instructional decisions. Teachers and students make decisions every day that drive learning—they need regular information about what each student has and has not yet learned. We make some decisions frequently, such as when we decide what comes next in student learning within lessons or when we diagnose problems. Typically, these decisions, made day to day in the classroom based on evidence gathered from classroom activities and assessments, are intended to support student learning—to help students learn more. These are known collectively as *formative assessment* practices: formal and informal processes teachers and students use to gather evidence for the purpose of improving learning.

We make other decisions periodically, such as when we assign report card grades or identify students for special services. In this case, we rely on classroom assessment evidence accumulated over time to determine how much learning has occurred. Other instructional decisions are made less frequently, such as when school districts assess to inform the community about the efficacy of school programs or to decide whether to continue or discontinue a particular program. Often these decisions are based on results of once-a-year standardized tests reported in broad categories of

FIGURE 1.3 Keys to Quality Classroom Assessment

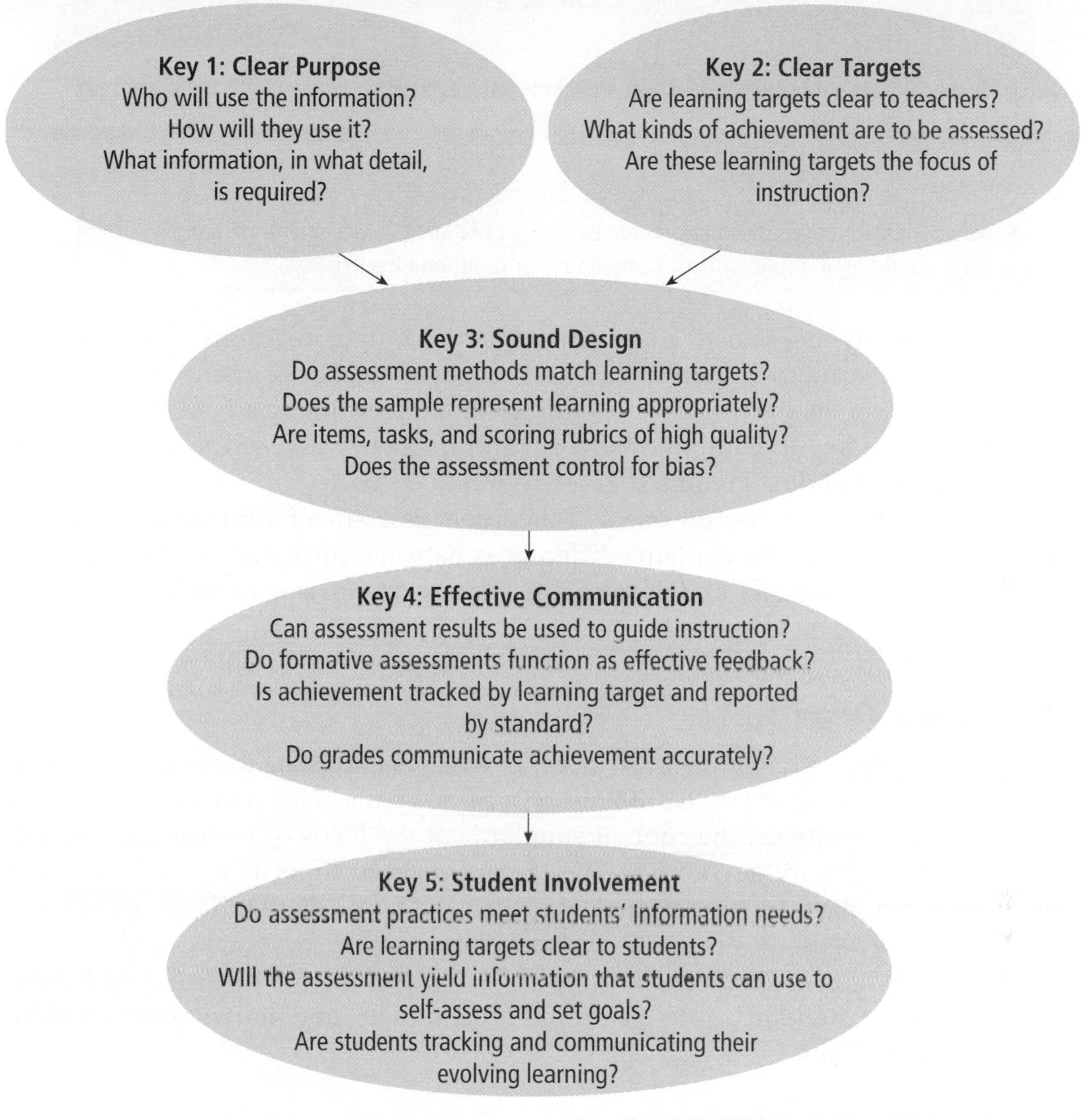

Key 1: Clear Purpose
Who will use the information?
How will they use it?
What information, in what detail, is required?

Key 2: Clear Targets
Are learning targets clear to teachers?
What kinds of achievement are to be assessed?
Are these learning targets the focus of instruction?

Key 3: Sound Design
Do assessment methods match learning targets?
Does the sample represent learning appropriately?
Are items, tasks, and scoring rubrics of high quality?
Does the assessment control for bias?

Key 4: Effective Communication
Can assessment results be used to guide instruction?
Do formative assessments function as effective feedback?
Is achievement tracked by learning target and reported by standard?
Do grades communicate achievement accurately?

Key 5: Student Involvement
Do assessment practices meet students' information needs?
Are learning targets clear to students?
Will the assessment yield information that students can use to self-assess and set goals?
Are students tracking and communicating their evolving learning?

learning. These are all examples of *summative assessment*: assessments that provide evidence of student achievement for the purpose of making a judgment about student competence or program effectiveness.

Formative and summative assessment can be thought of as assessment *for* learning and assessment *of* learning respectively (Figure 1.4). The purpose of one is to improve achievement, to *support* learning, and the purpose of the other is to measure, to *verify*, learning.

As you can see, assessment information can serve a variety of users—such as students, teachers, administrators, parents—and uses—both formative and

FIGURE 1.4 Formative and Summative Assessment

Formative Assessment

Formal and informal processes teachers and students use to gather evidence for the purpose of improving learning

Summative Assessment

Assessment information used to provide evidence of student achievement for the purpose of making a judgment about student competence or program effectiveness

summative. In any assessment context, whether informing decisions along the way (assessment *for* learning) or measuring achievement after it has happened (assessment *of* learning), we must start by understanding the information needs of the intended users. Those needs will determine the form and frequency of assessment, as well as the level and type of detail required in the results.

Chapter 2 describes the key users of classroom assessment information and their information needs. It also explains differences between formative and summative assessment (assessment *for* and *of* learning), the reasons for engaging in assessment *for* learning, and when to use each.

Key 2: Clear Targets

Besides beginning with intended use in mind, we must also start the assessment process with a clear sense of the learning to be assessed—the achievement expectations we hold for our students, the content standards at the focus of instruction. We call these *learning targets*. When our learning targets are clear to us as teachers, the next step is to ensure they are also clear to students. We know that students' chances of success improve when they start out with a vision of where they are headed.

Chapter 3 defines kinds of learning targets, explains how to turn broad statements of content standards into classroom-level targets, and shows ways to make them clear to students.

From the Field 1.1

Jim Lloyd

They say that "what gets measured gets done." While I believe there is some merit to this, I believe that a better way of phrasing this work is to say that "what is worthwhile, practical, and useful endures." Assessment *for* learning passes the worthwhile, practical, and usefulness tests.

In our district, we believe that all administrators play a vital role in helping classroom assessment for student learning gain traction. If our job is to educate all students up to high standards (a national education mission that is profoundly different from where it once started), then all the educators working within that system must have a clear focus and even clearer understanding as to what things make a profound impact on the achievement of the children. Clearly classroom assessments that are accurate and communicated appropriately are critical to our mission.

Our district leadership team set two goals that we wanted to be world-class at—clear learning intentions and high-quality feedback. We've had the good fortune of increasing our staffs' capacity in these areas through a partnership with Cleveland State University and have generated significant momentum, which in turn has impacted teachers' classroom practices and student learning. We have created local, cross-grade-level learning teams and are using our own teachers as a means to further our capacity and understanding of classroom assessment.

Classroom assessment *for* student learning isn't a simplistic instructional strategy. Rather, it is a way of being. It is a type of pedagogy that when used as a matter of practice makes a profound impact on the way the teacher engineers her learning environment and how the students work within it. We have witnessed firsthand how the learning environments in our school district have gone from great to greater as classroom assessment *for* student learning becomes more deeply embedded in our classrooms and in our students.

We believe that in order for systemic change to occur and endure it must be embraced by those it impacts most of all—teachers and students. Teachers who engage in quality classroom assessment *for* student learning as a matter of instructional practice have clearer student learning intentions, offer more regular and descriptive feedback, create more accurate assessments, communicate assessment results more effectively and involve students in the assessment process. All are ingredients for high levels of student engagement and learning. It has been our experience that Classroom Assessment *for* Student Learning impacts all learners—high, middle, and low achieving.

Jim Lloyd, Ed.D., *Assistant Superintendent*
Olmsted Falls City Schools, Olmsted, OH
January 2011

Key 3: Sound Assessment Design

Assessments can accurately or inaccurately reflect the current level of student learning. Obviously, our goal always is to generate accurate information. The previous two keys, *clear purpose* and *clear targets,* lay the foundation for quality assessment by telling us what needs to be assessed and what kind of results are needed. Next comes the challenge of creating an assessment that will deliver those results. This requires an assessment method capable of reflecting the intended target. Will it be selected response, written response, performance assessment, or personal communication? These four assessment methods are not interchangeable: each has strengths and limitations and each works well in some contexts but not in others. Our task always is to choose a proper method for the intended purpose and learning targets—the quality of our assessments hinges on it.

Chapter 4 describes the four assessment methods and provides practice in matching methods to learning targets. It also offers guidance on assessment planning with the intended purpose in mind.

After we have chosen a method, we develop it with attention to three other quality criteria. We must sample well by including just enough exercises to lead to confident conclusions about student achievement. We must build the assessment of high-quality items, tasks, or exercises accompanied by proper scoring schemes. And finally, every assessment situation brings with it its own list of things that can go wrong and that can bias the results or cause them to be inaccurate. To prevent these problems we must recognize and know how to eliminate or control for sources of bias.

Chapters 5 through 8 expand on these accuracy requirements for each individual assessment method: selected response (Chapter 5), written response (Chapter 6), performance assessment (Chapter 7), and personal communication (Chapter 8).

Key 4: Effective Communication

Once the information needs are clear, the learning targets are clear, and the information gathered is accurate, an assessment's results must be communicated to the intended user(s) in a timely and understandable way. When we do this well, we keep track of both formative and summative assessment results, and devise sharing options suited to the needs of whoever will act on the results. Communication of formative assessment information provides the kind of descriptive feedback learners need to grow. Communication in a summative assessment context leaves all recipients understanding the sufficiency of student learning such as when we convert summative assessment information into grades that accurately reflect achievement at a point in time.

Chapters 9 through 12 describe formative and summative record-keeping procedures, sound grading practices, and uses of portfolios and student-involved conferences to expand our communication options.

Key 5: Student Involvement

Student involvement is the central shift needed in our traditional view of assessment's role in teaching and learning. The decisions that contribute the most to student learning success are made, not by adults working in the system, *but by students themselves*. *Students* decide whether the learning is worth the effort required to attain it. *Students* decide whether they believe they are capable of reaching the learning targets. *Students* decide whether to keep learning or to quit working. It is only when students make these decisions in the affirmative that our instruction can benefit their learning. So an essential part of our classroom assessment job is to keep students in touch with their progress as learners in ways that keep them believing in themselves as learners so they will keep trying.

Techniques for involving students are woven throughout the chapters. Chapter 2 describes the research on the positive impact of student involvement on motivation and achievement. Chapter 3 provides specific ways to make learning targets clear to students. Chapters 5 through 8 include method-specific suggestions for involving students in self-assessment and goal setting. Chapters 9, 11, and 12 offer techniques for involving students in keeping track of and communicating about their own learning.

From the Field 1.2

Janna Smith

I used to think of assessment as an "ending" to a learning event. When preparing to teach a unit, my planning primarily consisted of looking at the objectives and crafting activities that would engage all students. The word *assessment* was a noun that referred only to a task generally used at the end to determine a grade. The things students were asked to do as part of an endpoint assessment task may—or may not—have been aligned to the key objectives. Items on an end-of-unit test were usually selected response or short-answer/essay, but for the most part that was just for variety's sake.

Now *assessment* is not a singular noun referring to an individual test or task, but refers to an ongoing process that is interwoven with instruction. The process no longer happens only at the end; in fact, it begins with pre-assessment. With my current group of 7th-grade mathematics students, I introduce a grid at the onset of each unit. The grid lists the learning targets for that unit, with space for students to record their analysis of the results of their pre-assessment, target by target.

Additional boxes are included for each target, where students list sources of evidence from daily work, quizzes, etc. Throughout the unit, we periodically pause for students to select which of the learning targets their evidence indicates they are doing well with and on which they need more support. I use their self-assessments along with my own records of their performance to determine mini-lessons, small-group instruction topics, and areas where we might move more quickly.

When I was first introduced to the principles of assessment *for* learning, I was a district-level administrator. My role consisted of providing professional development and supporting principals and teachers in implementing quality classroom assessment practices. I believed it could work and spoke passionately about how to integrate these strategies into instruction. I modeled lessons to demonstrate how learning targets could be turned into student-friendly language. I even taught a graduate-level course on classroom assessment in a school district, but I had never actually used assessment *for* learning in my own classroom! When I finally had that opportunity, I was determined to "walk my talk" with a group of 7th graders who have struggled with mathematics. I wanted to see my own "Inside the Black Box" (Black & Wiliam, 1998b) with my students, hoping it would result in increased achievement and motivation.

Making assessment *for* learning come to life in my own classroom has renewed my zeal for teaching. I am more focused on essential learning targets, and my students always know what we are learning, how they are doing, and what we can work on together to close any gaps. They have become fantastic self-assessors, using their "evidence files" to determine their own strengths and challenges. Most importantly, they are becoming more confident problem solvers who no longer avoid and complain about math. By going back to the classroom, I now know firsthand that using these strategies can have a significant positive impact on student learning.

Janna Smith, *classroom teacher*
Far Hills Country Day School, Far Hills, NJ
January 2011

CLASSROOM ASSESSMENT COMPETENCIES

Our mission with this book is to help improve the classroom assessment practices of all teachers wanting to do so. If we are successful, together we'll move assessment practices in the classroom from a collection of less-effective practices to a model that is grounded in the research of how to use classroom assessment to improve student learning. Figure 1.5 illustrates key shifts in thought and practice that are hallmarks of classroom assessment competency.

The teacher competencies listed in Figure 1.6 represent the big picture of what an assessment-literate teacher knows and can do within each of the five keys to quality.

FIGURE 1.5 Classroom Assessment: From . . . to . . .

From	To
Classroom tests disconnected from the focus of instruction	Classroom tests reflecting the written and taught curriculum
Assessments using only selected response formats	Assessment methods selected intentionally to reflect specific kinds of learning targets
"Mystery" assessments, where students don't know in advance what they are accountable for learning	Transparency in assessments, where students know in advance what they will be held accountable for learning
All assessments and assignments, including practice, "count" toward the grade	Some assessments and assignments "count" toward the grade; others are for practice or other formative use
Students as passive participants in the assessment process	Students as active users of assessments as learning experiences
Students not finding out until the graded event what they are good at and what they need to work on	Students being able to identify their strengths and areas for further study during learning

FIGURE 1.6 Classroom Assessment Competencies

Competency	Skills
1. *Clear Purpose* Assessment processes and results serve clear and appropriate purposes.	**a.** Identify the key users of classroom assessment information and know what their information needs are. **b.** Understand formative and summative assessment uses and know when to use each.
2. *Clear Targets* Assessments reflect clear student learning targets.	**a.** Know how to identify the five kinds of learning targets. **b.** Know how to turn broad statements of content standards into classroom-level learning targets. **c.** Begin instructional planning with clear learning targets. **d.** Translate learning targets into student-friendly language.
3. *Sound Design* Learning targets are translated into assessments that yield accurate results.	**a.** Design assessments to serve intended formative and summative purposes. **b.** Select assessment methods to match intended learning targets. **c.** Understand and apply principles of sampling learning appropriately. **d.** Write and/or select assessment items, tasks, scoring guides, and rubrics that meet standards of quality. **e.** Know and avoid sources of bias that distort results.
4. *Effective Communication* Assessment results function to increase student achievement. Results are managed well, combined appropriately, and communicated effectively.	**a.** Use assessment information to plan instruction. **b.** Offer effective feedback to students during the learning. **c.** Record formative and summative assessment information accurately. **d.** Combine and summarize information appropriately to accurately reflect current level of student learning.
5. *Student Involvement* Students are active participants in the assessment process.	**a.** Identify students as important users of assessment information. **b.** Share learning targets and standards of quality with students. **c.** Design assessments so students can self-assess and set goals on the basis of results. **d.** Involve students in tracking, reflecting on, and sharing their own learning progress.

They can be thought of as the *content standards* for this program of study. Within each of these competencies are specific understandings and actions, taught in each of the following chapters.

We understand that these classroom assessment competencies are not entirely new. Effective teachers already know a considerable amount about assessment; these practices have always been a part of good teaching. We offer our standards of good assessment practice to provide a cognitive structure for defining the domain, and to permit you to determine where you want to deepen your own assessment expertise.

Summary

Quality classroom assessment produces *accurate information* that is *used effectively* to increase student learning. This is the "do it right" and "use it well" of the book's title.

Accurate information comes from clearly identifying the purpose(s) for which information about student learning is being gathered, clearly defining learning targets for students, using the appropriate assessment method well, selecting a sample to accurately represent achievement of the intended learning, and avoiding circumstances that might bias results.

Effective use includes relying on accurate assessment results to plan instruction and interventions; using descriptive feedback and self-assessment tactics to help students understand their own progress; that is, their successes and areas for further study; and tracking and communicating achievement information clearly and in a way tailored to the user's needs.

These two overarching aspects of quality, *accuracy* and *effective use*, form the focus of the succeeding chapters of this book. Through the study and application of ideas in each chapter, you will learn to select, create, and use assessments that are of high quality and that engender student success.

CHAPTER 1 ACTIVITIES

End-of-chapter activities are intended to help you master the chapter's learning targets. They are designed to deepen your understanding of the chapter content, provide discussion topics for learning team meetings, and guide implementation of the practices taught in the chapter.

Forms and materials for completing each activity appear in editable Microsoft Word format in the Chapter 1 CD file. Documents on the CD are marked with this symbol:

Chapter 1 Learning Targets

1. Know what the five keys to classroom assessment quality are
2. Know why they are important to assessment accuracy and effective use of assessment information

---

Activity 1.1 Keep a Reflective Journal
Activity 1.2 Connect Your Own Experiences to the Keys to Quality
Activity 1.3 Complete the Assessment Practices Inventory
Activity 1.4 Survey Students
Activity 1.5 Gather Samples of Student Work
Activity 1.6 Reflect on Your Own Learning
Activity 1.7 Set up a Growth Portfolio

Activity 1.1

Keep a Reflective Journal

Keep a record of your thoughts, questions, and any implementation activities you tried while reading Chapter 1.

Reflective Journal Form

Activity 1.2

Connect Your Own Experiences to the Keys to Quality

After reading Chapter 1, complete this activity independently, with a partner, or with your team to understand the impact on students of sound and unsound assessment practices.

1. Think of a time you yourself were assessed and it was a *negative* experience. What made it negative?
2. Now think of a time you yourself were assessed and it was a *positive* experience. What made it positive?
3. Which of the five keys to assessment quality were involved in your *negative* experience?
4. Which of the five keys to assessment quality were involved in your *positive* experience?
5. What impact did each experience have on you?

Connect Own Experiences to Keys to Quality

Activity 1.3

Complete the Assessment Practices Inventory

In this independent activity, you conduct an ongoing self-assessment of your current understanding of classroom assessment practices.

1. Print the document "Assessment Practices Inventory" from the Chapter 1 file on the CD.
2. Answer the questions at the outset of your study of the text *Classroom Assessment* for *Student Learning: Doing It Right—Using It Well* (*CASL*). Use the 0–4 scale to fill in the column marked "Rating 1." Date the rating column. Then complete the reflection for Rating 1 at the end of the form.
3. Midway through your study of *CASL*, complete the survey again, filling in and dating the column marked "Rating 2." Complete the reflection for Rating 2 at the end of the form.
4. At the conclusion of your study, complete the survey for a third time, filling in and dating the column marked "Rating 3." Complete the reflection for Rating 3 at the end of the form.

This will provide you with an opportunity to look back and reflect on changes in your understanding and classroom practices that have resulted from your study. Consider using this as one of your first entries in a professional growth portfolio (described in Activity 1.7).

Assessment Practices Inventory

Activity 1.4

Survey Students

On the CD in the Chapter 1 file, you will find two sets of surveys—an elementary version and a secondary version—designed to elicit students' responses to important aspects of assessment. Each set has a pre-survey and a post-survey. The only difference between the pre- and post-surveys is the instructions; otherwise they are the same instrument. The surveys are anonymous—the information is intended to be examined and compared as a classroom set of data.

1. Select either the elementary or the secondary survey and print out the pre-survey form. Administer it to students at the start of your study of *CASL*.
2. Print out the post-survey. Administer it to students at the end of the school year (or semester).
3. Combine the class data and compare the results of the pre- and post-surveys. Use this information as one indicator of the impact of the practices you are using on students' attitudes about and understanding of assessment.

Elementary Student Pre-survey

Elementary Student Post-survey

Secondary Student Pre-survey

Secondary Student Post-survey

Activity 1.5

Collect Samples of Student Work

1. To document students' changes in achievement throughout the course of your study, collect samples of their work from the beginning. If you teach a large number of students or a number of subjects, you may want to focus on a handful of students—one or more typical strong learners, midrange learners, and struggling learners.
2. Collect samples periodically throughout the year.
3. Look for changes that are different from what you would normally expect to see.
4. Save these samples and include them in your own personal growth portfolio. These artifacts can be a powerful testament to your learning, as increased student growth is an important goal of your work.

None

Activity 1.6

Reflect on Your Own Learning

Review the Chapter 1 learning targets and select one or more that represented new learning for you or struck you as most significant from this chapter. Write a short reflection that captures your current understanding. If you are working with a partner or a team, either discuss what you have written or use this as a discussion prompt for a team meeting.

Activity 1.7

Set Up a Growth Portfolio

Part A: Growth Portfolio Option

We encourage you to collect evidence of your progress throughout the course of your study and recommend that you assemble the evidence in a growth portfolio—a collection of work selected to show growth over time—focused on classroom assessment literacy.

You may not want to include evidence of everything you have learned—you may want to narrow your focus somewhat. Each *CASL* chapter begins with a list of learning targets for that chapter. If one or more of those learning targets is an area of improvement for you, you may wish to complete the corresponding chapter activity or activities and use them as portfolio entries, along with anything else you develop along the way.

Many people find it helpful to keep a record of their thoughts and questions as they read each chapter and try out activities, both for their own learning and to prepare for learning team discussions. One of the activities for each chapter is to create a reflective journal entry that documents your thoughts, questions, and activities. This can also become part of a growth portfolio.

Part B: Portfolio Artifacts from Chapter 1

Any of the activities from this chapter can be used as portfolio entries for your own growth portfolio. Select activities you have completed or artifacts you have created that will illustrate your competence at the Chapter 1 learning targets:

1. Know what the five keys to classroom assessment quality are.
2. Know why they are important to assessment accuracy and effective use of assessment information.

If you are keeping a reflective journal, you may want to include Chapter 1's entry in your portfolio.

The portfolio entry cover sheet provided on the CD will prompt you to think about how each item you select reflects your learning with respect to one or more of these learning targets.

Chapter 1 Portfolio Entry Cover Sheet

CHAPTER

2

Clear Purpose: Assessment *for* and *of* Learning

If we can do something with assessment information beyond using it to figure grades, we can improve learning.

During the first decade of the twenty-first century, much was written about formative assessment—its impact on achievement, what it is and isn't, how to create formative assessments, how to use formative assessments, and how to use formative assessment teaching strategies in the classroom. In short, formative assessment has garnered the lion's share of assessment attention and established a pretty good name for itself.

Yet the reality is that most assessments in school remain summative—most "count" toward the grade. And, even though they only occur periodically, large-scale accountability assessments continue to dominate our thinking about what is most important.

This chapter begins our focus on the five keys to quality with Key 1: Clear Purpose (Figure 2.1). The questions of how to balance formative and summative assessments, when to use each, and why formative assessment is so important to student learning all trace back to the purpose for the assessment—who is going to use the information and how they intend to use it. This is the crux of Key 1.

Chapter 2 Learning Targets

At the end of this chapter you will know the following:

- How formative and summative assessment fit into a balanced assessment system
- The impact of formative assessment on student achievement
- Major differences between formative and summative assessment
- How formative and summative assessment relate to assessment quality
- What the Seven Strategies of Assessment *for* Learning are and how they connect to research on formative assessment

FIGURE 2.1 Keys to Quality Classroom Assessment

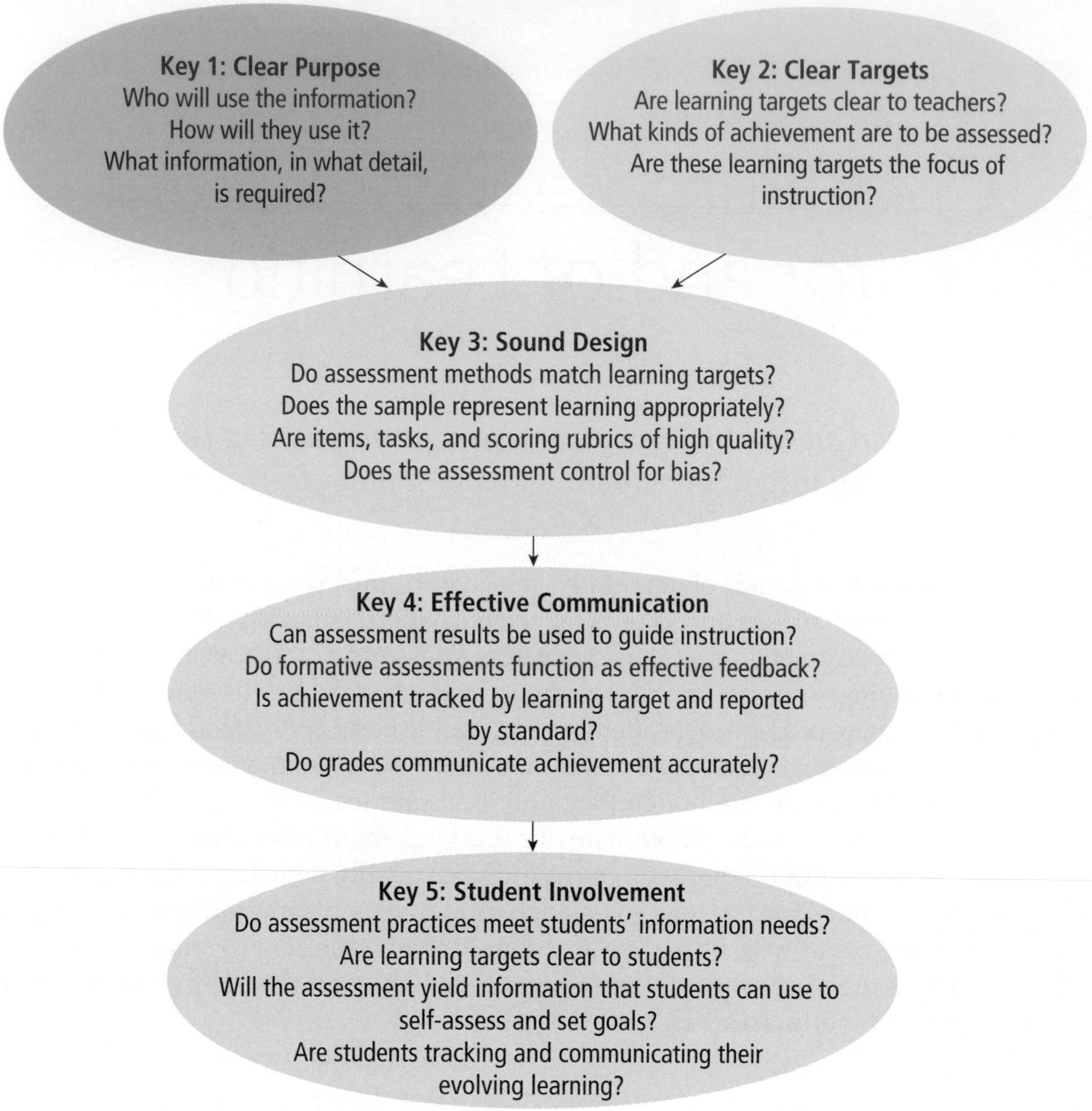

Key 1: Clear Purpose
Who will use the information?
How will they use it?
What information, in what detail, is required?

Key 2: Clear Targets
Are learning targets clear to teachers?
What kinds of achievement are to be assessed?
Are these learning targets the focus of instruction?

Key 3: Sound Design
Do assessment methods match learning targets?
Does the sample represent learning appropriately?
Are items, tasks, and scoring rubrics of high quality?
Does the assessment control for bias?

Key 4: Effective Communication
Can assessment results be used to guide instruction?
Do formative assessments function as effective feedback?
Is achievement tracked by learning target and reported by standard?
Do grades communicate achievement accurately?

Key 5: Student Involvement
Do assessment practices meet students' information needs?
Are learning targets clear to students?
Will the assessment yield information that students can use to self-assess and set goals?
Are students tracking and communicating their evolving learning?

A BALANCED ASSESSMENT SYSTEM

Who uses assessment information? The first answer that may come to mind is "the teacher," followed perhaps by parents, students, administrators, and the public. They all need assessment information to make decisions, but they make different kinds of decisions. No one assessment can fill everyone's information needs; different assessments are required. In a *balanced assessment system,* the key players' formative and summative information needs are identified and assessments are planned to meet their needs. Local district assessment systems serve to promote student success when they serve both formative and summative information needs across all three levels of assessment use: classroom assessment, interim or benchmark assessment, and annual testing (Chappuis, Commodore, & Stiggins, 2010). Figure 2.2 identifies the purposes a balanced assessment system serves. Note in this figure that the different users at each level face different decisions and therefore need different kinds of information to do their jobs of (1) supporting and (2) certifying student learning.

FIGURE 2.2 A Balanced Assessment System

Level: Classroom Assessment		
Key Issues	**Formative Context**	**Summative Context**
Key decision(s)	What comes next in the student's learning?	What standards has each student mastered? What grade does each student receive?
Decision makers	Students and teachers; parents	Teacher
Information needed	Evidence of where the student is now on learning progression leading to each standard	Evidence of each student's mastery of each relevant standard
Level: Interim/benchmark Assessment		
Key Issues	**Formative Context**	**Summative Context**
Key decision(s)	Which standards are our students consistently not mastering; that is, where can we improve instruction right away? Which students need specific help?	Did the program of instruction deliver as promised? Should we continue to use it?
Decision makers	Instructional leaders and teachers	Instructional leaders
Information needed	Standards our students are struggling to master; identification of who is struggling	Evidence of each student's mastery of each relevant standards
Level: Annual Testing		
Key Issues	**Formative Context**	**Summative Context**
Key decision(s)	What standards are our students consistently not mastering? Where and how can we improve instruction next year?	Are enough students meeting standards?
Decision makers	Curriculum and instructional leaders	School and community leaders
Information needed	Standards our students are struggling to master	Percent of students meeting each relevant standard

Source: Adapted with permission from Chappuis, S., C. Commodore, & R. Stiggins, *Assessment Balance and Quality: An Action Guide for School Leaders, 3rd ed.* (Portland, OR: Pearson Assessment Training Institute, 2010), pp. 14–15.

IMPACT OF FORMATIVE ASSESSMENT ON ACHIEVEMENT

Although Figure 2.2 balances information needs among the levels, of particular importance is how assessment information is used. Establishing a balance between formative and summative uses at the classroom and interim/benchmark levels is the most significant contributor to increased student achievement. In traditional classroom practice, most, if not all, of the assessments given have served summative purposes. And at the interim/benchmark level, even those assessments labeled as formative are often used only summatively, leading us to ask formative assessment expert Dylan Wiliam's question: "What's formative about it?"

We know now that formative assessment is reported to cause gains in student achievement, but we have to dig deeper into its many variations to learn what gains to expect and which practices are likely to lead to them. For this information, we look to the research.

The most well-known body of evidence was assembled and summarized by two British researchers, Paul Black and Dylan Wiliam. They conducted a comprehensive review of studies on formative assessment practices that collectively encompassed kindergarteners to college students; represented a range of subject areas, including reading, writing, social studies, mathematics, and science; and were carried out in numerous countries throughout the world, including the United States (Black & Wiliam, 1998a).

The gains they found were among the largest reported for any educational intervention. Typical effect sizes were between 0.4 and 0.7 (Black & Wiliam, 1998b). In some studies they reviewed, certain formative assessment practices increased the achievement of low-performing students to the point of approaching that of high-achieving students. To put the standard deviation numbers into perspective, a 0.4 to 0.7 achievement gain translates to 15 to 25 percentile points on commonly used standardized test score scales. For example, a student scoring at the 45th percentile on a standardized test such as the ITBS, who then attained a 0.7 standard deviation gain, would score at the 70th percentile. These are whopping achievement gains—we don't accomplish them with a good night's sleep the night before the test, snacks on the day of the test, or a pep rally. As one might guess, these formative assessment practices were not a matter of ingenious test preparation.

These are the reported gains that have launched a thousand "formative assessment" products. But the size of the achievement gains is only half of the story. The other half is what occurred to cause the gains. In reviewing the interventions featured in the highest-impact studies, Black and William (1998b) make the following observations:

- "Opportunities for students to express their understanding should be designed into any piece of teaching, for this will initiate the interaction through which formative assessment aids learning" (p. 143).

- "The dialogue between pupils and teachers should be thoughtful, reflective, focused to evoke and explore understanding, and conducted so that all pupils have an opportunity to think and to express their ideas" (p. 144).
- "Feedback to any pupil should be about the particular qualities of his or her work, with advice on what he or she can do to improve, and should avoid comparisons to other pupils" (p. 143).
- "If formative assessment is to be productive, pupils should be trained in self-assessment so that they can understand the main purposes of their learning and thereby grasp what they need to do to achieve" (p. 143).

Therefore, they suggest, the following practices are necessary to achieve the gains promised by formative assessment:

- Use of classroom discussions, classroom tasks, and homework to determine the current state of student learning/understanding, with action taken to improve learning/correct misunderstandings
- Provision of descriptive feedback, with guidance on how to improve, during the learning
- Development of student self- and peer-assessment skills

Unfortunately, none of these can be purchased as formative items or tests. They are all *practices*, not *instruments*. There is no magic test or tool—we cannot buy our way to achievement-through-assessment nirvana. Fortunately, the practices can all be learned. Even more fortunately, they are not new. Good teaching has included these components all along. However, in our accountability-saturated environment, we may have left more than children behind—we may have also left a few good teaching and assessment practices behind.

My Classroom Then and Now 2.1

Kristen Gillespie

I used to . . .

At the end of a class I would ask if there were any questions. I left it up to the individual to raise his or her hand to signal the level of understanding and ask questions.

Now I . . .

Each student is assigned a sticky note with his or her name on it. When prompted, students move their names to one of three boards. One board states that the child is on track and feels comfortable with the information from class. The second board signals to me that the child still has some questions and needs more practice. The third board lets me know that the child needs individual attention to understand the material. Students are asked to move their sticky notes approximately 3–5 times per week.

Why I changed. . .

I noticed that it was simply easier and less embarrassing for the student to not raise his or her hand when asked if anyone needed clarification. I realized that each student had to take more responsibility for his or her own learning. Student self-evaluation is priceless, not only to the student but also the teacher. I wanted to create an environment where students practiced self-monitoring and made deliberate decisions about their comprehension levels.

What I notice as a result . . .

The students look forward to moving their sticky notes. Those on the first board feel satisfied and proud of themselves. On the other hand, the students on the other two boards get the extra help they need, ultimately leading to a feeling of success.

Over the course of the school year, students realize that placing their sticky notes in the accurate location has rewards. My students are able to self-assess and get additional help thereby avoiding a poor test grade.

Source: Used with permission from 6th-grade mathematics, reading, and English teacher Kristen Gillespie, Olmsted Falls City Schools, Olmsted Falls, OH, January 2011.

Distinguishing Between Formative and Summative Assessment

To further understand the distinction between formative and summative assessment, we come back to our definitions:

> *Formative assessment:* Formal and informal processes teachers and students use to gather evidence for the purpose of improving learning
>
> *Summative assessment:* Assessment information used to provide evidence of student achievement for the purpose of making a judgment about student competence or program effectiveness

When engaged in formative assessment practices, teachers use assessment information during the learning to diagnose student needs, plan next steps in instruction, provide students with targeted practice, and offer effective feedback. Students use assessment information to offer each other effective feedback, to self-assess, and to set goals for improvement. They can also use it to track, reflect on, and share their progress. When engaged in summative assessment, teachers use assessment information after learning has taken place to determine the level of student achievement at a given point in time in order to determine a student's report card grade from chapter and unit tests, final exams, and term projects, for example. One form of assessment *supports* learning, the other *verifies* it.

We also call formative assessment by another term, *assessment* for *learning.* We do that in part because formative assessment has taken on a number of different meanings and is commonly interpreted as assessing frequently and using the results to plan the next steps in instruction. However, the research on formative assessment includes practices beyond those, as we have seen, so assessment *for* learning is the term we prefer to indicate the collection of practices necessary to realize significant achievement gains.

By the same token, we call summative assessment *assessment* of *learning.* If you prefer the terms "formative" and "summative," feel free to use them. We will use them throughout the book interchangeably with assessment *for* learning and assessment *of* learning. Just remember to include *descriptive feedback to students* and *student involvement in the assessment process* on the formative side. See Figure 2.3 for a summary of key differences.

FIGURE 2.3 Assessment *of* and *for* Learning: Summary of Key Differences

	Assessment *for* Learning	**Assessment *of* Learning**
Reasons for Assessing	Promote increases in achievement to help students meet more standards Support ongoing student growth and improvement	Document individual or group achievement or mastery of standards Measure achievement status at a point in time for purposes of reporting or accountability
Audience	Students about themselves	Others about students
Focus of Assessment	Specific achievement targets selected by teachers that enable students to build toward standards	Achievement standards for which schools, teachers, and students are held accountable
Place in Time	A process during learning	An event after learning
Primary Users	Students, teachers, parents	Policy makers, program planners, supervisors, teachers, students, parents
Typical Uses	Provide students with insight to improve achievement Help teachers diagnose and respond to student needs Help parents see progress over time Help parents support learning	Grading decisions Promotion and graduation decisions Certify student competence Sort students according to achievement

Source: Adapted from *Understanding School Assessment* (pp. 17–18), by J. Chappuis & S. Chappuis, 2002, Upper Saddle River, NJ: Pearson Education.

Why the Distinction Is Important

Understanding the distinction between assessment *for* learning (formative assessment) and assessment *of* learning (summative assessment) is pivotal to realizing gains in student achievement. The larger gains attributable to formative assessment practices will not materialize unless certain conditions are met:

1. The assessment instrument or event is designed so that it aligns directly with the content standards to be learned.
2. All of the instrument or event's items or tasks match what has been or will be taught.
3. The instrument or event provides information of sufficient detail to pinpoint specific problems, such as misunderstandings, so that teachers can make good decisions about what actions to take, and with whom.
4. The results are available in time to take action with the students who generated them.
5. Teachers and students do indeed take action based on the results. (Chappuis, 2009, p. 6)

If one or more of these conditions is missing, the assessment will not cause increased learning, no matter what it is called.

What This Has to Do with Clear Purpose

Establishing the purpose for an assessment is the first key to assessment quality. To ensure that our assessments and assessment practices are of high quality, we ask three questions at the planning stage:

1. Who is going to use the information?
2. How will they use it?
3. What information, in what detail, do they need?

Answers to the first question, at the classroom level, as we have seen in Figure 2.2, are generally *the student, the teacher,* or *the parent.* Answers to the second question follow one of two paths, formative or summative. What are the decisions to be made? Formative—intended to inform instruction (for teacher and student) during the learning? Or summative—used to report about learning that has already occurred?

The answer to the third question is directly dependent on answers to questions one and two—who needs the information and what they will do with it. As a matter of fact, all assessment design decisions flow from those two initial questions and so we will be revisiting them continuously throughout the book. As soon as we have identified who is going to use the information and what decisions the information will be used to make, we know which path, formative or summative, to take.

WHAT CLEAR PURPOSE HAS TO DO WITH ACHIEVEMENT. Let's think about the student for a moment. From a student's point of view, most every assignment is an assessment. Students complete assessments to meet teachers' needs, their district's needs, their state's needs, and their country's needs. How often do they experience assessments that meet *their* needs—not indirectly through the decisions that others make on their behalf, but directly? How long are we going to hammer away at increased achievement through changing teacher actions alone? Until we acknowledge the student's crucial role—if they would only show up/try/do their work—we will continue to change everything but the student. Formative assessment practices work to increase achievement because they change *the student's* interaction with assessment.

SEVEN STRATEGIES OF ASSESSMENT *FOR* LEARNING

Effective formative assessment practices all lead to action on the part of the teacher *and the student* that improves learning. As Chappuis (2009, p. 4) states, "Well-known educational researchers emphasize this point when they describe what is at the heart of formative assessment:"

> Formative assessment, therefore, is essentially feedback (Ramaprasad, 1983) both to the teachers and to the pupil about present understanding and skill development in order to determine the way forward. (Harlen & James, 1997, p. 369)
>
> [Formative assessment] refers to assessment that is specifically intended to provide feedback on performance to improve and accelerate learning. (Sadler, 1998, p. 77)
>
> Formative assessment is defined as assessment carried out during the instructional process for the purpose of improving teaching or learning . . . What makes formative assessment formative is that it is immediately used to make adjustments so as to form new learning. (Shepard, 2008, p. 281) [all items cited in Chappuis, 2009, p. 4]

In an often-cited article describing how formative assessment improves achievement, Australian researcher Royce Sadler (1989) concludes that it hinges on developing students' capacity to monitor and adjust the quality of their own work during production:

> The indispensable conditions for improvement are that the *student* comes to hold a concept of quality roughly similar to that held by the teacher, is able to monitor continuously the quality of what is being produced *during the act of production itself*, and has a repertoire of alternative moves or strategies from which to draw at any given point. (p. 121, emphasis in original)

Many teachers offer feedback regularly, as suggested by the research. Many teachers have engaged students in self-assessment and goal setting. These are good ideas that have been a part of effective teaching all along. Yet sometimes these practices work and sometimes they don't. Some students are more willing and able to

FIGURE 2.4 Seven Strategies of Assessment for Learning

Where am I going?

1. Provide a clear and understandable vision of the learning target.
2. Use examples and models of strong and weak work.

Where am I now?

3. Offer regular descriptive feedback.
4. Teach students to self-assess and set goals.

How can I close the gap?

5. Design lessons to focus on one learning target or aspect of quality at a time.
6. Teach students focused revision.
7. Engage students in self-reflection, and let them keep track of and share their learning.

Source: Reprinted from *Seven Strategies of Assessment* for *Learning* (p. 12), by J. Chappuis, 2009, Upper Saddle River, NJ: Pearson Education. Reprinted by permission.

take advantage of them than others. One contributing factor to success is how we set up the learning and assessment environment. Another is how we prepare students. Through careful reading of studies on formative assessment as well as on goal orientations (Ames, 1992; Butler & Neuman, 1995; Schunk, 1996; Shepard, 2008), we have organized these research-based recommendations into an instructional framework, the Seven Strategies of Assessment *for* Learning, which builds in the prerequisites to success.

The seven strategies, shown in Figure 2.4, are structured around three formative assessment questions, drawn from the work of Sadler and others:

- Where am I going?
- Where am I now?
- How can I close the gap?

Where Am I Going?

STRATEGY 1: PROVIDE STUDENTS WITH A CLEAR AND UNDERSTANDABLE VISION OF THE LEARNING TARGET. Share with your students the learning target(s), objective(s), or goal(s), either at the outset of instruction or before they begin an independent practice activity. Use language students understand, and check to make sure they do understand. Ask, "Why are we doing this activity? What are we learning?"

Convert learning targets into student-friendly language by defining key words in terms students understand. Ask students what they think constitutes quality in a product or performance learning target, then show how their thoughts match with the scoring guide or rubric you will use to define quality. Provide students with scoring guides written so they can understand them. For some learning targets, you can develop scoring criteria with them.

STRATEGY 2: USE EXAMPLES AND MODELS OF STRONG AND WEAK WORK. Use models of strong and weak work—anonymous student work, work from life beyond school, and your own work. Begin with work that demonstrates strengths and weaknesses related to problems students commonly experience, especially the problems that most concern you. Ask students to analyze these samples for quality and then to justify their judgments. Use *only* anonymous work. If you have been engaging students in analyzing examples or models, they will be developing a vision of what the product or performance looks like when it's done well.

Model creating a product or performance yourself. Show students the true beginnings, the problems you run into, and how you think through decisions along the way. Don't hide the development and revision part, or students will think they are doing it wrong when it is messy for them at the beginning, and they won't know how to work through the rough patches.

My Classroom Then and Now 2.2

Jessica Barylski, Audrey Eckert, & Robyn Eidam

We used to . . .

When concluding a writing lesson, we used to have students conduct a peer review of their work with a partner. We would provide them with checklists and tell them to use these checklists, assuming that they would know what to do. While students were giving each other feedback, we would monitor their conversations. We noticed that students simply read their writing pieces to each other and gave very few suggestions to improve their writing because they believed that was what peer review was.

Now we . . .

We have begun providing strong and weak examples in many of our lessons. To introduce peer review now, we list the criteria for quality peer feedback. Then we show the students a videotape of ourselves modeling weak and strong examples of peer feedback. Including this component adds a visual model to help the students engage. As students watch the clips, they are looking for the criteria that will help them identify the strong example. After thoroughly discussing each video clip, the students apply the peer feedback criteria to their own writing pieces.

Why we changed . . .

Peer feedback was often an area of difficulty for students due to its higher level of thinking. Students never really understood how to participate in the peer review process beyond reading the paragraph and we, as teachers, knew we needed to find a better way to teach them. When we began using formative assessment practices in our classrooms, we became more aware of how using strong and weak examples can impact student learning.

What we notice as a result . . .

First and foremost, the skills the students acquired from this activity were above and beyond our expectations. The students were engaged and focused throughout not only the videos but also during their peer feedback conferences. It was more meaningful for them to see their teachers engaged in a video that was outside of their normal routine. They took ownership of their peer review process, they followed the peer feedback model and criteria, and they took their time and allowed for corrections. They used constructive criticism and their conversations were more meaningful than in the past. We saw growth and improvement in our students' final writing pieces as well.

Source: Used with permission from 4th-grade language arts team teachers Jessica Barylski, Audrey Eckert, and Robyn Eidam, Olmsted Falls Intermediate School, Olmsted Falls, OH, January 2011.

Where Am I Now?

STRATEGY 3: OFFER REGULAR DESCRIPTIVE FEEDBACK. *Effective feedback* can be defined as information provided to students that causes an improvement in learning as a result. In our current system, most of the work students do is graded and often, these grades are the only formal feedback they receive. However, grades do not function as effective feedback. They deliver a coded evaluation without specific information about what students did well or what their next steps in learning might be.

Researchers and those interpreting their work have examined what causes assessment information to function as effective feedback to students—what kind of feedback will cause the most improvement in student (Ames, 1992; Butler, 1988; Hattie & Timperley, 2007; Shepard, 2001). Their major findings include the following:

- It isn't enough to be descriptive—a major contributor to effectiveness is *what* is described.

FIGURE 2.5 Characteristics of Effective Feedback

Effective Feedback

1. Directs attention to the intended learning, pointing out strengths and offering specific information to guide improvement
2. Occurs during learning, while there is still time to act on it
3. Addresses partial understanding
4. Does not do the thinking for the student
5. Limits corrective information to the amount of advice the student can act on

Source: Reprinted from *Seven Strategies of Assessment* for *Learning* (p. 57), by J. Chappuis, 2009, Upper Saddle River, NJ: Pearson Education. Reprinted by permission.

- Feedback directing attention to the learning leads to greater achievement than feedback directing attention to characteristics of the learner.
- Feedback is most effective when it points out strengths in the work as well as areas needing improvement.

We have translated feedback research findings into five characteristics of effective feedback, shown in Figure 2.5.

With that in mind, offer descriptive feedback instead of grades on work that is for practice. Descriptive feedback should reflect student strengths and weaknesses with respect to the specific learning target(s) they are trying to hit in a given assignment. Feedback is most effective when it identifies what students are doing right, as well as what they need to work on next. All learners, especially struggling ones, need to know that they did something right, and our job as teachers is to find it and label it for them, before launching into what they need to improve.

Remember that learners don't need to know everything that needs correcting all at once. Narrow your comments to the specific knowledge and skills emphasized in the current assignment and pay attention to how much feedback learners can act on at one time. Don't worry that students will be harmed if you don't point out all of their problems. Identify as many issues as students can successfully act on at one time, independently, and then figure out what to teach next based on the other problems in their work.

Providing students with descriptive feedback is a crucial part of increasing achievement. Feedback helps students answer the question, "Where am I now?" with respect to "Where do I need to be?" You are also modeling the kind of thinking you want students to engage in when they self-assess.

STRATEGY 4: TEACH STUDENTS TO SELF-ASSESS AND SET GOALS. Teaching students to self-assess and set goals for learning is the second half of helping students answer the question, "Where am I now?" Self-assessment is a necessary part of learning, not an add-on that we do if we have the time or the "right" students. Struggling students are the right students, as much as any others. The research described previously tells us it is they who gain the most (cf. White & Frederiksen, 1998).

Self-assessment includes having students do the following:

- Identify their own strengths and areas for improvement. You can ask them to do this before they show their work to you for feedback, giving them prior thoughts of their own to "hang" it on—your feedback will be more meaningful and will make more sense.
- Write in a response log at the end of class, recording key points they have learned and questions they still have.
- Using established criteria, select a work sample for their portfolio that proves a certain level of proficiency, explaining why the piece qualifies.
- Offer descriptive feedback to classmates.
- Use your feedback, feedback from other students, or their own self-assessment to identify what they need to work on and set goals for future learning.

How Can I Close the Gap?

STRATEGY 5: DESIGN LESSONS TO FOCUS ON ONE LEARNING TARGET OR ASPECT OF QUALITY AT A TIME. When assessment information identifies a need, adjust instruction to target that need. This strategy scaffolds learning by narrowing the focus of a lesson to help students master a specific learning goal or to address specific misconceptions or problems. If you are working on a learning target having more than one aspect of quality, build competence one block at a time.

For example, mathematics problem solving requires choosing a workable strategy as one component. A science experiment lab report requires a statement of the hypothesis as one component. Writing requires an introduction as one component. Look at the components of quality and then teach them one part at a time, making sure that students understand that all of the parts ultimately must come together.

My Classroom Then and Now 2.3

Jeff Overbay

I used to . . .

I used a CD-ROM to generate a topic match pre-test. The test would be mostly multiple-choice questions and a few short answer questions. These assessments would be administered at the beginning of the year and before each unit.

Now I . . .

I use the agree–disagree format to design a 10–12 question pre-assessment.

Example Topic:	Agree	Disagree	Depends	Don't Know
1. A ***Mixture*** cannot be separated using physical properties.				
2. A ***Compound*** is a pure substance composed of two or more elements.				

Why I changed . . .

The old pre-assessments had little value. I could never grade them all in a timely manner and as a result very little data could be gained or used in an effective way. The new agree–disagree format allows me to quickly check the students' prior knowledge about any given topic.

What I notice as a result . . .

This method serves several purposes for the classroom teacher. First, it helps me narrow the focus on where to begin teaching any given unit. Secondly, I could grade the assessment in a timely manner and use the data to drive my instruction. It gives me a starting point. Thirdly, it helps me to decide whether to review quickly or slowly depending on the students' answers to the questions. This *formative assessment* has great value in beginning a new unit of study.

This assessment is not given a score. This allows students to self-assess and takes some of the fear out of "getting a grade." Once they realize that they can be honest without the fear of failure, the information gathered will be more accurate. As a result, the data can be used in an effective way and the stage is set for learning for the individual student.

Source: Used with permission from 7th & 8th grade science teacher Jeff Overbay, Bell County School District, Pineville, KY, 2011.

STRATEGY 6: TEACH STUDENTS FOCUSED REVISION. This is a companion to Strategy 5. After focusing on an area of need, instead of retesting and grading, let students practice it in small segments and offer feedback focused just on that segment. This narrows the volume of feedback students need to act on at a given time and raises their chances of success in doing so, again especially for struggling learners—a time saver for you, and more instructionally powerful for students.

Some ways to help students practice revision include the following:

- Have students work in pairs to critique an anonymous sample and revise it using their own advice.
- Ask students to write a letter to the creator of an anonymous sample they have just critiqued, suggesting how to make it stronger for the aspect of quality discussed.
- Ask students to analyze your own work for quality and make suggestions for improvement. Revise your work using their advice. Ask them to again review it for quality.

These exercises will prepare students to work on a current product or performance of their own, revising for the aspect of quality being studied. You can then give feedback on just that aspect.

STRATEGY 7: ENGAGE STUDENTS IN SELF-REFLECTION, AND LET THEM KEEP TRACK OF AND SHARE THEIR LEARNING. Engage students in tracking, reflecting on, and communicating about their own progress. Any activity that requires students to reflect on what they are learning and to share their progress both reinforces the learning and helps them develop insights into themselves as learners. These kinds of activities give students the opportunity to notice their own strengths, to see how far they have come, and to feel in control of the conditions of their success. By reflecting on their learning, they deepen their understanding, and will remember it longer. In addition, it is the learner, not the teacher, who is doing the work.

Here are some examples of Strategy 7 activities:

- Students write a process paper, detailing how they solved a problem or created a product or performance. This analysis encourages them to think like professionals in your discipline.
- Students write a letter to their parents about a piece of work, explaining where they are now with it and what they are trying to do next.
- Students track their own progress toward mastery of learning targets.
- Students reflect on their growth. "I have become a better reader this year. I used to . . . , but now I . . . "
- Students help plan and participate in conferences with parents and/or teachers to share their learning.

The Seven Strategies as a Progression

These seven strategies reflect a progression that unfolds in the classroom over time. Students have trouble engaging in later steps (such as self-assessment) if they have not had experience with earlier steps (understanding learning targets and reliably assessing work). Likewise, it is much harder for students to communicate their progress if the learning targets are not clear, if they are not adept at assessing their work, and if they don't know what they need to do to improve.

Assessment *for* learning can have a powerful impact on student achievement if carried out thoughtfully. It enables students to take control of their own learning by providing a clear vision of the learning targets they are to attain, teaching them to assess where they are with respect to the target, and offering strategies they can use to close the gap between where they are and where they need to be. The research on goal orientations, feedback, and self-assessment comes together to support assessment for learning as the best use of assessment in the service of student learning and well-being.

We give suggestions throughout this book for how to implement each of the seven strategies. For a more in-depth treatment, see Chappuis, 2009.

Summary

In this chapter we have described the characteristics of a balanced assessment system—one that is designed to meet the information needs of all key instructional decision makers. All levels of the system—district, school, and classroom—have a role to play; however, the foundation of a truly effective assessment system is in the classroom—the one level that has shown that it can deliver improved achievement. We reviewed the impact of formative assessment noted by researchers, looking at the achievement gains and the high-impact practices associated with the gains.

We equated formative assessment with assessment *for* learning and summative assessment with assessment *of* learning. Assessment *for* learning occurs to regularly inform teachers and students about the progress of learning while that learning is taking place. Its purpose is to improve learning while there is still time to act—before the graded event. Assessment *of* learning occurs to sum up achievement at a particular point in time. It occurs after learning has happened.

We drew a clear distinction between assessment *for* and *of* learning to make the point that if we want to attain significant gains through formative assessment practices, certain conditions must be in place. Finally we provided an overview of the Seven Strategies of Assessment *for* Learning, a framework of practices structured to implement assessment *for* learning on a day-to-day basis in the classroom.

CHAPTER 2 ACTIVITIES

End-of-chapter activities are intended to help you master the chapter's learning targets. They are designed to deepen your understanding of the chapter content, provide discussion topics for learning team meetings, and guide implementation of the practices taught in the chapter.

Forms and materials for completing each activity appear in editable Microsoft Word format in the Chapter 2 CD file. Documents on the CD are marked with this symbol:

Chapter 2 Learning Targets

1. Know how formative and summative assessment fit into a balanced assessment system.
2. Understand the impact of formative assessment on student achievement.
3. Describe major differences between formative and summative assessment.
4. Understand how formative and summative assessment relate to the five keys of assessment quality.
5. Know what the Seven Strategies of Assessment for Learning are and how they connect to research on formative assessment.

Activity 2.1 Keep a Reflective Journal
Activity 2.2 Audit Your Assessments for Balance
Activity 2.3 Conduct a Team Self-evaluation
Activity 2.4 Assess Your Feedback Practices
Activity 2.5 Assess Prerequisites for Self-assessment and Goal Setting
Activity 2.6 Reflect on Your Own Learning
Activity 2.7 Select Portfolio Artifacts

Activity 2.1

Keep a Reflective Journal

Keep a record of your thoughts, questions, and any implementation activities you tried while reading Chapter 2.

 Reflective Journal Form

Activity 2.2

Audit Your Assessments for Balance

Use your grade book, a printout of one student's assessment data to date, or any other records you keep for assessment results to complete this activity.

1. Look over your record of assessments you have given in the past several months. Select an instructional unit or module of study spanning several weeks. If you don't have any that long, select several so that your data covers at least three weeks.
2. Make a photocopy of your assessment records for the instructional unit(s) or module(s) of study you have selected.
3. Mark on the photocopy whether each assessment's results were used formatively or summatively.
4. Reflect on the following questions:
    - What is the ratio of formative to summative use of assessment results for this instructional unit or module of study?
    - After having read Chapter 2, what do you think the ideal ratio of formative to summative use for this instructional unit or module of study might be?
    - What, if any, changes to the ratio would you make?
    - What would you do to make those changes?
5. If you are working with a partner or a team, discuss your results, your conclusions, and your questions.

Audit Your Assessments for Balance

Activity 2.3

Conduct a Team Self-evaluation

This group activity offers you and your team or school staff an opportunity to assess where you are now with respect to key assessment *for* learning practices.

For this activity, you will need the following:

- A copy of the self-evaluation survey for each person
- An open space with the numbers 1 through 5 posted about six feet high on a wall, spaced a few feet apart
- The graphing chart reproduced poster size
- A fat-tip marker

1. Have everyone individually evaluate their own classroom practice for each of the six statements on the self-evaluation survey, using the 1–5 scale described on the form. Don't put your name on your form.
2. After all have finished, crumple the surveys into snowball-sized wads, move to an open area, form a circle, and throw them at each other. Throw a few times until you are certain you have an anonymous snowball.
3. Open up the snowball you have now and become that person. Line up in front of the number on the wall that represents the rating you have on your paper for the rating for the first statement (e.g., if your paper ranks the first statement as a "4," line up in front of the number 4 on the wall).
4. Ask the person at the head of the line to count the people. Have one person graph the number of people standing in each line on the graphing chart, using a fat-tip marker. Then have that person read the corresponding statement aloud. Do the same for each of the remaining statements.
5. Debrief by finding partners and commenting on the results you see charted and implications for further learning. Then conduct a large-group discussion of your observations.

Source: Adapted with permission from *Assessment Balance and Quality: An Action Guide for School Leaders,* 3d ed. (pp. 138–139), by S. Chappuis, C. Commodore, and R. Stiggins, 2010, Portland, OR: Pearson Assessment Training Institute, 2010. Adapted by permission.

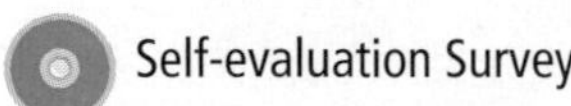

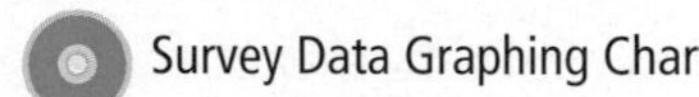

Activity 2.4

Assess Your Feedback Practices

After reading through the Seven Strategies of Assessment *for* Learning, think about the extent to which each of the characteristics of effective feedback is part of your regular classroom practice. Complete this personal inventory. If you are working with a partner or a team, discuss your results.

Characteristic	All	Some	Not Yet
1. My feedback to students links directly to the intended learning. Comments:			
2. My feedback points out strengths and/or offers information to guide improvement linked to the intended learning. Comments:			
3. My feedback occurs during the learning process. Comments:			
4. I have planned time for students to act on the feedback they receive. Comments:			
5. I don't use written feedback as instruction until the student's work exhibits at least partial understanding. Comments:			
6. My feedback encourages students to take action likely to lead to further learning. My intervention feedback does not do all of the thinking for the student. Comments:			
7. My intervention feedback limits correctives to the amount of advice the student can act on in time given. Comments:			

Which of the characteristics is your highest priority for continued learning?

What resources might you use?

 My Feedback Practices

Activity 2.5

Assess Prerequisites for Self-assessment and Goal Setting

After reading through the Seven Strategies of Assessment *for* Learning, think about the extent to which Strategies 1 through 3 are in place currently in your classroom. Complete this personal inventory. If you are working with a partner or a team, discuss your results.

Prerequisite	All	Some	Not Yet
1. Students have a clear vision of the learning targets. Targets are communicated to them in language they understand (including rubrics). Comments:			
2. Instruction centers on the learning targets. Comments:			
3. Assignments and assessments align directly with intended learning and instruction provided. Comments:			
4. Assignments and assessments are designed so that students can interpret results, in terms of intended learning. The results function as effective feedback. Comments:			

Which of the prerequisites is your highest priority for continued learning?

What resources might you use?

Prerequisites for Self-assessment and Goal Setting

Activity 2.6

Reflect on Your Own Learning

Review the Chapter 2 learning targets and select one or more that represented new learning for you or struck you as most significant from this chapter. If you are working individually, write a short reflection that captures your current understanding. If you are working with a partner or a team, either discuss what you have written or use this as a discussion prompt for a team meeting.

Reflect on Chapter 2 Learning

Activity 2.7

Select Portfolio Artifacts

Any of the activities from this chapter can be used as portfolio entries. Select activities you have completed or artifacts you have created that will illustrate your competence at the Chapter 2 learning targets:

1. Know how formative and summative assessment fit into a balanced assessment system.
2. Understand the impact of formative assessment on student achievement.
3. Describe major differences between formative and summative assessment.
4. Understand how formative and summative assessment relate to assessment quality.
5. Know what the Seven Strategies of Assessment *for* Learning are and how they connect to research on formative assessment.

If you are keeping a reflective journal, you may want to include Chapter 2's entry in your portfolio.

Chapter 2 Portfolio Entry Cover Sheet

CHAPTER

3

Clear Targets

Students can hit any target they can see and that holds still for them.

What do we want students to know and be able to do? In standards-based schools, what students are to learn drives all planning, instruction, and assessment. The curriculum documents are the roadmap we use and assessment is the global positioning system that guides us to our destination. Just as the GPS we use in our cars relies on an accurate map to accomplish its task, effective formative and summative assessment depend on the clear roadmap to important learning that a good curriculum provides.

Curriculum documents consist of statements of intended learning, known by more than a few labels. "Common Core State Standards," "content standards," "benchmarks," "grade level indicators," "grade level expectations," "essential learnings," "learning outcomes," "lesson objectives," "learning progressions," and "learning intentions" are a few examples. In this book we use one label to refer to these statements: *learning targets*.

Learning targets vary in complexity, clarity, and level of specificity. Some are written to represent the ultimate learning desired and others are written to reflect the day-to-day learning that students will engage in to reach the ultimate learning. When the content standards represented in our curricula aren't clear, they don't function as effective roadmaps for instruction and assessment won't help us reach our destination. If the curriculum side of the classroom is in disarray, the assessment side will be equally messy; the accuracy of any assessment hinges on clear targets, as we will see in the following chapters.

Learning targets are statements of the intended learning.

In this chapter, we explain the different kinds of learning targets; how to make them clear to everyone, including students; the importance of clear learning targets to teaching and learning; and how clear targets are a necessary foundation for classroom assessment quality. It focuses on the shaded portion of Figure 3.1.

Chapter 3 Learning Targets

At the end of this chapter, you will know how to do the following:

- Explain the connection between clear targets and assessment quality.
- Classify learning targets by type.
- Determine whether your learning targets are clear to you and to students.
- Clarify and deconstruct learning targets as needed.
- Create student-friendly versions of learning targets as needed.

FIGURE 3.1 Keys to Quality Classroom Assessment

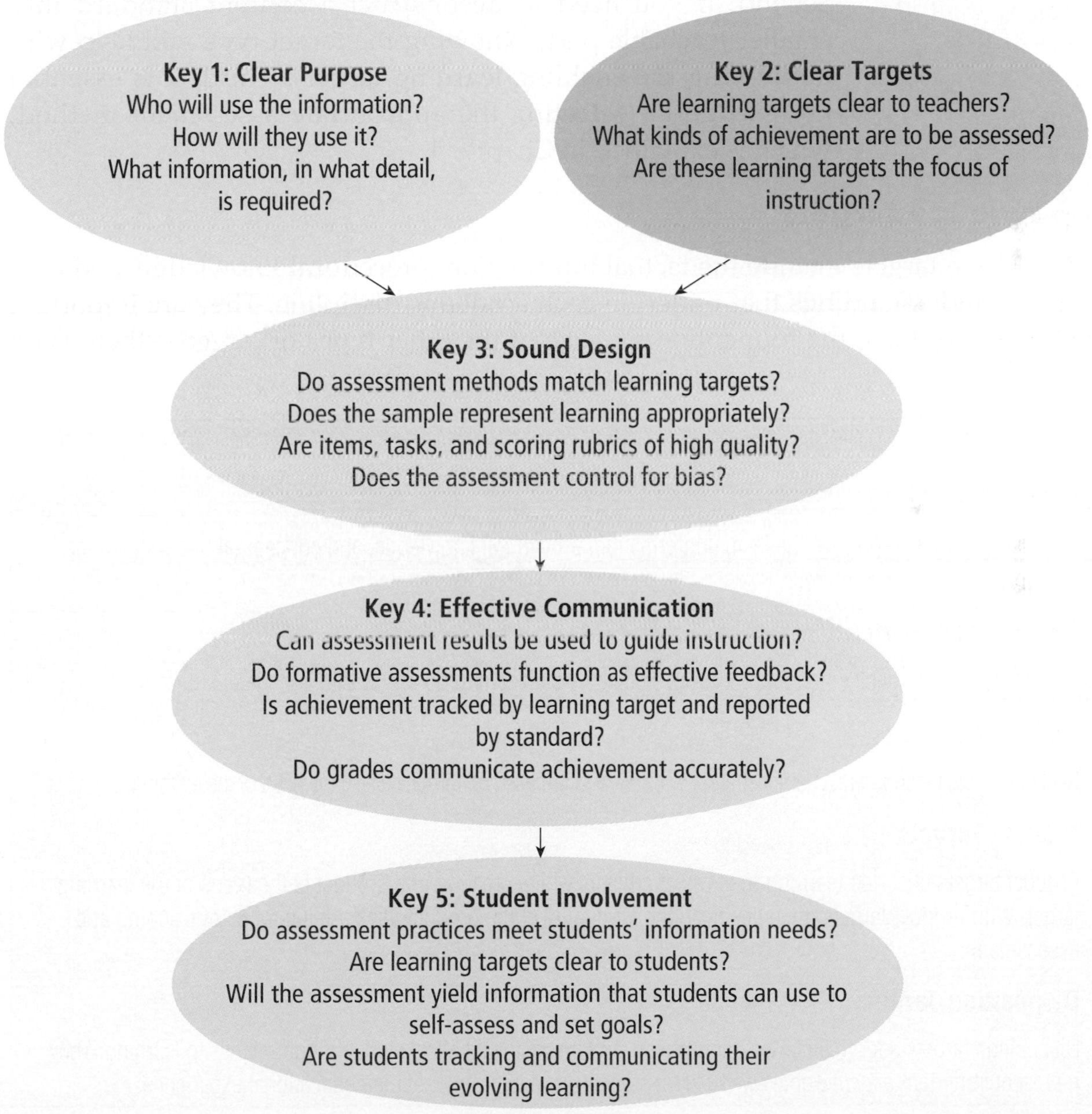

Key 1: Clear Purpose
Who will use the information?
How will they use it?
What information, in what detail, is required?

Key 2: Clear Targets
Are learning targets clear to teachers?
What kinds of achievement are to be assessed?
Are these learning targets the focus of instruction?

Key 3: Sound Design
Do assessment methods match learning targets?
Does the sample represent learning appropriately?
Are items, tasks, and scoring rubrics of high quality?
Does the assessment control for bias?

Key 4: Effective Communication
Can assessment results be used to guide instruction?
Do formative assessments function as effective feedback?
Is achievement tracked by learning target and reported by standard?
Do grades communicate achievement accurately?

Key 5: Student Involvement
Do assessment practices meet students' information needs?
Are learning targets clear to students?
Will the assessment yield information that students can use to self-assess and set goals?
Are students tracking and communicating their evolving learning?

TYPES OF LEARNING TARGETS

One way you will know that your targets are clear and usable is if you can determine what kind of learning is being called for. The accuracy of the assessments you develop will depend in part on your ability to classify learning targets in any written curriculum in a way that helps ensure a dependable assessment. We offer a categorization framework that identifies five kinds of learning targets: knowledge, reasoning, skill, product, and disposition, summarized in Figure 3.2.

Classifying learning targets is a necessary step in planning an assessment. It helps identify the assessment options appropriate to each target.

Our purpose in categorizing learning targets is threefold. First, the process will be useful when examining the targets in your own curriculum to determine if they are clear enough. Second, if you need to deconstruct a content standard into smaller teachable parts, knowing the target type will help with identifying the enabling learning targets. Third, it is essential knowledge for selecting the appropriate assessment method, which is explained in Chapter 4.

Knowledge Targets

Knowledge targets include the factual information, procedural knowledge, and conceptual understandings that underpin each academic discipline. They are important because they form the foundation for each of the other types of targets—there is no

FIGURE 3.2 Learning Target Types

Knowledge Targets

Knowledge targets represent the factual information, procedural knowledge, and conceptual understandings that underpin each discipline.

Reasoning Targets

Reasoning targets specify thought processes students are to learn to do well within a range of subjects.

Skill Targets

Skill targets are those where a demonstration or physical skill-based performance is at the heart of the learning.

Product Targets

Product targets describe learning in terms of artifacts where creation of a product is the focus of the learning target. With product targets, the specifications for quality of the product itself are the focus of teaching and assessment.

Disposition Targets

Disposition targets refer to attitudes, motivations, and interests that affect students' approaches to learning. They represent important *affective* goals we hold for students as a byproduct of their educational experience.

such thing as knowledge-free reasoning, knowledge-free skilled performance, or knowledge-free product development.

FACTUAL INFORMATION. Targets calling for *factual information* are often stated using verbs such as *knows, lists, names, identifies,* and *recalls.* Examples include "Identify and know the meaning of the most common prefixes and derivational suffixes" (Common Core State Standards Initiative, 2010a, p. 17 [hereafter cited as CCSSI, 2010a]), "Understand the absolute value of a rational number as its distance from 0 on the number line" (Common Core State Standards Initiative, 2010c, p. 43 [hereafter cited as CCSSI, 2010c]), and "Knows the nutritional value of different foods" (Kendall & Marzano, 1997, p. 552).

Some learning targets call for *procedural knowledge*: knowing how to do something. They often begin with the phrase *knows how to*, or the word *uses*, such as the target "Uses scientific notation to represent very large and very small numbers." Procedural knowledge usually involves knowing a protocol or memorizing a series of steps.

CONCEPTUAL UNDERSTANDING. When *conceptual understanding* is at the heart of a learning target, the target often begins with the word *understands*. A conceptual understanding learning target at the knowledge level means that the student can explain the concept. We would not consider this "low-level" knowledge; conceptual understanding is essential for reasoning effectively in any discipline. As the Common Core State Standards Initiative's description of the Standards for Mathematical Practice states: "Students who lack understanding of a topic may rely on procedures too heavily. Without a flexible base from which to work, they may be less likely to consider analogous problems, represent problems coherently, justify conclusions, apply the mathematics to practical situations, use technology mindfully to work with the mathematics, explain the mathematics accurately to other students, step back for an overview, or deviate from a known procedure to find a shortcut. In short, a lack of understanding effectively prevents a student from engaging in the mathematical practices" (CCSSI, 2010c, p. 8).

KNOWING VIA REFERENCE. Beyond knowing information outright, there is another way of knowing—knowing via reference. Not everything that we need to know needs to be learned "by heart." What, of the information students need, will we require they memorize, and what will we teach them to find if and when they need it? As our students become increasingly adept at using technology to search for information, we must carefully identify the information that it is important to have in memory. Will they memorize the list of prepositions (*above, aboard, about . . .*)? The table of periodic elements? The capitals of the 50 U.S. states? Maybe, maybe not. As we know, there isn't enough time to teach (or for students to learn) everything of importance—we can easily fill the year teaching facts, thereby losing instructional time for learning targets beyond the knowledge level. Where is the balance? One way to address this problem is to determine which knowledge learning targets will be important for students to know outright and which they will be required to know via reference.

CLASSIFYING TARGETS AS KNOWLEDGE. Classifying learning targets isn't a 100 percent foolproof process. Sorting by the verb in the target works well most of the time, but not always. A target beginning with the word *knows* very often is, but may not be, a knowledge target. For example, consider the two targets "Knows how healthy practices enhance the ability to dance" and "Knows folk dances from various cultures" (Kendall & Marzano, 1997, pp. 387, 386). Are they both knowledge targets? Before classifying each as *knowledge* because of the verb, we need to make sure that *knowledge* is the intent. "Knows how healthy practices enhance the ability to dance" is likely to be a knowledge target, but perhaps the intent of "knows folk dances from various cultures" is that students are able to perform a variety of folk dances. In that case, it is a skill target in its intent and should be rewritten to reflect that.

Sometimes a target that looks like procedural knowledge may not be. Consider the target "Knows how to narrow or broaden inquiry when appropriate." There is procedural knowledge involved, but figuring out when a topic is too broad or too narrow requires reasoning. And if the target's intent is that students actually broaden or narrow a topic, that is also reasoning. So while at first glance this may look like a knowledge target, it is in fact a reasoning target.

FIGURE 3.3 Examples of Knowledge Targets

Subject	Learning Target
Mathematics	1. Recognizes acute, obtuse, and right angles. 2. Knows the remainder theorem for polynomial division.
English Language Arts	3. Identifies nouns and verbs. 4. Knows how to use subject and object pronouns correctly.
Social Studies	5. Explains the difference between *power* and *authority*. 6. Knows the major reasons for the rapid expansion of Islam during the 7th and 8th centuries.
Science	7. Describes how organisms interact with each other to transfer energy and matter in an ecosystem. 8. Describes where mitochondria and chloroplasts come from.
Health/Physical Education	9. Identifies factors that determine the reliability of health information. 10. Knows influences that promote alcohol, tobacco, and other drug use.
The Arts	11. Identifies and describes elements of design in a work of art. (Visual Arts) 12. Identifies and writes notes on a treble clef. (Music)

Sources: Item 1 is from Common Core State Standards Initiative. 2010c. *Common Core State Standards for Mathematics.* Washington, DC: Council of Chief State School Officers & National Governors Association. Retrieved January 2011 from http://www.corestandards.org/assets/CCSSI_Math%20Standards.pdf, p. 32 (hereafter cited as CCSSI, 2010c)
Item 2 is from http://www.education.ky.gov/users/otl/KLN/Math/Arith%20with%20Poly%20and%20Ration%20St2%20Algebra.doc
Item 5 is from http://www.civiced.org/index.php?page=k4erica
Item 6 is from http://apcentral.collegeboard.com/apc/public/repository/ap-world-history-course-description.pdf
Items 11 and 12 are from North Thurston Public Schools K–12 Arts Curriculum

When a learning target begins with the word *understands*, it can either be a knowledge target or a reasoning target. Is the intent that students can explain something such as understanding of a concept? If so, it's a knowledge target. (Remember, calling it a knowledge target doesn't make it a simple target—in order to explain a concept clearly you have to know it well.) Or does the word *understand* in the context of the target call for reasoning in some way beyond an explanation? If so, it's a reasoning target.

Although looking to the verb often results in an accurate classification of a knowledge target, it's important to verify that knowledge is its intent.

Reasoning Targets

Reasoning targets specify thought processes students are to learn to apply effectively (do well) within a range of subjects; e.g., solve problems, make inferences, draw conclusions, form and defend judgments. Mastering content knowledge, while necessary, is not the sole aim of education today; more importantly, we want our students to develop the ability to *apply* knowledge in authentic contexts—that is, in contexts that transfer to work and life beyond school. This requires that they engage in reasoning using their knowledge.

All subject-area curricula include reasoning processes, such as *predict, infer, classify, hypothesize, compare, draw conclusions, summarize, estimate, solve problems, analyze, evaluate, justify,* and *generalize.* Reasoning processes can be thought of as falling into one of six overall patterns of reasoning: inference, analysis, comparison, classification, evaluation, and synthesis. Together, the six patterns of reasoning represent those most commonly found among various taxonomies, content standards documents, and assessments. They also represent the kinds of reasoning occurring most frequently in subject area curricula as well as in life beyond school.

FIGURE 3.4 Patterns of Reasoning

Inference: Making a reasonable guess based on information or clues

Analysis: Examining the components or structure of something

Comparison: Describing similarities and differences between two or more items

Classification: Sorting things into categories based on certain characteristics

Evaluation: Expressing and defending an opinion, a point of view, a judgment, or a decision

Synthesis: Combining discrete elements to create something new

INDUCTIVE AND DEDUCTIVE INFERENCE. An *inference* is a reasonable guess or conclusion based on information or clues. Inferences can take one of two forms: *inductive* or *deductive*. When we make an *inductive inference*, we use evidence or facts to infer a general rule or principle. It is sometimes referred to as "reading between the lines." Sound inductive reasoning requires that we select relevant evidence or facts, interpret them accurately, and then draw careful conclusions based on them. Examples of inductive inference include the following (Klauer & Phye, 2008, pp. 86–89):

- Finding common attributes
- Examining information to reach a conclusion
- Making analogies
- Generalizing
- Recognizing relationships
- Building and testing a hypothesis

A *deductive inference* also involves drawing a conclusion based on information. We can make a deductive inference one of two ways. The first is to begin with a general rule or principle and then infer a specific conclusion or solution. To do it well, we apply what the general rule tells us to a specific case and draw a plausible conclusion about that specific case.

General rule: *All people get mad sometimes.*

Application to specific case: *Mom is a person.*

Conclusion: *Mom gets mad sometimes.*

A second way to make a deductive inference is to begin with a set of premises that we know to be true, and then infer a specific conclusion or solution.

Premise 1: *Boston is east of Chicago.*

Premise 2: *Chicago is east of Salt Lake City.*

Conclusion: *Boston is east of Salt Lake City.*

ANALYSIS. When we reason analytically, we examine the components or structure of something. We undertake analysis to understand something more deeply or to provide an interpretation of it. Analysis often requires that we investigate how the component parts relate to each other or how they come together to form a whole. For students to be successful, they must be able to identify the parts of something and then have practice at describing relationships among those parts, or between the part and the whole.

Examples of analysis include the following:

- Analyzing a controversial decision, identifying the arguments for and against a particular action

- Conducting an experiment to analyze a compound to determine its component chemicals
- Determining the meaning of unknown words by breaking them into prefixes, suffixes, and root words

COMPARISON. Describing the similarities and differences between two or more items is at the heart of comparative reasoning. In this definition, comparative reasoning encompasses both *compare*—to find similarities, and *contrast*—to find differences. Venn diagrams and T-charts are two common graphic organizers used to help students understand the structure of comparative reasoning.

In the simplest form of comparison, students say how two things are alike or different. In its more complex form, students first select appropriate items to compare, then select salient features to base their comparison on, and last, perform the actual comparison (Marzano, Pickering, & McTighe, 1993).

The act of contrasting can also take the form of *juxtaposition*, whereby we place two significantly different things, such as objects, emotions, thoughts, melodies, colors, textures, arguments, or people, side by side to define each in sharp relief or to cause the differences between them to stand out distinctly. *Contrast*, used in this sense, is a device we manipulate for effect in areas such as writing, music, art, and drama.

CLASSIFICATION. *Classification* can be thought of as sorting things into categories based on certain characteristics. In its simplest form, classification consists of sorting objects into predetermined, clearly defined categories. To sort well at this basic level, students need practice at identifying and observing the pertinent characteristics that will help them determine which category the object belongs in.

A more complete exercise in classification requires students to select or create the categories and then to do the sorting. The game "Twenty Questions" is an exercise in creating categories. The first question could be, "Is it an animal?" to classify the object according to general type. The next question could be, "Is it bigger than a bread box?" to classify the object according to size. The third question might be, "Does it live around here?" to narrow the possibilities according to habitat, and so forth. The trick in Twenty Questions, as in all classification exercises, is to identify relevant categories that will provide the maximum information about the objects or concepts under consideration.

EVALUATION. Evaluative reasoning involves expressing and defending an opinion, a point of view, a judgment, or a decision. It can be thought of as having three facets—an assertion, criteria the assertion is based on, and evidence that supports the assertion. Students generally are able to make an assertion or judgment, but often do not follow up with the criteria or the evidence; instead, they express an opinion and then support it with further opinions. This can't be thought of as *evaluative* thinking until students are also able to identify criteria for making their assertion or judgment and are able to provide credible evidence that matches the criteria.

Content-specific examples of "assertion, criteria, and evidence" include the following:

- In mathematics problem solving, students choose a strategy by examining the options and judging the usefulness of each in the context of the problem, and then evaluate how well the strategy they selected is working as they use it.
- In science, students evaluate the validity of their conclusions based on what they know about experimental design.
- In social studies, students evaluate the quality of the arguments a politician makes against a set of criteria.

Similarly, when we ask students to evaluate the quality of their own work, they will need to use criteria describing levels of quality and then match their observations about their work to the criteria.

SYNTHESIS. *Synthesis* is the process of combining discrete elements to create something new. Cookies are an example of synthesis because the end product is something more than the sum of its parts—when we combine the ingredients (eggs, milk, flour, sugar, salt, and vanilla) we get something new, cookie dough, which some people bake before eating. Creating a tower out of blocks would not qualify as synthesis under this definition. Synthesizing involves selecting relevant ingredients to combine and then assembling them in such a way so as to create a new whole.

Writing a report is an act of synthesis; we want students to create something new (e.g., in their own words or with their own thoughts) from separate ingredients through a specific process. To do that they must locate and understand various bits of relevant information, sort through them, think about how they fit together, and assemble and present them in a way that does not copy any of the original sources. Sometimes we ask them to add their own thoughts as well. Although the assembly process differs according to the context, what all synthesis has in common is that it results in something different from the original ingredients.

RELATIONSHIPS AMONG PATTERNS OF REASONING. In line with current thought about reasoning, please note that we have not indicated a hierarchy of difficulty in the patterns of reasoning. However, some patterns of reasoning depend on other patterns to be carried out effectively. For example, before evaluating an issue, you might need to analyze it to identify the main problem, describe the different points of view on the issue, discover the assumptions that underlie various positions, and determine the information needed to inform a position on the issue; you also might need to compare positions to identify the most salient features of disagreement and agreement.

Also, the patterns are not necessarily mutually exclusive. For example, classifying and comparing are presented by some authors (e.g., Klauer & Phye, 2008) as types of inductive or deductive inferences because they involve either looking at the objects to be compared to detect commonalities (induction) or using the categories to identify examples (deduction). We present inference, comparison, classification, and evaluation as separate patterns here because they are commonly referred to separately in standards documents and they can be taught and assessed separately.

FIGURE 3.5 Examples of Reasoning Targets

Subject	Learning Target
Mathematics	1. Identifies shapes as two-dimensional or three-dimensional. 2. Uses data from a random sample to draw inferences about a population with an unknown characteristic of interest.
English Language Arts	3. With prompting and support, describes the relationship between illustrations and the story in which they appear. 4. Delineates and evaluates the argument and specific claims in a text, assessing whether the reasoning is valid and the evidence is relevant and sufficient.
Social Studies	5. Compares and contrasts points of view from an historical event. 6. Evaluates the strengths and weaknesses of candidates in terms of the qualifications required for a particular leadership role.
Science	7. Uses characteristic properties of liquids to distinguish one substance from another. 8. Draws conclusions from experiment results.
Health/Physical Education	9. Uses criteria to set goals for improving health and fitness practice. 10. Evaluates health and fitness information.
The Arts	11. Compares purposes of chosen musical examples. (Music) 12. Evaluates quality of own work to refine it. (Visual Arts)

Sources: Item 1 is from CCSSI, 2010c, p. 12
Item 2 is from CCSSI, 2010c, p. 50
Item 3 is from Common Core State Standards Initiative, 2010a. *Common Core State Standards for English Language Arts & Literacy in History/Social Studies, Science, and Technical Subjects.* Washington, DC: Council of Chief State School Officers & National Governors Association. Retrieved January 2011 from http://www.corestandards.org/assets/CCSSI_ELA%20Standards.pdf, p. 11 (hereafter cited as CCSSI, 2010a)
Item 4 is from CCSSI, 2010a, p. 40
Item 6 is from http://www.civiced.org/index.php?page=k4erica#4
Item 9 is from Central Kitsap Grade 5 Essential Learnings
Items 11 and 12 are from North Thurston Public Schools K–12 Arts Curriculum

CLASSIFYING TARGETS AS REASONING. While reasoning targets can most often be identified by the verbs they contain, many reasoning targets do not include a reasoning verb. For example, "Draws examples of quadrilaterals that do and do not belong to any of the subcategories" at first glance looks like a product target because the verb is *draws*, but the intent is clearly classification of quadrilaterals. The target, "Given a set of data or a word problem, creates an equation or inequality to solve the problem," may also look like a product target at first glance because the main verb is *creates*, but it is a reasoning target—the intent is that students are able to solve problems using equations and inequalities.

And, again, what about the verb *understands*? Many, many standards begin with it. When *understands* means something more than *conceptual understanding*, absent further explanation it is open to a wide spectrum of interpretations. To become a clear target, a content standard that begins with the word *understands* must be accompanied by information about how that understanding will be demonstrated. Most often, the explanation includes the application of one or more patterns of reasoning. The specific pattern or patterns of reasoning to be used should be specified: teaching to this target should include instruction on how to carry out the pattern or patterns of reasoning.

Sometimes a reasoning target on paper becomes a knowledge target in practice. For example, "Compares and contrasts main characters in a novel" is a reasoning target as written. If the teacher compares and contrasts the main characters in a novel, and then tests students' ability to replicate her reasoning about the same characters, she is not testing their reasoning; she is testing *recall* of the information she shared with them. It may have started out as a reasoning target, but as measured, it has devolved to a knowledge target. Seek to avoid this in your own assessments. To test a reasoning proficiency, we must provide students with a *novel* (new) application of the specific pattern of reasoning. The key to making the determination here lies in asking, "Who is doing the reasoning?" Are the students doing something more than remembering the answers the teacher previously demonstrated?

When there is a question about target type, we recommend using this guideline, developed by Carol Commodore in her work with deconstructing standards (personal communication, 2011):

> Look at how the state is measuring the target. For example, is the target "Understands the scientific method" a knowledge target or a reasoning target? To answer this question, first, look to see how the state measures it. If that information isn't available, then go for the more advanced target, which in this case is reasoning. We are preparing our students for their future life and work, not a state test. Application is what will be required of these students in real life, so when possible, teach it as the more advanced application.

FAQ 3.1

Identifying Target Types

Question

What kinds of targets are in the following language arts standard for grade 3?

Demonstrate command of the conventions of standard English capitalization, punctuation, and spelling when writing.

a. Capitalize appropriate words in titles.
b. Use commas in addresses.
c. Use commas and quotation marks in dialogue.
d. Form and use possessives.
e. Use conventional spelling for high-frequency and other studied words and for adding suffixes to base words (e.g., sitting, smiled, cries, happiness).
f. Use spelling patterns and generalizations (e.g., word families, position-based spellings, syllable patterns, ending rules, meaningful word parts) in writing words.
g. Consult reference materials, including beginning dictionaries, as needed to check and correct spellings. (CCSSI, 2010a, p. 29)

Answer

The standard is a series of *knowledge targets*. To double check our answer, let's test out the other possibilities.

Does the standard incorporate reasoning targets?

No. Confusion sometimes exists with the concept of "procedural knowledge"—in other words, if the standard stipulates that *students know how to do* something. If there is a rule to follow and the learning target represents right-or-wrong learning, chances are it is a knowledge target. But, knowing when and how to apply a rule in the case of conventions is still knowledge. It's a good example of knowledge targets not always being simple, a common bias against knowledge targets.

If, on the other hand, you have to make a judgment outside of a rule, if there are legitimate options from which to choose so that several options could be considered "right," it may represent a pattern of reasoning. For example, when we teach students to alter punctuation/conventions for rhetorical effect, we are teaching to a reasoning target. Students have to determine the effect they want to create and then experiment with conventions to create it. If the content standard doesn't call for that level of thinking, then it isn't reasoning. It doesn't mean you can't teach it, or that it's not a good thing to teach, just that the content standard, as written, doesn't ask for it.

Does the application of students' knowledge to their writing constitute a skill?

No. The target as stated does not specify a real-time demonstration or performance.

Couldn't it be a product target?

Even though the words "when writing" are in the standard, we would not classify this standard as a product target, either, since the intent is not about the creation of some specific product itself, but rather that students apply—or as the standard says, ***demonstrate***—the underlying knowledge whenever they write. Some of the components of this standard can be assessed through selected response methodology, some can be assessed through students editing text with embedded errors, and some are best assessed through students producing a sample of writing. In this last case, their writing becomes the ***context*** in which we assess their ***knowledge.*** So, even though we use a product as evidence of the learning, the learning itself is at the knowledge level.

Skill Targets

When we speak of skill targets, we are referring to those learning targets where a real-time demonstration or physical performance is at the heart of the learning. As defined, this is a somewhat narrow category. Subjects such as physical education, fine arts, performing arts, and world languages, have skill development as a central core of their discipline, and therefore have many skill targets in their curricula. Other subjects may have few or none. Examples of skill targets include oral fluency in reading, serving a volleyball, conversing in a second language, giving an oral presentation, directing scenes and productions, demonstrating movement skills in dance, and playing a musical instrument.

CLASSIFYING TARGETS AS SKILLS. A difficulty with the concept of *skill targets* arises from the broad use made of the word "skills": comprehension skills, research skills, writing skills, reading skills, reasoning skills, mathematics skills, science process skills, and so forth. While there is nothing wrong with calling each of those "skills," the ultimate goal of most of the underlying learning targets is some form of thinking: if you were to take each apart, you would discover a combination of knowledge and reasoning. In other instances you might discover skill targets as we have defined them here: the target as stated specifies a real-time demonstration or physical performance. This differentiation between reasoning (cognitive "skill") targets and skill targets becomes an important distinction in both teaching and assessing the learning, which will be illustrated in Chapter 4.

Additionally, the line between procedural knowledge and skill targets blurs when the target in question is a measurement skill requiring a certain level of manual dexterity and fine motor control, such as those often encountered in science and mathematics. For the purpose of explaining how to classify targets in preparation for assessing them, we will classify these as skill targets, even though they involve, for the most part, procedural knowledge—knowing how to use the tool correctly.

Product Targets

Some content standards specify the creation of a product. For product targets, the specifications for qualities of a good product are the focus of teaching and assessment.

FIGURE 3.6 Examples of Skill Targets

Subject	Learning Target
Mathematics	1. Measures the length of an object twice, using length units of different lengths for the two measurements. 2. Uses a protractor correctly.
English Language Arts	3. Pronounces, blends, and segments syllables in spoken words. 4. Propels conversations by posing and responding to questions that relate the current discussion to broader themes or larger ideas.
Social Studies	5. Learns how to greet people from other countries. 6. Participates in civic discussions.
Science	7. Measures properties of objects using balances and thermometers. 8. Uses laboratory equipment safely.
Health/Physical Education	9. Performs CPR correctly. 10. Dribbles to keep the ball away from an opponent; passes and receives on the move.
The Arts	11. Performs songs using appropriate expression to reflect music. (Band) 12. Integrates voice into character development. (Theater)

Sources: Items 1 and 2 are from CCSSI, 2010c, p. 32
Item 3 is from CCSSI, 2010a, p. 15
Item 4 is from CCSSI, 2010a, p. 50
Item 5 is from http://www.nationalgeographic.com/xpeditions/lessons/01/gk2/friends.html
Item 7 is from Ohio Science Academic Content Standards, p. 84, http://ode.state.oh.us/GD/Templates/Pages/ODE/ODEDetail.aspx?Page=3&TopicRelationID=1705&Content=88581
Items 11 and 12 are from North Thurston Public Schools K–12 Arts Curriculum

FAQ 3.2

Procedural Knowledge or Skill?

Question

How do I know if a target is calling for procedural knowledge or the demonstration of a skill?

Answer

If a target says "The student uses measuring tools," it is a skill target. If the target says "The student knows how to use measuring tools," then some discussion needs to take place. Does this mean just having the procedural knowledge; i.e., knowing the steps? If so, it is a knowledge target. If it means that they not only have the procedural knowledge but can also use those tools, then it is a skill target.

The example that brings this home to me is the target, "The student will know how to apply CPR." The intent of this target is clearly to be able to perform CPR. I know those steps very well as I took the CPR training a couple of times—I acquired the procedural knowledge. It is a whole new thing when I have to apply that knowledge and actually perform CPR. I don't feel yet that I do that well. I might save a life, but I don't feel I have that skill mastered. Thus, I still need to work on the skill target of performing CPR.

Source: Carol Commodore, personal communication, January 18, 2011

Product examples include "creates tables, graphs, scatter plots, and box plots to display data effectively," and "creates a quality personal wellness plan." Instruction and assessment focuses on the meaning of "effectively" and "quality" in these instances. Curricula generally include far fewer product targets than knowledge and reasoning targets.

Term papers, research reports, and lab reports are product targets when the curriculum guide specifically calls for students to create them. Such product targets are not only the vehicle by which we judge knowledge and reasoning proficiencies; the creation of the products themselves represents valued learning targets and is the focus of instruction. When these products are assessed they can yield evidence of the intended learning because the creation of the product *is* the stated learning.

CLASSIFYING TARGETS AS PRODUCTS. Sometimes when identifying product targets, the difference between the learning target and the activity to be used to teach or assess the learning gets cloudy. For example, is "Make a desk" a product target or an activity? It could be either. What does the content standard call for? Does it call for the creation of a desk? If so, it's a product target. If making a desk is the assessment—the way students will demonstrate the achievement of the learning targets—but the desk itself is not specified in the content standards, it is an activity. "Make a desk" is not generally a product target in the curriculum for a course such as Principles of Technology. Skillful use of machinery, knowing how to join pieces of wood, and how to finish surfaces *are* likely to be part of the curriculum. The task of making the desk may be the way we elicit evidence of the student's achievement of the relevant targets, but the learning target itself is not likely to be to make desks.

The key question in distinguishing the task or activity from the learning target is "What's the intended learning?"

Teaching to learning as specified in the written curriculum rather than teaching to an activity is sometimes a difficult transition to make. Confusing the activity with the learning target can cause difficulties when classifying product targets. If the learning target doesn't call for the creation of a product, but you want to classify it as a product target, it's possible that you are including the task or activity you will use to teach the target. The ability to distinguish between the *assignment*—the task or activity students will engage in—and the *learning target*—what they are to learn by doing the work—is crucial to classifying targets and therefore to creating an accurate assessment. The key question in classifying targets is "What is the intended learning?," not "How will students demonstrate it?"

Disposition Targets

Our last category of targets for students is one that may not be found in your written curriculum. Disposition targets reflect attitudes and feeling states, such as, "I look forward to coming to school each day," "Music is worth studying," or "I like reading." They represent important *affective* goals we hold for students as byproducts of their educational experience, and as such, are not assessed for the purpose of grading. Sometimes they are the overarching goals of schooling, often found in mission statements. The Common Core State Standards Initiative includes *productive disposition* in their summary of the Standards for Mathematics and defines it as "habitual inclination to see mathematics as sensible, useful, and worthwhile, coupled with a belief in diligence and one's own efficacy" (CCSSI, 2010c, p. 6).

Dispositions in any subject are influenced by experience and we strive to develop productive dispositions through the experiences students have in our classes. Because they are nonacademic, we typically do not hold students accountable for these targets in the same way that we hold them accountable for mastery of knowledge, reasoning, skill, and product targets, but that does not mean they are unimportant or that we would never assess for them. Understanding students' dispositions provides information into who they are as learners, insights that help us work more effectively with them as individuals and as a group. If we were to find that a majority of students on a survey, for instance, clearly indicated a dislike of reading, that information might cause us to review our current reading program.

We can think about disposition targets in terms of three characteristics (Stiggins & Chappuis, 2011). They have (1) a specific object as their focus, (2) a positive or negative

FIGURE 3.7 Examples of Product Targets

Subject	Learning Target
Mathematics	1. Draws a bar graph to represent a data set with up to four categories. 2. Constructs the inscribed and circumscribed circles of a triangle.
English Language Arts	3. Creates a visual display for use in a presentation to enhance the message. 4. Writes opinion pieces on topics or texts, supporting a point of view with reasons and information.
Social Studies	5. Creates a timeline to show the order of early explorations and settlements. 6. Produces maps to scale.
Science	7. Makes pictographs to describe observations and draw conclusions. 8. Creates an accurate, complete, and organized display of data obtained through scientific investigation.
Health/Physical Education	9. Develops a home fire escape plan. 10. Develops a personal health-related fitness plan.
The Arts	11. Creates drawings demonstrating one- and two-point perspectives. (Visual Arts) 12. Creates a scripted scene based on improvised work. (Theater)

Sources: Item 1 is from CCSSI, 2010c, p. 20
Item 2 is from CCSSI, 2010c, p. 77
Item 3 is from CCSSI, 2010a, p. 24
Item 4 is from CCSSI, 2010a, p. 20
Item 9 is from http://www.ode.state.or.us/teachlearn/subjects/health/standards/gradek-3contstan.rtf
Items 11 and 12 are from North Thurston Public Schools K–12 Arts Curriculum

direction, and (3) varied levels of intensity, from strong to weak. When we assess them, we are looking for information about both the direction and level of intensity of feeling toward the specific focus. For example, we might offer a series of statements such as, "I am good at reading," I like reading," and "I read for enjoyment in my spare time." After each statement, students would mark one answer choice from the following options: "strongly agree," "somewhat agree," "neutral or no opinion," "somewhat disagree," or "strongly disagree." In this case, students' attitude about reading is the focus; they are asked whether they feel positively or negatively about each statement, and how strongly. Examples of disposition learning targets appear in Figure 3.8.

FIGURE 3.8 Examples of Disposition Targets

Subject	Learning Target
English Language Arts	1. Chooses to read to learn more about something. 2. Looks forward to group discussions.
Mathematics	3. Views oneself as capable of doing mathematics. 4. Sees mathematics as important to learn.
Social Studies	5. Respects individual worth and human dignity. 6. Has the inclination to question the validity of various positions, including one's own.
Science	7. Seeks opportunities to understand how things work. 8. Is curious about the natural world.
Health/Physical Education	9. Enjoys playing a sport. 10. Chooses to avoid drugs and alcohol.
The Arts	11. Values practice for its own sake. 12. Wants to participate in community theater.

Source: Items 5 and 6 are from http://www.civiced.org/index.php?page=912erica#15

FAQ 3.3

Balance Among Target Types

Question

Should each subject's curriculum have all four types of targets in it?

Answer

No. Target type is entirely a function of the nature of the subject. Academic subjects generally have far more knowledge and reasoning targets than skill or product targets. Reading, for example, has no product targets. Performance-based disciplines, such as music, physical education, and other performing arts, have quite a few skill targets. Product-based disciplines such as fine arts have quite a few skill and product targets. They all have knowledge and reasoning targets as well, but the balance shifts more to the skill and product levels in some subjects.

WE NEED GOOD CURRICULUM GUIDES

We believe every teacher should have access to a practical curriculum guide, one that provides a clear vision of the intended learning and points the way for teaching and assessing. A good curriculum will link each year's learning targets to the previous and following year's targets, providing continuity among grade levels. The benefits of this to students and teachers are obvious: If we know that every student has had plenty of exposure to learning how to put a capital letter at the beginning of a sentence and a punctuation mark at the end in kindergarten through grade two, it would be reasonable to expect that knowledge in grade three, and to hold students accountable for demonstrating it. If we have no clear knowledge of what previous teachers have taught, we may spend time unnecessarily addressing things that students have learned before. Or, we may expect them to come to us having learned certain important concepts, only to find that they were not in their previous teacher's plan for the year.

Additionally, a good curriculum will clearly link to whatever standards form the basis for your accountability testing (Common Core State Standards or individual state or provincial standards). It will help you answer the question, "What specifically will my students be held accountable for having learned?" A curriculum that has been aligned to state or provincial standards, coupled with a test designed to measure them, allows you to use accountability test data to identify which portions of your curriculum students do well on and which portions students do not do well on, and to adjust teaching and resources accordingly.

Articulation between grade levels and alignment with accountability measures are only part of the picture. Another crucial aspect is the amount of learning represented by your grade level or course learning targets. Does your curriculum take into account the "180-day rule?" That is, does it acknowledge how much time you have to teach? It is not possible to teach everything that is important to learn, yet many curricula still include significantly more content standards than can be taught in the given time, thus turning a blind eye to the pace of learning. This is a big problem when teachers try to incorporate formative assessment strategies: there is not time for reteaching. A good curriculum guide will define your responsibility for what to teach and will allow you to pace instruction with student needs in mind.

Lastly, we recommend that the learning targets in your curriculum be stated so that everyone who teaches a subject interprets them the same way. Is it clear to everyone what to teach from the statements in your curriculum?

DECONSTRUCTING COMPLEX CONTENT STANDARDS

Even if your curriculum is comprised of clearly stated content standards, some of them may be complex. Others may require further refinement or translation in order to know exactly what to teach and assess. When you encounter a complex or unclear standard, we recommend the process of *deconstructing standards*. Often and ideally, this is work done by curriculum staff at the state or district level. But even when that is the case, engaging in the process with colleagues at the school level builds ownership for the expectations we hold in common for students, and helps ensure agreement of the intended learning, so that everyone responsible for teaching the standard has interpreted it the same way.

Deconstructing standards is the process of breaking a broad standard, goal, or benchmark into smaller, more explicit learning targets that can be used to guide daily classroom instruction.

During the deconstructing process, it is important to distinguish between learning targets—statements of what we want students to know and be able to do—and the manner in which we'll assess them—the tasks and assignments we'll give students to do. Remember, you are looking at what the content standard requires students to know and be able to do, not how you will assess it.

Once you have found a standard that needs deconstructing, follow these three steps.

1. Determine the Target Type

Is the content standard, as written, a knowledge, reasoning, skill, or product target? To determine this, consider whether the content standard's ultimate goal is the acquisition of knowledge, the development of reasoning capabilities, the demonstration of a physical skill, or the creation of a product. For Example 3.2 and For Example 3.3 show content standards deconstructed following this process.

When the standard includes several discrete learning targets, list each separately and identify the target type for each. Then proceed with steps 2 and 3 for each separate learning target. For Example 3.4 shows how you might carry out step 1 with a writing standard that is comprised of several separate learning targets. (Steps 2 and 3 are not completed in the example.)

2. Identify the Prerequisite or Underlying Knowledge, Reasoning, and/or Skills

At this step, answer the following four questions:

- What does a student need to know and understand to attain mastery of this standard?
- What patterns of reasoning, if any, are required to attain mastery of this standard?
- What skills, if any, are required for mastery of this standard?
- What products, if any, would students need to be proficient in creating to master this standard?

FIGURE 3.9 Process for Deconstructing Standards

1. Determine the ultimate target type represented in the standard.
2. Identify the prerequisite or underlying knowledge, reasoning, and/or skills.
3. Check your work for accuracy and reasonableness.

For Example 3.1

Kentucky's Deconstructing Standards Flowchart

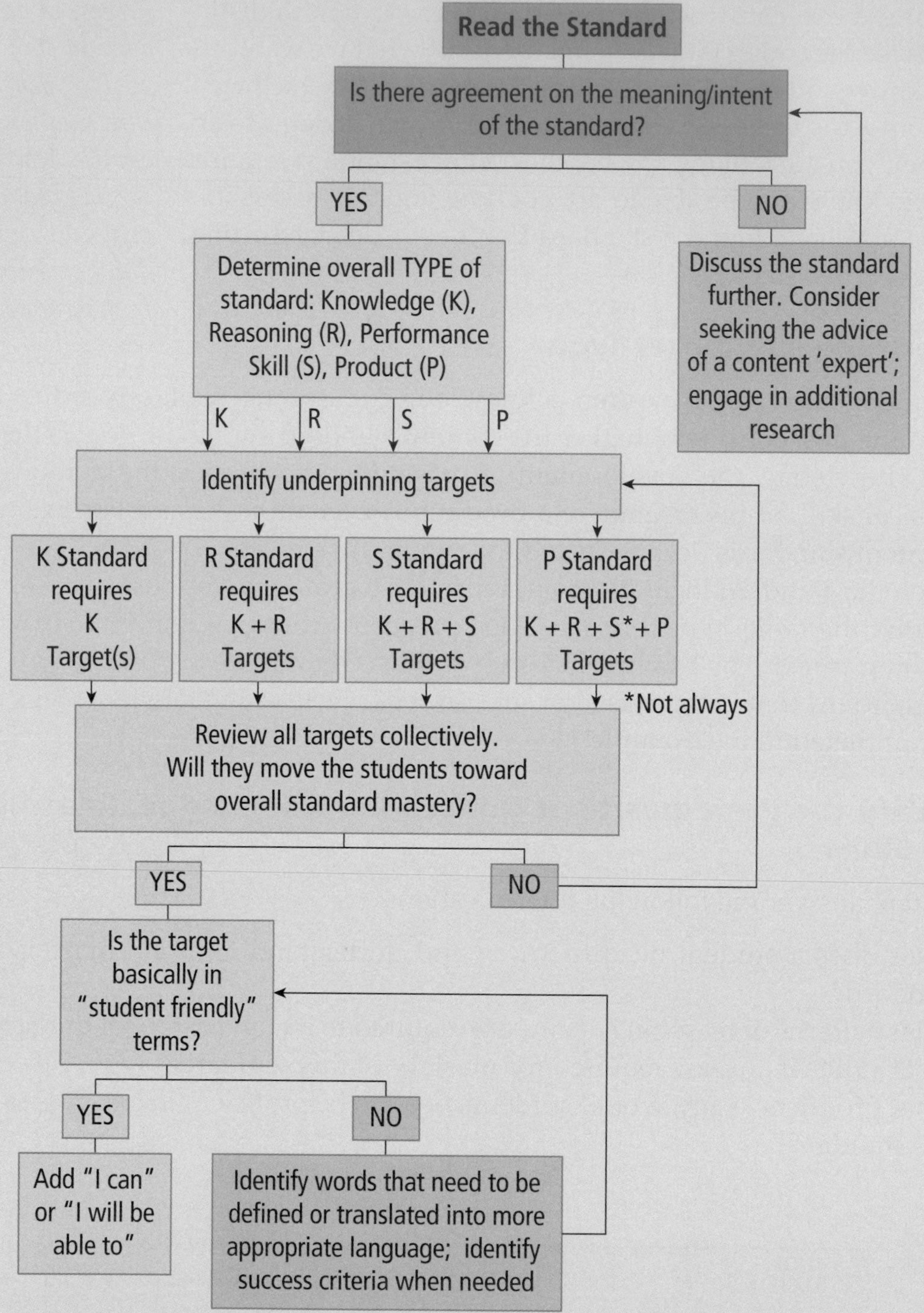

Adapted from *Classroom Assessment for Student Learning: Doing it Right, Using it Well.* Stiggins, Arter, Chappuis, and Chappuis, 2004

Source: Reprinted with permission from Kentucky Department of Education, Frankfort, KY. Downloaded May 20, 2011 from: http://www.education.ky.gov/users/otl/KLN/DeconstructingStandards.pdf

For Example 3.2

Deconstructing a Mathematics Standard

Grade Level/ Course: Algebra 1 Unit 4

Standard with code:	*A. REI.4a Solve quadratic equations in one variable.* *a. Use the method of completing the square to transform any quadratic equation in x into an equation of the form (x – p)2 = q that has the same solutions. Derive the quadratic formula from this form.*
Domain:	*Reasoning with Equations and Inequalities*
Cluster:	*Solve equations and inequalities in one variable.*

Type: _____Knowledge __X__Reasoning _____Performance Skill _____Product

Knowledge Targets	Reasoning Targets	Performance Skills Targets	Product Targets
Use the method of completing the square to transform any quadratic equation in x into an equation of the form (x – p)2 – q that has the same solutions.	*Derive the quadratic formula by completing the square on a quadratic equation in x.*		
Solve quadratic equations in one variable.			
Notes from Appendix A: Students should learn of the existence of the complex number system, but will not solve quadratics with complex solutions until Algebra II.			

Source: Reprinted from Kentucky Department of Education, Frankfort, KY. Reprinted by permission. Downloaded May 20, 2011 from http://www.education.ky.gov/NR/rdonlyres/C5603F9A-57F3-437E-AE0B-74A0CB5FDC07/0/HighSchoolAlgebra1.pdf

For Example 3.3

Deconstructing a Reading Standard

CCR: Analyze how and why individuals, events, and ideas develop and interact over the course of a text.

Strand: Reading Literature	*Cluster: Key Ideas and Details*	*Grade: 5*	*Standard #: 3*

Standard: Compare and contrast two or more characters, settings, or events in a story or drama, drawing on specific details in the text (e.g., how characters interact).

Type: ______Knowledge __X__Reasoning ______Performance Skill ______Product

Learning Targets

What are the knowledge, reasoning, performance skills, and products that underpin the standard?

Knowledge Target	Reasoning Target	Performance Skill Target	Product Target
Define terms: compare and contrast *Identify specific details that describe:* • *characters* • *settings* • *events* *in a story or drama* *Identify similarities of two or more:* • *characters* • *settings* • *events* *in a story or drama* *Identify differences between two or more characters in a story or drama*	*Compare two or more:* • *characters* • *settings* • *events* *in a text using specific details from a text* *Contrast two or more:* • *characters* • *settings* • *events* *in a text using specific details from a text*		

Source: Reprinted with permission from Kentucky Department of Education. Downloaded May 20, 2011 from http://www.education.ky.gov/NR/rdonlyres/F1E712E1-9083-4947-9493-F813B1830690/0/FifthGradeELA.pdf

For Example 3.4

Deconstructing a Writing Standard Comprised of Several Separate Learning Targets

Writing Standard 8, Grade 6 (CCSSI, 2010a, p. 44)

"Gather relevant information from multiple print and digital sources; assess the credibility of each source; and quote or paraphrase the data and conclusions of others while avoiding plagiarism and providing basic bibliographic information for sources."

This standard has multiple learning targets stated, so the first step is to separate them and classify each component:

Learning Target	Target Type & Rationale
Gather relevant information from multiple print and digital sources	*Evaluative reasoning: Gathering relevant information requires judging information against a standard of relevancy.*
Assess the credibility of each source	*Evaluative reasoning: Assessing credibility requires applying criteria for credibility to each source.*
Quote or paraphrase the data and conclusions of others while avoiding plagiarism	*Evaluative reasoning and synthesis: The first decision students will make is whether to quote or paraphrase; this involves making a judgment about which will be more effective in the context. When students paraphrase, they will be engaged in synthesis as well.*
Provide basic bibliographic information for source	*Procedural knowledge: There are steps to follow for citing sources correctly. Students will be following a learned protocol.*

The second step is to deconstruct each target.

TARGET: Gather relevant information from multiple print and digital sources.

Knowledge:

Reasoning:

TARGET: Assess the credibility of each source.

Knowledge:

Reasoning:

TARGET: Quote or paraphrase the data and conclusions of others while avoiding plagiarism.

Knowledge:

Reasoning:

TARGET: Provide basic bibliographic information for sources.

Knowledge:

While engaged in this step, take the following into account:

- If a target is at the knowledge level, all underlying targets will be at the knowledge level. There will be no reasoning, skill, or product components.
- Reasoning targets will have knowledge components, but they do not require skill or product components.
- Skill targets *always* have knowledge underpinnings. They usually require reasoning as well.
- Product targets will require knowledge and reasoning, and in some cases might be underpinned by skill targets as well.

3. Check Your Work for Alignment and Reasonableness

Checking for alignment means checking to be sure that all of the enabling learning targets you have listed are truly necessary to accomplish the ultimate target. Also check to be sure that you haven't included information about how you might assess it. For example, consider the standard, "Compare and contrast democracies with other forms of government," a reasoning target. It has knowledge underpinnings: knowledge of what a democracy is and knowledge of other types of government. It also has reasoning underpinnings: proficiency with comparing and contrasting. So, there are two, and only two, target types in the content standard—knowledge and reasoning. Let's say you want to assess the standard by having students create a product. You might be tempted to include learning targets relating to the product as you deconstruct the standard, *but don't*. The standard only requires knowledge and reasoning. As written, you can evaluate it several ways. If you do decide to have students create a product, you will want to make sure your evaluation reflects the knowledge and reasoning learning targets of the content standard and that creating the product hasn't interfered with students' ability to demonstrate mastery of the content standard.

Checking for reasonableness means paying attention to how many enabling targets you have listed. The deconstructing process always runs the risk of taking the ultimate target back to learning taught years before. This can helpful for diagnosing specific problems when students have difficulty, but it makes for a crazy-complicated curriculum if you take it too far and include all possibilities. Your deconstructed content standard then represents a multiyear curriculum, a progression spanning several years' worth of learning. When deconstructing, check to make sure you have not listed more learning targets than necessary for students *at your level* to achieve mastery of the ultimate content standard being deconstructed. If your K–12 curriculum is well thought out, the basic prerequisite knowledge from previous years will be represented in those years' content standards.

FAQ 3.4

Deconstructing Product Targets

Question

If an overall standard is a product learning target, will you have all four types of targets leading up to it?

Answer

This is a common question. The short answer is "Sometimes, but not always."

When the answer is yes:

Let's begin with a Visual Arts product target: "Creates drawings demonstrating one- and two-point perspectives." This target will have all three target types underpinning it. Students will need to know what one- and two-point perspectives are (knowledge), they will have to plan a drawing (reasoning), and they will have to employ drawing skills to create the product.

Now consider a geometry product target: "Creates formal models of regular solids." This target rests on students' knowledge and reasoning abilities: knowing what the regular solids look like and using analysis to figure out how to make them. There are skills involved, also. Students could accomplish this by creating a pattern on paper and then cutting, folding, and pasting. However, they could also create the models on a computer by creating or selecting the appropriate shapes and then dragging and dropping them to make a template. So, there are skills involved, but in this case they are context specific.

When the answer is no:

Let's look at a cross-subject product target: "Writes arguments focused on discipline-specific content." This target has knowledge and reasoning underpinnings such as knowing how to write a claim, identifying alternate or opposing views, evaluating sources to be used to support the claim for accuracy and credibility, and so forth. No skill targets are needed to accomplish it successfully (beyond handwriting or keyboarding, which we will assume are considered prerequisite and have already been taught).

My Classroom Then and Now 3.1

Jessica Cynkar

What we did . . .

One of the most important things that we did to expand on our formative assessment practices was to deconstruct the state standards and indicators. Our 6th-grade English department requested two professional development days to create common definitions and understandings of the content standards and indicators. We felt that we needed to be on the same page as to "what" we were teaching, but how we got there was up to us as professionals.

We wanted the focus of this time to be very intentional and specific, so we set norms at the beginning. We wanted to make sure that we stuck to one topic at a time and the time wasn't about sharing "this is what I do in my classroom," that it was more about what we need to teach and how we get there. During this time we reviewed several sources of information: standards and indicators at our grade level (6th), standards and indicators for 5th and 7th grades, standardized testing information, and a variety of classroom resources. Together we deconstructed the indicators into their underpinning learning targets. We created common definitions and "I can" statements, added resources, and developed assessment questions. We also began to note lessons and ideas we each had for teaching each target.

How we benefited . . .

These tips have been invaluable when I've started to plan a unit or concept to teach. They have become a bag of tricks to reference, especially when students need additional support or a way to stretch their learning. Another benefit is that that it has become very clear what lessons are not working or do not fit the content that we need to teach.

Source: Used with permission from Jessica Cynkar, 6th-grade language arts teacher, Olentangy Local School District, Lewis Center, OH, 2011

COMMUNICATING LEARNING TARGETS TO STUDENTS

Once our learning targets are clear to us, we need to make sure they will be clear to students (Figure 3.10). If you think back to the research on the effects of assessment *for* learning on student achievement, you will recall that a key feature to student success is students knowing where they are going—that is, understanding what they are to learn.

Making targets clear to students helps them understand that the assignment is the means *and the learning is the* goal.

Absent clear targets, students lack the information they need to self-assess, set goals, and act on the descriptive feedback they receive. Poorly defined learning expectations cause similar problems to poorly defined behavior expectations—confusion and conflict—which set students up for failure down the road.

Sharing learning targets with students can play out in several ways depending on the kind of target and its complexity. Some learning targets may be clear enough

FIGURE 3.10 Making Learning Targets Clear to Students

State it in its original form.

Or

Create a student-friendly definition and then share it.

Or

Create a student-friendly rubric.

to be stated to students in their original form—"Today, we're learning how to prepare microscope slides." Other targets, while clear to you, may not be clear to students, so you may want to translate them into student-friendly terms (Chappuis, 2009). This works especially well for reasoning targets—"We're learning to summarize text. This means we're learning to make a short statement of the central ideas of what we read." For reasoning, skill, and product targets that will be assessed with a rubric, you will need to find or create a student-friendly version of the rubric, which we will address in Chapters 6 and 7.

Converting Knowledge and Reasoning Learning Targets to Student-friendly Language

The process for converting learning targets into student-friendly language is especially useful with patterns of reasoning. Let us say we want students to learn to summarize text. How might we explain to fourth graders what that means? Here is a process you can use (Chappuis, 2009):

1. Define the word or words representing the pattern of reasoning. Use a dictionary, your textbook, your state content standards document, or other reference materials specific to your subject. If you are working with a colleague, come to agreement on definitions.
2. Convert the definition into language your students are likely to understand.
3. Rewrite the definition as an "I" or a "We" statement: "I am learning to _____"; "I can _______"; "We are learning to _____"; or "We can _______."
4. Try the definition out with students. Note their response and refine as required.
5. Let students try this process occasionally, using learning targets you think they could successfully define and paraphrase. Make sure their definition is congruent with your vision of the target.

For Example 3.5

Student-friendly Definitions of Reasoning Learning Targets

Inferring

I can infer. This means I can make a reasonable guess based on information.

Generalizing

I can generalize. This means I can compare pieces of evidence to see what they have in common. Then I can make an umbrella statement that is true for them and is also true for a broader array of instances.

Predicting

I can predict. This means I can use what I already know (or evidence) to guess at what will happen next.

Identifying Cause and Effect

I can identify causes and effects. This means I can describe relationships between events by answering two questions: "What happened?" and "Why did it happen?"

Drawing Conclusions

I can draw conclusions. This means I can begin with a general (an "umbrella") idea or statement and identify specific situations in which it is true.

Comparing

I can compare and contrast. This means that I can tell how things are alike and how they are different.

Evaluating

I can make evaluations. This means I can identify criteria upon which to make a judgment, apply it to a specific situation, and express an opinion based on the criteria. I can also justify my opinion by using the criteria.

Summarizing

I can summarize. This means I can make a short statement of the big ideas or main message of what I read (hear, view, observe).

Determining Main Idea and Supporting Details

I can determine main ideas and identify supporting details. This means I can find important ideas in the text and point out which facts or information help to make (or contribute to) that main idea.

My Classroom Then and Now 3.2

Elizabeth Schoo

I used to . . .

I used to teach my physical science class by following district objectives derived from state standards. These objectives were easy for me to understand and my lessons were based on these, but nowhere in my teaching was I telling my students what the goal for their learning of that day was to be. I just assumed it was obvious.

Now I . . .

Now my classroom units and lessons are all based on student-friendly "I can" statements. I have provided these statements to my students in numerous ways. In our science binders at the beginning of each chapter, I provide a sheet stating the chapter's new "I can" statements as well as any previous "I can" statements that will be reinforced. Our science team has developed a pre-assessment for the students to determine what level of knowledge they would rank themselves as having concerning the "I can" targets. Students rerank their level of knowledge at the end of the chapter and use the information to help them structure their studying for the final assessment.

To be even more student friendly, I have started to include the chapter "I can" statements on each set of notes, reinforcement worksheets, labs, quizzes, etc. that I give my students. When assessing my students at the end of a chapter, my review guide consists of revisiting these statements. I have taught my students to structure their studying based on how well they can answer the "I can" statement.

Why I changed . . .

I always told my students that there was no secret to what I was going to be teaching that day, but in reflection, by not writing student-friendly chapter targets and using them with my students, I was, in fact, keeping them in the dark.

What I notice as a result . . .

By providing my students with easy-to-understand targets for the day's lesson, they are able to focus their learning and understand the outcome for that day; they aren't left guessing what they were supposed to have learned. When surveyed to see if they liked this new format, most students responded that their study time was now more productive. They knew what to study—their time was spent more wisely on studying the statements that they lacked detail in answering rather than reviewing haphazardly everything from the chapter.

> My assessments are more accurate now because I create questions that match the "I can" statements. In turn, my students see more success. The secret is out and the light is on! Simply put, changing to writing student-friendly targets and providing them with those targets has allowed me to create a classroom environment that invites students to create ownership of their learning.
>
> *Source:* Used with permission from Elizabeth Schoo, 8th-grade science teacher, Community Unit School District 95, Lake Zurich, IL, 2011

WHEN THE WRITTEN CURRICULUM IS NOT THE TAUGHT CURRICULUM

Your curriculum is your first assessment guide. Problems arise when the written curriculum merely sits on the shelf. Absent an easily understood curriculum guide, teachers often rely on the textbook, a list of units or activities, or a series of projects to fill its role. Let's take a look at what happens in each of these cases.

Using the Textbook in Place of the Curriculum

If we rely on the textbook to stand in as our curriculum, we may think we have solved the problem of articulation between grade levels, and perhaps alignment with state or provincial standards. However, when textbooks serve as the curriculum, we face several problems.

First, many textbooks contain too much content to teach in a year, which is in part due to how they are designed. If you are a member of a district textbook review committee (searching for a new series to purchase), you will generally look for the best match between the text's coverage and the content standards you have adopted. Textbook companies know this; they include in their products as much as could be taught in that grade level in that subject, in order to align with all potential clients' curricular objectives. (Even when texts are aligned with a particular set of content standards, it does not mean they are aligned with those standards *alone*.) Therefore, by design, most textbooks address much more content than can be successfully taught in any one class in a year. In order to include so much content, textbooks can lack in-depth treatment of many concepts. In addition, textbooks seldom provide guidance on which information is of lesser and greater importance. When we cover material, we teach at a pace that far outstrips the pace required for learning for most students; when we select what to teach independently of our colleagues, we negate the benefit for students of experiencing an articulated curriculum.

In "Seven Reasons Why a Textbook Is Not a Curriculum," Shutes and Peterson (1994) assert the following:

> It is . . . time to recognize that in a curriculum vacuum, textbooks have fostered a preoccupation with content that has made content coverage an end in itself, has made didactic treatment of fact-level information the standard teaching method, and has overwhelmed learners with more information than they could possibly handle. Ironically, the teachers' strategies to cope with excess content may have alienated many of their students not only from the content but from school itself. (p. 12)

Note that they attribute use of textbooks as the curriculum to a curriculum vacuum. What is ironic today is that very few of us are operating in a curriculum vacuum, yet textbooks' tables of contents still function as the outline of the learning for many classes. Consider these facts as reported by Schmoker and Marzano (1999):

> Although U.S. mathematics textbooks attempt to address 175 percent more topics than do German textbooks and 350 percent more topics than do Japanese textbooks, both German and Japanese students significantly outperform U.S. students in mathematics. Similarly, although U.S. science textbooks attempt to cover 930 percent more topics than do German textbooks, and 433 percent more topics than do Japanese textbooks, both German and Japanese students significantly outperform U.S. students in science achievement as well (Schmidt, McKnight, & Raizen, 1996). (n.p.)

Using Units, Activities, or Projects in Place of the Curriculum

When used as our curriculum, a series of units, activities, or projects may well keep students busy and motivated. However, if activities are not consciously designed or selected with learning targets in mind, if we are not clear about the intended learning *in advance*, we may not be teaching what is most important to learn. If that is the case, we are also not adequately preparing students for the external high-stakes accountability tests they will encounter whose items are aligned to our written curriculum. And, if we do not begin with clear classroom learning targets, assessments cannot be counted on to provide accurate information about the learning.

In addition, without the unifying thread of underlying learning targets, we will not be able to build intentionally on previous learning, either from our own teaching or from the teaching in prior grades. Neither will subsequent teachers be able to build intentionally on what we have done with students. In essence, we are each in private practice, in our own teaching universe, unable to predict what our students will bring with them and unable to articulate what we send them off to the next grade with. As teachers come and go from a building, the instructional program changes course. Our scores on accountability measures are up or down, and we may have to rely on an outside program to straighten us out, imposing a "drop-in" remedial mini-curriculum.

Although such practices were common when many of us were students, today none of this is in the best interest of students or teachers.

THE BENEFITS OF CLEAR LEARNING TARGETS

Few educators would disagree that defining expectations for student behavior or conduct up front will head off discipline problems down the road. We can expect the same outcome when we clearly define what students are responsible for learning—we solve a number of problems before they surface. With the advent of the Common Core State Standards has come a renewed focus on academic rigor and on a *clear, teachable and assessable* curriculum at the state and district levels. This has also served to spark a renewed dialogue about what constitutes a clear learning target. Most certainly, teachers need to understand curriculum documents to be able to use them. But the benefits of making sure our targets are clear extend beyond that, for teachers, students, and parents (Figure 3.11).

Benefits to Teachers

1. KNOWING WHAT TO TEACH. First, begin with clear statements of the intended learning benefits instruction. Consider a reading curriculum that includes the content standard, "Students will comprehend fictional, informational, and task-oriented text."

FIGURE 3.11 Benefits of Clear Targets

To Teachers

1. Knowing what to teach
2. Knowing what to assess
3. Knowing what instructional activities to plan
4. Avoiding "coverage" at the expense of learning
5. Ability to interpret and use assessment results
6. System for tracking and reporting information
7. Common ground for working collaboratively with other teachers

To Students

1. Understanding what they are responsible for learning
2. Understanding and acting on feedback
3. Being prepared to self-assess and set goals
4. Being able to track, reflect on, and share their own progress

To Parents

1. Helping children at home
2. Understanding the grade report
3. Focusing discussions at conferences

While it is clear that the ultimate goal is reading comprehension in a variety of contexts, if the curriculum does not define "comprehend" and identify the kinds of fictional, informational, and task-oriented texts students should work with that year, interpretation is left up to the individual teacher and may involve guesswork. On the other hand, if the grade level curriculum breaks "comprehend" down into a set of learning targets such as, "identifies main idea and supporting details," "summarizes text," "makes inferences and predictions," and "uses context clues to determine the meaning of unfamiliar words," individual teachers are much better prepared to know what to teach.

2. KNOWING WHAT TO ASSESS. One of the most important contributors to accuracy of assessment information is the match to what was or will be taught. If we are not clear about the specific learning targets at the focus of instruction, we will not be able to create or select assessments that accurately measure achievement. Before planning instructional activities, it is a good idea to have a sense of what you will assess and how.

3. KNOWING WHAT INSTRUCTIONAL ACTIVITIES TO PLAN. Once we know what our learning targets are and have defined how we will assess them, we are able to think clearly about what combination of instruction and learning experiences will prepare students both to learn what they need to know and to demonstrate their learning.

My Classroom Then and Now 3.3

Jeff Overbay

I used to . . .

Over the years I had developed a routine for teaching a new unit. All assessments would be CD-Rom generated. Students would use the textbook to define vocabulary at the end of a chapter. All activities would be a topical match for the content being taught. These activities came from the textbook materials or those I had gathered over the years of teaching. I would use the state standards and the textbook to create objectives for a unit. The textbook was what I used to drive my teaching.

Now I . . .

I have developed a new procedure for teaching a new unit. State standards are deconstructed first. Assessments are now both formative and summative. The pre-assessment is 10 to 12 questions in the agree–disagree format. The vocabulary and activities are congruent with the deconstructed standards. Students are given a self-assessment guide that consists of student-friendly learning targets. This guide is also generated from the deconstructed standards. These work together to help students be more involved in both the learning and assessment process.

The daily classroom procedure has also changed. At the beginning of class I place a guiding question on the board. This question is based on one of the student-friendly learning targets. Under this question I put an "I can" statement. This is something that the students must master that day or in the next few days. When appropriate I give an exit-slip question to measure mastery of a concept. Quizzes are given as the unit progresses. Finally, the summative assessment is given after the content has been taught.

Why I changed . . .

There are many reasons for changing my methods of teaching. First, there never was congruency from the beginning to the end of a unit. Even though I had objectives there was never a true relationship between what was being taught and the state standards. The pre-assessment also needed to be changed. The information gathered is now useful in driving instruction. Next is that the vocabulary is now the critical vocabulary. Students are not wasting time looking up definitions. Finally, the assessment process needed to be changed. The self-assessment of learning targets is a valuable way of getting the students involved in their own learning process. Guiding questions and "I can" statements help the students stay focused from day to day. The quizzes match the targets so students know if they are succeeding as they go instead of waiting until the end of a unit. The summative assessment is now an accurate measurement of student achievement.

What I notice as a result . . .

This new format is helpful to both the students and myself. I now have a well-designed congruent "roadmap" to follow and the students have a better understanding of where they are going and how they are going to get there. As a result I have seen an increase in student achievement in the classroom and on the state assessment.

Source: Used with permission from Jeff Overbay, 7th-/8th-grade science teacher, Bell County School District, Pineville, KY, 2011

4. AVOIDING "COVERAGE" AT THE EXPENSE OF LEARNING. It's the beginning of May. You look at what is left to teach and the number of days left in the year and worry about how you'll get it all in. If it's world history, twentieth-century study may boil down to three quick wars. If it's math, geometry may be reduced to a few constructions, or statistics and probability to a few games of chance. If it's language arts, poetry may get the boot. A well-designed curriculum helps us avoid cramming large amounts of content into short periods of time, or "teaching by mentioning it" as Wiggins and McTighe put it (1998, p. 21). When your local curriculum is comprised of clear learning targets, it is easier to determine whether it is "doable," that is, "learnable" (as opposed to "coverable"), in the given time of a semester or year. The hard choices regarding what to leave in and what to take out should have been made before a local curriculum is finalized. Only then can you reliably use it to map out the year in advance, maximizing the chances that you will get students where they need to be by the end of the year.

5. INTERPRETING AND USING ASSESSMENT RESULTS. When you begin with well-defined learning targets, you are able to plan assessments that reflect exactly what you will teach and what you expect students to learn. Then the results of assessments can be used to further learning, because you can disaggregate the information learning target by learning target to identify areas of growth and areas needing further work. You can also use this information to provide students with effective feedback—feedback that relates directly to the intended learning—during the learning, while there is still time to act on it. The effectiveness of data-driven decision making depends on your ability to use assessment results in these ways, which all rely on a foundation of clear targets.

6. TRACKING AND REPORTING INFORMATION. When you know what learning targets each assessment represents, you can track achievement by learning target or content standard, rather than by assignment title or assessment type. This approach allows you to use your records to more accurately determine what students have and have not mastered and to keep records that track achievement in ways that facilitate the completion of standards-based report cards. (See Chapter 9 for an in-depth discussion of tracking and recordkeeping options for formative and summative assessment information.)

7. WORKING COLLABORATIVELY WITH OTHER TEACHERS. One of the most powerful benefits to teachers of having agreed-on clear targets and teaching to them is the common ground it offers in working with other teachers. Schmoker (2002, p. 2), well before the advent of common core state standards, suggests the following:

> The most enormous but peculiarly unsung benefit of common standards is that they provide the rich common context essential to focused, productive teacher collaboration, a sine qua non for improvement (Fullan 2000; Sparks 1998). Stated simply: If we want schools to improve, instruction—teaching lessons themselves —must improve (Stigler and Hiebert 1999). But there also must be a common set of standards. And there must be a commitment to reaching measurable achievement goals by making real adjustments to how we teach these common standards. There is no other way (Glickman 2002, 4–5).

Benefits to Students

1. UNDERSTANDING WHAT THEY ARE RESPONSIBLE FOR LEARNING. Explaining the intended learning to students is the crucial first step in helping them know where they are going. As Stiggins (2008, p. 1, emphasis added) states, "Students *can* hit any target they can see that holds still for them." However, if students have no idea what they are supposed to learn, if the only information they have is that we are doing "science" or "page 121" or "the odd-numbered problems," few of them are likely to infer the intended learning. They are more likely to believe that the ultimate aim of their effort is to complete the assignment. The assignment, however, is the means to the end, which is the intended learning.

2. UNDERSTANDING AND ACTING ON FEEDBACK. Effective feedback relates directly to the learning, pointing out strengths and offering specific guidance for improvement. If students don't understand what the learning targets are, they won't be likely to understand or act on the feedback intended to help them improve.

3. BEING PREPARED TO SELF-ASSESS AND SET GOALS. Students cannot accurately self-assess without a clear vision of what they are aiming for. When we make targets clear to students, they have a standard to compare their current status to, making self-assessment more objective (Sadler, 1989), and information to use when setting goals for next steps.

4. TRACKING, REFLECTING ON, AND SHARING THEIR PROGRESS. With learning targets that are clear from the outset, students can track their own mastery of expectations by target or standard. Without a direct, visible connection to the specific learning target, grades only tell them how *well* they have learned something. Students need to see how their grades connect to the learning targets represented on each assignment and assessment in order to *connect their work and level of achievement to learning*. This helps them become clear about what they have mastered and what they still need to work on. With that information, they are able to reflect on their progress and to share their thoughts at conference time.

Benefits to Parents

1. HELPING CHILDREN AT HOME. Understanding what the intended learning is helps parents focus their assistance with their children. It helps them know the intent of the assignment, which guides the assistance they provide. For instance, if you are teaching students how to edit their own papers and you communicate that learning to parents, you can ask that they not do the editing for their children. If you are working on map-reading skills and assistance at home would help, you can suggest that parents have their children practice using a map to give directions on a car trip. However, if you are asking students to complete a project and parents only have the project instructions to students to go by, they will be unlikely to know what they can and shouldn't do to support the intended learning, if and when their children need help.

2. UNDERSTANDING THE GRADE REPORT. Additionally, being clear about the intended learning helps parents understand what grades mean in terms of what their children have and have not learned. Sending home or posting on your website a list of learning targets written in parent-friendly language can help communicate the depth

My Classroom Then and Now 3.4

Sue Cho & Aaron Mukai

We used to . . .

We used to think we were doing great things with daily learning targets. Before beginning each chapter, we developed the learning target for each lesson in kid-friendly language. These learning targets would then be posted daily in our classrooms. In addition, we wrote these learning targets on our pre-assessments, exit tasks, and other formative assessments. We would even have our students self-assess on these learning targets at the beginning (pre-assessment), during (formative assessments), and after (summative assessments) each chapter.

Now we . . .

While we still do all of the things mentioned, we wanted to make these learning targets more meaningful to students. For starters, we revised our learning targets with quality indicators to make it clear to the students what they **should be able to do** and what they **need to do** to reach it. To do this, at the beginning of each lesson, we have the students write down the learning target with a fill in the blank option: "I can find equivalent fractions by __________." After we go through the lesson and before students work on the practice problems, we revisit the learning target and have the students fill in the blank: "I can find equivalent fractions by <u>multiplying or dividing the numerator and the denominator by the same number</u>." The students are now able to make a connection with the learning target and the problems they are solving.

We started having our students use the learning targets to set goals for each chapter. Each pre-assessment is sectioned by the learning targets aligned with the same state standards. After a student has received their scored pre-assessment, the student is able to identify areas of improvement based on the learning target.

Lastly, we began to use a Chapter Formative Tracking Sheet. We have each student keep track of their progress on different formative assessments throughout each chapter. The students are to record three items on their tracking sheet: the name of the formative, the learning target connected to the formative, and their score on the formative. This enables students to have a better understanding of how they are doing in regards to their learning throughout the chapter. It also provides students with a clear vision the targets they still may need work.

Why we changed . . .

We changed because there seemed to be a disconnect between the learning target and with what students were learning. Looking back, we felt that if the student was able to see the learning target, they would understand the learning target. This is why we tried to post it everywhere from the classroom wall to our formative and summative assessments. The problem was the learning target lacked ownership. Our students did not seem to do anything with the learning target. We wanted to make a connection between the learning target, student learning, and the student. We also wanted our students to be able to monitor their progress toward the target better and become more invested in the learning.

What we notice as a result . . .

Learning targets have become more than just words that our students read on the board or on a piece of paper. For starters, with the quality indicators, our students are able to make a connection between the math problems they are working on with the aligned learning target. When students now read their learning target, they not only understand what the goal is but what they need to do to reach this goal.

Students also seemed to have a better understanding of their progress throughout the chapter. The goal setting using the targets at the beginning of the chapter provides a direct focus of what areas students need to improve, so that they are able to meet or exceed the learning target. The formative tracking sheet helps students get into the habit of reflecting on their own learning. Having the students actively engaged in monitoring their own progress toward learning targets helps the students understand the importance of learning targets.

Source: Used with permission from Sue Cho & Aaron Mukai, 6th-grade mathematics teachers, Mukilteo School District, Mukilteo, WA, 2011

and breadth of the academic work their children are engaged in. When grades come home, parents can talk specifically with their children about the learning that underpins their strengths and areas for improvement. This helps parents and students understand what is behind the grade and helps them avoid damaging generalizations, such as, "My child is not good at reading."

3. FOCUSING DISCUSSION AT CONFERENCES. Similarly, having a set of clear and understandable learning targets focuses the discussions during conferences on what the student is learning and how well the student is learning it. Clear targets allow you to be specific about strengths and areas needing additional attention and to give specific advice about how the parent can best help the child.

CONCLUDING THOUGHTS

A good portion of this chapter has been devoted to the assessment benefits of a quality curriculum. It is not our purpose in this book to direct curriculum development, but to make as strong a case as we can for the necessity of framing clear and specific

FIGURE 3.12 Without Clear Targets . . .

We can't

- Know if the assessment adequately covers and samples what we taught.
- Correctly identify what students know and don't know and their level of achievement.
- Plan next steps in instruction.
- Give detailed, descriptive feedback to students.
- Have students self-assess or set goals likely to help them learn more.
- Keep track of student learning target by target or standard by standard.
- Complete a standards-based report card.

learning targets at the outset of teaching as an imperative to sound instruction and assessment (Figure 3.12). We emphasize the practical necessity of each teacher understanding each learning target clearly, and the need to be in agreement with others who teach the same subjects. We also emphasize the learning gains that come from formative assessment practices require first that our learning targets be clear to students. No one benefits in the long run when the intended learning is obscure or hidden.

Summary

Clear learning targets are essential for sound assessment. We can't assess accurately what is not clear. We began our exploration of clear targets by identifying five categories of learning targets, providing examples of each. Within those categories, we described a reasoning framework representing six patterns of reasoning that are commonly found in various taxonomies, content standards documents, and assessments. They also represent the kinds of reasoning occurring most frequently in subject area curricula as well as in life beyond school.

We described how to deconstruct complex content standards to make the prerequisite knowledge, reasoning, skill, and/or product targets clear. These form the scaffolding to each student's academic success. We offered suggestions for sharing learning targets with students, including ways to convert learning targets into student-friendly language so they can see the path to their success.

We gave examples of problems that arise when your curriculum or content standards are not yet clear.

Beyond this, clear targets benefit teachers, students, and parents by clarifying in the following ways what to assess and what instructional activities to plan:

- Help to avoid the problem of too much to teach and too little time.
- Provide a foundation for collaborative planning among teachers.
- Facilitate assessment for learning—when students understand the intended learning they are set up for productive self-assessment and goal setting.
- Facilitate communication with parents.

CHAPTER 3 ACTIVITIES

End-of-chapter activities are intended to help you master the chapter's learning targets. They are designed to deepen your understanding of the chapter content, provide discussion topics for learning team meetings, and guide implementation of the practices taught in the chapter.

Forms and materials for completing each activity appear in editable Microsoft Word format in the Chapter 3 CD file. Documents on the CD are marked with this symbol:

Chapter 3 Learning Targets

1. Explain the connection between clear targets and assessment quality.
2. Classify learning targets by type.
3. Determine whether your learning targets are clear to you and to students.
4. Clarify and deconstruct learning targets as needed.
5. Create student-friendly versions of learning targets as needed.

Activity 3.1 Keep a Reflective Journal
Activity 3.2 Connect Clear Targets to Assessment Quality
Activity 3.3 Classify Learning Targets
Activity 3.4 Identify Clear Learning Targets
Activity 3.5 Deconstruct a Content Standard
Activity 3.6 Create Student-friendly Learning Targets
Activity 3.7 Reflect on Your Own Learning
Activity 3.8 Select Portfolio Artifacts

Activity 3.1

Keep a Reflective Journal

Keep a record of your thoughts, questions, and any implementation activities you tried while reading Chapter 3.

Reflective Journal Form

Activity 3.2

Connect Clear Targets to Assessment Quality

After reading Chapter 3, explain three ways in which clear targets are a necessary precursor to assessment quality. Provide examples from your own experience to illustrate the connection between clear targets and assessment quality.

None

Activity 3.3

Classify Learning Targets

Work independently, with a partner, or with a team to complete this activity. The activity works best if all participants are familiar with the unit.

1. Select a short unit that you are currently teaching or will teach this year. (Alternatively, you can carry this activity out with a portion of the content standards listed in your curriculum guide.)
2. List the learning targets that will be the focus of the unit.
3. Classify each target as Knowledge, Reasoning, Skill, or Product (KRSP).
4. If you are unable to classify some targets as written, mark them with a question (?).

Template for Classifying Learning Targets

Activity 3.4

Identify Clear Learning Targets

Work independently, with a partner, or with your learning team to complete this activity. The activity works best if all participants are familiar with the unit.

1. Select a unit that you are currently teaching or will teach this year. List each learning target. You may want to use the learning targets you classified in Activity 3.3.
2. Decide which learning targets are clear as written. For these targets, you know what to teach and how to plan instruction without further clarification.
3. Identify any learning targets needing clarification. These are targets that are too vague, use terminology that you don't understand, or that just don't make sense. You will have to get clarification regarding meaning from another source.
4. Identify any learning targets that need to be deconstructed. There may be several learning targets described explicitly in one content standard. Or, there may be a number of underlying knowledge, reasoning, and/or skill targets that you will have to identify and then teach for students to attain mastery of the intended learning.

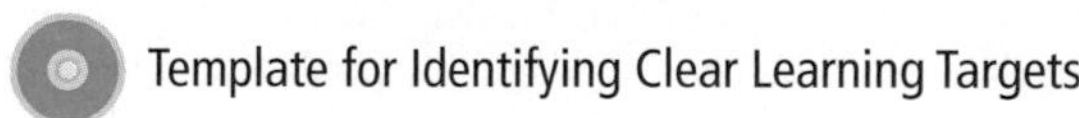
Template for Identifying Clear Learning Targets

Activity 3.5

Deconstruct a Content Standard

Work with a partner or your learning team to complete this activity.

1. Select a content standard that needs deconstructing.
2. Identify its component learning targets by answering these questions:

What knowledge will students need to know to be successful?
What patterns of reasoning, if any, will students need to master to be successful?
What skills, if any, will students need to master to be successful?
What products, if any, will students need to practice creating to be successful?

Template for Deconstructing a Content Standard

Activity 3.6

Create Student-friendly Learning Targets

Work independently, with a partner, or with your learning team to complete this activity.

1. Select a learning target that would benefit from being rephrased for students.
2. Follow the process described in the section, "Converting Knowledge and Reasoning Learning Targets to Student-friendly Language."
3. If you are working with a partner or a team, share any impact you noticed of using the student-friendly definition with your students.

Template for Student-friendly Learning Targets

Activity 3.7

Reflect on Your Learning

Review the Chapter 3 learning targets and select one or more that represented new learning for you or struck you as most significant from this chapter. If you are working individually, write a short reflection that captures your current understanding. If you are working with a partner or a team, either discuss what you have written or use this as a discussion prompt for a team meeting.

Reflect on Chapter 3 Learning

Activity 3.8

Select Portfolio Artifacts

Any of the activities from this chapter can be used as portfolio entries. Select any activity you have completed or artifact you have created that will illustrate your competence at the Chapter 3 learning targets:

1. Explain the connection between clear targets and assessment quality.
2. Classify learning targets by type.
3. Determine whether your learning targets are clear to you and to students.
4. Clarify and deconstruct learning targets as needed.
5. Create student-friendly versions of learning targets as needed.

If you are keeping a reflective journal, you may want to include Chapter 3's entry in your portfolio.

Chapter 3 Portfolio Entry Cover Sheet

CHAPTER

4

Sound Design

Varying assessment methods to give students practice or to accommodate learning styles is a thoughtful consideration. However, assessment methods are not interchangeable. To ensure accurate assessment results, the overriding criterion for selection of method is consideration of the type of learning targets to be assessed.

So far, we have examined two keys to assessment quality, clear purpose and clear targets. The first key, *Clear Purpose*, asks that we identify at the outset who will use assessment results and how they will use them. The second key, *Clear Targets*, asks that we identify the knowledge, reasoning, skill, and product learning targets that will be the focus of instruction. Now we consider the third key to classroom assessment quality—how to design assessments that align with our targets and serve our purposes.

In this chapter we describe four assessment methods, explain how to choose which method to use for any given learning target, and outline the steps in assessment planning and development. We explain each of the four assessment methods in depth in Chapters 5 through 8; in this chapter we offer an overview with an emphasis on selecting the proper method and on thoughtful assessment planning.

Chapter 4 Learning Targets

At the end of this chapter you will know how to do the following:

- Select the appropriate method(s) to assess specific learning targets.
- Follow the steps in the Assessment Development Cycle.
- Create an assessment blueprint.
- Use an assessment blueprint with students as assessment *for* learning.

FIGURE 4.1 Keys to Quality Classroom Assessment

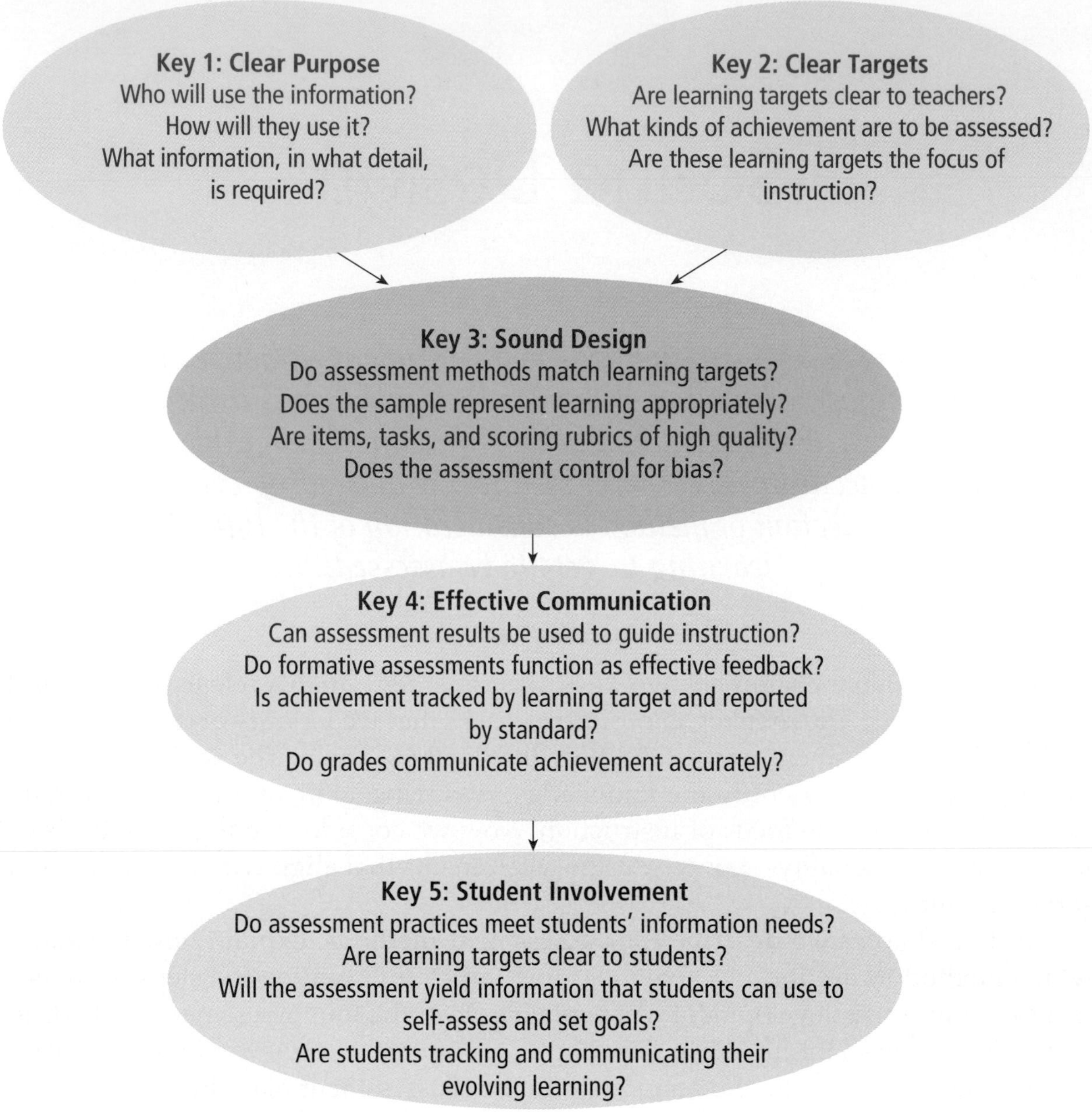

ASSESSMENT METHODS—A SET OF FOUR OPTIONS

Throughout your school career, both as a student and as a teacher, you have encountered thousands of different assessments. Although the variations are endless, all of the assessments you have experienced and give today fall into one of four basic categories of methods:

1. Selected response
2. Written response

3. Performance assessment
4. Personal communication

All four methods are legitimate options, but only when their use is closely matched with the kind of learning target to be assessed and the intended use of the information.

Selected Response

Selected response assessments are those in which students select the correct or best response from a list provided. Formats include the following:

- Multiple choice
- True/false
- Matching
- Fill-in-the-blank questions

Students' scores on selected response assessments are usually figured as the number or proportion of questions answered correctly.

How to develop and use selected response items is the focus of Chapter 5, "Selected Response Assessment."

FIGURE 4.2 Assessment Methods

Selected Response
- Multiple choice
- True/false
- Matching
- Fill in-the-blank questions

Written Response
- Short answer items
- Extended written response items

Performance Assessment
- Performance task
- Performance criteria

Personal Communication
- Questions during instruction
- Interviews and conferences
- Participation
- Oral exams
- Student journals and logs

Written Response

Written response assessments require students to construct an answer in response to a question or task rather than to select the answer from a list. They include *short answer* items and *extended written response* items. Short answer items call for a very brief response having one or a limited range of possible right answers. Extended written response items require a response that is at least several sentences in length. They generally have a greater number of possible correct or acceptable answers.

Examples of short answer items:

- Describe two differences between fruits and vegetables.
- List three causes of the Spanish-American War.
- What will happen if this compound is heated? Why will that happen?

Examples of extended written response items:

- Evaluate two solutions to an environmental problem. Choose which is better and explain your choice.
- What motivates (the lead character) in (a piece of literature)?
- Interpret polling data and defend your conclusions.
- Describe a given scientific, mathematical, or economics process or principle.

We judge correctness or quality of written response items by applying one of two types of predetermined scoring criteria. One type gives points for specific pieces of information that are present. The other type takes the form of a rubric, which describes levels of quality for the intended answer.

Example of the "points" approach: When students in a biology class are asked to describe the Krebs cycle, points might be awarded for including the following information:

- The cycle describes the sequence of reactions by which cells generate energy.
- It takes place in the mitochondria.
- It consumes oxygen.
- It produces carbon dioxide and water as waste products.
- It converts ADP to energy-rich ATP.

Example of the "rubric" approach: when students in an environmental science class are asked to evaluate two solutions to an environmental problem, their responses might be judged using these three dimensions: the criteria used for comparison, the accuracy of evidence brought to bear, and the strength of the argument for the supremacy of one over the other.

How to develop and use short answer and extended written response items and scoring procedures is the focus of Chapter 6, "Written Response Assessment."

Performance Assessment

Performance assessment is assessment based on observation and judgment. Even though it is called *performance* assessment, this method is used to judge both real-time performances, also called *demonstrations*, and products, or *artifacts*, that students create. It has two parts: the task and the criteria for judging quality of the response. Students complete a task—give a demonstration or create a product—that is evaluated by judging the level of quality using a rubric.

Examples of demonstrations (reflecting *skill* targets) include the following:

- Playing a musical instrument
- Carrying out the steps in a scientific experiment
- Speaking a foreign language
- Reading aloud with fluency
- Repairing an engine
- Working productively in a group

Examples of products (reflecting *product* targets) include:

- Term paper
- Lab report
- Work of art
- Wood shop creation
- Geometric solid

The criteria used to judge the demonstration or product can award points for specific features that are present, or it can describe levels of quality. For example, to assess the ability to carry out a process such as threading a sewing machine, doing long division, or safely operating a band saw, points might be awarded for each step done correctly and in the correct order. Level of achievement will be reported by the number or percent of points earned.

For more complex processes or products, you might have a scoring rubric for judging quality that has several criteria. In the case of evaluating an oral presentation, your rubric might cover four criteria: content, organization, presentation, and use of language. For a task requiring mathematical problem solving, the rubric might consist of these four criteria: analysis of the problem, reasoning processes and strategies used, communication, and accuracy. Level of achievement will be reported in terms of rubric levels (generally a number).

How to develop and use performance tasks and rubrics is the focus of Chapter 7, "Performance Assessment."

Personal Communication

Gathering information about students through *personal communication* is just what it sounds like—we find out what students have learned through structured and unstructured interactions with them. Examples include the following:

- Asking questions during instruction
- Interviewing students in conferences

- Listening to students as they participate or perform in class
- Giving examinations orally
- Having students keep journals and logs

Because these kinds of classroom assessments lead to immediate insights about student learning, they can reveal misunderstandings and trigger timely corrective action. This is why we usually think of them as formative, rather than summative assessments. As long as the learning target and criteria for judging response quality are clear, information gathered via personal communication can be used either way. It can serve as the basis for instructional planning, for feedback to students to guide next steps, and for student self-assessment and goal setting. If the event is planned well and recorded systematically, the information can also be used as part of the final grade.

Student responses in personal communication assessments are evaluated in one of two ways. Sometimes the questions we ask require students to provide a simple, short answer, and all we're looking for is whether the answer is correct or incorrect. This is parallel to scoring for short answer written response questions. Other times, our questions generate longer and more complex responses, which we can evaluate with scoring criteria. This is parallel to scoring for extended written response questions.

FAQ 4.1

Assessment Methods

Question

What about portfolios? I notice they aren't listed as a method. Where do they fit in?

Answer

Portfolios can be a powerful aid to learning and we devote Chapter 11 to their use. However, a portfolio is not an assessment method, but a vehicle for teachers and students to use to track, reflect on, and communicate about achievement. Typically, a portfolio contains a collection of evaluated work, each piece of which is the result of an assignment or task. The individual pieces represent responses to some form of assessment—selected response, written response, performance, or personal communication—but the portfolio itself is the *repository* of evidence, not the *stimulus* that produced its ingredients. So although a portfolio includes an array of assessments and plays a valuable role in assessment *for* learning, it is not an assessment method itself.

Question

What about exhibitions of mastery, group projects, worksheets, posters, brochures, PowerPoint® presentations, and the other ways that students show their achievement? Aren't they methods of assessment?

Answer

All of these performances and artifacts can be classified within one of the four basic assessment methods described. Exhibitions of mastery and group projects usually take the form of extended written response, performance assessment, or personal communication depending on how they are carried out. Worksheets contain various types of items, most frequently selected response or written response questions. Posters and brochures are generally tasks assigned in the context of performance assessment. If a content standard calls for students to develop and use a PowerPoint® presentation, there are two separate learning targets at work—the creation of the slides themselves and the skillful use of them in a presentation. Both would be assessed using a performance assessment.

MATCHING ASSESSMENT METHODS TO LEARNING TARGETS

The accuracy of any classroom assessment depends on selecting the appropriate assessment method that matches the achievement target to be assessed. Acceptable matches result in accurate information gathered as efficiently as possible. Mismatches occur when the assessment method is not capable of yielding *accurate* information about the learning target. Figure 4.3 summarizes when to use each assessment method. (Dispositional learning targets are not addressed because in this book, we focus our assessment information only on academic achievement targets.)

As you read through Figure 4.3, note that the descriptions of the matches are described as *Strong*, *Good*, *Partial*, and *Poor*. Here is what each means.

Strong: The method works for all learning targets of this type.

Good: The method works for many of the learning targets of this type.

Partial: The method works in some instances for learning targets of this type.

Poor: The method never works for learning targets of this type.

Assessing Knowledge Targets

Knowledge targets represent the factual information, procedural knowledge, and conceptual understandings that underpin each discipline.

SELECTED RESPONSE. This is labeled a **good match** in Figure 4.3 because selected response options do a good job of assessing mastery of discrete elements of knowledge,

FIGURE 4.3 Target–Method Match

	Selected Response	Written Response	Performance Assessment	Personal Communication
Knowledge	**Good** Can assess isolated elements of knowledge and some relationships among them	**Strong** Can assess elements of knowledge and relationships among them	**Partial** Can assess elements of knowledge and relationships among them in certain contexts	**Strong** Can assess elements of knowledge and relationships among them
Reasoning	**Good** Can assess many but not all reasoning targets	**Strong** Can assess all reasoning targets	**Partial** Can assess reasoning targets in the context of certain tasks in certain contexts	**Strong** Can assess all reasoning targets
Skill	**Partial** Good match for some measurement skill targets; not a good match otherwise	**Poor** Cannot assess skill level; can only assess prerequisite knowledge and reasoning	**Strong** Can observe and assess skills as they are being performed	**Partial** Strong match for some oral communication proficiencies; not a good match otherwise
Product	**Poor** Cannot assess the quality of a product; can only assess prerequisite knowledge and reasoning	**Poor** Cannot assess the quality of a product; can only assess prerequisite knowledge and reasoning	**Strong** Can directly assess the attributes of quality of products	**Poor** Cannot assess the quality of a product; can only assess prerequisite knowledge and reasoning

Source: Adapted from *An Introduction to Student-Involved Assessment FOR Learning*, 6th ed. (p. 78), by R. J. Stiggins & J. Chappuis, 2011, Upper Saddle River, NJ: Pearson Education. Adapted by permission.

such as important history facts, spelling words, foreign language vocabulary, and parts of plants. These assessments are efficient in that we can administer large numbers of questions per unit of testing time and so can cover a lot of material relatively quickly. It is easy to obtain a sufficient sample of student knowledge from which to draw a confident conclusion about level of overall knowledge acquisition.

WRITTEN RESPONSE. Written response is a **strong match** for knowledge targets. It is especially useful for assessing blocks of interrelated knowledge and conceptual understanding, such as causes of environmental disasters, the carbon cycle in the atmosphere, how one mathematical formula can be derived from another, or the concept of checks and balances in government. Not only can we determine if students know the correct answer, but we can also get at how students know, thus minimizing the chances of a right answer for the wrong reasons. Written response assessment is not as efficient as selected response in sampling broad domains of content because response time is longer. So, if time is limited or fixed, the assessment will include few exercises. But the tradeoff is the potential to get at deeper levels of knowledge and conceptual understanding.

PERFORMANCE ASSESSMENT. Performance assessment is a **partial match** for assessing knowledge targets. First we'll consider when it can be a good match. Then we'll explore the potential problems that make it a partial match at best.

It is a good match with primary students and with students who cannot read or write. To assess their acquisition of knowledge targets, we rely heavily on observation and judgment—performance assessment—as well as personal communication. Selected response and written response are obviously not viable choices for knowledge learning targets if students cannot yet read or write at a level that would allow them to show what they know.

In all other instances, it is a good match only if the student performs well. If we pose a performance task that asks a student to rely on the knowledge and reasoning to display a skill or create a product that meets certain standards of quality and the student does well, then we can draw the strong conclusion that the student was, in fact, a master of the prerequisite knowledge needed to be successful. However, because we can't be sure of the outcome in advance, we do not recommend that you use performance when the object is to assess solely mastery of knowledge. Three major barriers—accuracy, efficiency, and practicality—contribute to our recommendation.

Accuracy. A poor performance may not be the result of lack of knowledge. The key question is, Why did the student not perform well? Was it due to the lack of prerequisite knowledge? Failure to reason well using that knowledge? If it was a demonstration-based performance assessment, was the problem inadequate skills? If it was a product-based performance assessment, was the poor performance due to a problem with creating the product? For example, let's say we assign a complex performance, such as writing and executing a computer program, and let's say our learning target is student mastery of prerequisite knowledge. When a student's program works well, we can conclude she possesses the prerequisite knowledge. The problem comes in when the program does not run successfully. Because of factors beyond the prerequisite knowledge that could have contributed to the failure, we can't know that lack of prerequisite knowledge is the reason for failure. We will have to do some followup probing to find out if the prerequisite knowledge was there to start with. If our objective is to assess mastery of specific knowledge, to save time and increase accuracy, we are better off using selected response or written response assessments.

Efficiency. It is an extravagant use of time to rely on performance assessment to assess all content knowledge. A single performance task does require some subset of knowledge, and you can assess its presence with a particular performance task, but how many performance tasks would you have to create, administer, and score to cover all the knowledge you want students to acquire?

Practicality. It isn't always practical, or in some cases safe, to conduct certain performance assessments to assess knowledge. For example, if you want to assess students' ability to read bus schedules, although it would be most "authentic" to ask students to get around town on the bus, it would be highly inefficient and perhaps dangerous. Asking students to answer multiple-choice or short answer questions requiring understanding of a bus schedule would be a more efficient and safer way to get the information needed.

For these reasons we recommend as a general rule of thumb that you assess knowledge with a simpler method, when possible, and reserve performance assessment for those learning targets that really require it.

PERSONAL COMMUNICATION. Personal communication is a **strong match** with knowledge targets for most students at all grade levels. While for summative uses it tends to be inefficient if a lot of knowledge is to be assessed, recorded, and reported for lots of students, it works well in formative applications, such as real-time sampling of student understanding during instruction. Additionally, for some students such as those with special needs, English language learners, or younger students, it may be the only way to gather accurate information.

Assessing Reasoning Targets

Reasoning targets specify thought processes students are to learn to do well within a range of subjects—solve problems, make inferences, draw conclusions, form judgments.

SELECTED RESPONSE. Selected response is a **good match** for reasoning targets. A common misunderstanding is that selected response questions can tap only knowledge targets and can't assess reasoning proficiency. Selected response is not a good choice for all patterns of reasoning, but can be effective for some. For example:

- Which of the following statements best describes how dogs in real life are different from the dog in the story? (Comparative reasoning)
- What generalization can you make from this selection about how these plants lure their prey? (Inference—generalizing)

- Which answer best explains the author's purpose in writing this story? (Inference—determining author's purpose)
- Choose the sentence that best tells what the story is about. (Inference—identifying main idea)
- Which problem-solving strategy is the best choice for this problem? (Evaluation)

There are limits to selected response formats when assessing reasoning. If you want to assess how well students can select a strategy and work it through to completion to solve a problem requiring several steps, how well they can explain their choice or reasoning process, or how well they can defend an opinion, you must use another assessment method. For example, you might ask students to solve the following problem in mathematics: "Estimate the number of hours of TV advertising the typical U.S. fifth grader watches in a year. Describe the process you used to determine your answer." This is an extended written response question. If the learning target you want to assess falls into the category of student reasoning, a single number as the right answer is not the focus of the assessment—competence with the reasoning process is. So in instances such as these, you will need the deeper evidence of thinking that written response reveals.

WRITTEN RESPONSE. Written response represents a **strong match** for assessing reasoning targets. The trick here is to pose good questions, ones that require students to analyze, compare, contrast, synthesize, draw inferences, and to make an evaluative judgment. The criteria used to determine student scores must include the quality of each student's application of the pattern of reasoning in questions as well as the accuracy and appropriateness of the information or evidence brought to bear. These criteria were mentioned in Chapter 3 and will be detailed in Chapter 6.

Also, remember from Chapter 3 that to assess a student's ability to reason well, the question has to pose a novel problem (new to the student) to be solved at the time of the assessment. If students worked on the answer to the question during instruction, and that very question appears on a subsequent assessment, their answers are likely to represent a piece of remembered knowledge, which does not require reasoning.

PERFORMANCE ASSESSMENT. This is a **partial match** for assessing reasoning targets, for the same reasons as with performance assessment and knowledge targets. We can, for example, observe students carrying out science laboratory procedures and draw strong conclusions about their reasoning based on our observations if they succeed at the performance assessment. However, if they don't do well, it could be due to lack of prerequisite knowledge, lack of technique (skills), or to imprecise reasoning. In situations such as these, without engaging in additional assessment, we remain unable to judge level of achievement on reasoning targets.

As another example, students are sometimes asked to create a diorama in a shoebox as a reading assignment. This is a task we would assign only if it elicits evidence of specific reading learning targets. We have to be careful of assessing reading comprehension with a shoebox for the reason that it's fun. If the diorama project can be made to yield solid evidence of identifying main idea and supporting details, summarizing, determining cause and effect, or whatever reading comprehension targets are the focus of instruction, then it can be a match. If not, it's not good assessment.

PERSONAL COMMUNICATION. For gathering accurate information, personal communication is a **strong match** to reasoning targets. Teachers can ask students questions to probe more deeply into a response. Or, students can demonstrate their solution to a problem, explaining their reasoning out loud as they go. The drawbacks with using personal communication to assess reasoning proficiency are the amount of time it takes and the record-keeping challenge it poses.

FAQ 4.2

Target–Method Match

Question

To accommodate student learning styles, and/or to adhere to the call for "multiple measures," shouldn't I be using the widest variety of assessment methods possible?

Answer

In all contexts and cases, the driving force behind the selection of an assessment method must be matched to the learning target. If more than one method can work and you wish to have other factors such as student preference or learning style come into play, that's fine. But our goal always is to generate accurate results so we and our students can make sound decisions that advance learning.

Question

Shouldn't we only be using "authentic" assessments—performance assessments—to judge student progress?

Answer

It is somewhat of a misnomer to label one assessment method as "authentic," and thereby imply that the others are "inauthentic" and therefore inferior. None of these methods is inherently superior to any other, and all are viable if used well. Good assessment means clearly knowing what it is you want to assess and then choosing the best method to get the job done, which depends foremost on the kinds of learning targets being assessed. That is the point of the target–method matrix, which is grounded in principles of sound measurement. We would never advocate giving up accuracy to achieve authenticity, which happens when performance is the only acceptable method to use. However, within performance assessment methodology, authenticity is to be desired. We discuss the attribute of authenticity of performance tasks in Chapter 7.

Assessing Skill Targets

Skill targets are those where a demonstration or physical skill-based performance is at the heart of the learning.

SELECTED RESPONSE. Selected response is a **partial match** for skill targets. It is a **good match** only in a very limited number of cases. When the learning target calls for measuring with tools, there is a degree of manual dexterity involved and, although technically it is a skill target, we can evaluate it through selected response methodology. For example, we can construct a multiple-choice item to test whether a student measures with a ruler or a protractor correctly. We can present a drawing of a measuring cup containing liquid and showing the meniscus and ask students to determine the correct measurement.

Beyond those limited cases, selected response is a poor match for skill targets. We can use it to determine if students possess the prerequisite knowledge required to perform skillfully, but it cannot be used to judge the level of performance. As an example, assessing with a multiple-choice test whether a student can play his cornet clearly will not work. Also, in the measurement examples, we cannot diagnose problems easily, so if our intent is formative, we may want to watch students while they are measuring and correct their procedures as needed, which is performance assessment.

WRITTEN RESPONSE. Written response is also a **poor match** for skill targets, for the same reasons. Assessing with a written response whether a student can pronounce words correctly in Japanese will not yield accurate information about the student's proficiency. No one would think of doing that, yet if we only use selected response and written response methodology and our curriculum includes skill targets, we are not capturing the whole picture of student achievement.

PERFORMANCE ASSESSMENT. There is really only one assessment method that is a **strong match** for skill targets, and that is performance assessment. For example, we can determine whether students know how to conduct themselves during a job interview using another assessment method, but the only way to evaluate how well they can do it is to watch and listen to them during a simulated job interview and then judge their level of competence.

PERSONAL COMMUNICATION. Personal communication is a **partial match** for assessing skill targets. It is a good choice when the skills in question fall into the category of oral proficiency, such as speaking a foreign language or giving an oral presentation. In these instances, personal communication *is* the focus of the performance assessment. When the skill target in question is *not* related to oral proficiency, such as "dribbles a basketball to keep it away from an opponent," personal communication won't do.

Assessing Product Targets

Product targets describe learning in terms of artifacts where creation of a product is the focus of the learning target. With product targets, the specifications for quality of the product itself are the focus of teaching and assessment.

SELECTED RESPONSE. Selected response is a **poor match** for product targets. We can use it only to determine if students possess the prerequisite knowledge required to create the product, which is not the same as demonstrating the ability to create the product itself. If the learning target specifies that students will write opinion pieces on a topic or text supporting a point of view with reasons and information (CCSSI, 2010a, p. 20), no form of selected response assessment will provide accurate evidence.

WRITTEN RESPONSE. Written response is a **poor match** for product targets. When the learning target specifies the creation of a written product, such as an essay or a research report, the appropriate assessment method is performance assessment. Remember, by definition, *written response* is a short or extended answer to a question or task, and by definition, we limit it to assessing knowledge and reasoning targets. If the learning target states that students will construct scatter plots for bivariant measurement data, providing a written answer to a question does not go far enough to assess the intent of the target.

If the target requires creation of a product, only creating the product will give accurate evidence of achievement.

PERFORMANCE ASSESSMENT. Performance assessment is a **strong match** for determining whether students can create a specified product: Assign a task that calls for the creation of the product and then judge its quality using a rubric.

PERSONAL COMMUNICATION. Personal communication is a **poor match** for assessing product targets. We can use it only to determine if students possess the prerequisite knowledge required to create the product.

For Example 4.1

Examples of Target–Method Match—English Language Arts

Learning Target	Target Type	Assessment Method(s)
Understand the meaning of the terms *connotation* (associations) and *denotation* (definitions). (KY 1)	Knowledge	Selected Response, Written Response, or Personal Communication
Recognize and correct inappropriate shifts in pronoun number and person. (CCSSI, 2010a, p. 52)	Knowledge	Selected Response, Written Response, Performance Assessment, or Personal Communication

Learning Target	Target Type	Assessment Method(s)
Analyze text to locate figures of speech (e.g., personification) and interpret meanings in context. (KY 2)	Reasoning	Selected Response, Written Response, or Personal Communication
Make strategic use of digital media (e.g., textual, graphical, audio, visual, and interactive elements) in presentations to enhance understanding of findings, reasoning, and evidence and to add interest. (CCSSI, 2010a, p. 50)	Skill	Performance Assessment
Tell a story or recount an experience with appropriate facts and relevant, descriptive details, speaking audibly in coherent sentences. (CCSSI, 2010a, p. 23)	Skill	Performance Assessment or Personal Communication
Write informative/explanatory texts to examine and convey complex ideas and information clearly and accurately through the effective selection, organization, and analysis of content. (CCSSI, 2010a, p. 45)	Product	Performance Assessment

Sources: CCSSI, 2010a, pp. 23, 45, 50, & 52 KY 1 is from http://www.education.ky.gov/users/otl/KLN/ELA/Language%20St5%20Grade%207.doc KY 2 is from http://www.education.ky.gov/users/otl/KLN/ELA/Language%20St5%20Grade%208.doc

For Example 4.2

Examples of Target-Method Match—Mathematics

Learning Target	Target Type	Assessment Method(s)
Recognize that analog and digital clocks are objects that measure time. (KY 3)	Knowledge	Selected Response, Written Response, Performance Assessment, or Personal Communication
Distinguish between situations that can be modeled with linear functions and with exponential functions. (CCSSI, 2010c, p. 70)	Knowledge	Selected Response, Written Response, or Personal Communication

Learning Target	Target Type	Assessment Method(s)
Use ratio and rate reasoning to solve real-world and mathematical problems., e.g., by reasoning about tables of equivalent ratios, tape diagrams, double number line diagrams, or equations. (CCSSI, 2010c, p. 42)	Reasoning	Selected Response, Written Response, Performance Assessment, or Personal Communication
Given a two-digit number, mentally find 10 more or 10 less than the number without having to count; explain the reasoning used. (CCSSI, 2010c, p 16)	Reasoning	Personal Communication
Use a protractor correctly. (KY 3)	Skill	Performance Assessment
Draw (freehand, with ruler and protractor, and with technology) geometric shapes with given conditions. Focus on constructing triangles from three measures of angles or sides, noticing when the conditions determine a unique triangle, more than one triangle, or no triangle. (CCSSI, 2010c, p. 50)	Product	Performance Assessment
Construct two-way frequency tables of data when two categories are associated with each object being classified. CCSSI, 2010c, p. 82)	Product	Performance Assessment

Sources: CCSSI, 2010c, pp. 16, 42, 50, 70, & 82 KY 3 is from http://www.education.ky.gov/KDE/Instructional+Resources/Curriculum+Documents+and+Resources/Mathematics+DRAFT+Deconstructed+Standards.htm

ASSESSMENT DEVELOPMENT CYCLE

All assessments, regardless of method selected, need to go through the same development steps to ensure quality. Although the list (also shown in Figure 4.4) may look imposing at first, it outlines a commonsense process with several familiar steps. With a bit of practice, the process will become second nature.

FIGURE 4.4 Assessment Development Cycle

All assessments, regardless of method selected, need to go through the same development steps to ensure quality.

Planning Stage

1. Determine who will use the assessment results and how they will use them.
2. Identify the learning targets to be assessed.
3. Select the appropriate assessment method or methods.
4. Determine sample size

Development Stage

5. Develop or select items, exercises, tasks, and scoring procedures.
6. Review and critique the overall assessment for quality before use.

Use Stage

7. Conduct and score the assessment.
8. Revise as needed for future use.

Planning

1. Determine who will use the assessment results and how they will use them.
2. Identify the learning targets to be assessed.
3. Select the appropriate assessment method or methods.
4. Determine sample size.

Development

5. Develop or select items, exercises, tasks, and scoring procedures.
6. Review and critique the overall assessment for quality before use.

Use

7. Conduct and score the assessment.
8. Revise as needed for future use.

All assessments, regardless of intended use or method selected, need to go through the same development steps to ensure quality.

So far in Chapters 2 through 4, we have introduced the first three steps in the *Planning* stage: determining the intended users and uses of an assessment, identifying the learning targets to be assessed, and selecting the proper assessment method(s). Now we'll look at how to apply those first three steps when actually developing an assessment. We'll also address the fourth step, determining the appropriate sample size.

In Chapters 5 through 8, we'll work by method through the steps of selecting or creating items, tasks, and scoring procedures and checking them for adherence to the guidelines to quality. Also in those chapters, we'll offer suggestions for administering the assessment, noting any problems, and revising the assessment as needed.

The Assessment Development Cycle applies to any type of assessment intended for classroom use: formative or summative; practice assessments, quizzes, tests, projects; short-cycle, common, interim, or end-of-course assessments; developed or selected by individual teachers or by grade-level teams, content area departments, or district subject area teams. All need to adhere to standards of quality—all should follow the steps of the assessment development cycle.

Step 1: Determining Users and Uses

In a balanced classroom assessment system, each assessment represents a part of a long-term assessment map that parallels the curriculum map for the reporting period. Each assessment contributes to an accumulating body of evidence of each student's level of achievement. Some assessments will be used formatively—to guide further instruction and learning—while others will be used summatively—to report level of achievement. Our first planning decision is to determine the purpose for each:

- Who will use the information?
- How will they use it?
- Is the use formative or summative?

The answers to these questions guide design decisions. Summative assessments can function formatively and formative assessments can function summatively, but not without carefully thought-out design.

My Classroom Then and Now 4.1

Amy James

I used to . . .

When I began teaching, I would teach a concept over one to two weeks assuming that my students were "getting it" along the way and then would quiz students over that concept. The quiz did very little to inform my instruction, but instead rewarded those students who "got it" and punished those who didn't. Then we moved on and any misunderstandings only accumulated over the course of the unit. At the end of the unit, I was faced with trying to remediate several students over large amounts of material, while other students were ready to move on to the next unit.

Now I . . .

Now I am probing constantly for understanding with both formal and informal styles of formative assessment. I give both verbal and written feedback, as opposed to simply grades, so that both the student and I know what they understand and where they are struggling. I have broken units of study into manageable chunks, or specific learning targets, and assess students in a progressive manner on each learning target. Remediation occurs immediately, allowing students to revisit learning targets that they struggle with. This allows for easy differentiation and grouping, focusing on what each individual student needs help with and allowing those students who have reached understanding to delve deeper into the concepts.

Why I changed . . .

I felt as though I wasn't meeting the needs for all of my students, and there just wasn't enough of "me" to go around.

What I notice as a result . . .

I have found that by structuring instruction and assessment in this way, students take more ownership of their learning. Grades become less punitive and intimidating and instead are more of a gauge of the learning progression. Students who often struggle can more easily see their successes and can manage areas that they need to focus their attention on, which raises their confidence. I find that the classroom environment is more positive and focused. Students help each other and work together. I am more able to confer with individual students and groups, meeting more students' needs. And as a whole, I feel that I am more intentionally working to ensure that *all* students reach proficiency for each learning target in each unit. And isn't that the goal for every teacher?!

Source: Used with permission from high school science teacher Amy James, Oldham School District, Crestwood, KY, 2011.

CONDITIONS FOR FORMATIVE USE. As we saw in Chapter 2, if you have determined to use the assessment results formatively, certain conditions must be met. Because some of these conditions are often not met by assessments whose primary purpose is summative, you will need to consider them carefully if you are retrofitting a summative assessment for a formative purpose. The conditions are as follows:

1. The assessment instrument or event is designed so that it aligns directly with the content standards to be learned.
2. All of the instrument or event's items or tasks match what has been or will be taught.

3. The instrument or event provides information of sufficient detail to pinpoint specific problems, such as misunderstandings, so that teachers can make good decisions about what actions to take, and with whom.
4. The results are available in time to take action with the students who generated them.
5. Teachers and students do indeed take action based on the results. (Chappuis, 2009, p. 6)

Step 2: Specifying the Intended Learning Targets

List the learning targets to be assessed along with their classification (knowledge, reasoning, skill, or product). If the target is complex or unclear, clarify it or deconstruct it first, following the processes outlined in Chapter 3. Specifying the intended learning targets is important because the breadth and depth of a learning target will affect how much coverage it will need on the assessment and in instruction. Classifying the targets is important because different target types require different assessment methods.

My Classroom Then and Now 4.2

Christine Heilman

I used to . . .

I used to be unclear on what I was supposed to teach, what kids were supposed to learn, and what I should do with students who didn't demonstrate understanding. I carefully planned what I was teaching, but didn't pay much attention to what students were learning. I used textbook assessments and recorded percentages in my grade book, but did no reteaching. Tests were for grading purposes. There was no structure for collaboration or discussion of results. I taught what I thought was important and then "hoped" students would perform well on standardized tests.

Now I . . .

I now have essential learnings planned out for each content area. I focus instruction on student-friendly learning targets that are clearly posted. I write assessments based on state benchmarks with five to eight questions per learning target. I assess student understanding to fine-tune my instruction for the whole class and for individual students. I plan reteaching, interventions, and enrichment as necessary to ensure all students demonstrate understanding of learning targets. I include student reflection pieces, rubrics for student feedback, and error analysis opportunities. Student homework is aligned to learning targets. I send an essential learnings update to parents each month filled with suggestions for how they can follow up at home.

Our team now plans six-week instructional goals, action steps, and instructional strategies that support each goal. We use a variety of written response assessments, checklists, multiple-choice assessments, and student reflections to gather information about student understanding of targets. We share our goals and instructional plans with our resource support teachers so we are all working together to support goals. At the end of each six-week goal, our team comes together to share data. We display our data graphically, analyze student performance on each target, and make plans for intervention. We discuss instructional strategies that worked well in our individual classrooms so we all have an opportunity to learn from one another.

As a team, we are now very clear in what we are teaching, what we expect students to learn, and how they will demonstrate their learning. We use data to make plans for intervention and ensure remediation opportunities for those who need it. "Hope" is no longer our strategy for test preparation. We have data throughout the year that helps us measure progress on learning targets on an ongoing basis.

Source: Used with permission from 2nd grade classroom teacher Christine Heilman, ISD 196, Rosemount, MN, 2011.

Step 3: Selecting the Appropriate Assessment Method(s)

This is fairly straightforward. Once you have classified learning targets by type, decide which assessment method or methods to select by referring to the guidelines described in the section "Matching Assessment Methods to Learning Targets" and summarized in Figure 4.3.

Step 4: Determining the Appropriate Sample Size

Realistically, any test can include only a subset of all the questions we could have asked if testing time were unlimited. It never is unlimited, so we include a sample of the possibilities and then generalize from that sample to student mastery of the domain represented (Stiggins & Chappuis, 2011). Our sampling challenge is to answer two questions: *What will be the scope of coverage of this assessment? What will be the relative importance of the standards or learning targets to be assessed?* When we define the relative importance of each of the learning targets listed, we are mapping out how we will *sample* student learning.

Sampling means answering the question, "How much evidence is enough?"

Sample size is in large part determined by teacher judgment. In all cases, the assessment must include enough questions or tasks to lead us to a confident conclusion about how each student did in mastering each relevant standard or target. So we must decide how much evidence is enough for this target. How many multiple-choice test items, written response items, or performance tasks will we need for each learning target? The guiding principles for sampling are these:

1. The broader in scope the learning target, the larger the sample required to cover it thoroughly.
2. The more important the learning target is as a foundation of later learning—that is, the more confident you want and need to be about student mastery—the larger should be the sample.
3. The more important the decision to be made on the basis of results (formative or summative), the larger and more precise the sample must be.

Each assessment method brings with it specific rules of evidence for sampling within these guidelines. We will address those in more detail in Chapters 5 through 8 as we discuss assessment development with each method.

FAQ 4.3

Sampling

Question

How much evidence is enough?

Answer

Whenever we build an assessment, we face the practical issue of how many items to include. As a general rule, assuming an assessment built of quality items, the longer it is, the more dependable its results will be. But after that guideline, the matter of test length is a function of the context of that particular assessment. You have to rely on your own professional judgment. The assessor's challenge is to gather enough evidence to lead to a confident conclusion about student achievement without wasting time gathering too much.

How much is enough in any particular classroom situation is a function of several factors:

1. The assessment purpose—the decision to be informed by the results
2. The nature of the learning target to be assessed
3. The assessment method to be used
4. The students to be involved in the assessment

The matter of sampling student achievement in classroom assessment is as much about the art of assessment as it is the science. We suggest guidelines for each of these four factors individually. Just know that in the classroom they play out as a constellation of influences that can interact in complex ways—thus the need for your thoughtful choices.

1. ***The Assessment Purpose*** With respect to the instructional decision to be made based on assessment results, the more important the decision, the surer you must be about achievement status and, in general, the larger (more dependable) must be your sample. So, for example, when designing a formative assessment, the results of which will guide immediate action, you might be willing to limit sample size. If results lead to an incorrect decision about any student's current level of achievement, that fact will be revealed immediately and corrective action can be taken. On the other hand, in a summative context where, for example, a student's report card grade hangs in the balance, a larger sample might be indicated because it will be more difficult to reverse the decision later if the assessment is inaccurate.
2. ***The Nature of the Learning Target*** The broader the scope of the target or the greater its complexity, the larger should be the sample. For example, if we want to determine if a student has mastered a key piece of factual or procedural knowledge, we don't have to ask a number of times—once will probably be enough. But if we want to find out if a student is a competent writer, we will need to sample a number of different kinds of writing to evaluate properly.

   This sampling challenge is simplified to a certain extent by adopting clear content standards that identify and thus limit the scope of what students are responsible for learning. Teachers used to need to sample broad, vaguely defined domains of achievement such as a semester's worth of history. When content is defined in terms of a more focused set of achievement standards, the sampling challenge is to determine how each student did in mastering each standard.
3. ***The Assessment Method*** The more information provided by one assessment item, task, or exercise, the fewer items needed to cover the domain. For example, a multiple-choice test item typically provides one specific piece of evidence. Its focus and coverage is narrow. So typically we use several of them to cover the range of content. A written response or performance task, on the other hand, tends to provide relatively more evidence and thus samples broader targets in students' responses. So we typically need fewer of them.
4. ***The Students*** This factor comes into play more on the formative side than the summative; that is, during the learning. And, in this case, your professional judgment becomes very important. The key variable is where any given student is on the achievement continuum. If the student is clearly a master of the standard or clearly not, then you probably need few items. So, for example, if you ask a couple of questions and a particular student gets them all right or all wrong, then a trend is clear and you can decide based on relatively fewer items. But if the student gets some right and some wrong it may be necessary to keep asking

until that trend becomes apparent. Here is the guideline for thoughtful use: you probably have gathered enough evidence if, based on that evidence, you can guess with a degree of certainty how that student would do if you offered one more chance.

In summary, in high-stakes decision contexts with broader or more complex learning targets using a multiple-choice test, you will want to think about using relatively larger samples of items. But while the learning is under way in the classroom with narrower, more focused targets or when relying on assessment methods that yield more information per item, smaller samples may suffice.

COMBINING PLANNING DECISIONS INTO A TEST BLUEPRINT. Creating or selecting an assessment without having a blueprint can result in mismatches between instruction and assessment. Without such a plan, an assessment may not measure what you intend it to measure, which is a *validity* problem. From an assessment quality point of view, this is a bad thing. If you yourself have ever taken an exam that did not match what you understood to be the important aspects of the course, you know what this problem feels like to students.

Creating a good assessment blueprint requires starting with clear targets.

A *test blueprint* is simply a record of the decisions made in Steps 2, 3, and 4: what learning targets the assessment should cover, which assessment method or methods to use, and how much weight each learning target will receive in the overall score. Make a blueprint whether you intend to create the assessment from scratch, revise an existing one, or use an already-developed assessment.

1. List the major learning targets that will be the focus of instruction, being clear about target classification (knowledge, reasoning, skill, or product).
2. Write the learning targets into the appropriate spaces in the test blueprint format you select. (Which form you use depends on whether the test will include multiple assessment methods.)
3. If you will be using more than one assessment method, identify the appropriate method for each learning target.
4. Determine the relative importance of each target (weight it will receive) if the assessment is to include more than one.

Figure 4.5 is an example of a blueprint for a test employing multiple assessment methods: in this case, selected response items, written response items, and a performance task. Figure 4.6 is an example of a blueprint for a test comprised solely of selected response items.

FIGURE 4.5 Blueprint for a Unit Test with Multiple Assessment Methods

4th Grade Unit: The Physics of Sound (Selected Targets)

Learning Target	Type of Target	Assessment Method	Percent Importance
Acquire vocabulary associated with the physics of sound	Knowledge	Selected Response	20
Learn that sound originates from a source that is vibrating and is detected at a receiver such as the human ear	Knowledge	Written Response	10
Understand the relationship between the pitch of a sound and the physical properties of the sound source (i.e., length of vibrating object, frequency of vibrations, and tension of vibrating string)	Knowledge	Written Response	20
Use knowledge of the physics of sound to solve simple sound challenges	Reasoning	Written Response	10
Use scientific thinking processes to conduct investigations and build explanations: observing, comparing, and organizing (1) How sound travels through solids, liquids, and air; (2) Methods to amplify sound at the source and at the receiver	Reasoning & Skill	Performance Assessment	40

Source: Reprinted from the *FOSS® Physics of Sound Teacher Guide*. © The Regents of the University of California, 2005, developed by Lawrence Hall of Science and published by Delta Education, LLC. Reprinted by permission.

FIGURE 4.6 Blueprint for a Selected Response Quiz

5th Grade Reading

Learning Target	Problems	Total Points
Uses prefixes and knowledge of root words to determine meaning of unfamiliar words	1–6	6
Uses context to determine meaning of unfamiliar words	7–10	4
Summarizes text	11–15	5

The Steps in Test Development

So far, our planning has yielded an understanding of intended use, a list of learning targets or important concepts, a determination of appropriate method(s) to use, and an indication of each target's relative importance. At the *Development* stage, we adhere to guidelines for quality specific to each assessment method. This stage is comprised of Steps 5 and 6 of the Assessment Development Cycle.

Step 5 is to develop or select items, exercises, tasks, and scoring instruments adhering to guidelines for quality specific to each method. These are described in detail in each of the methods chapters, Chapters 5 through 8.

Step 6 is to review and critique the assessment before using it. Regardless of how carefully we plan, things can still go wrong that result in inaccurate measures of achievement. These are called *sources of bias and distortion*. A list of potential sources of bias and distortion common to all assessment methods is shown in Figure 4.7. Note that some problems, such as unclear targets, inappropriate assessment method, and

FIGURE 4.7 Potential Sources of Bias and Distortion Common to All Assessment Methods

Barriers that can occur within the student

- Language barriers
- Emotional upset
- Poor health
- Physical handicap
- Peer pressure to mislead assessor
- Lack of motivation at time of assessment
- Lack of testwiseness (understanding how to take tests)
- Lack of personal confidence leading to evaluation anxiety

Barriers that can occur within the assessment context

- Insufficient time allotted
- Noise distractions
- Poor lighting
- Discomfort
- Lack of rapport with assessor
- Cultural insensitivity in assessor or assessment
- Lack of proper equipment

Barriers that arise from the assessment itself

- Directions lacking or vague
- Poorly worded questions
- Misleading layout
- Poor reproduction of test questions
- Missing information

improper sampling, would be solved by adhering to the planning steps of the Assessment Development Cycle. Others are issues that can be hard to anticipate. Sources of bias and distortion specific to each method are discussed fully in Chapters 5 though 8.

Use and Refinement

Step 7 is to administer and score the test. Even if you are using an already-developed test, we recommend that you review it with each of the first six steps in mind. When we rely on textbook test writers to do the planning and development, we may have high-quality items, but we may have a partial or poor match to what we taught or to the relative balance of importance of each learning target in our curriculum. In addition, the test may not give students specific and detailed feedback regarding their strengths and areas of need.

Step 8, the last step, is to double check that the test did indeed do what we wanted it to. Were we able to use the results for all the decisions we intended to make? Were students able to use the results to understand their strengths and identify areas needing more work? How about how well it matched the intended learning? Consider asking students to help in this. Were parts of the test a surprise to them? Did it seem out of balance with what they thought it was most important to learn?

Did a source of bias or distortion creep in and affect the results? Were some questions or tasks confusing—students knew the material, but didn't know how to respond? It is almost impossible to eliminate *all* sources of bias and distortion up front. Some only become apparent when you give students the assessment. In any case,

- Do the best you can prior to administering the assessment.
- Watch for possible sources of mismeasurement during and after the assessment.
- If something goes wrong, either (1) don't use the results from the items or tasks in question, or (2) interpret the results with possible bias in mind.

Remember that our goal in the classroom is to get accurate information about student achievement, and if we know the information is not accurate, we have an obligation to discard it and to revise the assessment as needed before future use.

My Classroom Then and Now 4.3

Ken Mattingly

I used to . . .

I always believed I was a good teacher. My instructional activities engaged the students, confronting their preconceptions and misconceptions. Everything focused on the big idea of the unit and getting students to mastery of the standards.

Students were periodically assessed throughout the unit to determine how they were doing. I used the results to make adjustments in my teaching and hopefully fill in any gaps that appeared in student understanding. At the end of the unit students took an assessment that contained a mix of essay and multiple-choice questions.

The end-of-unit assessment was designed to address the big ideas of the unit. The multiple-choice questions had answers that attended to student misconceptions and identified specific problems. The essay questions were written to determine the depth of student understanding of key points. After taking the assessment, students received feedback on their performance in the form of a percentage grade.

Now I . . .

I begin my instructional design process long before I start a unit. I take the standards for the unit and deconstruct them into the knowledge, reasoning, skill, and product targets that make up each standard. I then decide how I will assess each target *during* the unit and at the *end* of the unit. A test plan for the end-of-unit assessment is created, paying attention to match the target to the correct assessment method and determining the proper question sample size.

With my targets developed and unit assessment determined, I now turn my attention to selecting instructional strategies that will enable my students to reach the targets. Whereas before I would pick activities that tied in to the big idea, I now select those that attend to a specific target or group of targets. Any activity, lesson, or strategy that doesn't move students toward mastery of a target is weeded out of my instructional plans.

Throughout the unit, students receive feedback on their performance on targets along with a discussion of how they can close the gap to mastery. Then on the unit assessment student performance is broken out by target so that students can see how they did on each individual target. This diagnosis allows for continued, focused work on gaining target mastery.

Why I changed . . .

I changed because it didn't make sense not to. Years of getting roughly the same results from group after group of students left me searching for a way to do things differently. After being exposed to assessment *for* learning practices and comprehending the classroom responsibility shift that would occur with its implementation, I slowly began to incorporate it into my teaching.

What I notice as a result . . .

Everything in my classroom now is more transparent than before. Students no longer have to guess about what they are supposed to learn. I am clearer on my instructional goals, and my students and their parents know what they are expected to learn and do. Involving students as partners in their learning, through feedback and self-analysis, encourages them to continue to try and improve. Student accountability and subject interest has improved, as has overall performance.

Source: Used with permission from 7th-grade science teacher Ken Mattingly, Rockcastle County School District, Mt. Vernon, KY, 2011.

ASSESSMENT *FOR* LEARNING USING ASSESSMENT BLUEPRINTS

Assessment *for* learning and student involvement activities (formative applications) can spin directly off the assessment blueprint. With the information provided by the blueprint you can do the following:

- Differentiate subsequent instruction after giving a quiz or test, by grouping students according to which learning targets they had trouble with.
- Share the blueprint with students at the outset to make the learning targets clearer.
- Share the blueprint with students and ask them to identify where each day's instruction fits.
- Share the blueprint with students and have them write practice test questions periodically for each cell, as a form of focused review.

We will offer more ideas for using test blueprints as instructional tools in Chapter 5 and 6.

Summary

None of the available assessment methods is inherently superior to others. Each brings its own unique strengths and limitations. Selected response, written response, performance assessment, and personal communication are all viable options. To ensure accuracy of results, we first consider the kind of learning target to be assessed and then take into account any special student characteristics such as age, English language proficiency, or specific learning disabilities that might compromise accuracy.

The Assessment Development Cycle proceeds through a series of commonsense stages: Planning, Development, and Use. There are eight steps in the cycle: (1) identify the purpose, (2) specify the targets, (3) select appropriate methods, (4) decide on relative importance of the targets and sample well, (5) write or select the items, exercises, tasks, and scoring instruments using guidelines for quality, (6) review and critique the assessment for quality, (7) administer and score the assessment; and (8) examine the results and revise as needed.

Complete these steps and you can have confidence that your formative and summative assessments are yielding accurate and usable results.

CHAPTER 4 ACTIVITIES

End-of-chapter activities are intended to help you master the chapter's learning targets. They are designed to deepen your understanding of the chapter content, provide discussion topics for learning team meetings, and guide implementation of the practices taught in the chapter.

Forms and materials for completing each activity appear in editable Microsoft Word format in the Chapter 4 CD file. Documents on the CD are marked with this symbol:

Chapter 4 Learning Targets

At the end of this chapter you will know how to do the following:

1. Select the appropriate method(s) to assess specific learning targets.
2. Follow the steps in the Assessment Development Cycle.
3. Create an assessment blueprint.
4. Use an assessment blueprint with students as assessment *for* learning.

Activity 4.1 Keep a Reflective Journal
Activity 4.2 Practice with Target-method Match
Activity 4.3 Audit an Assessment for Clear Purpose
Activity 4.4 Audit an Assessment for Clear Learning Targets
Activity 4.5 Make a Test Blueprint
Activity 4.6 Try an Assessment *for* Learning Application
Activity 4.7 Reflect on Your Own Learning
Activity 4.8 Select Portfolio Artifacts

Activity 4.1

Keep a Reflective Journal

Keep a record of your thoughts, questions, and any implementation activities you tried while reading Chapter 4.

Reflective Journal Form

Activity 4.2

Practice with Target–Method Match

After reading the section, "Matching Assessment Methods to Learning Targets," work independently, with a partner, or with your learning team to carry out this activity.

1. Select a short unit that you are currently teaching or will teach this year.
2. List the learning targets that will be the focus of the unit.
3. Classify each target as Knowledge, Reasoning, Skill, or Product (KRSP).
4. Using the information from "Matching Assessment Methods to Learning Targets," determine which assessment method to use for each.

Target–method Match Template

Activity 4.3

Audit an Assessment for Clear Purpose

After reading the section, "Step 1: Determining Users and Uses," work independently, with a partner, or with your learning team to complete the following activity.

1. Select an assessment to audit for clear purpose.
2. Answer the following questions:
   - Who will use the information?
   - How will they use it?
   - Is the use formative or summative?
3. If any of the answers indicate a need for revision, identify the problem and the revision needed.

Audit an Assessment for Clear Purpose

Activity 4.4

Audit an Assessment for Clear Learning Targets

After reading the section, "Step 2: Specifying the Intended Learning Targets," work independently, with a partner, or with your learning team to carry out the following activity.

First, select an assessment that you have not personally developed. Then follow these steps.

1. *Analyze the assessment item by item or task by task.*
   Identify and write down what learning each item or task assesses. Describe the learning in whatever terms you want. If two or more items or tasks address the same learning, use the same terms to describe that learning. Note the number of points each item is worth.
2. *Organize the learning targets into a test blueprint.*
   Transfer the information from step one to a test blueprint chart.
3. *Question the blueprint.*
   Does this match what you taught and what you expected students to learn?
   - Are some learning targets overrepresented? If so, which one(s)?
   - Are some learning targets underrepresented? If so, which one(s)?
   - Are any important learning targets you taught left out? If so, which one(s)?
   - Do all items on the test align directly with the content standards you have taught?

   Does the sample represent the learning appropriately?
   - Does the number of points for each learning target represent the amount of time you spent on it relative to the whole? If not, which ones are out of balance?
   - Does the number of points for each learning target represent its relative importance within the whole? If not, which ones are out of balance?
4. *Adjust the blueprint, as needed.*
   - Add or delete learning targets to reflect what you taught and what you deemed most important to learn and assess.
   - Adjust the number of points each target receives to reflect the amount of time you spent teaching each learning target and each target's relative importance to the content as a whole.

Audit an Assessment for Clear Learning Targets

Activity 4.5

Make a Test Blueprint

After reading the sections titled "Step 3: Selecting the Appropriate Assessment Methods" and "Step 4: Determining the Appropriate Sample Size," work independently, with a partner, or with a team to carry out this activity.

1. Select a short unit that you are currently teaching or will teach this year.
2. List the major learning targets that will be the focus of the unit. Be clear about the classification of each target (knowledge, reasoning, skill, or product).
3. Select or modify one of the test blueprint forms in Figures 4.4 and 4.5. Write your learning targets on the test blueprint.
4. If the learning targets will be assessed with multiple assessment methods, identify which method(s) you will use for each target.
5. Determine the relative importance of each target (the weight it will receive) and add that information to the test blueprint form.
6. If a test for the unit already exists, compare its content to the specifications in your test blueprint. Are there any discrepancies? Describe them.
7. Revise either the test blueprint or the test itself to accurately reflect achievement on the learning targets as needed.

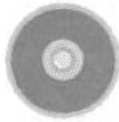 Test Blueprint Form A

 Test Blueprint Form B

Activity 4.6

Try an Assessment *for* Learning Application

After reading the section, "Assessment *for* Learning Using Assessment Blueprints," work independently, with a partner, or with your learning team to carry out this activity.

1. Select a unit that you are currently teaching or will teach this year.
2. Create a test blueprint for the unit, following the instructions in Activity 4.5.
3. Choose one or more of the ideas described in the section "Assessment *for* Learning Using Test Blueprints." Try the idea(s) with your students.
4. Briefly describe what you did, either in writing or as a discussion with a partner or your team.
5. Also describe the effect you noticed the activity had on students and their learning.

 Debrief the AFL Application You Tried

Activity 4.7

Reflect on Your Own Learning

Review the Chapter 4 learning targets and select one or more that represented new learning for you or struck you as most significant from this chapter. If you are working individually, write a short reflection that captures your current understanding. If you are working with a partner or a team, either discuss what you have written or use this as a discussion prompt for a team meeting.

 Reflect on Chapter 4 Learning

Activity 4.8

Select Portfolio Artifacts

Any of the activities from this chapter can be used as portfolio entries. Select any activity you have completed or artifacts you have created that will illustrate your competence at the Chapter 4 learning targets:

1. Know how to select the appropriate method(s) to assess specific learning targets.
2. Know how to follow the steps in the assessment development cycle.
3. Be able to create an assessment blueprint.
4. Know how to use an assessment blueprint with students as assessment *for* learning.

If you are keeping a reflective journal, you may want to include Chapter 4's entry in your portfolio.

Chapter 4 Portfolio Entry Cover Sheet

CHAPTER

5

Selected Response Assessment

Surprisingly, some of our most powerful formative assessment practices involve diagnostic uses of selected response items, quizzes, and tests, by both teachers and students.

Over the years selected response assessment has become almost synonymous with the concept of testing. In the 1920s and 1930s, however, it was known as the new, scientific assessment method, welcomed by those at the forefront of education innovation because it was considered objective—that is, free of teacher judgment. Although its luster dimmed over the years, it has reemerged as a predominant assessment method, fueled by the intersection of testing and technology. Computer adaptive testing, other forms of online testing, and software programs rely almost exclusively on selected response methodology. Two major reasons for its dominance, especially in accountability testing, are that it is easy to administer and cheap to score.

However, as we have seen in Chapter 4, if we use only selected response assessments, we are gathering data about only a portion of the important learning targets we teach. And teaching to the domain of what is covered on the accountability tests often requires that we give short shrift to learning targets not assessed with this method. For these reasons, many view selected response assessment in the classroom with distrust, even though it is still a valuable tool in our assessment repertoire and worthy of regular use as both assessment *for* learning and assessment *of* learning.

Selected response assessments can include one or more of four different item types: multiple choice, true/false, matching, and fill in the blank. In this chapter, we examine formative and summative uses for selected response assessments, how to choose from among selected response formats, how to create quality items, and how to use selected response assessments formatively, as assessment *for* learning.

Chapter 5 Learning Targets

At the end of this chapter you will know how to do the following:

- Make a test blueprint for a selected response assessment.
- Choose from among selected response formats.
- Create high-quality items.
- Audit any selected response test for quality.
- Use selected response assessments to plan further instruction.
- Use selected response assessments as feedback to students and for student self-assessment and goal setting.

FIGURE 5.1 Keys to Quality Classroom Assessment

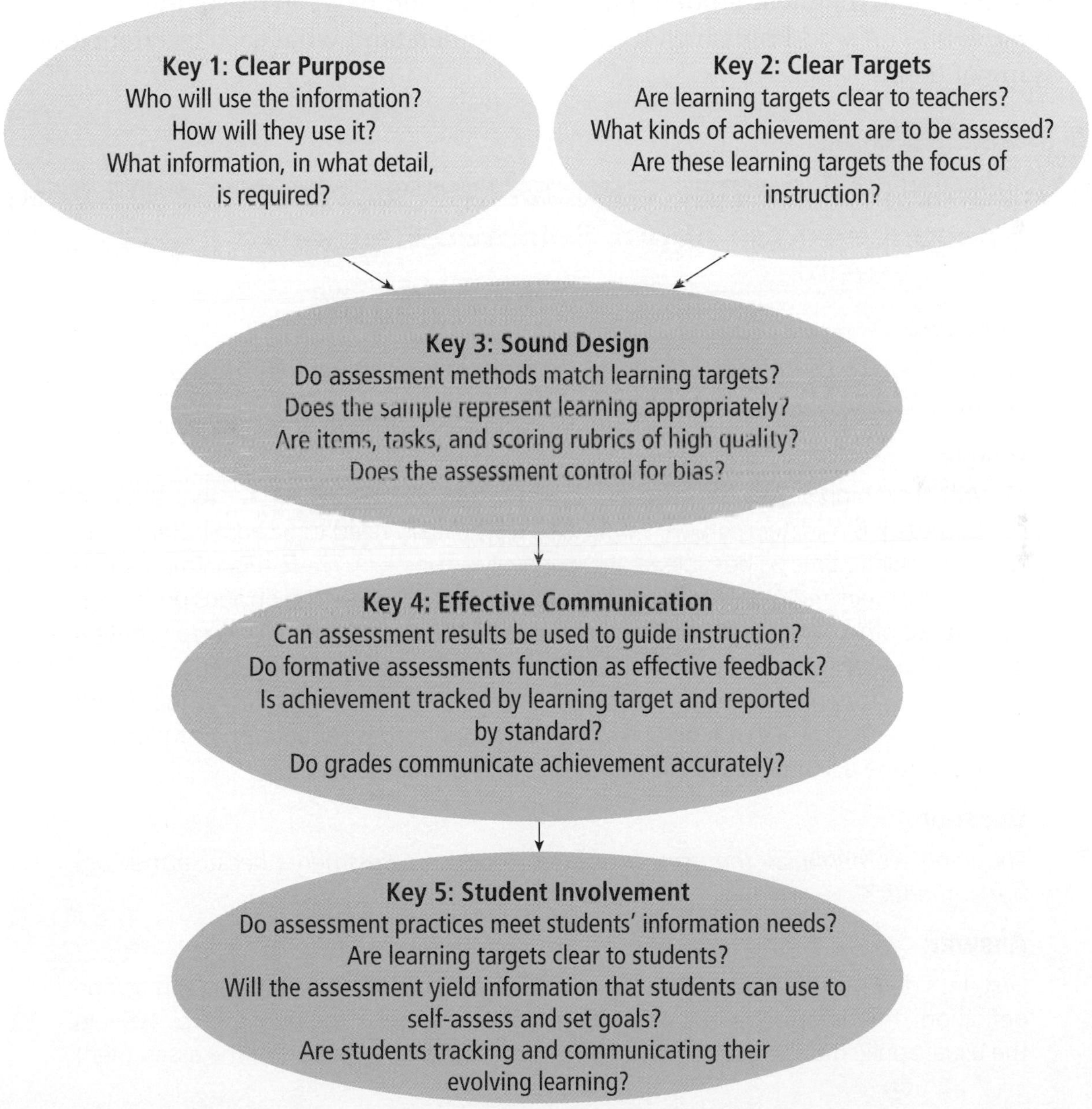

Key 1: Clear Purpose
Who will use the information?
How will they use it?
What information, in what detail, is required?

Key 2: Clear Targets
Are learning targets clear to teachers?
What kinds of achievement are to be assessed?
Are these learning targets the focus of instruction?

Key 3: Sound Design
Do assessment methods match learning targets?
Does the sample represent learning appropriately?
Are items, tasks, and scoring rubrics of high quality?
Does the assessment control for bias?

Key 4: Effective Communication
Can assessment results be used to guide instruction?
Do formative assessments function as effective feedback?
Is achievement tracked by learning target and reported by standard?
Do grades communicate achievement accurately?

Key 5: Student Involvement
Do assessment practices meet students' information needs?
Are learning targets clear to students?
Will the assessment yield information that students can use to self-assess and set goals?
Are students tracking and communicating their evolving learning?

WHEN TO USE SELECTED RESPONSE ASSESSMENT

The first condition for using selected response is that it must be capable of reflecting the type of learning target to be assessed. Selected response formats are ideal for assessing knowledge-level learning targets, some patterns of reasoning, and a very few number of skill targets, as described in Chapter 4.

Several other key conditions influence choosing the selected response method of assessment. Use it when

- The content to be assessed is broad, requiring wide-ranging coverage. Since the response time to one item is so short, you can include lots of items per unit of testing time and thus sample student achievement thoroughly.
- You want to diagnose student misconceptions and flaws in reasoning.
- Students can read English well enough to understand what each test item is asking of them.

FAQ 5.1

Misconceptions about Selected Response Assessment

Question:

Shouldn't we be using mostly multiple-choice tests because all the high-stakes tests use them?

Answer:

No. Although high-stakes tests use this format extensively, the reason for that choice is not because it is a better method. Large-scale tests usually need to be administered and scored in as little time as possible, as inexpensively as possible. These requirements lead to the use of selected response formats such as multiple choice. The obvious problem is that, unless other formats are also part of the assessment, learning targets representing important patterns of reasoning, skills, and products are going unmeasured.

Giving students practice on answering large-scale test items is one thing, but mirroring characteristics of high-stakes tests that are not instructionally useful or that do not provide accurate results in the classroom is not a good idea.

Question:

Shouldn't we minimize the use of selected response assessments because they are not authentic?

Answer:

First, let's define "authentic." The *New American Oxford Dictionary* offers this as one definition: "made or done in a way that faithfully resembles the original" (p. 107). In the usual application to assessment, *authentic* refers to the context of the assessment mirroring the use or application of the learning in a situation that would require it in life. (We prefer to call this "life beyond school" rather than "real-world" because school can and should be part of the real world for students.)

By that definition, selected response methodology is not "inauthentic." Life beyond school often calls for correct answers and solutions chosen from a variety of options. We believe it is more helpful to think of authenticity as a *dimension* of assessments, not as a label given to some forms rather than others. We can keep it as a consideration when writing assessments of any sort, as long as the application or context doesn't interfere with the accuracy of the item, task, or scoring guide.

DEVELOPING A SELECTED RESPONSE TEST

We will follow the steps in the Assessment Development Cycle described in Chapter 4.

Planning

1. Determine who will use the assessment results and how they will use them.
2. Identify the learning targets to be assessed.
3. Select the appropriate assessment method or methods.
4. Determine sample size.

Development

5. Develop or select items, exercises, tasks, and scoring procedures.
6. Review and critique the overall assessment for quality before use.

Use

7. Conduct and score the assessment.
8. Revise as needed for future use.

PLANNING STEPS

As we saw in Chapter 4, careful attention to each of the four planning steps is essential to ensuring that the resulting assessment will do what you want it to.

Step 1: Determine Users and Uses

We begin planning by answering these questions: How do we want to use the information? Who else will use it? What decisions will they make? Typically, we will use assessment information for one or more of the following purposes:

- To plan instruction, as with a pretest
- To offer feedback to students so they can self-assess and set goals for further learning
- To differentiate instruction according to student needs, as with a mid-unit quiz or an interim assessment
- To measure level of achievement to inform grading decisions, as with a post-test

Each one of these purposes can be accomplished with selected response formats, as long as we keep the intended use in mind while making further planning and design decisions.

Step 2: Identify Learning Targets

At this step we simply list the specific learning targets we have identified for the assessment. If one or more targets on the list are complex or unclear, clarify them or deconstruct them first, following the processes outlined in Chapter 3.

Step 3: Select Assessment Method(s)

Although we have already determined that we will use selected response, we must make sure the list of clarified targets only includes knowledge and reasoning learning targets and also that those targets can be assessed well with selected response methodology. So, review the list of learning targets to verify that they are knowledge and reasoning targets and that selected response items can capture an accurate picture of achievement.

Step 4: Determine Sample Size

This step requires that we assign a relative importance to each learning target. One simple way to do this with selected response questions is to decide how many points the test will be worth and then divide the points according to relative importance of each learning target. The number of points we assign to each learning target outlines our sample, which should represent the breadth of the learning targets and their importance relative to each other in the instructional period the test is to cover. At this step, you may want to review the sampling considerations described in Chapter 4.

When using a test that you didn't develop, check carefully that it matches the learning targets you taught and that the amount of emphasis each receives is appropriate.

Remember, when identifying the relative importance of each learning target, we consciously match our emphasis in assessment to our emphasis in the classroom. If, say, we spend 50 percent of the time learning how to read maps, then roughly 50 percent of the assessment should focus on map reading. If only 5 percent of the course deals with reading maps, then in most cases it would misrepresent learning to devote 50 percent of the final assessment to map reading.

If, on the other hand, the results are to be reported by individual learning target, or if the test only measures one single target, the sample must be sufficient to defend an inference about mastery of that individual target.

COMBINING PLANNING DECISIONS INTO AN ASSESSMENT BLUEPRINT. For selected response assessments, we offer two useful types of blueprints. One is a list of the learning targets and the other is a table crossing content with knowledge and

FIGURE 5.2 Blueprints for Third-Grade Mathematics and Reading Tests

Mathematics

Learning Targets	Number of Points
Identify place value to thousands	6
Read, write, order, and compare numbers through four digits	10
Use place value understanding to round whole numbers to the nearest 10 or 100	4

Reading

Learning Targets	Number of Points
Determine the lesson of a fable	1
Identify key supporting details	2
Infer a character's feelings	2
Distinguish literal from nonliteral language	2
Identify meanings of words in a text	3

pattern(s) of reasoning to be assessed. Each is suited to different types of content, but both are equally effective as test planning instruments.

Figure 5.2 shows plans for a third-grade mathematics test and a third-grading reading test consisting of a list of learning targets and how many points each will be worth. Note that on the reading test, only one to three points are assigned to each learning target. That is because, for any one reading passage, it can be difficult to develop more than one or two items to assess targets such as "Infer a character's feelings." So, especially with the shorter passages at the lower grades, you would want to construct similar items for a variety of reading passages at the same level of difficulty to obtain a sufficient sample size from which to draw conclusions about students' level of mastery.

Figure 5.3 shows a list of learning targets for a fifth-grade social studies unit on westward expansion. The test blueprint consists of a list of the content embedded in the learning targets in the left-hand column labeled "Content Categories." Each category represents many facts and concepts, some of which will be sufficiently important to test. The blueprint also includes columns labeled for the cognitive action to be carried out: know outright and reason comparatively. These patterns will be emphasized during the unit of study. The numbers in each cell represent its relative importance in the unit as planned. This kind of test plan is especially useful if we want to ensure that the test covers both recall of important information and reasoning processes we have taught. (Remember that there could be other learning targets taught during the unit—this blueprint represents only those covered by the selected response portion of the test.)

FIGURE 5.3 Learning Targets and Blueprint for a Fifth-Grade Social Studies Unit

1. Explain the concept of Manifest Destiny and its contribution to the migration of people in the development of the United States.
2. Compare the motives of the different groups who participated in the westward expansion by leaving the eastern United States and heading west.
3. Compare the lives of different Native American groups before and after westward expansion.
4. Identify significant individuals who took part in the westward expansion.
5. Explain how the westward migration led to conflict between Native Americans and settlers and between Mexicans and settlers.

Content Category	Knowledge	Compare/ Contrast	Totals
1. Manifest Destiny	2		2
2. Reasons settlers went west		6	6
3. Life of Native American groups	4	2	6
4. Significant individuals	6		6
5. Effects on Native Americans and Mexicans	6	4	10
TOTALS	28	8	36

DEVELOPMENT AND USE STEPS

The remaining four steps of the Assessment Development Cycle focus on developing the items and scoring procedures, critiquing the assessment for quality, administering the assessment, and revising it as needed.

Step 5: Develop or Select Items, Exercises, Tasks, and Scoring Procedures

The process for developing selected response items is as follows: identify the specific content to include, choose which kinds of items to write, write the items, and assemble the test.

IDENTIFYING SPECIFIC CONTENT TO INCLUDE. Even though people often think of selected response tests as objective measures of learning, selecting the content for the test is itself a subjective exercise. The test developer—you yourself, a textbook author, or a test publisher—chooses what will be on the test from a vast array of possible considerations. It is a matter of professional judgment, just as is determining how to teach the material in the first place. This element of subjectivity does not compromise the test's validity if the learning targets that underpin the content standards have been clearly and accurately identified.

Now that you have numbers on the test plan to indicate the relative importance of each learning target or content category, the next step is to identify what content you will test for each cell. In most cases, you won't test everything students are to have learned. Instead, you will select or create questions that cover as much of the important content as possible given the amount of testing time available, and that are prudent for the age of your students. You use the results to make an inference: a student who has scored 75 percent on the test has mastered about 75 percent of the material that was intended to be learned. You must carefully select the sample of all possible important aspects of knowledge and reasoning so that it allows you to accurately estimate level of achievement.

My Classroom Then and Now 5.1

Myron Dueck

I used to . . .

For the first decade of my teaching career, I constructed tests by section based on the type or style of the questions. For instance, my unit tests would have a structure such as this:

Section 1: True & False	(10 pts)
Section 2: Multiple Choice	(15 pts)
Section 3: Short Answers	(10 pts)
Section 4: Long Answer/Essay	(20 pts)

In each of the first three sections, I took a somewhat random sampling of concepts and facts from throughout the unit being tested. Therefore, from each section I had a basic idea of what the student knew of the unit as a whole. The last section could be general or specific, depending on the unit of study.

These tests were fairly easy to make and even easier to mark. As well, I thought that this was the best type of test to produce, but this is probably based on years of seeing this as 'the standard' way to construct a test.

Now I . . .

I divide my test by the learning outcomes or standards I want to evaluate. Now a test on the USA in the 1920s is structured like this:

Section 1: USA in the 1920s	(11 pts)
Section 2: Causes of the Great Depression	(8 pts)
Section 3: FDR's Efforts to End the Depression	(6 pts)
Section 4: Reactions to FDR's Actions	(7 pts)
Section 5: FDR's Overall Impact on the USA	(11 pts)

Once a student takes the test and I have evaluated it, the student notes his/her section scores on a custom tracking sheet. Each section is allotted a percentage score and this score is compared to the student's overall test score as well as his or her academic goal. Taking all of these numbers into account, the student determines which section(s) to retest. The student also has an opportunity to plan what he/she might do differently in preparation for the subsequent evaluation.

Why I changed . . .

1. Students are able to be evaluated according to each learning outcome and this has obvious benefits:
   a. I can reteach sections (learning outcomes) upon which the entire class scored poorly or below competency.
   b. An individual student can retest a single section or multiple sections depending on how he or she performed.
   c. A student can easily identify and focus on the areas in which they know they can improve.
   d. As the facilitator, I can effectively and efficiently administer retests as I am only retesting and remarking those sections that have been identified.
2. Struggling learners usually start with the section they know best, and research shows that success breeds success.
3. I am able to quickly evaluate if there is a strong correlation between the value of each section and the amount of time allotted to it in class.
4. I have constructed retests that have the same sections and values, but different questions or question formats. It is very easy to administer these retests and to determine if authentic learning has occurred.
5. This structure is a very good way to use both formative and summative assessments in the same way and at the same time.
6. Students feel a sense of ownership and control not present in conventional testing formats.

What I notice as a result . . .

1. Very positive student reactions to this system.
2. Incredible parent support and encouragement.
3. Increased student participation in 're-learning' activities.
4. Less stress and pressure at the time of the first evaluation.

Source: Used with permission from Myron Dueck, high school social studies teacher, SD 67 (Okanagan-Skaha), Penticton, BC, Canada, 2011.

WRITING PROPOSITIONS. *Propositions* are statements of important facts, concepts, or understandings that students will be held accountable for learning. Writing propositions is an efficient way to (1) identify the content that will be on the test and then (2) generate any type of selected response item you choose to reflect that content.

To write propositions, first review the material you have taught. For every cell in the test plan, note in writing the most important facts, concepts, or understandings you think every student should have at the end of instruction. State each as a clear sentence. *These sentences are propositions.* As you will see, they form a quick and easy basis for writing quality test items. Many teachers find it helpful to collect propositions over time while instruction is unfolding. This facilitates later test development. We recommend that you write more propositions than you will need. Additional propositions serve two purposes: (1) they allow you to create parallel forms of the test if you like and, (2) they provide a convenient supply of replacement propositions or test items if you find a weak item during test development. You will find that it is a time-saver to write propositions as you teach the material or to collect them afterwards.

Knowledge Propositions. Let's say we are writing propositions for the test planned in Figure 5.3. We will need a total of 30 knowledge items, two of which will relate to Manifest Destiny. As we read through the material we have taught, we identify and write down three or four statements that reflect important knowledge about the concept of Manifest Destiny. These are our propositions. They might include the following:

- Manifest Destiny represents a belief that it was natural and right to expand the territory of the United States westward.
- Manifest Destiny represents a mission to impart the government and way of life of United States citizens to people living in the land west of the United States during the 1800s.
- Manifest Destiny was first used as a justification for annexing Texas to the United States.
- Manifest Destiny represents a belief that was used to justify the taking of Native American lands.

The test plan also requires six items in the cell that crosses *Know* with *Effects on Native Americans and Mexicans*. Here are two sample propositions:

- Three effects of westward expansion on Plains Indians were increased disease, removal to reservation lands, and loss of food sources.
- Mexico lost the territory of Texas.

Reasoning Propositions. To write one of these, identify the knowledge to be applied, apply the pattern of reasoning, and state the result as a declarative sentence. In essence, you state a correct application of the pattern of reasoning to the content.

To write propositions for the cell in Figure 5.3 that crosses *Reasons settlers went west* with *Compare/Contrast*, we would identify two groups of settlers to focus on and then state a comparison of reasons each went west.

Examples of the resulting propositions might read like this:

- The Mormons went west to practice their religion without persecution, whereas the settlers in Texas went west because land was cheap or free and they wanted a place to start over.
- Both Mormons and settlers in Texas were searching for a better life.
- Settlers were encouraged to move to Texas by the Mexican government, while Mormons were led to settle in Utah by their religious leaders.

Remember that when we intend to evaluate students' ability to reason, we must provide them with a context different than that in which they practiced their reasoning. If we don't, as we saw in Chapter 3, we will not be capturing real evidence of their reasoning (ability to figure things out). Instead, we will assess what they remember from previous reasoning. If we want to assess the learning target as a reasoning proficiency, "Compare the motives of the different groups who participated in the westward expansion by leaving the eastern United States and heading west," we cannot have reasoned that through during instruction. It must appear on the test as a novel (that is, new to the student) item. If we did figure it out in class, then we certainly can assess student mastery of it, but it becomes a knowledge question.

Interpretive Exercises. This is a label used for those instances when we present students with a table of information, a diagram, or some other source of information and then ask them to use that information to figure out answers to reasoning questions. The most common version of this is found in reading comprehension tests, where a passage is accompanied by test items that ask for inferences based on the content of the passage. In this case, the propositions you write will be specific to the content of the information provided. For example, for the reading targets from the test planned in Figure 5.2, students might read a short passage recounting Odysseus's experience with the Cyclops.

Propositions for the learning target "infer a character's feelings" might look like this:

- Odysseus felt afraid in the Cyclops' cave.
- Polyphemus felt angry towards the sailors.

You might consider using the interpretive format in content areas other than English language arts when you are not sure that some (or all) of your students have mastered some body of basic knowledge, but nevertheless, you want to assess their reasoning proficiency. In this case, present the information and construct reasoning propositions. Or, if you simply want to assess reasoning and don't need to assess content knowledge, just give the content knowledge and write propositions to structure questions asking them to apply the pattern of reasoning.

When Writing Propositions Is Unnecessary. For some knowledge targets such as those identified in the third-grade mathematics test plan, writing propositions is unnecessary.

CHOOSING ITEM TYPES. Selected response methodology offers four choices of item types: multiple choice, true/false, match, and fill in the blank. Each has strengths and weaknesses. You can use Figure 5.4 to decide when to choose which format.

FIGURE 5.4 Comparison of Selected Response Item Types

Item	Used When	Advantage	Limitations
Multiple Choice	There is only one right answer. There are several plausible alternatives to the correct answer.	Can measure a variety of objectives. Easy to score. Can cover lots of material efficiently. Carefully crafted distracters can provide diagnostic information.	Guessing can skew score (up to 33% chance, depending on number of distracters). Can be hard to identify plausible distracters.
True/ False	A large body of content is to be tested, requiring the use of many test items.	Can ask many questions in a short time. Easy to score.	Can be trivial or misleading if not written carefully. Guessing can skew score (50% chance).
Matching	There are many related thoughts or facts; you want to measure association of information.	Can cover lots of material efficiently. Easy to score. Can serve as several multiple-choice items in one (each response is a distracter for the others).	Process of elimination can skew score if not written carefully.
Fill in the Blank	A clear, short answer is required. You want to determine if students know the answer, rather than if they can select it from a list.	Assesses production of a response. Reduces the possibility of getting the right answer by guessing. Can cover lots of material efficiently.	Takes longer to score.

WRITING ITEMS. Now here is the power of propositions: Once you have written them to reflect your important learnings, you can use them to almost instantly write whatever kind of selected response item you might want to use. Here's how it works with the following proposition from the Manifest Destiny example:

> Manifest Destiny represents a mission to impart the government and way of life of United States' citizens to people living in the land west of the United States during the 1800s.

Multiple-Choice Items. To create a multiple-choice item, turn the basic focus of the proposition into a question. Then turn the other part of the proposition into the correct answer. Add a number of plausible but incorrect answers and you have a multiple-choice item.

What was the mission of Manifest Destiny in the United States in the 1800s?

a. To have Lewis and Clark make friends with the Native Americans they met.
b. To move the U.S. form of government and way of life west.
c. To defeat General Santa Anna in the battle of the Alamo.
d. To establish religious freedom for all who lived in the west.

True/False Items. To create a true/false item that is true, include the proposition on the test as stated. In this example, for fifth graders, you may want to simplify the proposition so that it reads as follows:

> Manifest Destiny represents a mission the U.S. had in the 1800s to move its government and way of life westward.

To create a false true/false item, make one part false:

> Manifest Destiny represents a mission the United States had in the 1800s to guarantee religious freedom to all settlers.

Matching Items. This is a way to sample several interrelated propositions at once with great efficiency. Think of each entry in a matching exercise as a multiple-choice item, in that the task is to combine the trigger item (or "stem") with its proper match. You simply take your proposition and separate it into its subject (stem) and predicate (match) parts. Do this with several propositions at once, list the stems in order and then scramble the matches and you have a matching exercise.

The key to writing good matching items is to use them when they make sense: where the learning targets can be thought of as a series of closely linked propositions, such as states and their capitals or items to be categorized and their categories. Any individual match (stem and response) would state a single proposition. Matching items generally test knowledge propositions, but they can also be used to assess reasoning propositions.

Fill-in-the-blank Items. To create a fill-in item from a proposition, leave out the phrase defining the concept or dealing with the effect and ask a question:

What was the mission of Manifest Destiny in the United States in the 1800s?

____

For Example 5.1

Turning a Social Studies Proposition into Different Item Types

Proposition:

Three effects of westward expansion on Plains Indians in the 1800s were increased disease, removal to reservation lands, and loss of food sources.

Multiple-choice Item:

What were three effects of westward expansion on Plains Indians in the 1800s?

a. Access to health care, removal to reservation lands, and loss of food sources
b. Access to health care, population growth, and opportunities for better jobs
c. Increased disease, removal to reservation lands, and loss of food sources
d. Loss of their schools, removal to reservation lands, and private ownership of land

True/False Item:

(True) Three effects of westward expansion on Plains Indians were increased disease, removal to reservation lands, and loss of food sources.
(False) One effect of westward expansion on Plains Indians was access to better health care.

Matching Item:

Not applicable

Fill-in-the-blank Item:

What were three effects of westward expansion on Plains Indians in the 1800s?

For Example 5.2

Turning a Reading Proposition into Different Item Types

Proposition:

Odysseus felt afraid in the Cyclops' cave.

Multiple-choice Item:

How did Odysseus feel in the Cyclops cave?

a. Envious because Polyphemus was strong and fierce.
b. Ashamed because he lied to Polyphemus.
c. Worried that Polyphemus was going to hurt the goats.
d. Afraid that Polyphemus would eat him.

True/False Item:

(True) Odysseus felt afraid in the Cyclops' cave.
(False) Odysseus felt ashamed in the Cyclops' cave.

Matching Item:

Not applicable

Fill-in-the-blank Item:

How did Odysseus feel in the Cyclops' cave?

____

Here is one final quality-control idea linked to propositions. Before you do any item writing, list all of the propositions that are going to make up your test. Then review the list from top to bottom in one reading, asking yourself this question: Does this set of ideas really reflect the essential learnings of this unit of study? Remove and replace weak entries and fill any gaps you discover.

GUIDELINES FOR WRITING QUALITY ITEMS. We offer here the commonsense guidelines that test developers use to ensure item quality.[1] The first set of guidelines applies to all item types, and the rest are specific to each particular format.

General Guidelines.

1. *Keep wording simple and focused. Aim for the lowest possible reading level.* Good item writing first and foremost represents an exercise in effective written communication.

Right:

What are the poles of a magnet called?

a. Anode and cathode
b. North and south
c. Strong and weak
d. Attract and repel

Wrong:

When scientists rely on magnets in the development of electric motors, they need to know about poles, which are?

---

2. *Ask a full question in the stem.* This forces you to express a complete thought in the stem or trigger part of the question, which usually promotes students' understanding.

Right:

What was the trend in interest rates between 1950 and 1965?

a. Increased only
b. Decreased only
c. Increased, then decreased
d. Remained unchanged

Wrong:

Between 1950 and 1965

a. Interest rates increased.
b. Interest rates decreased.
c. Interest rates fluctuated greatly.
d. Interest rates did not change.

---

3. *Eliminate clues to the correct answer either within the question or across questions within a test.* When grammatical clues within items or material presented in other items give away the correct answer, students get items right for the wrong reasons.

Wrong:

All of these are an example of a bird that flies, except an

a. Ostrich
b. Falcon
c. Cormorant
d. Robin

(The article *an* at the end of the stem requires a response beginning with a vowel. As only one is offered, it must be correct.)

Also wrong:

Which of the following are examples of birds that do not fly?

a. Falcon
b. Ostrich and penguin
c. Cormorant
d. Robin

(The question calls for a plural response. As only one is offered, it must be correct.)

---

4. *Do not make the correct answer obvious to students who have not studied the material.*
5. *Highlight critical, easily overlooked words* (e.g., NOT, MOST, LEAST, EXCEPT).
6. *Have a qualified colleague read your items to ensure their appropriateness.* This is especially true of relatively more important tests, such as big unit tests and final exams.
7. *Double-check the scoring key for accuracy before scoring.*

Guidelines for Multiple-Choice Items. The following guidelines for writing multiple-choice test items allow students to answer questions more quickly without wasting time trying to determine what the question is saying. (The item *stem* refers to the part of the question that comes before the choices. The *distracters* are the incorrect choices.)

1. *Ask a complete question to get the item started, if you can.* This is important for clarity. It has the effect of directing the item's focus first to the stem, rather than the response options, to guide students' choices.
2. *Don't repeat the same words within each response option; rather, reword the item stem to remove the repetitive material from below.* This will clarify and focus the problem, not to mention making it more efficient for respondents to read.
3. *Be sure there is only one correct or best answer.* This is where that colleague's independent review can help. Remember, it is acceptable to ask respondents to select a "best answer" from among a set of correct answers. Just be sure to word the question so as to make it clear that they are to find the best answer and be sure there is one clearly best answer.
4. *Choose distracters carefully.* All distracters must be plausible—they must be choices that can't be ruled out without having the knowledge or reasoning proficiency being assessed. Carefully chosen distracters can function as formative assessment tools when they represent typical misunderstandings or flaws in reasoning. Student responses then become diagnostic. For example, when writing an item testing students' ability to generalize, typical errors include not generalizing at all (making a statement that is only true for the evidence at hand) and over-generalizing (making a statement that casts too wide a net). If you know

which kind of error each distracter represents, you can disaggregate the test results by answer choice (which most scoring machines and software can do) to diagnose common misconceptions or specific reasoning problems students are experiencing. Then you can plan instruction to address them. Figure 5.5 shows item formulas for creating distracters that can reveal difficulties with selected patterns of reasoning.

FIGURE 5.5 Item Formulas for Selected Patterns of Reasoning

Reasoning Learning Target	Item Formula
Makes inferences based on text	*Question:* Which sentence tells an idea you can get from this (selection)? *The right answer*—A guess based on clues you can find in the text *A wrong answer*—A guess that seams reasonable, but that evidence in the text does not support *A wrong answer*—Not a guess, just a detail recopied verbatim from the text
Summarizes information in text	*Question:* Which sentence best summarizes what this (selection) is about? *The right answer*—A brief statement of the main point(s) or idea(s) *A wrong answer*—A statement including an idea not found in the passage *A wrong answer*—A statement including an idea from the passage that is too narrow to be acceptable as a summary
Compares and contrasts elements of text	*Question:* Which sentence tells how (two or more items) are alike? *The right answer*—A statement of an appropriate similarity *A wrong answer*—A statement that does not identify a similarity *A wrong answer*—A statement that is true of one or the other but not both *Or* *Question:* Which sentence tells how (two or more items) differ? *The right answer*—A statement of an appropriate difference *A wrong answer*—A statement that does not identify a difference *A wrong answer*—A statement that claims an inaccurate difference
Makes generalizations based on information found in text	*Question:* Which statement can you support after reading this selection? *The right answer*—A statement that is true for the evidence presented and extends the application logically to a broader array of instances *A wrong answer*—A statement that is true for the evidence presented, but includes too broad an array of instances to be supported by evidence *A wrong answer*—A statement that is true for the evidence presented, but does not include an extension to other instances *A wrong answer*—A statement that is not true for the evidence presented

Source: Adapted from *Washington Assessment of Student Learning 4th-Grade Reading Test and Item Specifications*, 1998, Olympia, WA: Office of the Superintendent of Public Instruction. Adapted with permission.

If you find that you cannot think of enough plausible distracters, include the item on a test the first time as a fill-in-the-blank question. As your students respond, common wrong answers will provide you with a good variety of viable distracters for future use.

5. *Word response options as briefly as possible and be sure they are grammatically parallel.* This makes items easier to read and eliminates cues to the right answer.

Right:

Why did colonists migrate to the United States?

- **a.** To escape taxation
- **b.** For religious freedom
- **c.** For adventure
- **d.** More than one of the above

Wrong:

Why did colonists come to the United States?

- **a.** To escape heavy taxation by their native governments
- **b.** Religion
- **c.** They sought the adventure of living among native Americans in the new land
- **d.** There was the promise of great wealth in the New World
- **e.** More than one of the above answers

---

6. *Make all response options the same length.* Testwise students know that the correct answer may be the longest one because writers frequently need to add qualifiers to make it the best choice. If you need to do this, do it to all response options.
7. *Don't use "all of the above" or "none of the above" merely to fill space;* use them only when they fit comfortably into the context of the question. In general, test writers avoid using "all of the above" because if a student can determine that two responses are correct, then the answer must be "all of the above."
8. *Use "always" or "never" in your answer choices with caution.* Rarely are things always or never true. Absolutes are frequently incorrect; a student who knows this but is not sure of the correct answer can automatically eliminate those choices.
9. *It's okay to vary the number of response options presented as appropriate to pose the problem you want your students to solve.* While four or five response options are most common, it is permissible to vary the number of response options offered across items within the same test. It is more important to have plausible distracters than a set number of them.

Guidelines for True/False Exercises. You have only one simple guideline to follow here: Make the item entirely true or false as stated. Complex "idea salads" including some truth and some falsehood just confuse the issue. Precisely what is the proposition you are testing? State it and move on to the next one.

Right:

The Continental Divide is located in the Appalachian Mountains.

Wrong:

From the Continental Divide, located in the Appalachian Mountains, water flows into either the Pacific Ocean or the Mississippi River.

Guidelines for Matching Items. When developing matching exercises, follow all of the multiple-choice guidelines offered previously. In addition, observe the following guidelines:

1. *Provide clear directions for making the match.*
2. *Keep the list of things to be matched short.* The maximum number of options is 10. Shorter is better.
3. *Keep the list of things to be matched homogeneous.* Don't mix events with dates or with names.

Right:

Directions: New England states are listed in the left-hand column and capital cities in the right-hand column. Place the letter for the capital city in the space next to the state in which it is located. Responses may be used only once.

	States	Capital Cities
_____ 1.	Rhode Island	A. Concord
_____ 2.	Maine	B. Boston
_____ 3.	Massachusetts	C. Providence
_____ 4.	New Hampshire	D. Albany
_____ 5.	Vermont	E. Augusta
		F. Montpelier

Wrong:

_____ 1.	Texas	A. $7,200,000
_____ 2.	Hawaii	B. Chicago
_____ 3.	New York	C. Mardi Gras
_____ 4.	Illinois	D. Austin
_____ 5.	Alaska	E. 50th state

---

4. *Keep the list of response options brief in their wording and parallel in construction.*
5. *Include more response options than stems and permit students to use response options more than once when appropriate.* This has the effect of making it impossible for students to arrive at the correct response purely through a process of elimination.

Guidelines for Fill-in-the-blank Items. Here are three simple guidelines to follow:

1. *Ask respondents a question and provide space for an answer.* This forces you to express a complete thought.
2. *Try to stick to one blank per item.* Come to the point. Ask one question, get one answer, and move on to the next question.
3. *Don't let the length of the line to be filled in be a clue as to the length or nature of the correct response.* This may seem elementary, but it happens. Again, this can misinform you about students' real levels of achievement.

Right:

In what section of the orchestra is the kettle drum found? ____________________

Wrong:

In the percussion section of the orchestra are located ________, ______, ________, ________ and ______.

---

4. *Put the blank toward the end of the sentence.*

ASSEMBLING THE TEST. Begin the test with relatively easier items to maximize students' opportunity to start on a note of confidence. Consider arranging the items on your test according to the learning target each represents, especially if the results will be used formatively. If that presents a challenge in direction writing because you would be mixing item formats, consider indicating in some other fashion which learning target each addresses. However, do so only if this information will not give students unfair clues regarding the correct answer. Make sure your students know how many points each question is worth, so they can learn to prioritize their testing time. Put all parts of an item on the same page.

My Classroom Then and Now 5.2

Laura Anderson

We used to . . .

Our fourth-grade team had always grouped for math, written our own unit assessments, and given tests within a similar time frame. Our test questions were not grouped and often either did not have enough or had too many questions. Teachers only received an overall test score and not enough specific data about which skills were not mastered. We also did not collect the data. Even when questions obviously need revisions, it was easier to put the test away until next year. Unfortunately, we did not remember the changes a year later and gave the same test over again. Our old team discussions were based on the logistics of the school day (i.e., schedules, upcoming events, and running of materials).

Now we . . .

New to us was the test format that challenged us to identify our learning targets and group "like questions" together by targets. This new format with a percent score by target really helps teachers and students quickly see which targets are met. Students indicate whether they feel they made a simple mistake or if they need more study.

Why we changed . . .

This feature really holds the kids accountable for their own learning. We saw signs of students becoming more invested in the test-taking process and taking more ownership of their learning. Also, our instruction has become more focused as we started posting learning targets in our classrooms. Our students are now clearer about the learning targets of our daily lessons.

What we notice as a result . . .

The most powerful change we have seen since starting the common assessment process is the team discussion piece after the test data collection. Now, we meet as a team and examine our student data and test questions. When many kids miss a particular test question, we discuss whether we feel it was a test question issue or a teaching issue. If a question needs revising, it is done right away. We have continued to improve our tests over the last three years rather than using the same flawed tests over again. These collegial discussions focusing on test data are like nothing we have ever been a part of. Now, we focus much more of our team time on instructional strategies, remediation ideas, and curriculum/test development. It wasn't always easy to make the time or feel comfortable sharing our weaknesses. But, we have grown so much as teachers and have developed a professional community centered around improving our instruction.

> Our standardized math test scores (both state and district level) have shown dramatic improvement after our implementation of the common formative assessment process. We have felt such success that this school year we began designing and using common formative assessments in reading. We are now hopeful and excited to see the same improvement in our reading standardized scores.
>
> *Source:* Used with permission from Laura Anderson, 4th-grade teacher, District 196, Rosemount, MN, 2011.

Step 6: Review and Critique the Overall Assessment for Quality Before Use

At this step, we determine how much time to allow, adjust the time or the test as needed, and review the assessment for quality.

DETERMINING TESTING TIME. We advocate the development and use of "power" tests—this, as opposed to timed tests. We want each student to have time to address each item. If they don't, they will be marked wrong and you will infer nonmastery. But you may well be incorrect—you may be mismeasuring achievement. To prevent this, estimate time required to give the test as planned. Decide if this amount of testing is acceptable—if students in your grade level can reasonably be expected to maintain concentration for that long. If the testing time as planned is unreasonable, modify your test by one of the following means:

- Convert some of the more time-consuming item formats to true/false items.
- Test only some of the learning targets and hold others for a separate assessment later.

REVIEWING THE ASSESSMENT FOR QUALITY. There are three aspects of test quality to evaluate: how well it matches the assessment blueprint, how well the items are written, and how well the test avoids other sources of bias.

Matching the Assessment Blueprint. To check for the match between your test and its blueprint, you can use the following process:

1. Make a numbered list of the learning targets the test is to cover.
2. Next to each item on your test, write the number of the learning target it measures. Also indicate how many points the item is worth. For example, item number one on your test might measure learning target number five and be worth two points, so next to item number one, you would write 5/2.
3. On the list of learning targets, tally the points each receives on the test.
4. Compare these numbers to the blueprint.

Ensuring Item Quality. To evaluate the quality of the items you must do two things: check that each item tests what you intended and verify that each item is well-written.

To check that your items test what you intended, you can work backwards to turn them into the propositions you began with. Here's how:

- Combine the multiple-choice item stem with the correct response.
- True true/false items already are propositions.
- Make false true/false items true to derive the proposition.
- Match up elements in matching exercises.
- Fill in the blanks of short answer items.

If the result is a match with the proposition you wrote, then the item will measure what you intended it to.

You can verify that each item is well-written by using the Guidelines for Writing Quality Items and also by auditing each against the requirements of the first five sections of the checklist in Figure 5.6.

Avoiding Other Sources of Bias. Even with a match to learning targets, appropriate sampling, and high-quality items, there are a few things that can still go wrong that will compromise your results. The format of the test may be confusing or misleading, the directions may not be clear, or students may not have enough time to answer all questions. Example 5.3 shows two formats for the same item: Version 1 illustrates a problem with the layout that has been corrected in Version 2. You can check for sources of bias in your test by auditing it against the requirements in the last three sections of Figure 5.6: "Format," "Directions," and "Time."

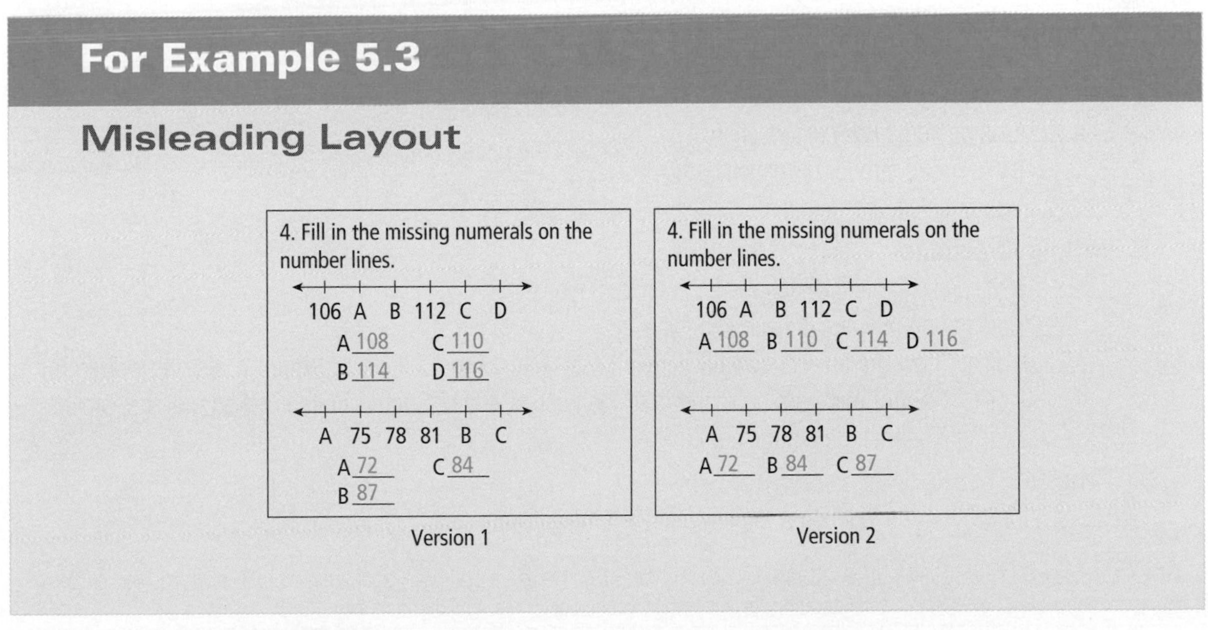

FIGURE 5.6 Selected Response Test Quality Checklist

1. **General guidelines for all formats**
   - ______ Keep wording simple and focused. Aim for lowest possible reading level.
   - ______ Ask a question.
   - ______ Avoid providing clues within and between items.
   - ______ Correct answer should not be obvious without mastering material tested.
   - ______ Highlight critical words (e.g., *most, least, except, not*).
2. **Guidelines for multiple-choice items**
   - ______ State whole question in item stem.
   - ______ Eliminate repetition of material in response options.
   - ______ Be sure there is only one correct or best answer.
   - ______ Keep response options brief and parallel.
   - ______ Make all response options the same length.
   - ______ Limit use of "all" or "none of the above."
   - ______ Use "always" and "never" with caution.
3. **Guideline for true/false items**
   - ______ Make them entirely true or entirely false as stated.
4. **Guidelines for matching items**
   - ______ Provide clear directions for the match to be made.
   - ______ Keep list of trigger items brief (maximum length is 10).
   - ______ Include only homogeneous items.
   - ______ Keep wording of response options brief and parallel.
   - ______ Provide more responses than trigger items.
5. **Guidelines for fill-in items**
   - ______ Ask a question.
   - ______ Provide one blank per item.
   - ______ Do not make length of blank a clue.
   - ______ Put blank toward the end.
6. **Formatting test items**
   - ______ Be consistent in the presentation of an item type.
   - ______ Keep all parts of a test question on one page.
   - ______ Avoid crowding too many questions on one page.
   - ______ Arrange items from easy to hard.
   - ______ Try to group similar formats together.
   - ______ Avoid misleading layout.
7. **Writing directions**
   - ______ Write clear, explicit directions for each item type.
   - ______ State the point value of each item type.
   - ______ Indicate how the answer should be expressed (e.g., should the word true or false be written, or T or F? Should numbers be rounded to the nearest tenth? Should units such as months, meters, or grams be included in the answer?)
8. **Time**
   - ______ Make sure the test is not too long for the time allowed.

Source: Adapted from *Student-Involved Assessment* for *Learning*, 5th ed. (p. 122), by R. J. Stiggins, 2008, Upper Saddle River, NJ: Pearson Education.

Step 7: Conduct and Score the Assessment
Step 8: Revise as Needed for Future Use

Even the best planning can't catch all problems with an assessment. Here are two things to watch for as you administer the test:

- *Students don't have enough time to complete all test items.* If students don't have the opportunity to attempt each item, their scores will not reflect what they have learned. Watch for students frantically marking items toward the end of the time allowed. Also look for large numbers of incomplete tests.
- *Students are confused by an item.* Make notes on the questions for which students ask clarifying questions.

While correcting the tests, make note of items that caused unexpected difficulties. Use the Guidelines for Writing Quality Items and the checklist in Figure 5.6 to troubleshoot these items as well as the items for which students required clarification and make any revisions as needed for future use.

My Classroom Then and Now 5.3

Shannon Braun

I used to ...

Testing in my classroom has always followed the traditional model. I would spend a couple of weeks teaching a unit, give a quiz partway through the chapter, and end the unit with a test. I rarely analyzed the results of my quizzes and tests. Instead, I corrected the summative assessments, entered them in my gradebook, and shared the results and class averages with the students. Were there questions that many students missed? What types of errors were students making? By not analyzing my assessments with any detail, I did not always have answers for parents or tutors wondering how they could help their children.

Now I ...

After doing some research on formative assessment and gathering ideas from others, I have started to implement some ideas in my own classroom. I now begin with essential targets or goals and guide students towards them. Students use responders to assess progress on certain targets. I am easily able to collect data from the students during the chapter and make spreadsheets to analyze the results. I return corrected summative unit tests with a slip of paper indicating the targets measured on the test. As we go through the test as a class, I match targets with test questions and students record tally marks for each target they missed. I post additional review worksheets for each target on my webpage and give students a week to work on them. I then allow retakes on these targets for students who have completed the extra practice. I also convey information to parents and tutors about the areas in which students need help.

Why I changed ...

These practices help both students and me decide what areas they are doing well on and what areas they need to improve. Besides helping students understand their tests better, it helps me improve instruction. Prior to using formative assessment strategies I would give parents a very vague response when they asked what to do to help their children, but now I am able to give parents very detailed guidance.

What I notice as a result ...

Using formative assessment in a structured way has transformed the way I look at instruction. I found improvements in student achievement in almost all cases. Communication between myself and students and parents has improved. Other members of my department are also using these strategies and we are now able to compare results and share insight on how we might improve certain targets. We all have different techniques to share!

Source: Used with permission from Shannon Braun, high school mathematics teacher, District 196, Rosemount, MN, 2011.

SELECTED RESPONSE ASSESSMENT *FOR* LEARNING

As we saw in Chapter 2, formative assessment can be thought of as actions that involve both the teacher and the student as decision makers. We also saw that motivation to learn and level of achievement both rise when students are engaged in the assessment process. The following suggestions represent ways selected response tests can serve to help students answer the three essential questions at the heart of assessment *for* learning: "Where am I going?"; "Where am I now?"; and "How can I close the gap?" These seven strategies as applied to selected response tests are summarized in Figure 5.7.

Where Am I Going?

STRATEGY 1: PROVIDE STUDENTS WITH A CLEAR AND UNDERSTANDABLE VISION OF THE LEARNING TARGET. Once you have an assessment blueprint, you can use it, not just for test development, but also as assessment *for* learning. Give students a list of the learning targets, in terms they understand, at the outset of instruction, along with your assessment blueprint. You can also use the blueprint as a way to summarize the day's or week's learning by asking students to identify which cells the instruction has focused on.

FIGURE 5.7 Assessment *for* Learning with Selected Response Methodology

Where am I going?

1. Provide students with a clear and understandable vision of the learning target.
   _____ Write targets in student-friendly language.
   _____ Share assessment blueprints at the outset.
   _____ Have students match propositions with blueprint cells.
   _____ Have students generate propositions for each blueprint cell.
2. Use examples and models of strong and weak work.
   _____ Students identify wrong multiple-choice and fill-in answers and say why.

Where am I now?

3. Offer regular descriptive feedback.
   _____ Use distracters to intentionally frame corrective feedback.
   _____ Use the blueprint to provide feedback target by target on a test.
4. Teach students to self-assess and set goals.
   _____ Students "traffic light" the blueprint.
   _____ Students use assessment blueprints as a basis for evaluation of strengths and areas for study.

How can I close the gap?

5. Design lessons to focus on one learning target or aspect of quality at a time.
   _____ Use student-generated information from Strategy 4 to differentiate instruction.
   _____ Students use item formulas to write items.
   _____ Students answer question: *How do you know your answer is correct?*
   _____ Students turn propositions into items and practice answering the items.
   _____ Students create test items for each cell and quiz each other.
   _____ Students use graphic organizers to practice patterns of reasoning.
6. Teach students focused revision.
   _____ Students answer the question: *How do I make this answer better?*
7. Engage students in self-reflection and let them keep track of and share what they know.
   _____ Students track their progress and use that information to engage in self-reflection: I have become better at _____. I used to _____, but now I _____.

Propositions play a role in assessment *for* learning. Explain to students that a proposition is a statement of important learning and then do one or more of the following:

- Ask students to note what they understand to be the proposition(s) at the center of the day's instruction. Have them keep a list and add to it each day. Help students see how well their lists match your own.
- Give groups of students the assessment blueprint and sample propositions representing the learning thus far. Have them match the propositions to the correct cell in the blueprint.
- Have students create propositions for each cell in the blueprint. Check these for misunderstandings and reteach as needed.

STRATEGY 2: USE EXAMPLES AND MODELS OF STRONG AND WEAK WORK. Give students a reasoning item formula, such as the ones in Figure 5.6. (For younger students, you will need to translate the item formula into student-friendly language.) Show them a test item created with the formula. Ask them to identify which answers are wrong and which one is right by identifying the response pattern each follows. See the example "Using Item Formulas as Strong and Weak Examples" for an illustration of how this can work when teaching fourth-grade students to infer.

For Example 5.4

Using Item Formulas as Strong and Weak Examples

Which one of these answers is a good inference, based on the reading selection from *The BFG*? Mark the good inference with a star. The right answer is a good inference because it is a guess based on clues from the story.

a. The BFG could hear extremely well because he could not see very well.
b. The author loved his father very much.
c. The father did not finish high school.
d. The father had a good imagination.
e. The father wanted people to think he was a serious man.
f. The father had a well-developed sense of hearing.
g. The father was a funny person.

Some of these answers are wrong because they are not inferences at all! They are just facts that the story tells you outright. Write the letters of those wrong answers here:

____

Some of the answers are wrong because, even though they are guesses, there are no clues in the story to support them. Write the letters of those wrong answers here:

____

Be careful—you might think there is evidence for them, so look closely!

Where Am I Now?

STRATEGY 3: OFFER REGULAR DESCRIPTIVE FEEDBACK. To offer effective feedback with selected response assessments, you must know what learning target each item addresses. Your students must also understand the targets they are responsible for learning. If you are using multiple-choice items, the distracters students choose can pinpoint problems to address. After taking a test, students can use the assessment blueprint to figure out which learning targets they have mastered and which ones they still need to work on.

STRATEGY 4: TEACH STUDENTS TO SELF-ASSESS AND SET GOALS. Hand your assessment blueprint out at the beginning of instruction. Have students self-assess on the learning targets or concepts as you teach them, using "traffic light" icons. Students mark the learning target or concept with a large dot—green to indicate confidence in having mastered it ("I've got it"), yellow to indicate a judgment of partial mastery ("I understand part of it, but not all of it"), or red to indicate little or no understanding ("I don't get it at all"). Then let the "greens" and "yellows" partner to fine-tune their understanding while you work with the "reds." (Black, Harrison, Lee, Marshall, & Wiliam, 2002).

You can structure a quiz or test to function as both effective feedback and a means for self-assessment and goal setting. This works best if there is opportunity for students to improve their achievement before the assessment that counts for the mark or grade. Here is the process (adapted from Chappuis, 2009, pp. 111–112):

1. Identify what each item on the quiz or test measures by filling out the first two columns of the form "Reviewing My Results" shown in Figure 5.8.
2. Administer the quiz or test, correct it, and hand it back to students, along with the form, "Reviewing My Results."
3. Have students review their corrected quizzes or tests and mark the appropriate column "Right" or "Wrong" for each item.
4. Then have students review the items they got wrong and ask themselves, "Do I know what I did wrong? Could I correct this myself?" If the answer is "Yes," they mark the "Simple Mistake" column. If the answer is "No," they mark the "Don't Get It" column.
5. Hand out the form "Analyzing My Results" shown in Figure 5.9 and have students transfer their results to one (or more) of three categories: "I am good at these"; "I am pretty good at these, but need to do a little review"; and "I need to keep learning these."
6. Last, students make a plan to improve. Figure 5.10 offers two examples of goal-setting frames you might have them use.

Figure 5.11 shows an example of a form designed for secondary students. To use it, you make a numbered list of the learning targets to be assessed and then put only the learning target number on the form. Students use the form while they are taking the quiz or test to mark "Confident" or "Unsure" as they answer each item. After you have corrected the quizzes or tests, students fill in the "Right," "Wrong," "Simple Mistake," and "Don't Get It" columns. Then they combine that information

FIGURE 5.8 Reviewing My Results

Reviewing My Results

Name: ________________ Assignment: ________________ Date: ________

Please look at your corrected test and mark whether each problem is right or wrong. Then look at the problems you got wrong and decide if you made a simple mistake. If you did, mark the "Simple Mistake" column. For all the remaining problems you got wrong, mark the "Don't Get It" column.

Problem	Learning Target	Right	Wrong	Simple Mistake	Don't Get It
1					
2					
3					
4					
5					
6					
7					
8					
9					
10					

Source: Reprinted from *Seven Strategies of Assessment* for *Learning* (p. 112), by J. Chappuis, 2009, Upper Saddle River, NJ: Pearson Education. Reprinted by permission.

FIGURE 5.9 Analyzing My Results

Analyzing My Results

I AM GOOD AT THESE!

Learning targets I got right:

I AM PRETTY GOOD AT THESE, BUT NEED TO DO A LITTLE REVIEW

Learning targets I got wrong because of a simple mistake:

What I can do to keep this from happening again:

I NEED TO KEEP LEARNING THESE

Learning targets I got wrong and I'm not sure what to do to correct them:

What I can do to get better at them:

Source: Reprinted from *Seven Strategies of Assessment* for *Learning* (p. 113), by J. Chappuis, 2009, Upper Saddle River, NJ: Pearson Education. Reprinted by permission.

FIGURE 5.10 Student Goal-Setting Frames

To get better at____________________________________, I could . . .

-
-
-
-

Some things I am going to start doing are . . .

-
-
-

I'll start doing this on _________________ and work on it until__________________.
(date) (date)

One way I'll know I'm getting better is . . .

____

____

Goal	**Steps**	**Evidence**
What do I need to get better at?	How do I plan to do this?	What evidence will show I've achieved my goal?
Time Frame: Begin ________________ End ________________ Date ________________ Signed ________________		

Source: From *Self-Assessment and Goal-Setting*, (p. 45) by K. Gregory, C. Cameron, and A. Davies, 2000, Merville, BC: Connections. Reprinted by permission.

along with the "Confident" or "Unsure" information to fill out the form "Analyzing My Results."

How Can I Close the Gap?

STRATEGY 5: DESIGN LESSONS TO FOCUS ON ONE LEARNING TARGET OR ASPECT OF QUALITY AT A TIME. You can use the information provided by students in reviewing and analyzing their quiz or test results to differentiate instruction, to have students form study groups, or as the basis for general review.

Other focused activities include the following:

- Let students create test items using an item formula. See the example "Student-generated Inference Questions" for an illustration of how this might work as a followup to the activity described in Strategy 2.
- Follow each selected response item with the question, "How do you know your answer is correct?," providing several lines for a response. Discuss common reasons for right and wrong choices when you pass back the test.

FIGURE 5.11 Reviewing and Analyzing My Results—Secondary Version

Name: ________________ Assignment: ____________________ Date: ________

As you answer each question, decide whether you feel confident in your answer or unsure about it and mark the corresponding box.

Problem #	Learning Target #	Confident	Unsure		Right	Wrong	Simple Mistake	Don't Get It
1								
2								
3								
4								
5								
6								

My Strengths

To identify your areas of strength, write down the learning targets for problems you felt confident about **and** got right.

Learning Target #	Learning Target or Problem Description

My Highest Priority for Studying

To determine what you need to study most, write down the learning targets for problems you marked "Don't Get It" (problems you got wrong, NOT because of a simple mistake).

Learning Target #	Learning Target or Problem Description

What I Need to Review

To determine what you need to review, write down the learning targets for problems you were unsure of and for problems on which you made simple mistakes.

Learning Target #	Learning Target or Problem Description

Source: Adapted from *Assessment FOR Learning: An Action Guide for School Leaders* (pp. 198, 199), by S. Chappuis, R. Stiggins, J. Arter, and J. Chappuis, 2004, Upper Saddle River, NJ: Pearson Education. Adapted by permission.

My Classroom Then and Now 5.4

Kim Urban

I used to ...

To prepare for tests or quizzes, I used to do a whole-class review (either worksheets or a game). This would mean that students who have mastered a concept reviewed the material for the same amount of time as a student struggling. I also did not separate concepts (learning targets) for the chapter. Rather, students would study for the chapter as a whole. The review was completed in class the day before the test so there was limited opportunity for students to ask for help or identify the areas they needed help with.

Now I ...

Two days before the scheduled test (summative assessment), I separate learning targets into "I can" statements and give students a formative assessment. Students must answer the questions (1–2 per learning target) and bring their paper to me. If there are mistakes, I provide immediate feedback and have students correct and bring their paper back to me. When students have shown through the formative assessment that they have mastered a concept, they are able to receive enrichment on those learning targets. Students who have made corrections on a learning target may benefit from further review. Additional practice materials are made available to those students. Students who are unable to make corrections can then sit with me and review in a small group. The next day, students who have mastered the learning targets and feel that they are ready may begin their test. Students who worked with me the previous day and students who are still working on learning targets will be offered additional review individually or with me. They are given the test the next day

Why I changed ...

All students do not need to review the same targets for the same amount of time. The use of formative assessments and separating review into learning targets allows me to differentiate instruction for the students. With 30 or more students in a class, formative assessments provide a quick way to assess the level of understanding of all students before testing, and provide for each student's individual needs.

What I notice as a result ...

Students used to be overwhelmed by studying for a "chapter" in math class. Now, I show students the learning targets that they have mastered so they can focus on studying the learning targets that they are struggling with. Even students unwilling to ask for help benefit from formative assessments because they receive the feedback from me and are forced to correct their mistakes. Test scores have improved and the majority of students are willing to ask for help on targets they do not understand.

Source: Used with permission from Kim Urban, 6th-grade mathematics teacher, Olmsted Falls School District, Olmsted Falls, OH, 2011.

- Assign groups of students to each cell of your test plan. Have them create questions that might be on the test, based on the propositions they generated for each cell during instruction. Have the groups take each others' practice tests.
- Teach students to use graphic organizers as a means to understand the specific kind of reasoning called for. After doing activities from Strategies 1 and 2, let students create their own graphic organizer for a specific pattern of reasoning.

For Example 5.5

Student-generated Inference Questions

How to Write an Inference Question

Here is a recipe that test writers use to create multiple-choice inference questions and answers.

Question:

Which idea does this selection suggest?

Possible responses

(these include the right answer and several wrong answers):

- The correct response is a guess that is supported by clues in the text.
- One incorrect response is a guess that a quick glance might suggest, but there really isn't enough evidence to support it.
- One incorrect response is a wild guess, because there aren't any clues in the text to support it.

Now it's your turn! First, read the assigned passage in the text. Then, work with a partner to create the right and wrong answers to the inference question below.

Here's the inference question:

Which idea does this selection suggest?

You write a correct answer and two incorrect answers. You can mix up the order—the correct answer doesn't have to come first.

a.
b.
c.

STRATEGY 6: TEACH STUDENTS FOCUSED REVISION. Anything we do to give students practice with applying what they know about quality or correctness to rework their own answers or to offer suggestions on someone else's work causes them to engage in revision. Consider letting them first practice on anonymous responses by answering one or both of the following questions: "What is wrong with this answer?" "What would make this answer better?"

STRATEGY 7: ENGAGE STUDENTS IN SELF-REFLECTION AND LET THEM KEEP TRACK OF AND SHARE THEIR LEARNING. We may think of this strategy as best suited to performance assessment, but it is equally effective with selected response assessment. Students should be thinking about their achievement with respect to the knowledge and reasoning targets measured by this method, both because they play an important role in their education, and also because it is these fundamental targets that struggling students often have not mastered. As we stated in Chapter 2, any activity that requires students to reflect on what they are learning and to share their progress both reinforces the learning and helps them develop insight into themselves as learners. These are keys to enhancing student motivation.

Some software programs have built-in mechanisms for students to track their progress and communicate their results. Students answer a variety of questions and get immediate feedback on how they did. They are able to monitor their own progress and experience the satisfaction of watching themselves improve. Many students come to enjoy the assessment experience, even if they are not wildly successful at first, and are motivated by seeing progress to continue trying.

We share more ways for students to track their learning in Chapter 9 and to share it in Chapters 11 and 12.

For specific examples of how each of these strategies can be used with selected response assessment across grade levels and subject areas, see Chappuis (2009).

Summary

In this chapter we revisited the idea that selected response items are a good way to measure knowledge and reasoning learning targets, as long as students can read at the needed level to understand the questions. Selected response is an efficient way to cover a lot of content in a short period of time.

Although we reviewed all steps in test development—from planning to critiquing the final product—we focused on creating assessment blueprints, generating propositions to identify important content, and adhering to guidelines for writing high-quality selected response items of all types.

Finally, we offered concrete examples of how to use selected response assessment as assessment *for* learning, meeting both the teacher's and the students' information needs. These strategies focused on how to use items, quizzes, and tests to answer the three questions that define assessment *for* learning: "Where am I going?"; "Where am I now?"; and "How can I close the gap?"

NOTES

1. Portions of these writing guidelines have been reprinted and adapted from Chapter 5, pp. 91-119, of R. J. Stiggins, and J. Chappuis, *Introduction to Student-involved Assessment FOR Learning*, 6th ed., 2011, Upper Saddle River, NJ: Pearson Education. Copyright © 2011 by Pearson Education, Inc. Reprinted and adapted by permission of Pearson Education, Inc.

CHAPTER 5 ACTIVITIES

End-of-chapter activities are intended to help you master the chapter's learning targets. They are designed to deepen your understanding of the chapter content, provide discussion topics for learning team meetings, and guide implementation of the practices taught in the chapter.

Forms for completing each activity appear in editable Microsoft Word format in the Chapter 5 CD file. Documents on the CD are marked with this symbol:

Chapter 5 Learning Targets

At the end of this chapter, you will know how to do the following:

1. Make a test blueprint for a selected response assessment.
2. Choose from among selected response formats.
3. Create high-quality items.
4. Audit any selected response test for quality.
5. Use selected response assessments to plan further instruction.
6. Use selected response assessments as feedback to students and for student self-assessment and goal setting.

Activity 5.1 Keep a Reflective Journal
Activity 5.2 Audit Items for Quality
Activity 5.3 Create a Test
Activity 5.4 Develop an Assessment *for* Learning Activity
Activity 5.5 Prepare Quiz or Test for Formative Use
Activity 5.6 Reflect on Your Own Learning
Activity 5.7 Select Portfolio Artifacts

Activity 5.1

Keep a Reflective Journal

Keep a record of your thoughts, questions, and any implementation activities you tried while reading Chapter 5.

 Reflective Journal Form

Activity 5.2

Audit Items for Quality

This activity has two parts. The first part is an exercise in identifying item problems and the second part is an exercise in applying the Selected Response Test Quality Checklist in Figure 5.6 to an existing selected response quiz or test.

Part 1: Test of Franzipanics

After reading the section, "Step 5: Develop or Select Items, Exercises, Tasks, and Scoring Procedures," work independently, with a partner, or with a team to review this test of an imaginary subject, "Franzipanics." The correct answers can be guessed at without any knowledge of Franzipanics.

Directions: Circle the correct answer for each question. Then identify the item flaw that allowed you to obtain the correct answer without knowing the subject.

1. The purpose of the cluss in furmpaling is to remove

- **a.** cluss-prags
- **b.** tremalis
- **c.** cloughs
- **d.** plumots

2. Irassig is true when

- **a.** lusp trasses the vom
- **b.** the viskal fans, if the viskal is donwil or zortil
- **c.** the belgo frulls
- **d.** dissles lisk easily

3. The sigla frequently overfesks the trelsum because

- **a.** all siglas are mellious
- **b.** siglas are always votial
- **c.** the trelsum is usually tarious
- **d.** no trelsa are feskable

4. The fribbled breg will minter best with an

- **a.** derst
- **b.** morst
- **c.** sorter
- **d.** ignu

5. Among the reasons for tristal doss are

- **a.** the sabs foped and the foths tinzed
- **b.** the kredges roted with the orots
- **c.** few rakobs were accepted in sluth
- **d.** most of the polats were thonced

6. The mintering function of the ignu is most effectively carried out in connection with

- **a.** a raxma tol
- **b.** the groshing stantol
- **c.** the fribbled breg
- **d.** a frally sush

Test of Franzipanics

Answers to Franzipanics Test

Part 2: Critique a Selected Response Test

Now select a short selected response quiz or test from your resources. Work independently, with a partner, or with a team to evaluate its quality by following the steps described in the section, "Reviewing the Assessment for Quality."

1. Check for the match between your test and its blueprint. If it doesn't have a blueprint, make one by completing Activity 4.5. You can use one of the blueprint forms from Activity 5.3, also.
2. Evaluate the quality of each item by checking that it tests what you intend it to and verifying that each item is well written. Use the Selected Response Test Quality Checklist (Figure 5.6) to help you with this step.
3. Audit the test against the sources of bias described in the text.
4. Make a revision plan for the test, if needed.

Test Blueprint Form A

Test Blueprint Form B

Selected Response Test Quality Checklist

Activity 5.3

Create a Test

Select a short unit that you are currently teaching or will teach this year. Work independently, with a partner, or with a team to carry out this activity.

Planning Stage

1. Follow the steps described in the Planning Stage. Use either "Test Blueprint A" or "Test Blueprint B," or modify one to make your own test blueprint.

Development Stage

2. Identify the content to be tested by writing propositions following the suggestions in Chapter 5.
3. Next, determine which item type(s) you will use for each target. Refer to Figure 5.4 "Comparison of Selected Response Item Types" for guidance.
4. Follow the Guidelines for Writing Quality Items to create each type of item you have specified.
5. Assemble the items following the guidelines in the text.
6. Review and critique the test for quality following the instructions in the text. Revise it as needed before use. You can also use the Selected Response Test Quality Checklist to help with this.
7. If you created the test for formative use, use the blueprint to create a second version of it for summative use. If you created the test for summative use, use the blueprint to create a second version for formative use.

Test Blueprint Form A

Test Blueprint Form B

Selected Response Test Quality Checklist

Activity 5.4

Develop an Assessment *for* Learning Activity

1. After reading the section, "Selected Response Assessment *for* Learning," select one formative application to try.
2. Develop the materials, use them with students, and note any changes in students' motivation, interest, or achievement.
3. Share the materials you developed and your observations about the effects the activity had on students with a colleague or your learning team.

(Note that directions for the application described in Strategy 4 and illustrated in Figures 5.8 to 5.11 are provided in Activity 5.5.)

 Debrief the AFL Activity You Tried

Activity 5.5

Prepare a Quiz or Test for Formative Use

This activity is set up so that both teachers and students can use quiz or test results formatively: teachers to plan further instruction and students to self-assess and set goals for further learning. It has two parts—preparing for formative use and creating the forms students will use.

Begin by choosing a selected response quiz or test you intend to give to students. Work independently or with one or more colleagues who will also give the quiz or test to carry out the two parts of this activity.

Part 1: Preparing for Formative Use

At this point, you need to ensure two things. The first is that the items on the quiz or test match exactly to what you have been teaching. The second is that you have planned instructional interventions and built in time for them after the quiz or test is given.

For the first consideration, making sure that each item on the quiz or test matches what you are teaching, if you have developed the test or quiz yourself following Chapter 5 guidelines, you will have taken care of the match. If you are using a quiz or test that you did not develop, use Activity 4.4, "Audit an Assessment for Clear Learning Targets" to ensure the match.

For the second consideration, think about how many learning targets you will be assessing as well as their complexity. How much remediation time do you anticipate students will need after the assessment? What kinds of activities will you prepare for review and reteaching? Identify specific resources and activities that could be used for further instruction on each learning target you are assessing. Plan for a mix of independent work and direct instruction to meet different student needs.

Part 2: Creating the Forms

You can use one of two versions. Option A, illustrated in Figures 5.8 and 5.9, is the simpler version and Option B, illustrated in Figure 5.11, is more detailed.

When working with a cumulative-type test, this activity is most powerful as a learning experience if students will have an opportunity to take some version of the test again because it can direct their studying for a retake of the test. Students can follow up their self-analysis with a specific study plan, using a form such as one of those shown in Figure 5.10.

Option A

1. Identify which learning target each item on the quiz or test represents.
2. Fill out the first two columns of the form "Reviewing My Results": *Problem Number* and *Learning Target*. In this version, you write the actual learning target (in student-friendly language) on the form.

3. Give the quiz or test. Correct it as usual and hand it back to students, along with the forms "Reviewing My Results" and "Analyzing My Results."
4. Have students mark whether each problem is right or wrong on the form "Reviewing My Results." Then have them revisit the problems they got wrong to determine the cause. They mark "Simple Mistake" if they know what they did wrong and can correct it without help. They mark "Don't Get It" if they do not understand how to answer the problem correctly.
5. Now have students fill out the form "Analyzing My Results." They begin by listing learning targets they got right. Then they list those with simple mistakes and make a plan to keep from making those mistakes again. Last they list the learning targets that they don't get and write down options for how to get better at them. It's good to have students think about this, but you can also give them suggestions, such as an activity to complete, a section in the text to re-read, or a series of problems that build understanding to work.
6. You can use the students' self-identified "I need to keep learning these" lists of targets to group students for focused instruction.
7. You can also ask students to use the results to complete a goal-setting form.

Option B

1. Make a numbered list of the learning targets represented on the test. Write the learning targets in the same student-friendly language you have used when sharing them with students. Save this list.
2. Fill out the first two columns of the form, "Reviewing My Results": *Problem Number* and *Learning Target Number*. For this version, you write the learning target number only, not the learning target itself, on the form, because you will be handing the form out with the test.
3. Copy the form, "Reviewing and Analyzing Results" for each student and hand it out with the quiz or test.
4. As students take the quiz or test, they note on the form whether they feel confident or unsure of the correct response to each item.
5. Correct the tests as usual and hand them back, along with the numbered list of learning targets (from Step One), and the form "Reviewing and Analyzing My Results."
6. Have students mark whether each problem is right or wrong on the first portion of the form. Then have them revisit the problems they got wrong to determine the cause. They mark "Simple Mistake" if they know what they did wrong and can correct it without help. They mark "Don't Get It" if they do not understand how to answer the problem correctly.
7. Now have students fill out the second half of the form to analyze their results. They begin by listing learning targets they got right as their strengths. Then they list the learning targets they don't get as their highest priority for study. Last

they list those with simple mistakes and those they got right, but were unsure of what they need to review.

8. You can use the students' self-identified "I need to keep learning these" lists of targets to group students for focused instruction, such as an activity to complete, a section in the text to re-read, or a series of problems that build understanding.
9. If this is a summative assessment and you are going to offer students a chance to retake it, you may want to have them complete a goal-setting form based on the results of this first assessment.

Reviewing and Analyzing My Results, Option A

Reviewing and Analyzing My Results, Option B

Goal-Setting Form

Activity 5.6

Reflect on Your Own Learning

Review the Chapter 5 learning targets and select one or more that represented new learning for you or struck you as most significant from this chapter. If you are working individually, write a short reflection that captures your current understanding. If you are working with a partner or a team, either discuss what you have written or use this as a discussion prompt for a team meeting.

Reflect on Chapter 5 Learning

Activity 5.7

Select Portfolio Artifacts

Any of the activities from this chapter can be used as portfolio entries. Select any activity you have completed or artifacts you have created that will illustrate your competence at the Chapter 5 learning targets:

1. Make an assessment blueprint for a selected response assessment.
2. Choose from among selected response formats.
3. Create high-quality items.
4. Audit any selected response test for quality.
5. Use selected response assessments to plan further instruction.
6. Use selected response assessments as feedback to students and for student self-assessment and goal setting.

If you are keeping a reflective journal, you may want to include Chapter 5's entry in your portfolio.

 Chapter 5 Portfolio Entry Cover Sheet

CHAPTER

6

Written Response Assessment

A farmer lost his entire crop.
Why might this have happened?

STUDENT 1: Drought

STUDENT 2: Floods and heavy rains destroyed them.

Drought destroyed them.

The birds ate all the seeds.

The crop was demolished for business construction.

He didn't take proper care of his crops.

He went bankrupt, so was unable to look after his crop.

The soil was unsuitable for growing his crops.

(ARTER & BUSICK, 2001, P. 137)

Written response assessment acts as a window into students' knowledge, conceptual understanding, and reasoning abilities, but it only provides a clear view if it is well done. At first glance a written response assessment may seem fairly easy to create—what's so hard about writing a question?—yet as the preceding student responses show, we may not get what we expected or hoped for without carefully thought-out questions and plans for scoring the answers.

Written response assessments include *short answer* items and *extended written response* items. Short answer items call for a very brief response having one or a limited range of possible right answers. Extended written response items require a response that is at least several sentences in length, and generally have a greater number of possible correct or acceptable answers. In this chapter, we examine how to develop items of both kinds, how to score them accurately, and how to use written response assessments formatively, as assessments *for* learning.

Chapter 6 Learning Targets

At the end of Chapter 6, you will know how to do the following:

- Develop short answer items and scoring guides.
- Develop extended written response items and scoring guides.
- Use written response assessments formatively, as teaching tools.
- Structure written response assessments so that students can use the results to self-assess and set goals for further learning.

FIGURE 6.1 Keys to Quality Classroom Assessment

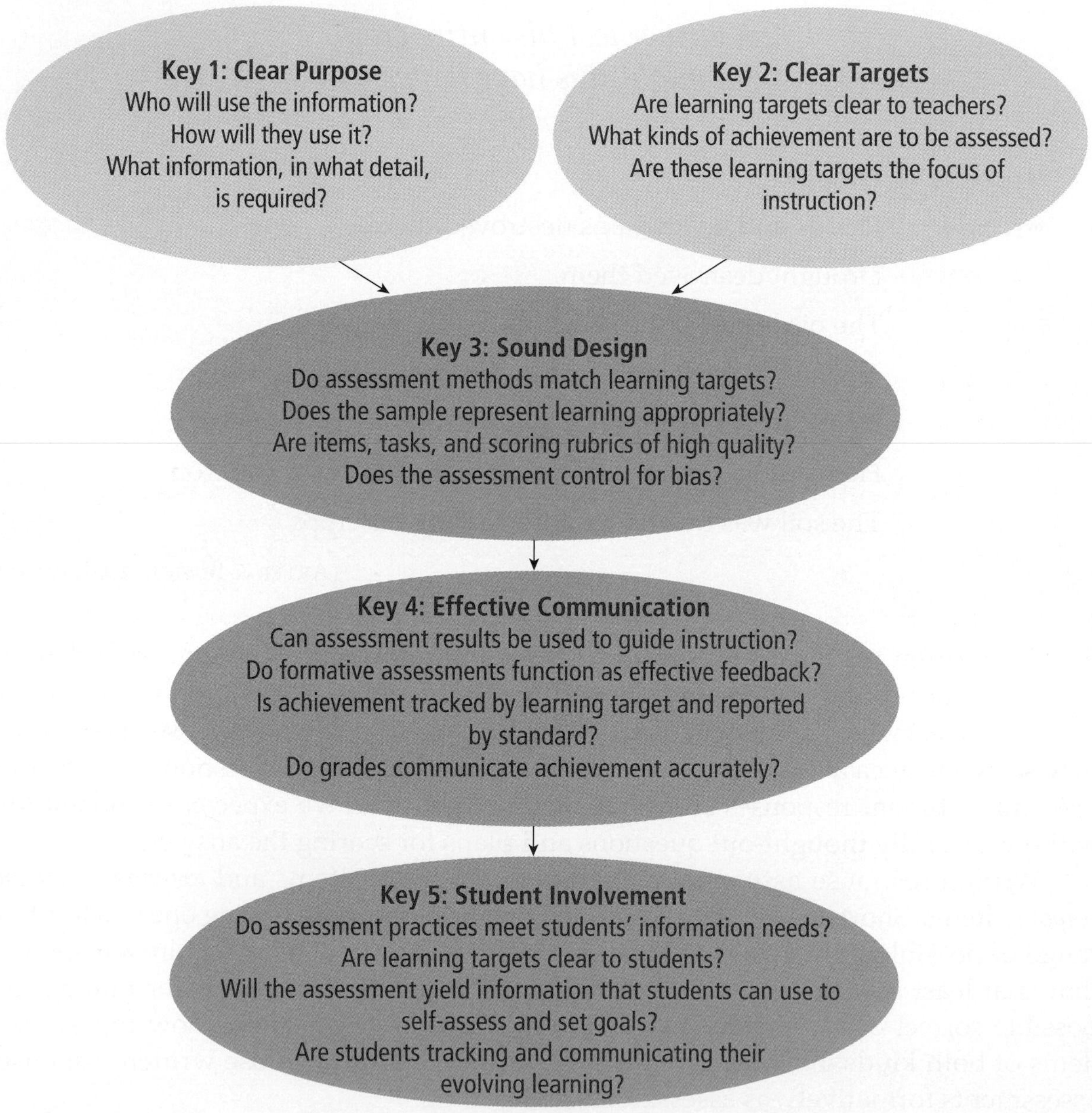

Key 1: Clear Purpose
Who will use the information?
How will they use it?
What information, in what detail, is required?

Key 2: Clear Targets
Are learning targets clear to teachers?
What kinds of achievement are to be assessed?
Are these learning targets the focus of instruction?

Key 3: Sound Design
Do assessment methods match learning targets?
Does the sample represent learning appropriately?
Are items, tasks, and scoring rubrics of high quality?
Does the assessment control for bias?

Key 4: Effective Communication
Can assessment results be used to guide instruction?
Do formative assessments function as effective feedback?
Is achievement tracked by learning target and reported by standard?
Do grades communicate achievement accurately?

Key 5: Student Involvement
Do assessment practices meet students' information needs?
Are learning targets clear to students?
Will the assessment yield information that students can use to self-assess and set goals?
Are students tracking and communicating their evolving learning?

WHEN TO USE WRITTEN RESPONSE ASSESSMENT

Not surprisingly, the first consideration for using written response assessment is the type of learning target to be assessed. Written response assessment is a strong match for knowledge targets, especially when assessing mastery of chunks of knowledge that interrelate, rather than individual pieces of knowledge assessed separately. (Selected response is more efficient for individual pieces of knowledge.) For example, in science, we might want students to explain how atoms combine to form other substances. In social studies, we might want students to describe the factors that led to development of centers of habitation, and why each factor is important. In English, we might want students to explain the difference between connotation and denotation.

Written response is also a strong match for reasoning targets. Reasoning occurs in the mind—we can't "see" it as it's happening, but we can ask students to describe their thinking using a written form of communication. In doing so, we can discover not only what they know, but also how well they understand it. For example, in mathematics we might ask students to explain the process they used to arrive at an answer. In science, we might ask students to explain their rationale for an experiment design.

Through written response, students can show their ability to infer, analyze, compare, determine cause and effect, and evaluate information. In a unit on pollution, for example, we might ask students to determine which solution to a problem is most likely to have the greatest benefit and to explain the reasons for their choice. In social studies, we might ask students to trace the line of an argument in a political speech. In English, we might ask students to interpret the meaning of a metaphor in a poem.

Several other conditions influence the selection of the written response method of assessment. Use it when

- Your students are capable of writing in English. Written response, especially extended written response, probably won't work well for primary students, English language learners, and students with special needs involving English or writing.
- You can't get the information you need through the less time-consuming selected response method.
- You know that the scoring guides are of high quality and that scorers will apply them consistently.

THE PLANNING STAGE FOR A WRITTEN RESPONSE ASSESSMENT

The Planning Stage has four steps: determine who will use the assessment results and how they will use them, identify the learning targets to be assessed, select the appropriate assessment method or methods, and determine sample size.

Determining Users and Uses

We begin planning by answering these questions: How do we want to use the information? Who else will use it? What decisions will they make? Typically, we will use assessment information for one or more of the following purposes:

- To plan instruction, as with a pretest
- To differentiate instruction based on student needs derived from the assessment
- To offer feedback to students so they can act on it during the learning
- To give students the opportunity to self-assess and set goals for further learning
- To measure level of achievement for a final grade, as with a post-test

Each one of these purposes can be accomplished with written response formats, as long as we keep the intended use in mind while making further planning and design decisions.

Identifying Learning Targets

At this step we simply list the specific learning targets the assessment is to measure. (If a target is complex or unclear, clarify it or deconstruct it first, following the processes outlined in Chapter 3.)

Selecting Assessment Method(s)

Although we have already determined that we will use written response, it's important to make sure we have identified only knowledge and reasoning learning targets as the subject of this assessment and also that the targets can be assessed well with written response methodology. So review the list of learning targets (from Step 2) with this in mind. (Refer to Chapter 4 for an in-depth discussion of which types of targets are best assessed with written response methodology.)

Determining Sample Size

At this step, we establish priorities. Which of the learning targets or topics are most important, next most important, and so on? This will serve as the basis for the distribution of points or ratings in the overall assessment plan. The prioritization should parallel the amount of time and emphasis given the various targets or topics in teaching.

Remember, when identifying the relative importance of each learning target, we consciously match our emphasis in assessment to our emphasis in the classroom. If, say, we spend 20 percent of the time learning how to trace a line of argument in a political speech, then roughly 20 percent of the assessment points should focus on tracing a line of argument. If only 5 percent of the course deals with tracing lines of argument, then in most cases it would misrepresent learning to devote 20 percent of the final assessment to it.

However, if it's a standards referenced assessment in which we are documenting how students have done in mastering one or more standards of equal importance, then we simply apportion the points to adequately sample each standard.

COMBINING PLANNING DECISIONS INTO AN ASSESSMENT BLUEPRINT. We can create a blueprint for a written response assessment in one of two ways—a list of learning targets or a table—as described in Chapter 4.

A blueprint in the form of a list of learning targets is useful when the assessment will be fairly simple. Example 6.1 shows a blueprint for a written response assessment focusing on selected learning targets from the "Physics of Sound" unit described in Chapter 4.

For Example 6.1

Assessment Blueprint in List Format

Unit on Physics of Sound

Learning Target	Points
Learn that sound originates from a source that is vibrating and is detected at a receiver such as the human ear	6
Understand the relationship between the pitch of a sound and the physical properties of the sound source (i.e., length of vibrating object, frequency of vibrations, and tension of vibrating string)	6
Use knowledge of the physics of sound to solve simple sound challenges	8

A blueprint in the form of a table is useful when the assessment is more complex and will include both knowledge and reasoning learning targets in combination. These plans are similar to those used with selected response assessments, but they differ in how numbers are assigned to each cell. With selected response assessments, the numbers represent how many items will be needed. With written response assessments, the numbers represent the total point value for each cell. The points may come from a single item or more than one item. Example 6.2 shows the table form of a blueprint for a written response test covering a unit on pollution. The teacher has translated the learning targets to be tested into categories of content students are to know and the patterns of reasoning they are to master. The categories of content are represented in the lefthand column and the patterns of reasoning are listed across the top. The numbers in each cell represent the relative emphasis assigned to each.

For Example 6.2

Assessment Blueprint in Table Format

Unit on Pollution

Content	Pattern of Reasoning			
	Know	Compare	Evaluate	Total
Concentrations	10	0	0	10
Effects of Pollutants	7	8	0	15
How to Reduce Pollution	6	10	9	25
Total	23	18	9	50

Given 50 points for the entire exam, this plan emphasizes how to reduce pollution, requiring that students rely on that understanding to compare and evaluate.

THE DEVELOPMENT STAGE FOR A WRITTEN RESPONSE ASSESSMENT

The Development Stage for a written response assessment has three steps: develop the items, prepare the scoring guide or guides, and critique the overall assessment for quality. As described in the following sections, written response items can take one of two forms: short answer or extended response. They can be designed to assess mastery of knowledge and reasoning proficiencies together or separately. Scoring guides can take one of three forms: a list, a task-specific rubric, or a general rubric. The items and scoring guides can be critiqued using the Quality Guidelines for Written Response Assessments (Figure 6.4) and the Rubric for Rubrics (which will be introduced in Chapter 7 and presented in Figure 7.10) prior to use.

DEVELOPING THE ITEMS

One of the advantages of written response tests relative to other test formats is that items are easier and less time consuming to develop. Keep in mind, however, that "easier to develop" does not mean they require little thought, as illustrated by

FIGURE 6.2 Options for Item Design

Short Answer Items

- Require a brief response
- Have one or a limited range of possible right answers
- Can be used for knowledge and some reasoning targets

Extended Written Response Items

- Require a response that is at least several sentences in length
- Have a greater number of possible correct or acceptable answers
- Can be used for knowledge and reasoning targets

Interpretive Items

- Can be either short answer or extended written response in format
- Knowledge provided; students demonstrate reasoning
- Used for reasoning targets

the question about the farmer's crops. If we are not careful at this stage, students who know the material may not perform well, and students who have not mastered the material may be able to look as though they have. Poorly framed written response items can be a nightmare for students to answer and for teachers to score.

Short Answer or Extended Response?

Use short answer items when the learning target calls for demonstration of conceptual understanding and the concept is fairly narrow, such as the learning target "Understand that the Earth's rotation causes day and night." (A "narrow" concept is not necessarily easy to understand. It just has a straightforward explanation.) Some patterns of reasoning can also be assessed with short answer items. For example, students can summarize the main idea of a paragraph in a sentence or two.

If, however, they are summarizing a longer passage, the response could be one to several paragraphs in length, in which case, extended written response may be a better choice. For learning targets that are more complex and therefore require greater depth in an explanation or demonstration of reasoning capability, develop extended written response items.

Devising Short Answer Items

A short answer item should be short and clearly worded, while giving students enough information to frame an acceptable response. If you are looking for two examples, three instances, or five characteristics, put that information in the item. Here are some examples:

Learning target:

Understand that shapes in different categories (e.g., rhombuses, rectangles, and others) may share attributes (e.g., having four sides). (Grade 3 Mathematics) (CCSSI 2010c, p. 26)

This:

Name four ways that rhombuses, rectangles, and squares are alike.

Not this:

How are rhombuses, rectangles, and squares alike?

Also not this:

What do rhombuses, rectangles, and squares have in common?

Learning Target:

Understand that human capital refers to the quality of labor resources, which can be improved through investments. (Grade 4 Social Studies) (Council for Economic Education, 2010, p. 3)

This:

Define *human capital* and give two examples of how you can improve your own human capital.

Not this:

What is human capital?

Learning Target:

Describe characters, settings, and major events in a story, using key details. (Grade 1 Reading) (CCSSI, 2010a, p. 11)

This:

Who is the main character of the story? What is the main character like? Give two details from the story that help you know this.

Not this:

Describe the main character.

If you are working with students who do not write sentences yet, you can ask written response questions orally. You can also ask them to draw a picture to supplement the answer, if a picture will help show their thinking. If you are requiring a picture, make sure your item asks for a picture that will show their thinking and not just illustrate the topic.

Learning Target:
Understand that day and night are caused by the earth's rotation. (Grade 2 Science)

This:

Everyone knows about day and night. Write what you think makes day and night. Draw a picture to show what you think.

Not this:

Explain day and night.

And not this:

Everyone knows about day and night. Write what you think makes day and night. Draw a picture of day and night.

Devising Extended Written Response Items

We have all experienced "essay" questions on tests, some of which may have been painful. "Discuss photosynthesis." "Analyze *King Lear*." "Explain the causes of the Civil War." High-quality extended written response items, in contrast to these, carefully frame the task so that students who have learned the material know how to tackle it.

ITEMS ASSESSING KNOWLEDGE MASTERY. Extended written response items that assess factual and conceptual knowledge do three things: (1) set a clear and specific context, (2) indicate what students are to describe or explain, and (3) point the way to an appropriate response without giving away the answer.

To assess the learning target "Understand the importance of the carbon cycle and how it works," we could create this item:

1. Set the Context

We have been studying the importance of the carbon cycle and how it works.

In this example, the context is stated as a paraphrase of the learning target. With extended written response questions, especially if they are included in a test with other items, it helps students to be reminded of the specific body of knowledge they are to use when framing their responses.

2. Tell What to Describe or Explain

Based on your understanding of the carbon cycle, describe why we need to know about it and how it works.

The task they are to carry out is stated in the second part—with a knowledge or conceptual understanding learning target, students are generally explaining or describing something. Notice this sentence doesn't just say "Describe the carbon cycle," for two reasons. First, that would not be sufficient to assess the learning target, and second, it doesn't give enough guidance—describe what? If you want students to describe how it works, make sure the item lays out that expectation.

3. Point the Way to an Appropriate Response

Be sure to include the following:

- Why it is important to understand the carbon cycle (5 points)
- The four major reservoirs where carbon is stored (4 points)
- At least six ways that carbon gets transferred from one place to another (6 points)

The third part helps students know what will be considered an appropriate and complete response; students who know the material will be able to answer well, and students who don't know it won't be able to bluff their way through.

ITEMS COMBINING KNOWLEDGE MASTERY WITH REASONING. Extended written response items that ask students to reason with knowledge they have learned are similar in structure to items that assess knowledge mastery. They also have three components, slightly altered to account for the addition of reasoning: (1) set a clear and specific context; (2) specify the kind of reasoning to be used; and (3) point the way to an appropriate response without giving away the answer.

For example, to assess the sixth-grade learning target, "Explain how an author develops the point of view of the narrator or speaker in a text," (CCSSI 2010a, p. 36), the Common Core State Standards document offers this extended written response task as a possibility: "Students explain how Sandra Cisnero's choice of words develops the point of view of the young speaker in her story 'Eleven'" (CCSSI, 2010b, p. 89).

Applying our item frame to the task it might look like this:

1. Set the Context

We have been studying "point of view"—what it means and how to identify it in a story.

2. Describe the Reasoning Task

After reading the story "Eleven," explain how the author uses word choice to show the point of view of the young speaker.

3. Point the Way to an Appropriate Response

Choose at least three examples. Make sure you explain what the young speaker's perspective is and how each example shows that.

(Written response items should also include information about how they will be evaluated, whether with a list of a number of points or with a rubric. Both options are described in the next section.)

As another example, to assess the learning target, "Evaluate opposing positions on humankind's role in global climate change," we could create this item:

1. Set the Context

There are those who contend that global climate change is a naturally occurring phenomenon and others who contend it is caused by the actions of humans.

2. Describe the Reasoning Task

Analyze the evidence we have studied to support each claim. Decide whom you think has the stronger argument. Defend your judgment with reasons.

3. Point the Way to an Appropriate Response

In doing so, consider the evidence from geologic history, the history and levels of emissions, and the political and economic interests of each side.

Here are two simpler examples:

- Explain the mathematics formula we studied today in a memo to a student who was absent.
- Teach younger students how to read a contour map by creating a list of instructions accompanied by diagrams and/or illustrations.

DEVISING INTERPRETIVE ITEMS. Interpretive items allow you to assess mastery of specific patterns of reasoning disentangled from student mastery of the prerequisite content knowledge. As you will recall from Chapter 4 we do this by supplying a passage, table, chart, or map of background information about a given topic and then asking students to write a response demonstrating the targeted pattern of reasoning: describe certain relationships, draw comparisons, conduct analyses, or create and fill categories, for example.

Interpretive items also do three things: (1) set the context, (2) describe the reasoning task, and (3) point the way to an appropriate response without "over helping."

To assess the learning target "Summarize text," we could create this item:

1. Set the Context

We have been learning how to write a summary—a brief statement of the main ideas of a text.

2. Describe the Reasoning Task

After reading (the assignment provided), write a paragraph that summarizes the main ideas.

3. Point the Way to an Appropriate Response

In your paragraph, be sure to do the following:

- focus only on the main ideas (2 points)
- include enough information to cover all of the main ideas (2 points)

or

Your paragraph will be evaluated with the Summary Rubric, attached.

FAQ 6.1

Analyze This

Question:

Some learning targets beginning with the word analyze *seem to require more than* "examining the components or structure of something." *How do we know what to teach and assess?*

Answer:

When a learning target begins with the word *analyze,* it also often requires students to do something with the components or structure. You will have to think through the whole target to determine the full extent of the reasoning required. Basically, you have to **analyze** an *analyze* target to know what to teach and assess.

For example, a sixth-grade Common Core State Standard in Reading states:

> Analyze in detail how a key individual, event, or idea, is introduced, illustrated, and elaborated in a text (e.g., through examples or anecdotes). (CCSSI, 2010a, p. 39)

In this case, we would suggest that to *analyze* here means this:

Explain how a key individual is introduced, illustrated, and elaborated and support the explanation with examples or anecdotes from the text.

Offering Choices

Typically, we recommend that you don't offer choices where the choices don't all provide comparable evidence of the same learning target. Regardless of the assessment format being used, especially in summative assessment contexts, the question should always be, "Can you hit the agreed-on target(s)?" It should never be, "Which (or which part of the) target are you most confident that you can hit?" or "Which target are you most interested in?"

When students select their own sample of performance, it can be a biased one when it avoids revealing that which they have yet to master. If what they don't know is essential for mastering what comes next, we won't know it and they won't learn it. However, in a formative assessment environment, we might relent somewhat because,

FIGURE 6.3 Scoring Guide Options for Written Response Items

Task-specific list—a list of possible correct answers or desired features of the response along with information about how points will be awarded

Task-specific rubric—a rubric describing features of quality as they appear in a single item or task

General rubric—a rubric describing the features of quality as they apply across items or tasks

hopefully, key gaps in learning will be revealed in recurring diagnostic assessments down the road.

PREPARING THE SCORING GUIDES

Again not surprisingly, a key to successful use of written response assessment is having clear and appropriate criteria by which to judge the quality of student responses. We recommend that you don't use "floating standards," in which the evaluator waits to see what responses come in before deciding what will count and thus how to score. Floating standards destroy the validity and reliability of the assessment. Teachers and students alike need to be clear in advance regarding which aspects of the response are important—this is as essential to a quality assessment as is thoughtful item development. In this section, we explain three scoring guide options and describe how to create each.

Scoring Guide Options

A *scoring guide* is simply a way to assign points to specific features of a response. Three types of scoring guides are appropriate for assessing written response items: lists, task-specific rubrics, and general rubrics.

LISTS. A scoring guide in list form identifies the possible correct answers or desired features of the response and specifies how points will be awarded. Use a list when the desired answer has several parts and each one represents a specific category of knowledge or reasoning with knowledge.

For an item asking students to cite instances where Spanish literature and politics may have influenced each other in the twentieth century, the scoring guide might look like this:

3 points for each instance cited, maximum 9 points

Quality of inferences about prominent novelists

Quality of inferences about political satirists

Quality of inferences about prominent political figures of Spain

For an item asking students to explain the Krebs cycle, the scoring guide might look like this:

One point for each of the following, maximum five points:

Cycle describes the sequence of reactions by which cells generate energy

Cycle takes place in the mitochondria

Cycle consumes oxygen

Cycle produces carbon dioxide and water as waste products

Cycle converts ADP to energy-rich ATP

For an item requiring students to explain how carbon moves from one place to another, the scoring guide might look like this:

One point for any six of the following, maximum six points:

Carbon moves from the atmosphere to plants through photosynthesis.

Carbon moves from the atmosphere to oceans by dissolving in places it is cold.

Carbon moves from the oceans to the atmosphere by evaporation where it is hot.

Carbon moves from land to the atmosphere through fires.

Carbon moves from land to the atmosphere through volcanic eruptions.

Carbon moves from land to the atmosphere through burning fossil fuels.

Carbon moves from the land into the oceans through erosion.

Carbon moves from plants/animals to the ground/sediments through decay.

For Example 6.3 shows an extended written response item and its scoring list.

Creating Lists. Because a scoring list is simply a description of specific information along with its point value, it is fairly easy to create one. Notice in the last two examples the correct responses are propositions, which we explained in Chapter 5. One good way to create a list of correct responses is to follow the instructions for proposition development found in that chapter. Another form of list useful for scoring is one that describes the characteristics of a correct response. For Example 6.3 shows a mathematics extended written response item scored by a task-specific list following this pattern.

Sharing Lists. Because the item should communicate to students what is most important to attend to in a quality response, it should include information about how their work will be scored. In the first "Spanish literature and politics" example, we suggest including the scoring list as written. However, in the second and third examples, the scoring list is the answer key, so we would not recommend including it in the item. Instead,

For Example 6.3

Extended Written Response Item Scored by a List

"Label the Graph" (Grade 3)

Content Standard: Draw a scaled bar graph to represent a data set with several categories (CCSSI 2010c, p. 25).

Learning Targets:

Know how to make equal-interval scales on axes

Interpret data from a bar graph

Extended Written Response Item:

Bar graphs can be used to compare things. This graph has four bars. What might the bars be comparing?

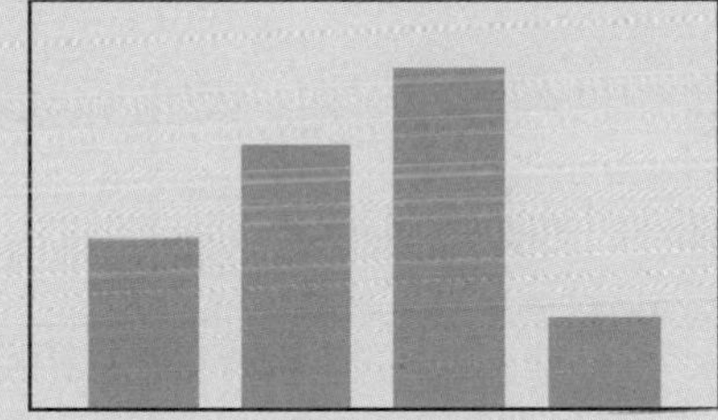

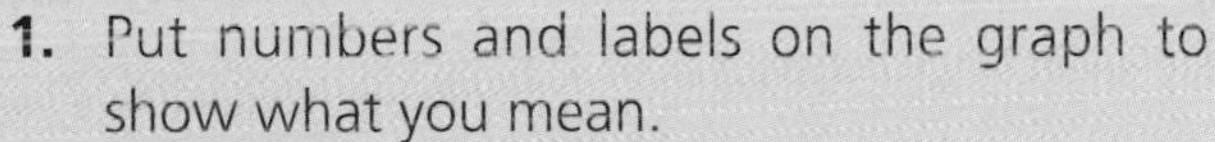

1. Put numbers and labels on the graph to show what you mean.

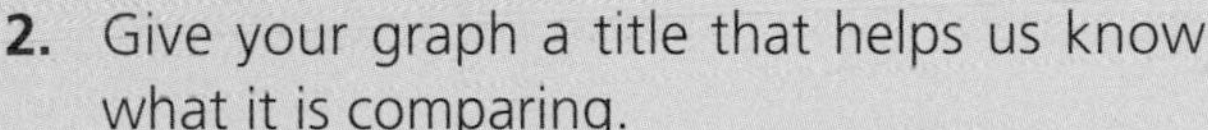

2. Give your graph a title that helps us know what it is comparing.

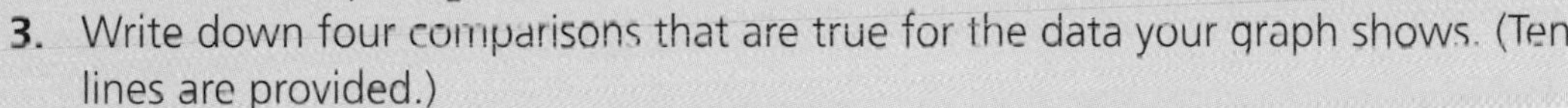

3. Write down four comparisons that are true for the data your graph shows. (Ten lines are provided.)

Scoring List

8 points total

1 point: Each bar on the X axis has label below it.

1 point: Labels identify categories that can be compared.

1 point: The Y axis is marked with an equal-interval scale.

1 point: The title accurately communicates the comparison.

1 point for each accurate comparison listed (4 points)

for the second "Krebs cycle" example, the item might conclude with the statement, "5 points possible, one for each key feature described correctly." For the third "carbon cycle" example it might look like this: "6 points possible, one for each correct explanation."

RUBRICS. A scoring guide in the form of a *rubric* is a detailed description of the features of work that constitute quality. In a rubric, the features of quality are described at different levels, representing a continuum of "novice" to "proficient" or "weak" to "strong." The levels can be labeled with words, symbols, or numbers. With a rubric, the level is the score.

There are two basic forms of rubrics: *task-specific* and *general*. A *task-specific* rubric describes the features of quality as they appear in a single item or task. For Example 6.4 shows a rubric used to evaluate a task given to assess the learning target "Interpret data from a graph." It can only be used to score one item, so it is called a *task-specific* rubric. A *general* rubric describes the features of quality as they apply across items or tasks. Example 6.5 shows a rubric that can be used to score any item that tests students' ability to interpret information from a graph. It is *general* because it is *generalizable* across tasks.

Remember from Chapters 3 and 4 that when the characteristics of effective writing are evaluated, we would classify the learning as a product target and evaluate it with a performance assessment.

We recommend the use of general rubrics over task-specific rubrics whenever practical for several reasons:

- Task-specific rubrics can't be handed out to students in advance because they give away the "answer."
- You have to create a new one for each assignment.
- With task-specific rubrics, it's easy to award points to features that are idiosyncratic to the specific assignment and not essential to the accomplishment of the learning target.

However, there are times when a task-specific rubric makes sense to use.

For Example 6.4

Task-specific Rubric for Interpreting a Graph

This rubric is an example of a task-specific rubric. It can only be used on one task, the math problem "Going to School" (not included here).

4 points:

Has all five points on the graph labeled correctly. Indicates that Graham and Paul ride their bikes to school. Provides accurate and complete explanation of how those conclusions were drawn. Indicates that Susan walks, and Peter takes a car as a part of the explanation.

3 points:

Has four or five points on the graph labeled correctly. Indicates that Graham and Paul ride their bikes to school. Explanation of reasoning is correct but incomplete and requires interpretation. May indicate that Susan walks and Peter takes a car as a part of the explanation.

2 points:

Has three points on the graph labeled correctly. Indicates that Graham or Paul ride a bike. Chooses the incorrect mode of transportation for the other. Explanation of reasoning is partially correct, but also includes faulty reasoning. Explanation may indicate that information about Susan or about Peter was interpreted incorrectly.

1 point:

Has one or two points on the graph labeled correctly. Indicates that Graham or Paul ride a bike. Chooses the incorrect mode of transportation for the other. Explanation of reasoning, if offered, is incomplete and incorrect. Explanation may ignore information about Susan and Peter or have interpreted it incorrectly.

0 points:

Has no points on the graph labeled correctly. Indicates incorrect mode of transportation for Graham and Paul. Explanation of reasoning, if offered, is faulty.

For Example 6.5

General Rubric for Interpreting a Graph

This is an example of a general rubric. It can be of use to judge responses to all problems requiring interpretation of a graph.

4 points:

Interprets information from graph to provide correct answers. Provides accurate and complete explanation of how conclusions were drawn.

3 points:

Interprets information from graph to provide correct answers. Provides accurate explanation of how conclusions were drawn, but explanation is incomplete and requires interpretation.

2 points:

Interprets information from graph to provide partially correct answers. Provides partially accurate explanation of how conclusions were drawn, but includes faulty reasoning. Explanation may also be incomplete and require interpretation.

1 point:

Interprets information from graph to provide partially correct answers. Explanation, if offered, consists of faulty reasoning and does not support correct conclusions drawn.

0 points:

Provides incorrect answers. Explanation, if offered, represents faulty reasoning.

Creating Task-Specific Rubrics

Task-specific rubrics are appropriate for assessing conceptual understanding. An example of a second-grade learning target for which we might create a task-specific rubric is, "Understand that the Earth's rotation causes night and day."

To write a task-specific rubric, we refer back to selected response methodology for the "bones." First we create a proposition—a sentence that accurately states the conceptual understanding—and from that we identify statements representing partial understanding, misunderstanding, and lack of understanding. These become our rubric levels.

Here is the process illustrated with the rubric for the item "Day and Night" shown in For Example 6.6:

1. Create a proposition—a sentence that accurately states the conceptual understanding.

> **Proposition:**
>
> "Night and day happen because the earth turns so that the same side is not always facing the sun."

2. Identify typical characteristics of partial understanding. You can also include misconceptions that aren't egregious; that is, they don't contradict the central understanding.

> **Statements of partial understanding:**
>
> "Night and day happen because the moon and sun are on different sides of the Earth."
>
> "The Earth rotates facing the sun and then the moon."

(These are partial understandings because the Earth's rotation does cause day and night, but facing the moon is not a factor. The misunderstanding does not contradict the explanation of Earth's rotation being the central cause.)

3. Identify typical characteristics of misunderstanding or lack of understanding. Also identify any egregious misconceptions that contradict the central understanding, which we call "fatal flaws."

> **Statement of misunderstanding:**
>
> "Night and day happen because the sun moves across the sky."

(This is also the "fatal flaw.")

4. Determine how many levels the rubric will have.

> **Levels:**
> "2," "1," and "0"

For Example 6.6

Short Answer Item Scored by a Task-specific Rubric

"Day and Night" (Grade 2)

Learning Target:

Understand that the Earth's rotation causes day and night.

Item:

Everyone knows about day and night. Write what you think makes day and night. (Four lines are provided.)

Draw a picture to show what you think. (A 5 × 5-inch box is provided.)

Scoring Guide:

2 The response indicates that the Earth turns so that the same face is not always facing the sun.

Example: "The Earth turns every 24 hours and for 12 hours we are facing the sun."

1 The response indicates that the moon and sun are on different sides of the Earth and the Earth rotates facing one and then the other. There is no implication that the sun moves.

Example: "In the day we face the sun and in the night we turn to face the moon."

0 The response indicates that the sun moves to cause night and day (possibly across the sky).

Example: "The sun moves and makes way for the moon."

Essay 3: "Day and Night" reprinted from *Exemplary Assessment Materials – Science* (p. 15), by Australian Council for Educational Research, Ltd., 1996, Hawthorn, Victoria, Australia.

For many task-specific rubrics, it makes sense to have three levels. You can use this formula to create one:

2 points = The response indicates ______ *insert statement(s) showing complete understanding*

1 point = The response indicates _______ *insert statement(s) showing partial understanding*

0 points = The response indicates _______ *insert statement(s) showing lack of understanding, complete misunderstanding, or partial understanding with a "fatal flaw"*

Notice that in the "Day and Night" rubric in Figure 6.6 an explanation can demonstrate partial understanding and also include a misunderstanding and still earn partial credit, but if it includes reference to the sun moving, it earns no credit because that is considered a "fatal flaw" in understanding the concept. A fatal flaw wipes out partial credit.

A three-level ("2," "1," and "0") rubric is a formula for awarding two, one, or no points. It can be used for a short answer or an extended response item, if the conceptual understanding is not too complex.

For conceptual understanding with more variables, it may make sense to have four levels, following this formula:

3 points = The response indicates _______ *insert statement(s) showing complete understanding.*

2 points = The response indicates _______ *insert statement(s) showing partial understanding. You may also include a statement of simple misunderstanding at this level.*

1 point = The response indicates _______ *insert statement(s) showing partial understanding with some misunderstandings, but no "fatal flaw."*

0 points = The response indicates ______ *insert statement(s) showing lack of understanding, misunderstanding, or partial understanding with the inclusion of a "fatal flaw."*

A four-level ("3," "2," "1," and "0") rubric is a formula for awarding three, two, one, or no points. It is best used with extended written response items. However, if you find yourself stretched to differentiate clearly between the two-point level and the one-point level, you may want to combine them into a three-level ("2," "1," and "0") rubric.

FAQ 6.2

Rubric Levels

Question:

Sometimes I see rubrics that have five levels but only the level 5, the level 3, and the level 1 are defined. What's the difference between that kind of rubric and the three-level rubric defined here?

Answer:

The first difference is that the five-level rubrics do have five distinct levels and the three-level rubrics only have three distinct levels. Five-level rubrics are commonly used for more complex learning targets with multiple scales, such as the Six-trait Writing Rubric. It has a separate scoring scale for six different criteria, called *traits*: Ideas and Content, Organization, Voice, Word Choice, Sentence Fluency, and Conventions. Each of the traits has its own five-level scale. Within each trait, multiple facets are described at the "five" level, the "three" level, and the "one" level. For example, the trait of Organization includes phrases at each of the three levels that describe these things: the quality of the introduction, the sequence of ideas, transitions, pacing, and the conclusion. Students could be doing well on some of those and not others. So the rubric is designed to let you award a "four" or a "two" to those papers that have some of the characteristics of each of the adjacent levels. It keeps us from having to assign a rubric score that doesn't match the work in front of us.

Chapter 7 provides further explanation of these kinds of rubrics.

Creating General Rubrics

Although we often use task-specific scoring, either in the form of lists or rubrics, for assessing student understanding of content, it is not our only option. We can also use a general rubric designed to assign points to student understanding of any concepts within a body of knowledge.

To create a general rubric for conceptual understanding, we can use the task-specific rubric formula itself. Instead of including the content-related statements of understanding, partial understanding, misunderstanding, or lack of understanding, we leave the descriptions in general terms:

2 points = Evidence shows complete understanding

1 point = Evidence shows partial understanding, with no serious misunderstandings

0 points = Evidence shows lack of understanding, complete misunderstanding, or partial understanding with a "fatal flaw"

Or

3 points = Evidence shows complete understanding

2 points = Evidence shows partial understanding with few, if any, simple misunderstandings

1 point = Evidence shows partial understanding with some misunderstanding, but no "fatal flaw"

0 points = Evidence shows lack of understanding, misunderstanding, or partial understanding with the inclusion of a "fatal flaw"

If we are using interpretive items to assess reasoning alone, then all we need is a general rubric for the pattern of reasoning we are assessing, such as the Rubric for a Generalization shown in For Example 6.7 and the Rubric for Analysis shown in For Example 6.8. Additional rubrics designed to evaluate inference, classification, comparison, synthesis, and evaluation can be found on the CD in the Chapter 6 file.

For Example 6.7

Rubric for a Generalization

2 points

- Statement is true for evidence presented and extends application logically to a broader array of instances.

1 point

- Statement is true for evidence presented, but application to other instances includes too broad an array of instances to be supported by evidence (overgeneralization).

0 points

- Statement is true for evidence presented, but application to other instances is flawed.
- Statement is true for evidence presented, but no application to other instances is attempted.
- Statement is not true for evidence presented.

For Example 6.8

Rubric for Analysis

Definition: *Analysis* is the examination of the components or structure of something to determine how the parts relate to each other or how they come together to form a whole.

Strong	Developing	Beginning
The response reveals a thorough and accurate understanding of the component parts and how they come together to form a whole, identifies the important information in a problem statement, or has a clear sense of the order of steps in a process, if that is the nature of the target, and why that order is important. This is indicated by • Specific and appropriate references to elements, components, or steps • Correct and relevant description of most elements, components, or steps • Correct relationships among or interconnectedness of parts or steps • Correct use of vocabulary	*The student understands some component parts but gaps or inaccuracies are apparent. Thus, the student has a general sense of key parts of a whole, the important information in a problem statement, or steps in a process but lacks key insights as to the contribution of each. This is indicated by* • Accurate identification and discussion of only part of the relevant elements, components, or steps • Accurate description of only some elements, components, or steps • Some of the relationships of parts are appropriate, some not • Some incorrect use of vocabulary	*The student has a superficial or inaccurate understanding of the component parts, has little sense of how parts work together to form a whole, incorrectly identifies the information needed to solve a problem, or has an inaccurate sense of steps in a process and why the order is important. This is indicated by* • The object, issue, or event treated as a vague whole, there are few references to elements, components, or steps • Inaccurate or irrelevant description of most elements, components, or steps • Incorrect use of most vocabulary

Source: Adapted from *Introduction to Student-Involved Classroom Assessment*, 6th ed. (p. 53), by R. Stiggins and J. Chappuis, 2011, Upper Saddle River, NJ: Pearson Education. Adapted by permission.

The situation is different if we're also scoring how well students reason with the knowledge given in the item. In this case, we need both a way to assess content knowledge and a way to assess the pattern of reasoning. For example, if the extended written response item calls for students to make a generalization based on content, you might use a task-specific list to assess content understanding, and then a general rubric to analyze the quality of the generalization, such as the one shown in For Example 6.7. The process for starting from scratch to develop general rubrics is explained in Chapter 7.

We recommend general rubrics for assessing the quality of various patterns of reasoning because they are versatile:

- You can give them to students in advance to help them understand what high quality looks like.
- You can use them to give students feedback on practice work, highlighting strengths and areas for improvement.
- Students can self-assess with them while practicing, evaluating their own strengths and areas for improvement.
- Students can offer peer feedback with them.
- You can use them again and again, for any task calling for the pattern of reasoning.

My Classroom Then and Now 6.1

Kelly Dye

I used to . . .

On tests and quizzes, I would give an extended response or short answer question and assess it based on my idea and criteria of what a 4-point, 3-point, 2-point, 1-point, and 0-point response would be. I would score the students' work and give it back with an attached rubric. We would discuss it briefly and I would attach comments as to what was well done and what needed improvement in their answers.

Now I . . .

The students learn how to answer extended response and short answer questions by practicing, and by assessing each other's work. I show strong and weak models of the different answers and we discuss what criteria are needed to achieve the different point values. Students then have a chance to practice answering questions on their own. I scan them into the electronic whiteboard anonymously and we as a class assess them. This can be done in pairs, groups or a whole class.

Why I changed . . .

I feel that student involvement is a key piece in having them understand and focus on the learning target. I believe that students needed to have a more active role in their learning and academic growth, as well as their weaknesses. When they take ownership and responsibility, they are more likely to achieve and feel confident in their work.

What I notice as a result . . .

Students have a clearer picture of the learning target and have much more success when answering extended response and short answer questions. Frequent practice of scoring and repeated exposure to strong and weak examples allows them to better assess their own work. This has led them to more accurately answering these types of questions not only in my classroom, but also on the state test.

Source: Used with permission from Kelly Dye, 6th-grade mathematics teacher, Olmsted Falls City Schools, Olmsted Falls, OH, 2011.

CRITIQUING THE OVERALL ASSESSMENT FOR QUALITY

An excellent way to check the quality of your items is to try to write or outline a high-quality response yourself. If you can, you probably have a properly focused item. If you cannot, it needs work. Or you can ask a colleague to write a response and discuss the item and its scoring guide to see if either needs revision.

If your scoring guide will take the form of a general rubric, you can use the Rubric for Rubrics (Figure 7.10 in Chapter 7) to check it for quality.

Remember that there can be sources of bias specific to extended written response assessment. Figure 6.4 summarizes the factors to think about when devising extended written response items and scoring procedures. Answering these questions assists in constructing effective, high-quality items—those that avoid bias and distortion.

THE USE STAGE

The Use Stage has two steps: conduct and score the assessment and revise as needed for future use.

Conducting and Scoring the Assessment

Even the best planning can't catch all problems with an assessment. Here are two things to watch for as you administer the test:

- Students have enough time to complete their responses. If students don't have the opportunity to attempt each item, their scores will not reflect what they have learned. Watch for large numbers of incomplete items.

FIGURE 6.4 Quality Guidelines for Written Response Assessments

Quality of the Items

- Is written response the best assessment method for this learning target?
- Do items call for focused responses?
- Is the knowledge to be used clearly indicated?
- Is the reasoning to be demonstrated (if any) clearly indicated?
- Is the item itself written at the lowest possible reading level—will all students understand what they are to do?
- Will students' level of writing proficiency in English be adequate to show you what they know and can do?
- Is there anything in the item that might put a group of students at a disadvantage regardless of their knowledge or reasoning level?
- Are there enough items to provide a defensible estimate of student learning on intended targets?

Quality of the Scoring Guide(s)

- For the knowledge aspect of the response, is it clear how points will be awarded? If a task-specific rubric is used, does the item clearly call for the features described in the highest level of the rubric?
- For the reasoning portion of the response (if any), does the rubric capture the essence of high-quality thinking at the highest level? Does it identify flaws in reasoning at the lower levels?
- Does the scoring guide sufficiently represent the intent of the learning target(s)?

Scoring Considerations

- Is the total number of items to be scored (number of items on the assessment times number of students responding) limited to how many the rater(s) can accurately assess within a reasonable time?
- If the scoring guide is to be used by more than one rater, have raters worked together to ensure consistent scoring?

- Students ask for clarification of an item. Make notes on the items for which more than one or two students ask for clarification. Clarify the directions or the item itself for the next time you use it.

Revising for Future Use

While correcting the tests, make note of items that caused unexpected difficulties. After you conduct, score, and interpret the assessment, if it has flaws you will see them clearly and can then correct them before future use. You also will notice where any instruction may have fallen short on particular targets, which allows you to reteach your current students and revise your plans for instruction next year.

My Classroom Then and Now 6.2

Michele Buck

I used to . . .

I used to show students examples of work after a summative assessment.

Now I . . .

Now I do an activity we call "Scoring Camp for Kids." First, the students complete math problems relating to a specific learning target using real-life problems. Upon completion of the pretest the student and teacher use student models to create a rubric to score the student answers. Finally, the kids rate the models while discussing the strong and weak points for each math problem. When the "Scoring Camp for Kids" lesson is complete the students attempt and score additional practice problems.

Why I changed . . .

I changed my teaching focus to include formative assessments and clear learning targets. I found that many of my students questioned why I was taking off points on the extended response questions on the chapter tests. A few students did not even attempt the essay questions because they were not able to make a connection between a math skill and how it relates to a real-life math story.

What I notice as a result . . .

Now my students understand how to read a question and determine what they need to include in their answer in order to get a perfect score. Most importantly, the students now know why points are taken off of their score. Clear learning target instruction directly impacts student achievement, because my students are earning higher scores on summative assessments.

Source: Used with permission from Michele Buck, 6th-grade mathematics teacher, Olmsted Falls City Schools, Olmsted Falls, OH, 2011.

WRITTEN RESPONSE AS ASSESSMENT *FOR* LEARNING

As we have seen, student motivation and achievement both improve when we use the assessment process to help students answer the following three questions: "Where am I going?"; "Where am I now?"; and "How can I close the gap?" Here are some suggestions for assessment *for* learning practices with written response formats.

- Engage students in devising practice items like those that will appear on a future test. This will help them learn to center on important content and to become sufficiently comfortable with patterns of reasoning that they can build them into practice items. If they write practice items, trade with classmates, and write practice responses, both we and they gain access to useful information on what parts of the standards they are and are not mastering.

- Provide students with practice items and see if they can place them in the proper cells of the test plan. Then have them defend their placement.
- Design written response assessments so they function as feedback to students. Let students self-assess on the basis of results. Have them set goals for further learning based on their assessments of what they have mastered and what they still need to learn.
- Make use of general, but not task-specific, rubrics as instructional tools. Students can't use task-specific lists or rubrics while developing their responses because they outline the exact answers. However, they can use general rubrics, such as those for patterns of reasoning, to guide their responses. We offer more suggestions for using rubrics formatively at the end of Chapter 7.
- Provide sample items and let students practice scoring each other's responses to those items. By repeating this process as they proceed through a unit of study, students can watch themselves improve.
- Give students a list of misconceptions and design instruction to address the misconceptions. As students can correct each misconception, they date the list and write the correct understanding (see Example 6.9).

My Classroom Then and Now 6.3

Jeff Overbay

I used to . . .

In the past I would use the combined curriculum document as a guide for teaching. I never felt confident that I was covering the necessary content or that I was being effective in the classroom. It was more of a topical approach to teaching content. Having objectives has always been a part of my teaching but having clear learning targets for both myself and my students was something that seemed to always be out of reach.

Now I . . .

I now use the deconstructed standards to design a student-friendly self-assessment of the learning targets. These are broken down into knowledge, reasoning, and skills targets.

Knowledge Targets: "What do I need to know?"		
Yes	**No**	
1. ______	______	1. I can give examples of **adaptations** that allow organisms to survive their environment.
Reasoning Targets: "What can I do with what I know"		
1.______	______	1. I can use models to show how energy flows through an ecosystem (food chains, food webs, and energy pyramids).

Why I changed . . .

The use of learning targets ensures assessment accuracy. The targets are much clearer and guide the day-to-day learning.

What I notice as a result . . .

Students now know where we are going and can self-assess along the way. This process helps students to quickly recognize areas that they are struggling with. These templates can also be used as a guide to create more accurate assessments. They actually become the guide for designing the assessments.

Source: Used with permission from 7th/8th-grade science teacher Jeff Overbay, Bell County School District, Pineville, KY, 2011.

For Example 6.9

Correcting Misconceptions

Misconception	Date	Correction
1.		
2.		
3.		

Source: Reprinted from *Seven Strategies of Assessment* for *Learning* (p. 133) by J. Chappuis, 2009, Upper Saddle River, NJ: Pearson Education. Reprinted by permission.

For more examples of how each of these strategies can be used with written response assessment across grade levels and subject areas, see Chappuis (2009).

Summary

Written response assessments are excellent for assessing conceptual understanding, extended bodies of knowledge, and reasoning learning targets. We followed the creation of these assessments through eight steps, with an in-depth focus on the development stage. Items need to specify what knowledge and patterns of reasoning, if any, students are to use in developing their response. They also need to indicate what features of performance will count, by pointing the way to the correct answer without giving away the answer. Items must avoid other potential sources of bias and distortion such as unclearly written instructions, instructions at too high a reading level, and features that might disadvantage any group. Scoring procedures and guides must be developed along with the items. We explored three options: the list, the task-specific scoring guide, and the general rubric. The first two are most typically used to call out content knowledge that must be present in a correct response, while the third is useful for evaluating patterns of reasoning. We offered examples of general rubrics, as well.

We concluded with suggestions for strategies that use written response items as assessment *for* learning, where students share the item development and scoring responsibility. These strategies connect assessment to teaching and learning in ways that can maximize both students' motivation to learn and their actual achievement.

CHAPTER 6 ACTIVITIES

End-of-chapter activities are intended to help you master the chapter's learning targets. They are designed to deepen your understanding of the chapter content, provide discussion topics for learning team meetings, and guide implementation of the practices taught in the chapter.

Forms for completing each activity appear in editable Microsoft Word format in the Chapter 6 CD file. Documents on the CD are marked with this symbol:

Chapter 6 Learning Targets

At the end of Chapter 6, you will know how to do the following:

1. Develop short answer items and scoring guides.
2. Develop extended written response items and scoring guides.
3. Use written response assessments formatively, as teaching tools.
4. Structure written response assessments so that students can use the results to self-assess and set goals for further learning.

Activity 6.1 Keep a Reflective Journal
Activity 6.2 Evaluate a Written Response Assessment for Quality
Activity 6.3 Create a Short Answer Item and Scoring Guide
Activity 6.4 Create an Extended Written Response Item and Scoring Guide
Activity 6.5 Apply an Assessment *for* Learning Strategy
Activity 6.6 Reflect on Your Own Learning
Activity 6.7 Select Portfolio Artifacts

Activity 6.1

Keep a Reflective Journal

Keep a record of your thoughts, questions, and any implementation activities you tried while reading Chapter 6.

Reflective Journal Form

Activity 6.2

Evaluate a Written Response Assessment for Quality

Work independently, with a partner, or with a team to carry out this activity. It helps if those you are working with are familiar with the content being assessed.

1. Select an already-developed assignment or assessment that includes short answer and extended written response items from a unit you have taught or will teach. It can be one that you or another teacher created, or one that comes from district or published materials.
2. Write out the answers to each short answer and extended written response on the assignment or assessment yourself. Or trade assessments with a colleague and answer each others' assessment items. Score your answers with whatever scoring guide is provided. Note any difficulties either in answering items or in using the scoring guide.
3. Review the guidelines for developing short answer and extended written response items. Then use the checklist version of Figure 6.4, "Quality Guidelines for Written Response Assessments," to check each item and scoring guide for quality.
4. If this activity reveals flaws in one or more items, revise them and rewrite them.
5. If this activity reveals problems with one or more scoring guides, revise them and rewrite them.

Evaluate a Written Response Assessment for Quality

Checklist of Quality Guidelines for Written Response Assessments

Activity 6.3

Create a Short Answer Item and Scoring Guide

Work independently, with a partner, or with a team to complete this activity. It helps if those you are working with are familiar with the content being assessed.

1. After reading the section, "Short Answer or Extended Response?" select one or more learning targets for which short answer items are a good match.
2. Follow the guidelines in the section, "Devising Short Answer Items" to write one or more short answer items to assess the learning target(s) you selected.
3. Follow the recommendations for when to use which type of scoring guide option in the section, "Scoring Guide Options" to select a scoring guide option (list, task-specific rubric, or general rubric) for each item.
4. Follow the instructions for creating the type(s) of scoring guide(s) you selected.
5. Use the checklist version of Figure 6.4, "Quality Guidelines for Written Response Assessments," to check your item(s) for quality. Revise as needed.
6. Ask a colleague to answer your item(s) and then score the response(s) using the scoring guide(s) you have created. Discuss any difficulties in responding or scoring.
7. Revise your item(s) and scoring guide(s) again as needed.

Template for a Short Answer Item and Scoring Guide

Checklist of Quality Guidelines for Written Response Assessments

Activity 6.4

Create an Extended Written Response Item and Scoring Guide

Work independently, with a partner, or with a team to complete this activity. It helps if those you are working with are familiar with the content being assessed.

1. After reading the section, "Short Answer or Extended Response?" select a learning target for which an extended written response item is a good choice.
2. Follow the guidelines in the section, "Devising Extended Written Response Items" to write the item.
3. Follow the recommendations for when to use which type of scoring guide option in the section, "Scoring Guide Options" to select a scoring guide option (list, task-specific rubric, or general rubric) for each item.
4. Follow the instructions for creating the type(s) of scoring guide(s) you selected.
5. Use the checklist version of Figure 6.4, "Quality Guidelines for Written Response Assessments," to check your item(s) for quality. Revise as needed.
6. Ask a colleague to answer your item(s) and then score the response(s) using the scoring guide(s) you have created. Discuss any difficulties in responding or scoring.
7. Revise your item and scoring guide(s) again, as needed.

Templates for Extended Written Response Items and Scoring Guides

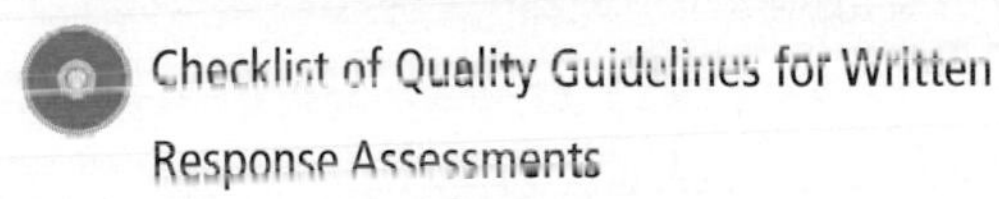

Checklist of Quality Guidelines for Written Response Assessments

Activity 6.5

Apply an Assessment *for* Learning Strategy

Work independently, with a partner, or with your team to complete this activity.

1. After reading the section, "Written Response as Assessment *for* Learning," choose one of the suggestions to try in your classroom.
2. Create the materials needed to carry out the suggestions.
3. Try the suggestion with your students.
4. If you are working with a partner or team, discuss one or more of the following:
   - What did you do? What did you notice happening with students as a result?
   - How might the activity benefit student learning?
   - Would you conduct the activity again?
   - What, if anything, would you change?

Debrief the AFL Strategy You Tried

Activity 6.6

Reflect on Your Own Learning

Review the Chapter 6 learning targets and select one or more that represented new learning for you or struck you as most significant from this chapter. If you are working individually, write a short reflection that captures your current understanding. If you are working with a partner or a team, either discuss what you have written or use this as a discussion prompt for a team meeting.

Reflect on Chapter 6 Learning

Activity 6.7

Select Portfolio Artifacts

Any of the activities from this chapter can be used as portfolio entries. Select activities you have completed or artifacts you have created that will illustrate your competence at the Chapter 6 learning targets:

1. Develop short answer items and scoring guides.
2. Develop extended written response items and scoring guides.
3. Use written response assessments formatively, as teaching tools.
4. Structure written response assessments so that students can use the results to self-assess and set goals for further learning.

If you are keeping a reflective journal, you may want to include Chapter 6's entry in your portfolio.

 Chapter 6 Portfolio Entry Cover Sheet

CHAPTER

7

Performance Assessment

As we reflect on our most valued twenty-first century proficiencies, such as skill at collaboration, complex problem solving, or functioning effectively in the digital age, it's startling to notice how few can be translated into multiple-choice tests for evaluation. This is why methods such as performance assessment will be increasingly important as we look to the future of assessment in our schools.

Performance assessment, assessment based on observation and judgment, has been used for at least 3,000 years to evaluate mastery of essential competencies. To obtain a government position in ancient China, applicants had to demonstrate their skill at shooting with a bow and arrow and their proficiency at writing poetry. Although what we consider essential to measure may have changed over the centuries, performance assessment remains the same valuable process for collecting information about performances and products central to each academic discipline.

A performance assessment has two parts: the task to be completed by the respondent and the criteria for judging quality of the response. Students complete the task—give a demonstration or create a product—and we evaluate it by judging the level of quality using a rubric.

Performance assessment is essentially subjective and can take more time to conduct and score than do the other methods we have studied so far. So we must ensure that our use of this form of assessment is as objective (free of bias and distortion) as possible and that we get maximum possible instructional value from time spent. Research and practice over the last several decades have strengthened both the accuracy and usefulness of our applications of this method. Specifically, this work has taught us how to create high-caliber rubrics for rating the quality of student work and how to help teachers learn to make consistent evaluations of those performances. It has enabled performance assessment to be used dependably outside the classroom as part of standardized, large-scale assessments. But more importantly, this work has made it possible for teachers to use performance assessments formatively to support learning. Good rubrics give us information we can use to differentiate instruction, direct students' attention to the features of work that constitute quality, allow us to give focused feedback, and enable students to self-assess.

Even though it is called performance *assessment, this method is used to judge both real-time performances, also called demonstrations, and products, or artifacts that students create.*

As with any other method, performance assessment can be constructed and used well or poorly. In this chapter, we examine the characteristics of a good task, the characteristics of a good rubric, how to develop and evaluate each, and how to use performance assessment formatively, as assessment *for* learning.[1]

Chapter 7 Learning Targets

At the end of Chapter 7, you will know how to do the following:

- Select, revise, and develop high-quality performance tasks.
- Select, revise, and develop high-quality rubrics.
- Use performance assessment formatively, as teaching tools.
- Structure performance assessments so that students can use the results to self-assess and set goals for further learning.

WHEN TO USE PERFORMANCE ASSESSMENT

In Chapter 4 we advocated reserving performance assessment for those learning targets that really require it: skills, products, and some forms of reasoning. The most important determiner for using performance assessment is the nature of the learning target. For example, if the learning target states "Sets personal fitness goals," it is a *reasoning* target. The student could list personal fitness goals, which could be evaluated with a simple rubric or checklist, and we would consider this a written response assessment. If the learning target states "Creates a personal fitness plan," then the target calls for an *artifact*, a fitness plan, and it would be classified as a *product* target. The plan itself will be more extensive than a list of fitness goals—presumably it will include actions and timelines as well—and we would use a performance assessment to evaluate it because the task is more complex and the characteristics we are evaluating are also more complex than a list of personal fitness goals.

FIGURE 7.1 Keys to Quality Classroom Assessment

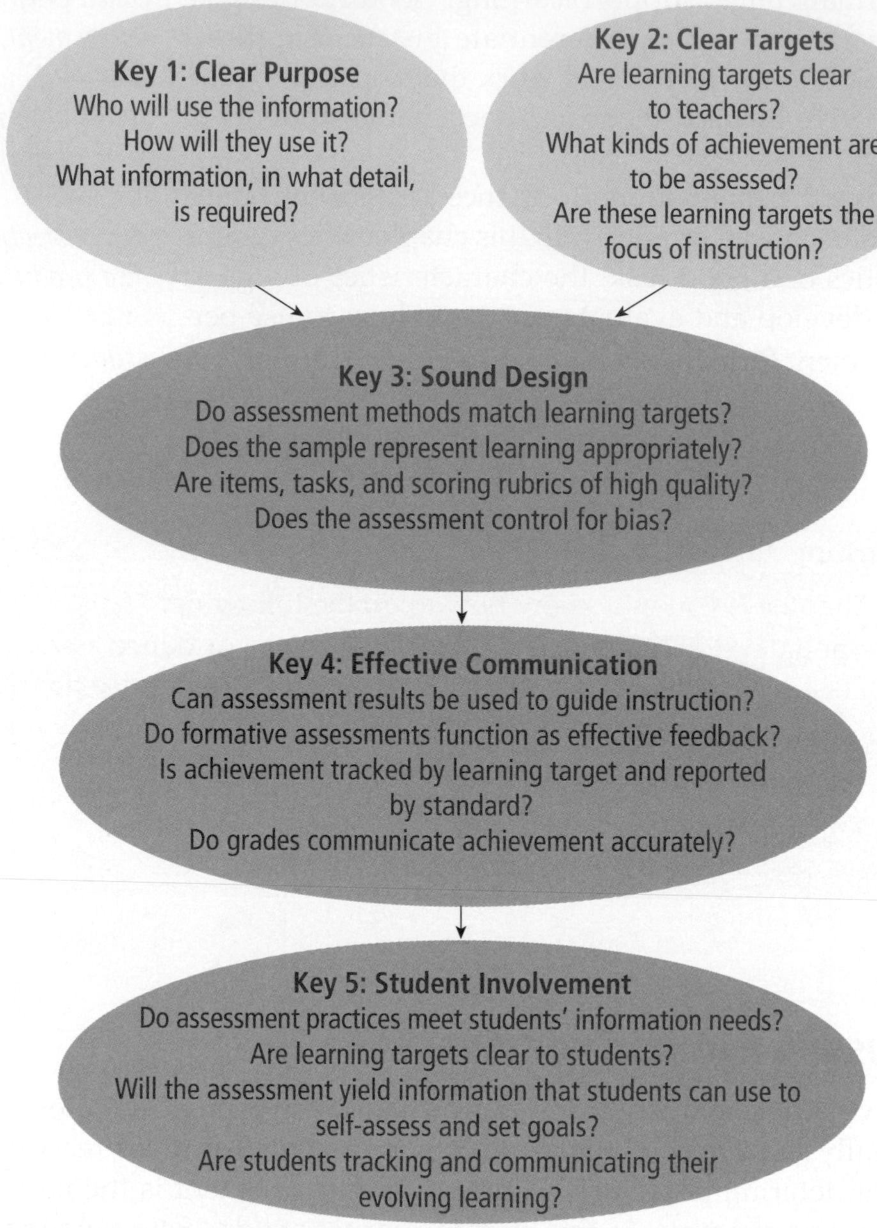

Two other conditions influence the selection of performance assessment. Use it when either or both of the following are true:

- You work with young primary students or students who cannot read or write in English. In this case, you will be using it to assess knowledge as well as reasoning, skill, and product targets.
- You can't get the information you need through written response assessment methodology.

ASSESSMENT DEVELOPMENT CYCLE FOR A PERFORMANCE ASSESSMENT

Developing a performance assessment begins with the same four steps at the Planning Stage as do all other assessment methods: (1) determine who will use the assessment results and how they will use them; (2) identify the learning targets to be assessed; (3) verify that performance assessment is the best method for the purpose and the targets; and (4) attend to sampling issues. At the Development Stage, performance assessment requires four steps: (1) select, revise, or develop the task; (2) evaluate the task for quality; (3) select, revise, or develop the rubric; and (4) evaluate the rubric for quality. At the Use Stage, we follow the same two steps as with other methods: (1) conduct and score the assessment; and (2) revise as needed for future use (Figure 7.2).

This is somewhat challenging work. So you should approach it from the perspective that, once developed, your performance assessments will be reusable (perhaps with ongoing improvements) well into the future. That is, don't think of this as one-shot development; this is not to use and toss. Take advantage of this valuable resource for as long as you can.

Determining Users and Uses

Again, we begin by answering these by now familiar questions: How do we want to use the information? Who else will use it? What decisions will they make? Typically,

FIGURE 7.2 Assessment Development Cycle for a Performance Assessment

Planning

- Determine who will use the assessment results and how they will use them.
- Identify the learning targets to be assessed.
- Select the appropriate assessment method or methods.
- Determine sample size.

Development

- Select or develop the task.
- Evaluate the task for quality.
- Select or develop the rubric.
- Evaluate the rubric for quality.

Use

- Conduct and score the assessment.
- Revise as needed for future use.

we will use performance assessment information for one or more of the following purposes:

- To plan instruction, as with a pretest
- To differentiate instruction, as with a mid-unit quiz
- To offer feedback to students so they can act on it during the learning
- To give students the opportunity to self-assess and set goals for further learning
- To measure level of achievement for a final grade, as with a post-test

Each of these purposes can be accomplished with performance assessment, as long as we keep the intended use in mind while making further planning and design decisions.

Identifying Learning Targets

At this step we simply list the learning target or targets the assessment is to measure. (If a target is complex or unclear, clarify it or deconstruct it first, following the processes outlined in Chapter 3.)

Selecting Assessment Method(s)

Although we have already determined that we will use performance assessment, it's important to make sure we have identified targets that require it and also that the targets can be assessed accurately with this methodology. So review the list of learning targets with this in mind. (Refer to Chapter 4 for an in-depth discussion of which types of targets are best assessed with performance assessment.)

Determining Sample Size

As we have seen in previous chapters, the sampling challenge is gathering just enough evidence to make a relatively confident judgment of level of achievement. In the context of a performance assessment, sampling issues are addressed by the task. Does the task provide enough evidence to support a valid conclusion about level of mastery of the intended target or targets? The answer depends on a number of factors—the complexity of the learning target, the decision the evidence will inform, consistency of the student's performance, and proximity of the student's performance to an important cutoff mark. For each of these factors, we offer general guidelines, not rigid rules. Sampling well requires our professional judgment in the simultaneous weighing of all factors.

COMPLEXITY OF THE TARGET. The first sampling consideration is the complexity of the learning target to be assessed. If the target is a simple one, it may require fewer instances—a smaller sample—to judge level of achievement. If the target is a complex one, it may require more. For example, you may be able to judge a primary student's reading rate with one or two performances. This target is relatively narrow and sharply focused. However, if you want to judge proficiency at reading aloud with fluency, you may need several performances because the target is more complex—the definition of *reading fluency* often includes accuracy, phrasing, and expression. You may need more demonstrations to hear and evaluate all of the parts.

DECISION THE EVIDENCE WILL INFORM. How you intend to use the results also affects sampling decisions. If you will use the results in a low-stakes assessment *for* learning context, a smaller sample size will often do. If you are deciding how to regroup for instruction, one task may provide sufficient information to work from, because if the small sample size leads you to an incorrect judgment, you can easily see and correct it. In a high-stakes assessment *of* learning context, it is important to consider the consequences of an incorrect decision and enlarge the sample to minimize that possibility. If you are deciding, for example, who passes and who fails, you are going to want more rather than fewer samples to be sure you are making the correct inference about level of proficiency—an incorrect high-stakes decision is much harder to fix after the fact.

CONSISTENCY OF PERFORMANCE. A third key sampling variable, as described in Chapter 4, is the consistency of the student's performance. If the student is clearly a master of the standard or clearly not, then we need few tasks to determine level of achievement. A student whose assessment results are consistently at one level of proficiency on a given learning target can with some confidence be said to be at that level. However, a student whose assessment results are all over the map for a given learning target does not engender the same level of confidence. If the student's performance fluctuates, it may be necessary to assign one or more subsequent tasks until we are able to make a stable estimate of level of achievement. Here is the rule of thumb: we have gathered enough evidence if we can guess with a degree of certainty how that student would do if we gave him one more task.

PROXIMITY TO THE CUTOFF MARK. In addition, when a student's level of achievement is very close to or on the dividing line between two levels of proficiency, such as very close to "meets the standard," or teetering between two grades, it is helpful to have more samples to justify assigning the level of grade. But when a student's performance is considerably above or below an important cutoff point, more data are not likely to change the outcome.

FAQ 7.1

Difference Between Extended Written Response and Performance Assessment

Question:

If both extended written response and performance assessment are evaluated by rubrics, what is the difference between them?

Answer:

The differences lie in the nature of what is evaluated and what criteria are used to evaluate results. Written responses call for composition of original text. Performance assessments can call for an infinite array of products, performances, or demonstrations. Depending on the context, written responses can be evaluated using criteria reflective of content mastery or the quality of the reasoning used in formulating the answer. Performance assessments rely on criteria reflective of the quality of the particular product or performance called for by the context. It becomes difficult to differentiate written response and performance assessment when a composition is called for that is to be evaluated in terms of the form of the response; that is, the quality of the writing. We categorize that as a *product* target and assign it to the category of *performance assessment*.

SELECTING, REVISING, OR DEVELOPING THE TASK

A performance task can be thought of as all the material you prepare to let students know what they are supposed to do to demonstrate their current level of proficiency. It can take one of several forms, depending on the learning target it is intended to assess: a physical demonstration of skill, a verbal presentation or dialogue, or the creation of a product. The purpose of the task is to elicit the correct demonstration or artifact from the student so that it can be assessed by the rubric.

Although much of the emphasis in performance assessment is on the rubric, the quality of the task must receive equal attention. Chances are you have had experience with a poorly designed task, either on the giving or receiving end. Here are just a few of the problems that can result:

- Student work doesn't provide evidence of the intended learning, even if the work itself is of high quality.
- Students aren't sure what to do and consequently don't produce what you expected or don't produce the level of quality they are capable of producing.
- You spend a great deal of time responding to "Is this what you want?" and "I don't get it" during task completion time.
- The task takes much longer to complete than expected.

FIGURE 7.3 Characteristics of a Good Task

Content of the Task

- *Target Alignment*: Aligns to the intended learning target and elicits the right performance or product
- *Authenticity*: Provides as realistic a context as possible
- *Choice*: If choice is offered, all options are equivalent
- *Level of Scaffolding*: Information points the way to success without "overhelping"
- *Interference*: Successful completion does not depend on unrelated skills or a specific linguistic or cultural background
- *Availability of Resources*: Necessary resources and materials are available to all

Structure of the Task

- *Knowledge students are to use*: What knowledge is to be applied?
- *What students are to accomplish*: What are students to do with the knowledge specified?
- *Performance or product students are to create*: What form will the finished performance or product take?
- *Materials to be used*: What materials should students use?
- *Timeline for completion*: How much time will students have?
- *Conditions*: If the task calls for a demonstration or performance, under what conditions will it take place?
- *Help allowed*: What assistance will be permitted? From whom?
- *Criteria*: What criteria will be the focus of the assessment?

Sampling

- *Use of information*: How many tasks will be assigned? Does this task sample adequately for the intended use?
- *Coverage of the target*: Does the breadth of the task or the number of tasks adequately cover the breadth of the target?

Figure 7.6, the *Rubric for Tasks*, also found on the accompanying CD in the Chapter 7 file, can be used to evaluate tasks for each of these dimensions of quality.

- The resources necessary for completion turn out to be hard to acquire for some or all students.
- Students find it necessary to get outside help doing the work and therefore parts of the task are completed by well-meaning parents or other helpers.
- Students go into a tailspin and conclude they are not good at the subject.

In this section we will examine the characteristics of a good task—what needs to be in place to avoid these and other problems—by considering three dimensions: content, structure, and sampling. Figure 7.3 summarizes the criteria for a good task.

The Content of the Task

The ultimate goal of a performance task is to produce accurate evidence of the intended learning in a context that approximates realistic conditions, while avoiding sources of bias and distortion. Though the task need not be a complex assignment, it introduces a number of variables that must be managed thoughtfully for it to reflect student achievement accurately. Whether you are selecting, revising, or creating a task, the *content* of the task is the first aspect to consider. What learning will completion of this task demonstrate? What context will it be set in? Will the task allow for choice? Does the content set up a fair and unbiased assessment for all students?

TARGET ALIGNMENT. The requirements of the task should produce evidence of the learning target(s) it is intended to assess. This is known as *content validity*. For example, this writing task was intended to assess narrative writing: "You have all heard stories of how the elephant got its trunk or how the camel got its hump. Think of something in nature and make up a story about how it got that way." Instead, it elicited expository writing from a number of students and could not be used to judge their competence at narrative writing. If we don't elicit the right performance or product, we can't use the results as evidence of level of achievement.

In addition, requirements unrelated to the learning targets (e.g., neatness) should not be included. If you are going to require something and evaluate it, it should be part of the learning target you have been teaching to and students have been practicing.

AUTHENTICITY. The content of the task should provide as realistic a context as practical. It should model what application of the learning looks like in life beyond the classroom where possible. This helps students see the links among what they are learning, how they can use it, and why it might be valuable. This characteristic is often referred to as *authenticity*.

CHOICE. Student choice can increase student motivation. Yet, giving students a choice of tasks can cause the assessment to yield inaccurate results; with choice comes the chance that one or more options will include requirements unrelated to the learning target, or that they will represent different levels of difficulty. If the task allows students to select from a menu of tasks, all options should be equivalent. They should all provide evidence of achievement on the same learning targets at the same level of difficulty. If this requirement is not satisfied, students will select the option they feel most confident with and this can keep us (and them) from understanding and working on areas in need of improvement.

LEVEL OF SCAFFOLDING. The information in the task should be sufficient to let students know what they are to do without giving so much information that the task will no longer measure level of mastery of the intended learning target. The task should point the way to success without doing the thinking for the student.

INTERFERENCE. In addition, successful completion of the task cannot depend on unrelated skills, such as intensive reading in a task intended to evaluate a mathematics learning target or complex mathematical problem solving in a task intended to evaluate reading. Nor can the task depend on having had one particular cultural or linguistic background for successful completion. This can happen when a task uses a context such as sewing or baseball that is not familiar to some students. Including unrelated skills or a context relying on cultural or linguistic background can interfere with the accuracy of results for groups of students, due to conditions beyond their control.

AVAILABILITY OF RESOURCES. All resources and materials necessary for the completion of the task need to be available to all students. If, for example, some students have difficulty obtaining materials required for a display or cannot get to a library or an Internet connection for required research, their performance on the task will be compromised by factors other than the level of achievement the task was intended to assess. Again, these factors are out of some students' control.

Structure of the Task

After having thought through content considerations, we are ready to look at the structure of the task. Imagine students receive the following "Physics of Motion" science task to assess their comprehension of physics equations, understanding of the principles of experiment design, and ability to collect and explain experiment results:

> Conduct an experiment to determine the percentage of vehicles that exceed the speed limit as they pass the school. Report your results.

Although the task represents a good portion of what students need to know to successfully complete it, if this is all the information they receive, many students may be unable to demonstrate their learning accurately. What kinds of information do students need in order to know what to do? What materials can or should they use? If the task calls for a demonstration or a performance, under what conditions will they be demonstrating or performing? What is the timeline for completion? How much and what kinds of help are allowed? How will success be judged?

KNOWLEDGE STUDENTS ARE TO USE. Good tasks remind students of the knowledge they are to use in completing them. Tasks that give students only partial content information cause teachers to spend an inordinate amount of time filling in the missing pieces. We cannot overstate the importance of avoiding this problem. When faced with incomplete information, some students conclude that because they don't understand what to do, the problem is with them and not the task. For the duration of the assignment, these students don't regain a sense of confidence that they can be successful, and some of them give up. Such tasks are not a fair measure of achievement.

Therefore, it is important to include in the task a statement of the knowledge to be applied. This reminds students of which part of all that they have been studying they are to focus on. It might appear that this could go without saying, but many students are thinking about a number of different things besides our course at any given time, and it is helpful to give them a general cue to the knowledge they will apply in completing the task.

In the "Physics of Motion" task, the knowledge students are to use is the knowledge of the physics of motion.

WHAT STUDENTS ARE TO ACCOMPLISH. Most tasks will ask students to reason or perform in some way with the knowledge specified. Often, as in the "Physics of Motion" task, this is the only information given.

In this example, students are told to conduct an experiment to determine the percentage of vehicles that exceed the speed limit as they pass the school.

If part of the learning to be assessed is ability to design an experiment, the task should include the instruction to design as well as conduct the experiment.

PERFORMANCE OR PRODUCT STUDENTS ARE TO CREATE. Most tasks include some version of describing the performance or product that will ultimately be evaluated, but the description may not include enough details. In the "Physics of Motion" task, students are told to report their results. Yet the intended learning targets relate to student ability to collect and explain experiment results. Without more information, students' reports will not likely include evidence of experimental design. Also, students could prepare a one-sentence summary and be at a loss as to how to turn it into a report.

For the "Physics of Motion" task, students would benefit from a statement such as "Write a report in which you explain your experimental design and share your results."

MATERIALS TO BE USED. If students are required to use certain materials, it is better to include this information on the written task than to rely on students to guess or remember what you said. However, if part of what you are assessing is the knowledge of what materials to use, then don't list them in the task.

In the "Physics of Motion" task, it may be helpful to let students know they are to use a stopwatch and a measuring tape.

TIMELINE FOR COMPLETION. The time given for completion should be reasonable, given the task requirements. We often underestimate the amount of time a complex task will take, which can compromise the accuracy of its results and create stress for students and teachers alike. It is best to check this carefully before assigning a task. If the task is to be completed entirely in class, specify enough time so that almost all students can finish with no problem, and then offer options as needed for those who

FAQ 7.2

Individual or Group Work

Question:

To make tasks more like what occurs in the workplace, shouldn't students work in groups to complete them?

Answer:

In an attempt to make assessments as realistic as possible, teachers often have students work in a group. This is fine if your target is to determine how well students work in a group. But, if your target is to ascertain individual achievement, a group product or presentation will not yield accurate information. To get around this problem, some test developers recommend having students work in groups to make sure everyone is beginning the task with a similar knowledge base. Then have students create the product or perform the skill individually. In general, when assessing individual student reasoning proficiency, skill level, or product development capabilities, the task must be completed individually to give an accurate picture of each student's level of achievement.

don't. Or plan enough time for all to finish and have a followup activity available for those who finish early.

It is a good idea to include the timeline for completion in the task. If it has intermediate due dates, those should be included as well. Seeing the timeline in writing helps students get or stay organized and it helps you rethink whether the timeframe is reasonable.

In the "Physics of Motion" task, it might look like this: "You will have three days to design and conduct the experiment and two days to write your report. The report is due in one week."

CONDITIONS. If a task calls for a demonstration or performance, it should specify the conditions under which the demonstration or performance is to take place. For example, if students are to give a speech, you may want to specify the audience and the length of time required for the speech.

In the "Physics of Motion" task, there may be no need to specify conditions.

HELP ALLOWED. Accuracy of assessment requires that we assess each student's level of achievement and no one else's. For tasks accomplished in one day, you can control who does the work and what parts students get help with. When completion of a task will span more than one day, some students may have a great deal of parent help while others have none. If you want to increase the odds that the work is the student's alone, the task should explicitly state that as a requirement. If help is allowed, how much and what kind? If, for example the task requires a written product and you don't intend to evaluate it for spelling, capitalization, or punctuation, you could recommend that students use a peer or parent editor to help with that part.

In the "Physics of Motion" example, you might tell students that they can work with a partner for designing and conducting the experiment, but they will each have to submit a separate, individually written report.

CRITERIA. The task should include a reminder of the elements of quality you will use to assess it. You can either attach the rubric that you will use or remind students of the criteria that will be the focus of this assessment from a rubric you have already distributed.

In the "Physics of Motion" task, it might look like this: Your report will be scored on understanding of physics equations, experimental design, and collection and explanation of results. Rubrics are attached.

Students should have had prior experience with the standards of quality represented on your rubrics before being held accountable for demonstrating them. A process for familiarizing students with rubrics is explained later in this chapter.

So, if the "Physics of Motion" task had all of these components, it would look like this (see For Example 7.1): Using a stopwatch and a measuring tape, you are to use your knowledge of the physics of motion to design an experiment to determine the percentage of vehicles that exceed the speed limit as they pass the school. Then you are to conduct your experiment. Last, you are to write a report in which you explain your experimental design and share your results.

You will have three days to design and conduct your experiment and two days to write your report. The report is due in one week.

You may work with a partner or alone to design and conduct the experiment, but you must submit an independent report that you alone have written. Your report will be scored on understanding of physics equations, experimental design, and collection and explanation of results. Rubrics are attached.

Sampling

Last, in selecting, revising, or developing a task we check the sample size. The task should offer enough evidence to satisfy its intended purpose and to adequately represent the breadth of the learning target. If it is a summative assessment, you will be able to draw a confident conclusion about student mastery of the intended target(s). If it is a formative assessment, you and/or students will have enough evidence to guide further instruction and learning.

For Example 7.1

"Physics of Motion" Task

Knowledge students are to use	Use your knowledge of the physics of motion.
What students are to accomplish	Design and conduct an experiment to determine the percentage of vehicles that exceed the speed limit as they pass the school.
Performance or product students are to create	Write a report in which you explain your experimental design and share your results.
Materials to be used	Use a stopwatch and a measuring tape.
Timeline for completion	You will have three days to design and conduct the experiment and two days to write your report. The report is due in one week.
Conditions	N/A
Help allowed	You can work with a partner or alone to design and conduct the experiment. You must each submit a separate report that you alone have written.
Criteria	Your report will be scored on understanding of physics equations, experimental design, and collection and explanation of results. Rubrics are attached.

USE OF INFORMATION. There are three ways that tasks can sample adequately for the intended use. The first is breadth of the task. This means the complexity and coverage of the task. Sometimes one sufficiently broad task can provide enough information for its intended use. The second is the number of tasks. For some purposes you may need one, while for others you may need several separate tasks to adequately sample for the intended use. The third is repeated instances of performance. In this case, you may be able to use one task and ask students to perform it as many times as needed to support the intended use of the information.

COVERAGE OF TARGET. The breadth of the task or the number of tasks should adequately cover the breadth of the target(s). Is the task broad enough to cover the important dimensions of the learning target? If the target is complex, you may need several tasks, each focusing on one part of the learning target. One way to gather samples that show student progress and achievement status is to have students collect work in a portfolio. If we carefully outline the types of entries along with the learning targets they represent, we can get a good sample. With a portfolio, we can gather evidence over time to make the sample adequately reflect the breadth and depth of the learning target being assessed. In Chapter 11 we describe how to assemble and use portfolios to accomplish this purpose.

Creating Tasks to Elicit Good Writing

In certain writing tasks, especially those in the English Language Arts classroom, students benefit from a more in-depth explanation of the knowledge they are to apply and the product they are to create. Writer Donald Murray tells us that "a principal cause of poor writing received from students is the assignment . . . they have to be well prepared so that the students know the purpose of the assignment and how to fulfill it. Far too many teachers blame the students for poor writing when the fault lies with the teacher's instructions—or lack of instructions" (Murray, 2004, p. 98). When a task is intended to measure writing learning targets, we can use a more explicit formula in its design, one that answers the questions that writers must ask to write well:

- What is my role?
- Who is my audience?
- What is the format?
- What is the topic?
- What is the purpose?

These questions are represented by the acronym RAFTS and are illustrated in Figure 7.4. (In the acronym, the "S" stands for "strong verb," which directs the student's attention to the purpose of the writing.)

FIGURE 7.4 RAFTS Writing Task Design

R ole: Writers must imagine themselves as fulfilling specific roles—for example, as tour guides or scientists or critics—when they write.
A udience: Writers must always visualize their audiences clearly and consistently throughout the writing process. If they don't, the writing will fail.
F ormat: Writers must see clearly the format that the finished writing should have, whether brochure, memo, letter to the editor, or article in a magazine.
T opic: Writers have to select and narrow their topics to manageable proportions, given their audiences and formats.
S trong verb: Words like "cajole," "tempt," "discourage," when serving as definers of the predominant tone of a piece of writing, will guide writers in innumerable choices of words.

Source: Reprinted from "Why Grade Student Writing?" by E. Smith, 1990, *Washington English Journal, 13*(1), p. 26. Reprinted by permission.

ROLE. Sometimes we ask students simply to write as themselves, as students, but we can often increase their motivation and the relevance of a task if we ask them to assume a role. Think about these questions to devise student roles: Who might be writing about this topic? If it is a content-area topic (social studies, science, mathematics, health, art, and so on), who in the practice of this content area might be writing about this topic? What job might they have?

AUDIENCE. When we don't specify an audience, students are writing to us, their teachers, by default. Yet they don't often know how to envision their audience's needs when they write, even if it is us. For writers to make good decisions about what information to include, what terminology to use, and what tone to adopt, they need to think about who they are writing to. When we ask students to write thorough explanations, it is helpful if we specify an audience who is not familiar with the topic. If we are the audience, either stated or unstated, students often conclude that we know plenty about the topic already. It is hard to write about something to someone who knows more about it that you do, and that particular circumstance doesn't occur in life beyond school very often. In life beyond school, when we are writing to inform, generally, the audience doesn't have the same level of expertise as the writer does. So, in tasks calling for informational writing, consider specifying an audience who might need to know the information and who doesn't already know it.

FORMAT. This is a simple component of the task. If a beyond-school application of the writing would take the form of a report or an essay, then by all means specify that format. Decisions about format are driven by three considerations: audience, topic, and purpose. If our audience is primary students, our topic is insects, and our purpose is to inform, a report may not be the best format. We can convey interesting and important information about insects in an alphabet book, on a poster, in a sticker book, or on playing cards. If, on the other hand, our audience is a politician, our topic is water quality (as measured by the number and diversity of stream bugs found in water samples), and our purpose is to persuade the politician to take an action, a combination of a letter and a report will be more suited to the task.

TOPIC. We rarely leave this out of a task or assignment. However, even this aspect can cause student writing to be better or worse, depending on how it is crafted. When we specify the topic for students, we must exercise caution in how we state it. The question here is, are we going to narrow the topic for students or are we going to expect students to narrow it for themselves? If we have been studying the foundations of the U.S. economic system and we want students to write about the Industrial Revolution, we will have to narrow the topic considerably for them to handle it successfully. Or we can teach students how to narrow topics and let them determine the aspect they will focus on. Considerations in narrowing topics include who the audience is and how much time the writer will have. Generally, the less time, the narrower the topic. We can write all about the topic of friendship if we have a year or two and want to produce a book, but if we have only a week or so, we may wish to write a simple set of instructions for how to be a friend.

STRONG VERB. This does not refer to strong verbs in the students' writing. Rather, in this context, *strong verb* refers to the verb we use in the task itself. What is the *purpose* for the writing? Most often writing tasks in school are set to accomplish one of three purposes—to narrate, to inform, or to persuade—and the forms of writing produced are often referred to as narrative, expository, and persuasive. In narrative writing, the purpose is to tell a story, either real (personal narrative or anecdote) or imagined (fictional narrative). In expository writing, the controlling purpose is to inform. In persuasive writing, we may have one of four purposes: to initiate thought, to change thought, to initiate action, or to change action. We may use both narrative and expository writing in service of persuasion, but the ultimate purpose for persuasive writing is to cause something different to happen. Figure 7.5 gives

FIGURE 7.5 Specifying *Purpose* in a Writing Task: Strong Verbs

Purpose	Sample Verbs and Phrases	
To narrate	Chronicle Depict Describe an experience Give an account of Recount	Relate Set forth Tell the story of Tell about a time when
To inform	Brief Clarify Compare Define Discuss Describe	Explain Familiarize Inform Teach Tell Update
To persuade	Argue Challenge Compel Convert Convince Defend Enlist Exhort	Impel Incite Induce Influence Inspire Justify Persuade Sway

For Example 7.2

Using the RAFTS Formula

To Your Health

Imagine that a fifth-grade teacher from the elementary school you attended has asked for your help. Because she knows that younger children look up to teenagers, she has asked you to help teach her students how healthy childhood habits lead to becoming healthy adults.

Your assignment:
In a report to be read by fifth graders, explain three or more habits they can establish now to help them become healthy adults.

In framing your report, consider the following questions:

- What are healthy childhood habits?
- What does good health involve beyond healthy eating habits?
- What should a child do, and what should a child avoid?

Role	Well-informed older student
Audience	Fifth graders
Format	Report
Topic	Health habits
Purpose	To teach (inform)

Your report will be judged on the basis of the attached criteria.

examples of verbs that help students understand what kind of writing they are to produce.

For Example 7.2 shows how we might use these questions to plan the ingredients or a written task in a content area.

Evaluating the Task for Quality

We have developed the Rubric for Tasks to help you evaluate any performance task for the degree to which it meets the standards of quality on the three criteria described in this section: *Content*, *Structure of the Task*, and *Sampling*. The Rubric for Tasks, Figure 7.6, also can be found in the Chapter 7 CD file.

FIGURE 7.6 Rubric for Tasks

Content: What learning will the task demonstrate?

Indicator	Level 3: Ready to Use	Level 2: Needs Some Revision	Level 1: Completely Revise or Don't Use
Target Alignment	All requirements of the task are directly aligned to the learning target(s) to be assessed. The task will elicit a performance that could be used to judge proficiency on the intended learning targets.	Some requirements of the task are not aligned to the learning target(s) to be assessed. There is extra work in this task not needed to assess the intended learning targets.	Requirements of the task are not aligned to the learning target(s) to be assessed. The task will not elicit a performance that could be used to judge proficiency on the intended learning targets.
Authenticity	The task provides as realistic a context as possible, given the learning target and intended use of the information. The conditions model application of the learning to a practical situation found in life beyond school.	The task provides an artificial context. The conditions do not provide a clear link to application of the learning to situations found in life beyond school.	The task either provides no context, when it would be appropriate to provide one, or the context does not lead students to see how the learning could apply to situations found in life beyond school.
Choice	If the task allows students to choose different tasks, it is clear that all choices will provide evidence of achievement on the same learning targets. All choices ask for the same performance or product, with approximately the same level of difficulty, and under the same conditions.	If the task allows students to choose different tasks, some of the choices may relate to different learning targets, or there is some variation in performance or product called for, level of difficulty, or conditions.	If the task allows students to choose different tasks, none of the choices relate to the same learning target, or there is considerable variation in performance or product called for, level of difficulty, and/or conditions.

Indicator	Level 3: Ready to Use	Level 2: Needs Some Revision	Level 1: Completely Revise or Don't Use
Interference	Successful completion of the task does not depend on skills unrelated to the target being measured (e.g., intensive reading in a mathematics task).	Successful completion of the task may be slightly influenced by skills unrelated to the target being measured.	Successful completion of the task depends on skills unrelated to the target being measured (e.g., intensive reading in a mathematics task).
	The task is culturally robust. Successful completion is not dependent on having had one particular cultural or linguistic background.	Successful completion of the task may be slightly influenced by having had one particular cultural or linguistic background.	The task is not culturally robust. Successful completion depends on having had one particular cultural or linguistic background.
Resources	All resources required to complete the task successfully are available to all students.	Some students may have difficulty obtaining the necessary resources to complete the task successfully, or one or more of the resources required will be difficult for most students to obtain.	Many or most students will have difficulty accessing the resources necessary to complete the task successfully.

Information Provided: Are the directions and guidance given clear and sufficient?

Indicator	Level 3: Ready to Use	Level 2: Needs Some Revision	Level 1: Completely Revise or Don't Use
Instructions	The instructions are clear and unambiguous.	The instructions may leave room for erroneous interpretation of what is expected.	The instructions are confusing and frustrating to students.

(*continued*)

FIGURE 7.6 Rubric for Tasks (*continued*)

Indicator	Level 3: Ready to Use	Level 2: Needs Some Revision	Level 1: Completely Revise or Don't Use
Supplemental Information	The task includes the following information: • The knowledge students are to use in creating the task • The performance or product students are to create—what form it should take • The materials to be used, if any • Timeline for completion	Some of the following information is clear; some is unclear or missing: • The knowledge students are to use in creating the task • The performance or product students are to create—what form it should take • The materials to be used, if any • Timeline for completion	The task does not include the following information: • The knowledge students are to use in creating the task • The performance or product students are to create—what form it should take • The materials to be used, if any • Timeline for completion
Time Allowed	The time allowed for the task is sufficient for successful completion.	The time allowed is too long or too short, but either the timeline or the task can be adjusted.	The task will take considerably more time than is allowed and cannot be broken into shorter segments.
Level of Scaffolding	The task information is sufficient to let students know what they are to do without giving so much information that the task will no longer measure level of mastery of the intended learning target. The content points the way to success without doing the thinking for the student.	Some parts of the task may give students too much help. In some places, the task does the thinking or the work for the student, compromising the results or the learning.	The task is over-scaffolded. If used for summative purposes, the task cannot measure students' ability to create the product or performance independently, because the content is so explicit that students can follow it like a recipe. If used formatively, students can satisfactorily complete the task without having learned anything. The task measures only students' ability to follow directions.
Conditions	If a task assesses a performance skill, it specifies the conditions under which the performance or demonstration is to take place.	If a task assesses a performance skill, it does not sufficiently specify the conditions under which the performance or demonstration is to take place.	If a task assesses a performance skill, it does not give any indication of the conditions under which the performance or demonstration is to take place.

Indicator	Level 3: Ready to Use	Level 2: Needs Some Revision	Level 1: Completely Revise or Don't Use
Help Allowed	Multi-day tasks specify the help allowed.	Although there is some reference to what kind of help is allowed for multi-day tasks, it could be misinterpreted.	Multi-day tasks do not specify the help allowed.
Criteria	The task includes a description of (or reference to) the criteria by which the performance or product will be judged. Students are familiar with the criteria.	Although described or referred to, the criteria by which the performance or product will be judged are vague or unclear (see *Rubric for Rubrics*).	The task includes no reference to the criteria by which the performance or product will be judged. or The students are not familiar with the criteria to be used.

Sampling—Is there enough evidence?

Indicator	Level 3: Ready to Use	Level 2: Needs Some Revision	Level 1: Completely Revise or Don't Use
Use of Information	The breadth of the task or the number of tasks or repeated instances of performance is sufficient to support the intended use of the information.	The task is broader than needed to support the intended use of the information. There are more tasks or repeated instances of performance than are needed to support the intended use of the information.	The breadth of the task or the number of tasks or repeated instances of performance is not sufficient support the intended use of the information.
Coverage of Target	The breadth of the task or the number of tasks or repeated instances of performance is sufficient to cover the breadth of the intended learning target.	The task is broader than needed to cover the breadth of the intended learning target. There are more tasks or repeated instances of performance than are needed to cover the breadth of the intended learning target.	The breadth of the task or the number of tasks or repeated instances of performance is not sufficient to cover the breadth of the intended learning target.

SELECTING, REVISING, OR DEVELOPING RUBRICS

In the context of performance assessment, rubrics represent the criteria for evaluating the quality of a reasoning process, a performance, or a product. You may be familiar with a variety of rubrics, some of which you may have seen used in large-scale assessments. Although rubrics used in large-scale assessments share many features of quality with rubrics designed for classroom use, those rubrics are generally designed to yield a quick, overall summary judgment of level of achievement. As a result, they don't tend to provide the level of descriptive detail about strengths and weaknesses in individual student work, and are therefore of limited usefulness in day-to-day instruction. To function effectively in the classroom, either formatively or summatively, rubrics must provide such detail.

A good classroom-level rubric serves multiple communicative and evaluative purposes:

- Defines quality
- Makes expectations clear and explicit for students
- Describes quality to parents
- Focuses teaching
- Guides interventions
- Promotes descriptive feedback to students
- Promotes student self-assessment and goal setting
- Tracks student achievement
- Makes judgments more objective, consistent, and accurate
- Improves grading consistency

If you search for rubrics on the Internet, you'll be confronted with hundreds of choices, some of which could accomplish all of the purposes listed here and many of which could not. How do you know which is which? Whether you plan to use an existing rubric or develop one of your own, it is helpful to understand the characteristics of rubrics that make them capable of serving all intended purposes. In this section, we'll introduce the terminology commonly used to describe rubrics and then examine the three dimensions of a high-quality rubric: *Content*, *Structure*, and *Descriptors*.

Rubric Terminology

You may have heard rubrics described as *holistic* or *analytic*. Those terms refer to how many scoring scales the rubric is comprised of—one or more than one. A *holistic* rubric has only one scale—all features of quality are considered together in determining a score. An *analytic* rubric has two or more scales—features of quality have been organized into separate categories and are rated separately from one another. These are sometimes known as *multi-trait rubrics*. The reasoning rubrics we examined in Chapter 6 are examples of holistic rubrics—one for each pattern of reasoning. The Oral Presentation Rubric shown in Figure 7.7 is an example of an analytic rubric.

The structure of each rubric takes the form of *criteria*, *indicators*, *levels*, and *descriptors*. See Figure 7.7 for illustrations of each of these terms.

CRITERIA. The categories of quality in an analytic rubric are known as *criteria*. Criteria represent key, independently varying dimensions of quality. Each criterion has its own rubric. You can teach each criterion separately, students can practice and receive feedback on each criterion separately, students can self-assess on each criterion separately, and you can assign grades to each criterion separately, if desired. Criteria are also sometimes called *traits*.

INDICATORS. Criteria for complex performances or products can be broken down further into subcategories called *indicators*. Indicators are the bulleted list of features assessed in each criterion. Occasionally indicators are represented on the rubric as subheads dividing the descriptors of quality. All criteria have indicators, but not all criteria call them out with structured subheads within a rubric.

LEVELS. *Levels* on a rubric are the points on a scale defining degrees of quality. They can be labeled with numbers (e.g., 1–5), phrases (e.g., "Just Beginning"; Halfway There", "Success"), and/or symbols representing "basic" to "proficient" (e.g., parts of a hamburger, ice cream cone, or pizza). On an analytic rubric each criterion generally has the same number of levels.

DESCRIPTORS. *Descriptors* refer to the sentence or phrases representing each indicator at each level. Descriptors provide the details used to flesh out the indicators and differentiate the levels. In assessment *for* learning applications, the descriptors function as diagnosis and feedback about student strengths and weaknesses within the criterion.

Content of the Rubric

The *content* of the rubric defines the elements of quality essential to achieve the intended learning target. What does it assess? What are we looking for in a student's product or performance? What will "count?" We examine this characteristic first when selecting rubrics. If the rubric under consideration falls seriously short on content, there is no need to consider it further.

A good rubric defines the intended learning target by describing what is required to do it well. If the rubric misrepresents the intended learning, students will work toward producing evidence of something other than what is desired—what students see on the rubric is how they will define quality. To make sure a rubric's content is in good shape, we pay attention to two factors, target alignment and match to essential elements.

TARGET ALIGNMENT. Just as the task should align to the learning target(s) to be assessed, so should the rubric. The rubric's criteria and descriptors should not focus

FIGURE 7.7 Structure of a Rubric

To illustrate the structure of a rubric, we will use an oral presentation rubric as our example.

CRITERIA

The oral presentation rubric has four *criteria*:

1. Content
2. Organization
3. Delivery
4. Language Use

INDICATORS

Each of the four criteria has several *indicators*:

1. Content
    - Clear main topic
    - All information is important to understanding the topic
    - Facts, details, anecdotes, and/or examples make topic come alive for audience
2. Organization
    - Opening introduces topic and catches audience's interest
    - Sequence of ideas supports meaning and is easy to follow
    - Transition words guide audience
    - Conclusion wraps up topic and leaves audience feeling satisfied
3. Delivery
    - Maintains eye contact with audience throughout presentation
    - Voice is loud enough for audience to hear
    - Articulates clearly
    - Speaks at a pace that keeps audience engaged without racing
    - Avoids "filler" words ("and," "uh," "um," 'like," "you know")
    - Uses gestures and movement to enhance meaning
    - Uses notes only as reminders
    - Visual aids and props, if used, add to meaning
4. Language Use
    - Chooses words and phrases to create a clear understanding of the message
    - Uses language techniques (e.g., humor, imagery, simile, and metaphor) effectively as appropriate to topic, purpose, and audience
    - Explains unfamiliar terminology, if used
    - Matches level of formality in language and tone to purpose and audience
    - Uses words and phrases accurately
    - Uses correct grammar

LEVELS AND DESCRIPTORS

Each criterion has a separate scoring scale, divided into *levels*. The oral presentation rubric has three levels. Each indicator for each criterion is fleshed out into one or more *descriptors* at each level. Here is what the rubric looks like for the criterion of *Content*. Each of the other three criteria also has a rubric organized the same way.

ORAL PRESENTATION CRITERION 1: CONTENT

5: Strong

- My presentation had a clear main topic.
- All of the information in my presentation related to and supported my topic.
- The information I included was important to understanding my topic.
- I chose facts, details, anecdotes, and/or examples to make my topic come alive for my audience.

3: Part-way There

- My topic was fairly broad, but the audience could tell where I was headed.
- Most of my details related to and supported my topic, but some might have been off-topic.
- Some of my information was important, but some details might have been too trivial to be included. Maybe I should have left some details out.
- Some of my information may not have been interesting or useful to my audience.

1: Just Beginning

- I wasn't sure what the focus of my presentation was, or I got mixed up and changed topics during my presentation. I think I wandered through a few topics.
- I didn't really know how to choose details to share, so I just used whatever came into my mind.
- I forgot to think about what information might be most interesting or useful to my audience.

Source: Adapted from *Seven Strategies of Assessment for Learning (p.* 194), by J. Chappuis, 2009, Upper Saddle River, NJ: Pearson Education. Adapted by permission.

on features that do not contribute to doing well on the learning target. Sometimes rubrics stray in their focus, as when students are asked to produce a poster to demonstrate a reasoning learning target and the rubric includes features of the poster more closely related to direction following or art than to the reasoning target. "Homegrown" rubrics, absent careful consideration of the intended learning, often suffer from this problem. If we are evaluating reasoning, the rubric should represent levels of quality for the reasoning target. Features unrelated to the learning targets should be left out or assessed separately for another purpose.

Judge the performance (demonstration) or the product (artifact) only if the performance or product is specified in the learning target. If a performance or product is not called for, make sure the rubric measures the learning target.

FAQ 7.3

Length of Rubrics

Question:

Aren't shorter rubrics better? Shouldn't the rubric fit on one page?

Answer:

Whether a rubric fits on one page depends on the use to which it will be put and the complexity of the learning target. For a rubric with more than one criterion, each criterion needs enough descriptive detail so that teachers can be consistent in judging student work and students can understand the strengths and/or weaknesses that underlie each score point.

With a lengthy rubric keep two points in mind. First, you don't have to evaluate all criteria for each piece of work. One of the strengths of multicriteria rubrics is that you can teach to, and assess, one aspect of quality at a time. Second, once students are familiar with a rubric, you can use a list of indicators for each criterion to remind them of the definition of quality, keeping the whole rubric handy for reference.

We would not advocate trading clarity for conciseness in either summative or formative applications.

Source: Adapted with permission from *Creating and Recognizing Quality Rubrics* (p. 43), by J. A. Arter and J. Chappuis, 2006, Upper Saddle River, NJ: Pearson Education. Adapted by permission.

MATCH TO ESSENTIAL ELEMENTS. The rubric's criteria and descriptors should also represent best thinking in the field about what it means to perform well on the intended learning target. Everything of importance for students at your level should be included. Three unfortunate things happen when important things are omitted: (1) we send the message that what is left out is unimportant; (2) we generate incomplete information on which to plan future instruction; and (3) we provide no feedback to students on the quality of valued elements.

By the same token, trivial features, those not important to success, *should* be left out. Some rubrics with a problem here require one way of demonstrating the learning, but the requirement may not be essential to demonstration of quality for the learning target. These rubrics inaccurately limit the definition of what it means to do well and penalize students who achieve the intended learning through a different path. If the feature is essential to the learning target, leave it in. If not, consider taking it out.

FIGURE 7.8 Characteristics of a Good Rubric

Content of the Rubric

- *Target Alignment*: Focuses on features that contribute to doing well on the learning target.
- *Focus on Essential Elements*: Represents best thinking in the field about what it means to perform well on the intended learning target.

Structure of the Rubric

- *Number of Criteria*: Sufficient to reflect the complexity of the learning target and its intended use.
- *Independence of Criteria*: If multiple criteria, they are independent of one another.
- *Grouping of Descriptors*: If multiple criteria, descriptors are grouped logically.
- *Number of Levels*: Fits the complexity of the target and intended use of the data.

Descriptors in the Rubric

- *Kind of Detail*: Wording is descriptive of the work and can be used diagnostically in describing strengths and weaknesses.
- *Content of Performance Levels*: Levels of performance quality are parallel in content.
- *Formative Usefulness*: Language can function as effective feedback to the student and the teacher.

Structure of the Rubric

Structure refers to how the rubric is organized: criteria are defined that represent important dimensions of quality. A good rubric organizes the criteria and its associated descriptors in ways that make it possible for the user to create an accurate picture of strengths and weaknesses. Good clear structure contributes to ease of use. To maximize a rubric's structure, we pay attention to four factors: number of criteria, independence of criteria, grouping of descriptors, and number of levels.

NUMBER OF CRITERIA. The number of criteria should be sufficient to reflect the complexity of the learning target and its intended use. If the rubric is holistic, the single scale needs to sufficiently represent all important parts of the target in one scale. If the target is complex, the rubric needs to include whatever number of criteria is needed appropriately define all important categories of proficiency.

INDEPENDENCE OF CRITERIA. If there are multiple criteria, they should be independent of one another. The same or similar descriptors should appear in only one criterion. When the same feature is rated in more than one criterion, it may indicate that the criteria aren't separable. If they are separable, they can be rated independently and each feature should appear in only one criterion.

GROUPING OF DESCRIPTORS. If there are multiple criteria, all descriptors should fit under the criterion they are assigned to. In other words, the categories defined by the criteria should suit the descriptors contained within them. Grouping of descriptors is a classification challenge. If descriptors don't fit where they're placed, they should be moved, or the categories should be redefined.

NUMBER OF LEVELS. The number of levels of proficiency defined within each criterion should fit the complexity of the target and intended use of the data as well. The levels should be useful in diagnosing student strengths and next steps: there should be enough of them to reflect typical stages of student understanding, capabilities, or progress. However, there should not be so many levels that it is difficult or impossible to define each or to distinguish among them.

When a scoring guide is comprised of several categories, each of which is assigned a number of points, it is sometimes referred to as a scoring rubric. In truth, it is often a list of criteria with few or no descriptors and lots of levels. Here is an example:

Ideas and Content: 10 points

Organization: 20 points

Word Choice and Sentence Structure: 10 points

Conventions: 20 points

When a scoring guide looks like this, it's not a rubric because it's not a description of levels of quality. It is just a way to assign points, and not a very reliable one. If there are 20 points possible for Organization, there are 20 levels of quality with no guidance on how to differentiate among them—what's the difference between a 13 and a 14?

Descriptors in the Rubric

The *descriptors* are the "goes-unders"—the detail that fleshes out each level. A high-quality rubric includes descriptors that accurately represent the criteria, are complete, and are clear enough so that teachers and students are likely to interpret them the same way. To evaluate a rubric's descriptors we pay attention to three factors: kind of detail, content of the levels, and formative usefulness.

KIND OF DETAIL. The wording should be descriptive of the work. To be used formatively, a rubric's descriptors should be helpful in defining levels in ways that diagnose student strengths and weaknesses. Evaluative language should not be used in the descriptors. When a rubric uses only these kinds of evaluative terms to differentiate levels, it offers no insight into why something is good or not; it just repeats the judgment of the level.

Also, if counting the number or frequency of something is included in a descriptor, we need to ensure that changes in such counts *are* indicators of changes in quality. Under

FAQ 7.4

Number of Levels

Question:

Shouldn't we always use an even number of levels? With an odd number, won't it be too easy to gravitate toward the middle?

Answer:

The number of levels depends on the learning target being assessed and the intended use of the information the rubric yields. Raters can easily be trained to avoid the problem of over-assigning the middle score.

Some simpler learning targets can truly only be divided into three levels of proficiency, so it makes sense to have only three levels. Others, such as the criterion *Content* in the Oral Presentation example in Figure 7.7, can be divided into five levels. This rubric has three defined levels, but it is easy to see that a student's performance might contain some descriptors from Level 5 and some descriptors for Level 3, or some descriptors from Level 1 and some from Level 3. With such rubrics, when a performance falls between two score points, highlight the phrases that describe it from each of the defined levels and then assign it the intermediate score, e.g., 4 or 2.

Source: Adapted with permission from *Creating and Recognizing Quality Rubrics* (p. 36), by J. A. Arter and J. Chappuis, 2006, Upper Saddle River, NJ: Pearson Education. Adapted by permission.

the guise of increasing the objectivity of scoring guides, it is tempting to count things—the number of sentences, the number of pieces of information, the number of topics covered, and so on. But this backfires when quality is not primarily defined by quantity. See For Example 7.3 for a sample of descriptive, evaluative, and quantitative language.

CONTENT OF LEVELS. The levels of the rubric should be parallel in their references to keys to quality. If an indicator of quality is referred to in one level, it should be mentioned in all levels. If an indicator is missing at one or more levels, there should be a logical rationale. For example, in a writing rubric, if "focus" is described at the "strong" level, it should also be described at all of the other levels. Or in a mathematics problem-solving rubric, one indicator may be "reasonableness of the solution." In this case, even though you may have a three-level rubric, you may only describe reasonableness of the solution at the "strong" and "weak" levels, because the solution is either within a reasonable range or it isn't.

For Example 7.3

Descriptive, Evaluative, and Quantitative Language

One criterion of a rubric for a science report may include descriptors for display of information. These three examples show the differences among descriptive language, evaluative language, and quantitative language. We recommend whenever possible to use descriptive language.

Descriptive language:

4: Display of information is accurate, complete, and organized so that it is easy to interpret.
3: Display of information is accurate, mostly complete, and is mostly organized so that it is easy to interpret. It may have one or two small omissions.
2: Display of information is partially accurate, partially complete, and may have some organization problems.
1: Display of information is inaccurate, incomplete, and not well organized.

Evaluative language:

4: Excellent display of information
3: Good display of information
2: Fair display of information
1: Poor display of information

Quantitative language:

4: Displays four pieces of information
3: Displays three pieces of information
2: Displays two pieces of information
1: Displays one piece of information

Source: Adapted from *Seven Strategies of Assessment* for *Learning* (p. 39), by J. Chappuis, 2009, Upper Saddle River, NJ: Pearson Education. Adapted by permission.

FORMATIVE USEFULNESS. If the rubric is intended for formative use, its levels and descriptors should function as effective feedback to the student and the teacher, leading to clear conclusions about strengths and areas needing work that provide sufficient detail to guide further learning. Students should be able to use the ingredients of the rubric to self-assess, to revise their own work, and to plan their own next steps in learning. They should be able to use the criteria, levels, and descriptors to

FAQ 7.5

Including Task-specific Requirements in the Rubric

Question:

The tasks I assign have very specific requirements and I include them in the rubric to make sure students do them and get credit for them. Can I still do this?

Answer:

It depends. If the requirements relate directly to a definition of quality regarding the learning target, they may legitimately belong in the rubric. However, if the requirements have to do with following directions—e.g., includes three characters, has five sentences—unless they are integral to the successful demonstration of the intended learning, they don't belong in the rubric and may not belong in the task.

offer one another feedback. Teachers should be able to use the rubric to determine what to teach next, to identify needs for differentiated instruction, or to identify topics for whole-group reteaching. All of the student uses require a version of the rubric in language they can understand—a student-friendly rubric.

Process for Developing Rubrics

Often existing rubrics can be revised to meet standards of quality. However, when a survey of available rubrics yields no promising candidates, you will need to start from scratch. Because you will want to use the rubric both formatively and summatively in the classroom, we recommend that you develop *general* rather than *task-specific* rubrics.

The process of rubric development involves collecting samples of existing rubrics, brainstorming features of quality, creating a draft, examining and scoring student work with the draft, and revising it. We have organized this path into six steps which we strongly recommend be carried out by teachers *working as a team* (Figure 7.9):

1. Establish a knowledge base.
2. Gather samples of student performances or products.
3. Sort student work by level of quality.
4. Cluster the descriptors into traits.
5. Identify samples that illustrate each level.
6. Test the rubric and revise as needed.

STEP 1: ESTABLISH A KNOWLEDGE BASE. To create a rubric that meets standards of quality, we have to be clear ourselves about what the performance or product looks like when it is done well. If you're an expert in creating the product or performance

FIGURE 7.9 Steps in Rubric Development

1. Establish a knowledge base.
2. Gather samples of student performances or products.
3. Sort student work by level of quality.
4. Cluster the descriptors into traits.
5. Identify samples that illustrate each level.
6. Test the rubric and revise as needed.

yourself, you may be able to work alone, but we recommend going through this process with a team as mentioned previously. A rubric development team should include some level of expertise. If you are not an expert at it, make sure you are working with someone who has experience with creating the performance or product.

As a team, begin by listing what you believe to be the characteristics of a high-quality performance or product, as called for by the learning target the rubric is intended to assess.

Next, collect as many existing rubrics as you can. These documents may provide you with inspiration and rubric language. Review the rubrics and add to your list any characteristics that you believe should be added.

STEP 2: GATHER SAMPLES OF STUDENT PERFORMANCES OR PRODUCTS. Gather a range of student performances or products that illustrate different levels of quality on the intended learning target. Good sources include your own students' work, your colleagues' students' work, books on teaching your subject, your State Department of Education's website, and other Internet sites. If the learning target requires a performance, this will require gathering audio or videotaped examples.

In general, try to gather at least 20 samples representing more than one topic or task. Using samples from only one topic or task may lead you to develop a rubric that is too task-specific to be useful across tasks. A variety of samples helps ensure that all important criteria are included on the final rubric.

A note of caution: If the samples come from your own school, once you are finished with this process, don't publish them as "anchors" for the rubric. Any published anchors require permission from the student and more anonymity than can be guaranteed in one school.

STEP 3: SORT STUDENT WORK BY LEVEL OF QUALITY. Begin by examining the samples of student work and sorting them into three stacks representing your evaluation of them as Strong, Medium, or Weak. Write down your reasons for placing each sample in each stack as you go. Have each member of the team do this independently.

The goal of sorting is not to get every sample in exactly the correct stack. The goal is to develop a complete list of the *reasons why* a sample should be placed in a particular stack. Eventually, the rubric you develop will be capable of judging samples accurately and consistently, but for now, focus on being descriptive in your reasons.

For each sample, write down exactly what you are saying to yourself as you place it into the stack. Don't wait until you have the samples sorted—it's harder later to remember all of the details of your reasons. Include as much detail as you can. Dig below general statements to a description of the evidence that leads to the general conclusion. For example, "logical" might be on your list of desired characteristics, but that is a general statement and does not describe the features present that lead you to determine whether or not a solution or argument is logical.

As another example, if "fluency" is on your list, students may not understand "lacks fluency," but they will understand "speaks slowly with hesitation." To generate detail, ask yourself questions such as these: "What specific features made me judge that the speech lacks fluency?" "What am I saying to myself as I categorize the performance?" "What descriptive feedback might I give to this student?" If you want the rubric to provide descriptive feedback and to function as a self-assessment and goal-setting tool for students, it is to your advantage to include those descriptive phrases from the outset. The descriptive phrases that you create now will form the core of your rubric descriptors.

Then, as a team, compile all of your descriptions of the samples in each stack. Ask yourself, "What makes the Strong stack different from the Middle stack? What makes it different from the Weak stack?" Use the samples to create a list of descriptors of quality at each level. We recommend trying to come up with as broad and long a list as possible.

As people sort samples, they sometimes discover that three levels is too few. Their eye develops to the point that they find work that is between two of the levels and they want to have four to six stacks. This is the beginning of determining your final number of levels. If three levels seem adequate, that's your number. If you can distinguish more than three independent levels, sort student work into the number of stacks you think you need and create the list of descriptors for each level. That is fine as long as you can find descriptors and/or sample performances that differentiate the levels. As long as you and students can differentiate performance levels, identify however many performance levels you need.

STEP 4: CLUSTER THE DESCRIPTORS INTO TRAITS. Your sorting and describing will result in a hodgepodge of descriptors at each level of performance. Some descriptors will be closely linked and can be assigned to a category: someone will say "Wait a minute. We have a whole lot of statements that refer to fluency. Why not group them together?" Some descriptors will overlap: you may hear, "Wait a minute. 'Speaks in paragraphs' is the same as 'Combines several sentences.' Why not delete one?"

FAQ 7.6

Student-developed Rubrics

Question:

To maximize student motivation, shouldn't we develop our rubrics with them?

Answer:

Involving students in developing criteria has several advantages and some drawbacks. It helps them internalize the standards of quality and it helps us refine our thinking. But most often we as teachers know more about the criteria for quality than students do, so developing criteria with students requires a robust sample set to help them refine their vision. For example, if students come up with criteria along the lines of "three colors" for a quality poster, we need to be prepared to broaden their thinking by showing them examples of effective posters with fewer (or more) than three colors. If they say that work has to be two pages long, we need to be ready to show them effective work that is only one page long, or that is six pages long.

A teacher should not begin instruction aimed at helping students perform well on a performance assessment without a clear vision of what the rubric should contain. The role of instruction is to bring students to a sufficient understanding of the keys to quality to be able to perform well. If you want to develop criteria with students, be prepared to assist them in their discovery of good criteria through use of thoughtfully chosen examples. Leading students through a process of devising a student-friendly version of the already-created rubric is one excellent instructional strategy. But the original articulation of keys to quality is the responsibility of the teacher.

Other descriptors may need to be separated into two categories: "I had trouble placing a student performance in a single category because it was strong in fluency but weak in pronunciation. Let's score those two dimensions separately."

This is the beginning of an analytical structure for the rubric—when you can sort out broad, independently varying categories of strengths and weaknesses, these indicate separate criteria. Once you have drafted the categories, it's time to refine them. You might decide that two criteria really refer to the same thing, or that one criterion should be divided into two or more criteria because of their independence from one another and the importance of being able to assess each separately. Most rubrics go through several stages of criteria definition and organization.

STEP 5: IDENTIFY SAMPLES THAT ILLUSTRATE EACH LEVEL. Return to the samples categorized as Strong, Middle, and Weak and select examples that illustrate well what is meant by each trait at each achievement level. These samples—also called *models, exemplars, examples,* and *anchors*—help teachers attain consistency with each other and within their own scoring across time, students, and assignments. Samples also help students understand what each achievement level looks like in concrete terms. Be sure to have more than one sample to illustrate each level. If you show students only one example of good performance, all performances might come out looking the same. Rather, show several performances that illustrate each level and trait.

Here are rules of thumb for selecting samples to illustrate criteria and levels:

1. *Start with the extremes.* Identify what you consider to be classic examples of strong and weak performances or products—ones that match a good number of the descriptors in the highest and lowest categories. Choose samples that everyone on the development team can agree on. When students are first learning to analyze samples for quality, they need examples that are fairly straightforward. Leave the more ambiguous examples for later, when students have more fully developed their sense of quality.
2. *Find examples for the middle level(s).* If you are using an odd number of levels, find samples that represent the approximate midpoint in the progression to excellence for each criterion. These samples will demonstrate the partial understanding or developing proficiency that is described by the phrases attached to your Middle level. If you are using an even number of levels, you will need to find two or four sets of midrange examples. For example, if your rubric has four levels, you will select samples for each criterion that typify the descriptors at level 2 (weaker, rather than stronger) and samples for each criterion that typify the descriptors at level 3 (stronger, rather than weaker).
3. *Find several different examples across assignments that illustrate each level.* The purpose of the samples is to help with training raters to apply the criteria consistently, whether those raters are teachers or students. Teachers and students need to be able to apply the rubric across tasks, so the samples should help in learning how to do that.
4. *Keep your eye out for examples illustrating typical problems.* Select examples that illustrate common errors students make, misconceptions they are likely to have, and flaws in reasoning. Carefully selected examples of typical problems can function well as teaching tools if students will be using them to practice scoring with the rubric.

The process of finding examples of performances or products at each level for each criterion usually results in revisions to the descriptors and criteria.

STEP 6: TEST THE RUBRIC AND REVISE AS NEEDED. Now is the time to test the rubric and note how you might improve it. Score student samples with your draft rubric and ask students to score anonymous samples as well. Unless you're spectacularly good at rubric development or spectacularly lucky, you'll identify some combination of the following problems:

1. Some student performances or products include features not mentioned in the rubric. If the features are indeed salient to quality, add descriptors and perhaps, indicators. Especially try to add descriptors that clarify general features or concepts. Don't despair that your rubric is becoming unwieldy. It's part of the revision process: we expand text to include all possible options before paring it down to the most-needed elements.
2. Features of student work seem to be rated in more than one criterion. Note this when it occurs. It might be that some descriptors are repeated across criteria. You will need to decide in which criterion the feature fits best. In some cases you may need to merge two criteria into one because they overlap to the extent that they can't be scored separately.
3. Criteria seem too broad. Sometimes there are a number of indicators in a criterion that could be separated out to form two or more separate criteria. Do this if you would like to teach, diagnose, and assess the parts separately. Make sure that the new criteria structure does represent independently varying features of quality.
4. The content of some levels is not parallel. You find that some descriptors at one level are not represented at other levels. In this case, write the descriptors for the other levels.

Evaluating the Rubric for Quality

We have developed the Rubric for Rubrics to help you evaluate any performance rubric for the degree to which it meets the standards of quality on the three criteria described in this section: *Content*, *Structure*, and *Descriptors*. The Rubric for Rubrics, Figure 7.10, can also be found in the Chapter 7 CD file.

USE STAGE

At this stage we conduct and score the assessment and revise it as needed for future use. As we noted previously, problems can still crop up even with the best planning. It is a good idea to keep notes of any potential sources of mismeasurement that may have compromised students' ability to show what they know and can do. If something appears to have gone awry and you can't identify the problem, use the Rubric for Tasks and the Rubric for Rubrics to troubleshoot the performance assessment.

FIGURE 7.10 Rubric for Rubrics

Rubric for Rubrics: *Content*

Indicator	Level 3: Ready to Use	Level 2: Needs Some Revision	Level 1: Don't Use
Target Alignment	Criteria and descriptors align directly with the content standards or learning targets they are intended to assess.	The rubric includes one or two small features that are not related to the intended content standards or learning targets.	The rubric focuses on features that are not related to the intended content standards or learning targets. One or more of the following applies: • The criteria and descriptors inappropriately focus on dimensions of the task rather than the learning targets. • The learning targets are not clear.
Focus on Essential Elements	Criteria and descriptors represent best thinking in the field about what it means to perform well on the content standards or learning targets. • Everything of importance (for students at your level) has been included. Trivial and unrelated features are left out. • If the rubric is a developmental continuum, the content represents the best thinking in the field about how proficiency develops over time.	A few descriptors might be irrelevant or unimportant for defining proficiency, but most are relevant.	You can think of many important indicators of quality that are missing, the rubric focuses on irrelevant features, or you find yourself asking, "Why should students have to do it *this* way?"

(*continued*)

FIGURE 7.10 Rubric for Rubrics (*continued*)

Rubric for Rubrics: *Structure*

Indicator	Level 3: Ready to Use	Level 2: Needs Some Revision	Level 1: Needs Major Revision
Number of Criteria	The number of criteria reflects the complexity of the learning target and its intended use. • If the rubric is holistic, a single scale sufficiently represents the target or the use is solely summative. • If the target is complex and the use is formative, the rubric is analytic; the number of criteria appropriately define categories of proficiency.	If a rubric is analytic, the number of criteria needs to be adjusted: either a single criterion should be made into two or more criteria, or two or more criteria should be combined.	The rubric is holistic (a single scale) when it needs to be analytic (multiple criteria) to better reflect the level of complexity of the learning targets to be assessed and the intended use of the data.
Independence of Criteria	If there are multiple criteria, they are independent of one another—the same or similar features are represented in only one criterion.	The criteria are mostly independent of one another, but in some cases features are represented in more than one criterion.	The criteria are not independent of one another. The same or similar features are represented in multiple criteria throughout the rubric, to the extent that the criteria do not function as separate categories.
Grouping of Descriptors	If there are multiple criteria, indicators and descriptors are grouped logically within each criterion. All descriptors fit under the criterion in which they are placed.	Most indicators and descriptors under a criterion are placed correctly, but a few need to be moved to a different criterion.	Indicators and descriptors that go together don't seem to be placed together; descriptors that are different are placed together; the categories don't work.

Indicator	Level 3: Ready to Use	Level 2: Needs Some Revision	Level 1: Needs Major Revision
Number of Levels	The number of levels fits complexity of the target and intended use of the data. There are enough levels to reflect typical stages of student understanding, capabilities, or progress, but not so many that it is impossible to distinguish among them.	There are a few too many levels of quality to distinguish among, so some will need to be merged; or, there are not quite enough levels to reflect typical stages of student growth, so more will have to be created.	The number of levels is inappropriate for the learning target being assessed or the intended use of the rubric. One or more of the following is true: • There are so many levels it is impossible to reliably distinguish among them. • There are far too few levels to be useful in tracking student growth. • It is impossible to define the number of levels indicated.

Rubric for Rubrics: *Descriptors*

Indicator	Level 3: Ready to Use	Level 2: Needs Some Revision	Level 1: Needs Major Revision
Kind of Detail	Wording is descriptive of the work. There is enough detail that it is possible to match a student performance or product to the appropriate level. Descriptors provide an accurate explanation of the characteristics of quality. If counting the number or frequency of something is included as an indicator, changes in such counts *are* indicators of changes in quality.	Wording is mostly descriptive, but has one or more problems: • The rubric includes a few terms that are vague. • Some language is evaluative rather than descriptive of the work. • Only the top level of quality is described sufficiently; the other levels include insufficient or no descriptive detail. • The rubric mostly avoids frequency counts, but there are a few times that counts are used even though changes in such counts do not equate to changes in level of quality.	Wording is not clear. One or more problems exist: • Descriptors consist of vague terms without clarification, e.g., "extremely," "thoroughly," "completely," or "insightful." • Descriptors rely heavily on evaluative language to differentiate levels of quality, e.g., "mediocre," "clever," or "above average." • The rubric is little more than a list of categories and a rating scale. • Descriptors consist almost solely of counting the number or frequency of something, when quantity does not equate to quality.

(*continued*)

FIGURE 7.10 Rubric for Rubrics (*continued*)

Indicator	Level 3: Ready to Use	Level 2: Needs Some Revision	Level 1: Needs Major Revision
Content of Levels	The features described across the levels are parallel in content. If a feature is present in one level, it is present in all levels. If a feature is missing at one or more levels, there is a logical rationale.	The levels of the rubric are mostly parallel in content. One or a few descriptors of quality at one level are missing at other levels when they should be present.	The levels of the rubric are not parallel in content. Most descriptors of quality are not represented at all levels and there is not an adequate rationale for their omission.
Formative Usefulness	If the rubric is intended for formative use, its language can function as effective feedback to the student and the teacher, describing strengths and areas needing work in sufficient detail to guide further learning. • Students can easily use the rubric to revise their own work and plan their own next steps. • Teachers can easily translate results into instruction.	If the rubric is intended for formative use, some parts can function as effective feedback to the student and the teacher, describing strengths and areas needing work in sufficient detail to guide planning for further learning. Descriptors in other parts need refining to accomplish this purpose.	If the rubric is intended for formative use, it cannot be used provide effective feedback to students and teachers because it doesn't describe strengths and areas needing work in sufficient detail to guide next steps in learning.

SEVEN STRATEGIES FOR USING RUBRICS AS INSTRUCTIONAL TOOLS IN THE CLASSROOM

You're all set with a great task and rubric. But how do you get students to understand and internalize your standards of quality? Performance assessment is a prime context for using assessment to help students learn. The instructional power here resides in using high-quality performance criteria to help students answer the three questions introduced in Chapter 2 to define assessment *for* learning: "Where am I going?"; "Where am I now?"; and "How can I close the gap?" Try out these seven strategies for using a rubric as a teaching tool to help students become competent, confident self-assessors and improve their performance in any subject.

Where Am I Going?

STRATEGY 1: PROVIDE STUDENTS WITH A CLEAR AND UNDERSTANDABLE VISION OF THE LEARNING TARGET. Motivation and achievement both increase when instruction is guided by clearly defined learning targets. Activities that help students answer the questions, "What's the learning? What am I responsible for accomplishing?" set the stage for all further formative assessment actions.

In the context of performance assessment:

Teach students the concepts underpinning quality in your scoring rubric by asking them what they already know ("What makes a good ____?"), then show how their prior knowledge links to your definition of quality.

Rationale:

Showing the connection between new information and knowledge students already have helps it all make sense and provides a link to long-term memory. It also lays the foundation for students understanding upcoming learning.

STRATEGY 2: USE EXAMPLES AND MODELS OF STRONG AND WEAK WORK. Carefully chosen examples of the range of quality can create and refine students' understanding of the learning goal by helping students answer the questions, "What defines quality work? What are some problems to avoid?"

In the context of performance assessment:

- Use models of strong and weak work.
- Share anonymous strong and weak student work. Have students use the scoring rubric to evaluate the samples, then share their reasons, using the language of the scoring rubric.
- Share published strong (and weak, if available) work. Let students comment on the quality of published examples and your own work, using the language of the scoring rubric.
- Share your own work. Model the "messy underside" of creating the performance or product for students.

Rationale:

Student performances improve when they understand the meaning of quality. This strategy teaches students to distinguish between strong and weak products or performances, and to articulate the differences. It also encourages teachers to share different aspects of the beauty of their discipline. What does it look/sound/feel like when it's done especially well? Modeling the messy underside for students reassures them that high-quality work doesn't always start out looking like high-quality work. As teachers, we tend to smooth over this part, so when the going gets messy for students, they may infer that they are "doing it wrong." What does high-quality work look like at its beginning stages? Model it.

Where Am I Now?

STRATEGY 3: OFFER REGULAR DESCRIPTIVE FEEDBACK. Effective feedback shows students where they are on their path to attaining the intended learning. It answers for students the questions, "What are my strengths?" "What do I need to work on?" "Where did I go wrong and what can I do about it?"

In the context of performance assessment:

If students have become familiar with the language of the rubric, we can use that language as the basis for descriptive feedback. If we are focusing on one trait at a time, we only need give descriptive feedback on that one trait. This has the effect of narrowing the scope of work for both the teacher and the student. With struggling students, we can show them they do indeed know some things and we can limit the things they need to work on at one time to less daunting, more manageable number. Our feedback may be verbal, such as that given in a brief student-teacher conference, or we may choose to offer written feedback.

Rationale:

Students need descriptive feedback while they're learning. It tells them how close they are to reaching the target and it models the kind of thinking we want them to be able to do, ultimately, when self-assessing.

STRATEGY 4: TEACH STUDENTS TO SELF-ASSESS AND SET GOALS. Strategy 4 teaches students to identify their strengths and weaknesses and to set goals for further learning. It helps them answer the questions, "What am I good at?"; "What do I need to work on?"; and "What should I do next?"

In the context of performance assessment:

Strategy 4 includes anything students do to identify where they are with respect to mastery of the desired learning and to set goals for improvement. Black and Wiliam (1998a) assert that for assessment to bring about learning gains, it has to include student self-assessment: "self-assessment by the students is not an interesting option or luxury; it has to be seen as essential" (pp. 54–55). In performance assessments, you can ask students to use the rubric to identify their own strengths and areas for improvement. If you have given them descriptive feedback based on the rubric, you have modeled for them the kind of thinking they are to do when self-assessing. You can teach them to set specific, achievement-related goals and to make a plan to accomplish them.

Rationale:

Periodic articulation about their understanding of quality and about their own strengths and weaknesses is essential to students' ability to improve.

How Can I Close the Gap?

STRATEGY 5: DESIGN LESSONS TO FOCUS ON ONE LEARNING TARGET OR ASPECT OF QUALITY AT A TIME. When assessment information identifies a need, we can adjust instruction to target that need. In this strategy, we scaffold learning by narrowing the focus of a lesson to help students master a specific learning goal or to address specific misconceptions or problems.

In the context of performance assessment:

Students who are not yet proficient at creating a complex performance or product have a difficult time improving simultaneously on all elements of quality. This strategy suggests that you may want to teach lessons that address your rubric one criterion at a time. In some instances, you may need to focus on only one *part* of one criterion at a time. For example, a writing rubric might have a criterion called *Organization.* Within that criterion are descriptors about the quality of the introduction, the sequencing of ideas, transitions between ideas, pacing, and the conclusion. If your students are not writing effective and inviting introductions to their papers, give them some practice with that single aspect of the whole rubric. You could use strategies 1 through 3: Ask "What makes a good introduction?"; share examples of strong and weak introductions; have students write an introduction to something they are working on; and offer descriptive feedback based on strengths and weaknesses of introductions as described in your rubric.

Rationale:

Novice learners cannot improve simultaneously all elements of quality of a complex skill or product. If your scoring rubric represents a complex skill or product, students will benefit from a "mini-lesson" approach, wherein they are allowed to learn and master a portion at a time.

STRATEGY 6: TEACH STUDENTS FOCUSED REVISION. When a concept, skill, or competence proves difficult for students, we can let them practice it in smaller segments and give feedback on just the aspects they are practicing.

In the context of performance assessment:

Any activity that allows students to revise their initial work with a focus on a manageable number of aspects of quality, problems, or learning targets is a logical next step after teaching focused lessons. Alternatively, let them create a revision plan, detailing the steps they would take to improve their product or performance, and let that stand in for the actual revision. This is especially useful in an assessment *for* learning context; students can think about revision more frequently, because each instance takes less time. Strategy 6 gives students practice using the rubric to self-assess and to guide their revisions.

Rationale:

Students need the opportunity to practice using the scoring guide as a guide to revision. When they do this, it is the students and not you who are doing the thinking about and the work of revision; this translates into deeper learning.

STRATEGY 7: ENGAGE STUDENTS IN SELF-REFLECTION AND LET THEM KEEP TRACK OF AND SHARE THEIR LEARNING. Long-term retention and motivation increase when students track, reflect on, and communicate about their learning. In this strategy, students look back on their journey, reflecting on their learning and sharing their achievement with others.

In the context of performance assessment:

Set up a system, such as a portfolio, that lets students track their learning along the way. Along with the artifacts, include the scoring rubrics you and they have used for feedback, self-assessment, and goal setting. Ask them to reflect on the contents of their portfolio, summarize their progress, and to comment on it: What changes have they noticed? What is easy that used to be hard? Where have they been surprised? Disappointed? Excited? What insights into themselves as learners have they discovered?

Rationale:

Any activity that requires students to reflect on what they are learning and to share their progress with an audience both reinforces the learning and helps them develop insights into themselves as learners. By reflecting on their learning, students are learning more deeply and will remember it longer.

(See Chapter 9 for information about how students can track their learning, Chapter 11 for how to set up and use portfolios for tracking and reflecting on progress, and Chapter 12 for the kinds of conferences students can participate in to share their learning.)

For a more detailed treatment of how each of these strategies can be used with performance assessment across grade levels and subject areas, refer to Chappuis (2009).

My Classroom Then and Now 7.1

Bruce Herzog

I used to ...

I have been an elementary school teacher for over twenty-five years. For the first fifteen years of my career I ended every year feeling disheartened by the fact that most of the students who were not meeting grade-level standards when they entered my room the previous fall were still below grade-level standards when the year ended. So each new year I worked even harder to improve my instruction because, throughout my career, I had been told over and over that good instruction would lead to good learning. I embraced new strategies and new programs of instruction that promised to lead to high achievement for all students, yet success still remained out of reach for far too many of my students.

Now I ...

When I first heard about formative assessment I was skeptical, but when I read the research that showed that effective assessment practices could lead to unprecedented achievement gains it convinced me to give it a try. I began by having my students set goals and reflect on their learning. It became immediately apparent that most students weren't exactly sure about what they were supposed to be learning. This led me to focus on making sure that the learning targets I expected students to meet were clear. I did this through the use of rubrics, study guides, and continued student goal setting and reflection. Having clear learning targets helped me focus my instruction on those clearly identified learning targets and enabled me to refine my assessments to reflect exactly what students were learning.

What I notice as a result ...

I saw almost immediate results. Within the first month that I began using formative assessment practices in my classroom I saw achievement gains from virtually all students with the greatest gains being made by the lowest-achieving students. Using these practices has completely changed the learning environment in my classroom. Good instruction is still important, but the focus has shifted from teaching to learning and from the teacher to the student. Now that learning targets are clear to students they are able to take responsibility for meeting those learning targets. By regularly reflecting on where they are in relation to the targets they are able to decide what action they need to take or what help they need in moving toward meeting those targets. Formative assessment has removed the barriers to learning in my classroom.

Do all students reach grade level standards in my room now? No, but many more do now than before I began using formative assessment practices and I am seeing dramatic improvement in those students who still have a way to go. More importantly, all students now know that, when they take responsibility for their own learning, they can be successful. One of my students probably put it best when he wrote in one of his reflections, "Now I know what I need to know and I know when I know it."

Source: Used with permission from 5th-grade teacher Bruce Herzog, Nooksack Valley School District, Nooksack Valley, WA, 2011.

USING A PERFORMANCE TASK AS AN ASSESSMENT *FOR* LEARNING

In the context of performance assessment, opportunity to practice and improve can be configured several ways, all variations of assessment *for* learning strategies 3, 4, 5, and 6 described in the previous section. These three approaches are summarized in Figure 7.11, "Performance Assessment Tasks As Opportunities for Practice."

1. You can set up one or more practice tasks, use the rubric to give students feedback on their strengths and areas to work on, and let them revise their performance or product before assigning the task you will grade. This often works well with performance tasks that don't take days or weeks to complete. For example, in mathematics you may use several tasks, all assessing the same learning target, as practice. On the first task, use the rubric to offer students feedback, showing them what they are doing well and what they still need to master. Have them revise their work based on the feedback. On the second task, let them use the rubric to give each other feedback, again having them revise their work based on the feedback. On the third task, have them use the rubric to self-assess and then revise as needed. Use the fourth task as the graded event. If you have access to multiple tasks addressing the same learning target, consider a progression such as this rather than assigning them all for a grade.

FIGURE 7.11 Performance Assessment Tasks As Opportunities for Practice

1. Schedule feedback, self-assessment, and revision on short practice tasks before assigning a task to be graded.
2. Break complex tasks into parts and schedule feedback, self-assessment, and revision on each part before students put the pieces together and turn the product in for a grade.
3. Schedule feedback, self-assessment, and revision multiple times while students are developing a complex performance or product that will ultimately be graded.

Source: Adapted from *Creating and Recognizing Quality Rubrics* (p. 134), by J. A. Arter and J. Chappuis, 2006, Upper Saddle River, NJ: Pearson Education. Adapted by permission.

2. On a more lengthy assignment, such as a science laboratory experiment, you may want to break the task into smaller pieces. Students can write just the hypothesis and receive feedback on it from the portion of the rubric describing levels of quality for the hypothesis. Or you may give them practice at writing hypotheses by offering an experiment context and having them draft a hypothesis and then revise it using rubric-based feedback from you, from other students, or from their own self-assessment. You can follow the same procedure to practice any other parts of the experiment process or report that students have not yet mastered.
3. Another approach, often used in English language arts classes, is to use the same task as assessment *for* and *of* learning through the writing process, as illustrated in Figure 7.12. Here, the teacher assigns a writing task and gives students time to assemble their ideas and organize them into a draft, with instruction as needed. Students then share their drafts with peers and receive feedback focused on one or more criteria from the rubric. For example, if the instruction focused on the two criteria of *Ideas and Content* and *Voice*, students' feedback to each other

FIGURE 7.12 The Writing Process As Assessment *for* Learning

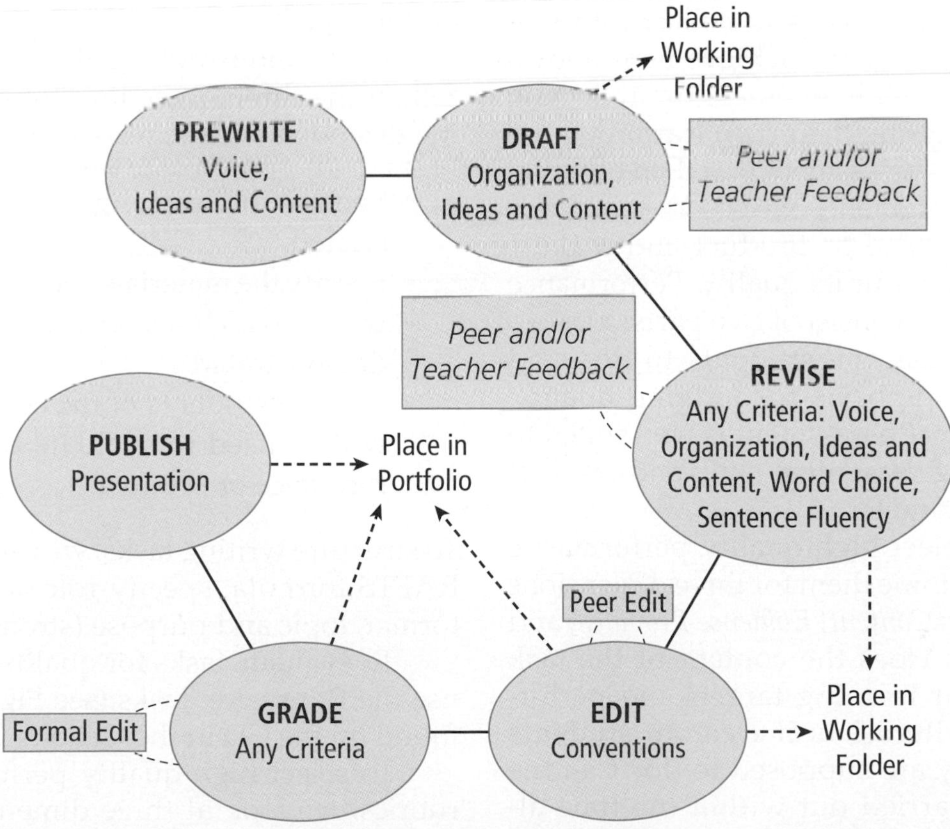

Source: Adapted with permission from *Creating and Recognizing Quality Rubrics* (p. 136), by J. A. Arter and J. Chappuis, 2006, Upper Saddle River, NJ: Pearson Education. Adapted by permission.

would also focus on *Ideas and Content* and *Voice*. Students then use this feedback as well as their own thoughts to revise the draft. They may repeat the draft/receive feedback/self-assess/revise cycle one or more times before submitting the paper to the teacher for feedback. Last, students revise their paper based on the teacher's (and perhaps others') feedback and turn it in for a grade. This process approach can also be used for shorter practice pieces, where students work on improving a paper for a selected number of criteria and then put the paper into a working folder. At a later date, students choose one piece from their writing folder to develop further through the whole writing process and then turn it in for a grade.

Summary

Performance assessment, described by some as the most authentic of assessment methods and yet viewed with suspicion by others due to its inherently subjective nature, has evolved into one of our most valuable ways to collect information about student achievement and to involve students in assessing, reflecting on, and sharing their own learning.

This is assessment based on observation and judgment—we observe or review a performance or product and make a judgment about its quality. Performance assessments consist of two parts: a task—what we ask the students to do—and criteria—the basis for judging quality. Performance assessment is well suited to evaluating reasoning, skill, and product learning targets.

To select high-quality performance tasks, examine them for three dimensions of quality: *Content*, *Evidence Provided*, and *Sampling*. Does the content of the task match our learning targets and performance criteria? Is it clear to students what they are supposed to do? Can the task be carried out within the time allowed given the materials at hand? Is there anything in the task that might disadvantage any particular student or group of students? Do we have enough tasks that cover enough dimensions of the targets to ensure that we will be able to infer overall level of student mastery of the target?

To develop high-quality tasks, we follow the same procedure for developing extended written response items:

- Specify the learning to be demonstrated.
- Specify the materials and constraints within which achievement is to be demonstrated.
- Remind students of the criteria that will be used to evaluate their performance or product.

To structure writing tasks, we can use the RAFTS formula: specify role, audience, format, topic and purpose (strong verb).

To evaluate tasks for quality, we can use the Rubric for Tasks (see Figure 7.6), found on the CD in the Chapter 7 file.

To select high-quality performance rubrics, we look at three dimensions of quality: *Content*, *Structure*, and *Descriptors*. Do the criteria cover features of work that really define quality? Are the criteria and descriptors organized to portray an accurate picture of strengths and weaknesses? Do the descriptors accurately represent the criteria? Are they complete? Are they clear enough so that teachers and students are likely to interpret them the same way?

To develop rubrics, we follow six steps: (1) establish our knowledge base, (2) gather samples of student performance, (3) sort the samples by level of quality and describe the features of the work at each level, (4) cluster the features into traits, (5) identify samples to illustrate each level, and (6) test the rubric and revise as needed.

To evaluate rubrics for quality, we can use the Rubric for Rubrics (see Figure 7.10), found on the CD in the Chapter 7 file.

The rubrics associated with performance assessments provide the classic example of how to involve students in assessment. Rubrics can be used to help students understand where they are going, where they are now, and how to close the gap. With respect to understanding where they are going, good rubrics define quality so that students can see it. They provide a vocabulary for talking about features of quality work. Using models of anonymous strong and weak performance not only helps students deepen their understanding of the features of a quality performance or product, but also allows students to become accurate raters of performance. This accuracy is essential before students begin to self-assess.

Rubrics also help students to know where they are now in their learning and how to improve. Teachers can use them to provide descriptive feedback to students and students can use them to self-assess, set goals for further learning. Rubric information can form the basis of students' tracking, reflecting on, and sharing their progress.

NOTES

1. Portions of this chapter have been reprinted and adapted from J. A. Arter and J. Chappuis, *Creating and Recognizing Quality Rubrics*, 2006, Upper Saddle River, NJ: Pearson Education. Copyright © 2006 by Pearson Education, Inc. Reprinted and adapted by permission of Pearson Education, Inc.

CHAPTER 7 ACTIVITIES

End-of-chapter activities are intended to help you master the chapter's learning targets. They are designed to deepen your understanding of the chapter content, provide discussion topics for learning team meetings, and guide implementation of the practices taught in the chapter.

Forms for completing each activity appear in editable Microsoft Word format in the Chapter 7 CD file. Documents on the CD are marked with this symbol:

Chapter 7 Learning Targets

At the end of Chapter 7, you will know how to do the following:

1. Select, revise, and develop high-quality performance tasks.
2. Select, revise, and develop high-quality rubrics.
3. Use performance assessment formatively, as teaching tools.
4. Structure performance assessments so that students can use the results to self-assess and set goals for further learning.

Activity 7.1 Keep a Reflective Journal
Activity 7.2 Evaluate a Performance Task for Quality
Activity 7.3 Create a Performance Task
Activity 7.4 Create a Writing Task Using the RAFTS Format
Activity 7.5 Evaluate a Rubric for Quality
Activity 7.6 Create a Rubric
Activity 7.7 Create a Student-friendly Version of a Rubric
Activity 7.8 Use Rubrics as Assessment *for* Learning
Activity 7.9 Structure a Task for Formative Use
Activity 7.10 Reflect on Your Own Learning
Activity 7.11 Select Portfolio Artifacts

Activity 7.1

Keep a Reflective Journal

Keep a record of your thoughts, questions, and any implementation activities you tried while reading Chapter 7.

 Reflective Journal Form

Activity 7.2

Evaluate a Performance Task for Quality

Work with a partner or a team to carry out the following activity.

1. After reading the section titled "Selecting, Developing, or Revising the Task," find a performance task you have used or will use to assess student learning.
2. Make a copy of the task you have selected and the Rubric for Tasks for each person.
3. Individually, evaluate the task for each criterion on the Rubric for Tasks. Refer to the text in Chapter 7 for clarification of the terms used on the Rubric for Tasks. Note any areas needing improvement and suggestions for revision.
4. Share your evaluation and notes with your partner or team.
5. Together, revise the task so that it meets all applicable standards of quality as described in the Rubric for Tasks.

 Performance Task Evaluation Form

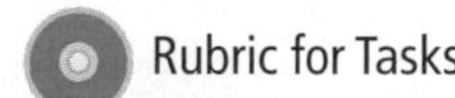 Rubric for Tasks

Activity 7.3

Create a Performance Task

Work independently, with a partner, or a team to carry out the following activity.

1. Select a learning target for which performance assessment is a good match.
2. Identify the intended use and intended users of the assessment information the task will provide.
3. Create the major components of the task by answering these four questions:
    - What knowledge are students to use?
    - What are they to perform or create?
    - What conditions are they to adhere to?
    - How much time will they have?
4. Working with the information from Step 3, draft the task. Use the criteria from the Rubric for Tasks as a guide.
5. Consider the intended use and the learning target to answer the following sampling questions:
    - How many tasks will be needed to sample well?
    - How should these tasks differ to cover the breadth and depth of the learning to be assessed?
6. Identify the criteria that will be used to judge the performance or product. If you do not have a high-quality rubric available, revise or create one following the steps in Activity 7.5 or Activity 7.6.
7. Evaluate your task using the Rubric for Tasks. Note any areas needing improvement and suggestions for revision.
8. Revise your task so that it meets all *applicable* standards of quality as described in the Rubric for Tasks.

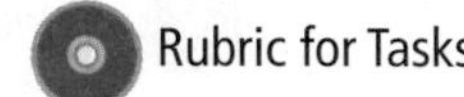

Activity 7.4

Create a Writing Task Using the RAFTS Format

If the learning targets you are teaching specify that students will write to inform or explain, persuade or express and defend an opinion, or narrate real or imagined experiences or events, you may want to create a writing assignment using the RAFTS format. If so, use the text in the section titled "Creating Tasks to Elicit Good Writing" as a guide to complete the following activity.

1. Brainstorm possibilities for *role, audience, format, topic*, and *strong verb* (purpose). Refer to Figure 7.5 for *strong verb* suggestions.
2. Considering your students, the context (subject area content? literature content? personal experience content?), and the length of time you want the task to take, select one option for *role, audience, format, topic*, and *strong verb*.
3. Assemble the ingredients into a draft-writing task, following the format illustrated in Example 7.2.
4. Share your draft task with a partner or your team. Together, use the Rubric for Tasks to evaluate it for quality. Note any areas needing improvement and suggestions for revision.
5. Revise your task so that it meets all *applicable* standards of quality as described in the Rubric for Tasks.

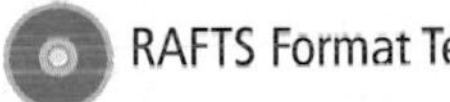
RAFTS Format Template

Rubric for Tasks

Activity 7.5

Evaluate a Rubric for Quality

Work with a partner or a team to carry out the following activity.

1. After reading the section titled "Selecting, Revising, or Developing Rubrics," find a rubric you have used or will use to assess student learning.
2. Make a copy of the rubric, the Rubric Evaluation Form, and the Rubric for Rubrics for each person.
3. Individually, evaluate the rubric for each criterion on the Rubric for Rubrics. Refer to the text in Chapter 7 for clarification of the terms used on the Rubric for Rubrics. Note any areas needing improvement and suggestions for revision.
4. Share your evaluation and notes with your partner or team.
5. Together, revise the rubric so that it meets all applicable standards of quality as described in the Rubric for Rubrics.

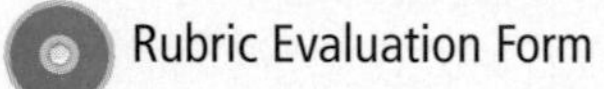

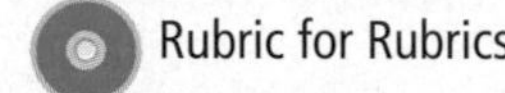

Activity 7.6

Create a Rubric

If you have decided that no suitable rubric exists to evaluate the form of reasoning, skill, or product called for in a learning target, you will need to create one. This work is ideally done with a team, but can be completed with a partner, if more people are not available.

1. Reread carefully the section titled "Selecting, Devising, or Developing Rubrics." Also read the Rubric for Rubrics carefully. Work with your team to discuss and answer any questions you may have about aspects of quality rubrics.
2. Work through the six steps explained in the section titled "Process for Developing Rubrics" to create a draft rubric.
3. Make notes of what needs revising after carrying out Step 6 and make the revisions.
4. Audit your sample collection from Step 5 against the revised rubric. Note which work well and which don't. Revise your sample selection, adding and deleting as needed.
5. Using the Rubric for Rubrics, evaluate your revised rubric for quality. Refer to the text in Chapter 7 for clarification of the terms used on the Rubric for Rubrics. Note any areas needing improvement and suggestions for revision.
6. Share your evaluation and notes with your partner or team.
7. Together, revise the rubric so that it meets all applicable standards of quality as described in the Rubric for Rubrics.

Rubric Development Template

Rubric Evaluation Form

Rubric for Rubrics

Activity 7.7

Create a Student-friendly Version of a Rubric

Once you have found or created a rubric that meets standards of quality, create a student-friendly version by following these steps. We recommend that you work with a partner or a team to complete this activity. In some cases, students can also be enlisted to work with you on this.

1. Examine each phrase and decide if you want to leave it out, leave it as is, or convert it to student-friendly language. (Only leave phrases out if you do not need to evaluate the feature they represent.)
2. To convert phrases to student-friendly language, look words up in the dictionary or in textbooks as needed. Discuss with colleagues the best phrasing choices for your students.
3. Convert the definitions into wording your students will understand. Sometimes you need to convert one word into one or more phrases or sentences.
4. Phrase the student-friendly version in the first person.
5. Try the rubric out with students. Ask for their feedback.
6. Revise as needed.

Source: Adapted from *Creating and Recognizing Quality Rubrics* (p. 83), by J. A. Arter and J. Chappuis, 2006, Upper Saddle River, NJ: Pearson Education. Adapted by permission.

Create a Student-friendly Version of a Rubric

Activity 7.8

Use Rubrics As Assessment *for* Learning

After reading the section titled "Seven Strategies for Using Rubrics As Instructional Tools in the Classroom," complete one or more of the following activities.

1. Select a rubric that you plan to use with students, but have not yet introduced to them. Follow the instructions in Strategies 1 and 2 to help students understand the concepts represented by the rubric and to improve their ability to use the rubric to determine levels of quality. (For a more detailed explanation of how to implement Strategies 1 and 2 with rubrics, refer to Chapter 2 of *Seven Strategies of Assessment* for *Learning* [Chappuis, 2009].) Have students keep the rubric for future use when engaging in the reasoning or creating the performance or product assessed by the rubric.
2. After having introduced the language of a rubric to students, offer them feedback on their work by highlighting phrases on the rubric that match the level of quality they have produced. Ask them to revise their work based on the feedback before turning it in for a grade.
3. After having offered feedback with the rubric, ask students to revise their work and then self-assess using the same rubric. If you are highlighting phrases on the rubric, have them use a different color highlighter to self-assess their revised work.
4. Select one portion of the rubric and plan a series of lessons to help students get better at just that one part. You may want to include Strategy 2 activities as a part of the focused instruction. Ask them to practice on just that one part, then give them feedback on it. Let them revise their work, just for the characteristics that were the focus of instruction.
5. Have students keep evidence of their growing proficiency—the tasks they have completed along with the formative and summative information from the rubrics. Refer to Chapters 11 and 12 for more information on how to help students track, reflect on, and share their growth and achievement using these artifacts.
6. Reflect on the quality of the final performances or products your students are creating after experiencing these activities: how does it compare to the quality of their previous work (or to that of classes in the past)?
7. Discuss with a partner or your team any impact the strategies might have had on students' motivation and achievement. Also discuss how you might modify the activities for future use.

Activity 7.9

Structure a Task for Formative Use

After reading the section titled "Using a Performance Task as an Assessment *for* Learning," select a performance assessment task that you use to structure for formative use.

1. Choose one of the three options best suited to your students, intended learning target(s), and task(s). Adapt it as needed.
2. Find or create the materials required to carry out the option.
3. Try it out with students, noting their responses to the activities.
4. Reflect on the quality of their final performance or product: how does it compare to the quality of their previous work (or to that of classes in the past)?
5. Discuss with a partner or your team any impact this activity might have had on students' motivation and achievement. Also discuss how you might modify the process for future use.

Debrief Structuring a Task for Formative Use

Activity 7.10

Reflect on Your Own Learning

Review the Chapter 7 learning targets and select one or more that represented new learning for you or struck you as most significant from this chapter. If you are working individually, write a short reflection that captures your current understanding. If you are working with a partner or a team, either discuss what you have written or use this as a discussion prompt for a team meeting.

Reflect on Chapter 7 Learning

Activity 7.11

Select Portfolio Artifacts

Any of the activities from this chapter can be used as portfolio entries. Select activities you have completed or artifacts you have created that will illustrate your competence at the Chapter 7 learning targets:

1. Select, revise, and develop high-quality performance tasks.
2. Select, revise, and develop high-quality rubrics.
3. Use performance assessment formatively, as teaching tools.
4. Structure performance assessments so that students can use the results to self-assess and set goals for further learning.

If you are keeping a reflective journal, you may want to include Chapter 7's entry in your portfolio.

 Chapter 7 Portfolio Entry Cover Sheet

CHAPTER

8

Personal Communication as Classroom Assessment

"What's in a question, you ask? Everything. It is a way of evoking stimulating response or stultifying inquiry. It is, in essence, the very core of teaching."

—John Dewey (1933)

"Who remembers what a noun is?" "How would you describe the workings of a food web to someone who had never heard of one?" "What patterns do you notice in this sequence of numbers?" "What do you think of when you hear the word *power*? What do you think of when you hear the word *authority*? Are *power* and *authority* the same?" While we may not have considered the questions we ask in the course of a day as a form of assessment, they are. Asking instructional questions is both a teaching and an assessment strategy; through careful questioning, we can access prior knowledge, pique curiosity, check for understanding, provoke and explore thinking, and create new learning.

Asking instructional questions is one personal communication assessment option. Others include class discussions, conferences and interviews, oral examinations, and student journals and logs. As with all assessment methods, personal communication can be used formatively or summatively. However, some options are better suited to each use than others. When personal communication is used formatively as assessment *for* learning, it can serve teachers' needs to gauge students' knowledge and understanding in order to diagnose problems and misconceptions and adjust instruction accordingly, one part of the formative picture. An equally important part is its ability to affect student learning directly. Done well, it can hook students' interest, deepen their conceptual understanding, and strengthen their reasoning proficiencies. And with careful attention to rules of accuracy,

FIGURE 8.1 Keys to Quality Classroom Assessment

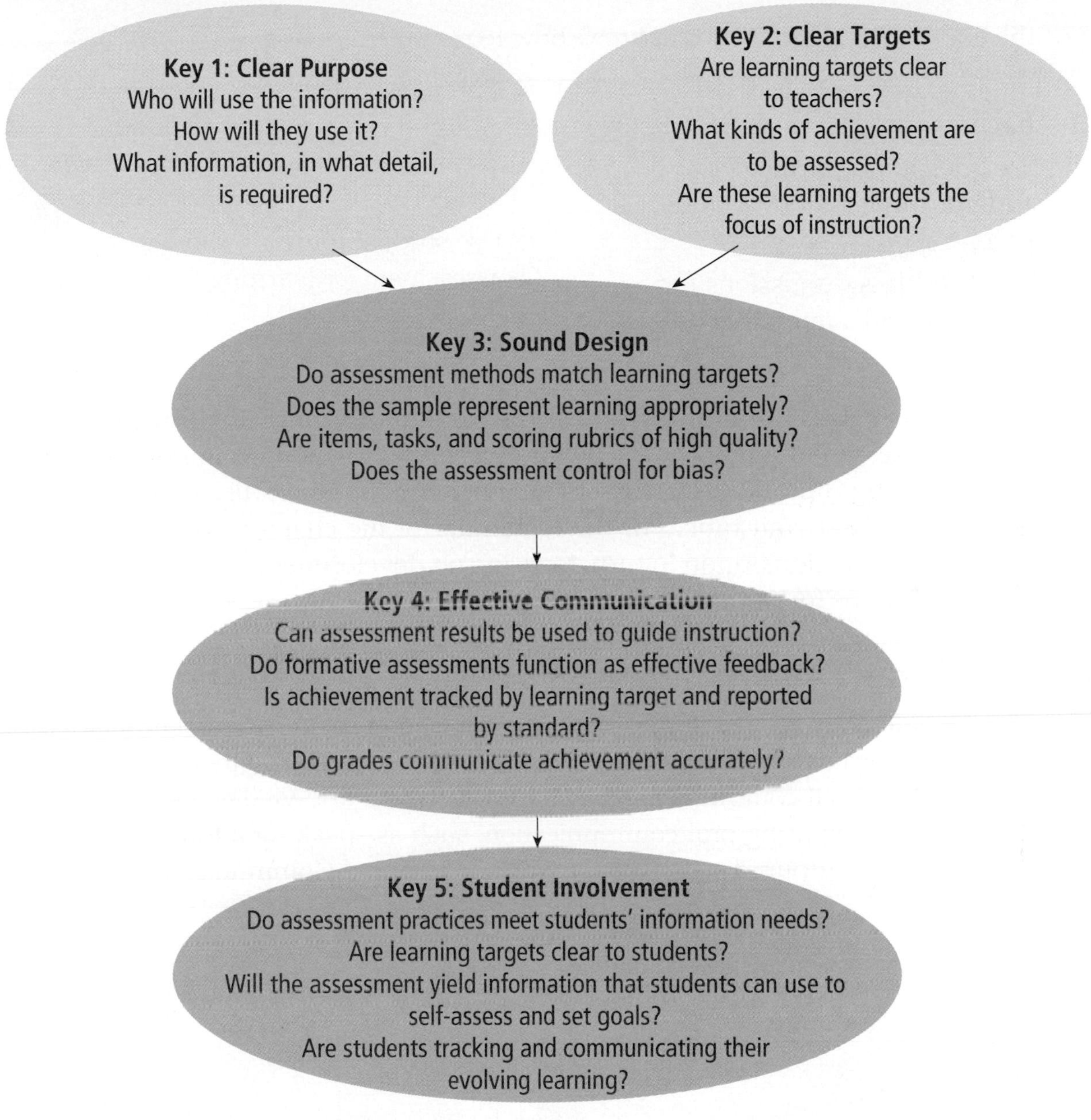

Key 1: Clear Purpose
Who will use the information?
How will they use it?
What information, in what detail, is required?

Key 2: Clear Targets
Are learning targets clear to teachers?
What kinds of achievement are to be assessed?
Are these learning targets the focus of instruction?

Key 3: Sound Design
Do assessment methods match learning targets?
Does the sample represent learning appropriately?
Are items, tasks, and scoring rubrics of high quality?
Does the assessment control for bias?

Key 4: Effective Communication
Can assessment results be used to guide instruction?
Do formative assessments function as effective feedback?
Is achievement tracked by learning target and reported by standard?
Do grades communicate achievement accurately?

Key 5: Student Involvement
Do assessment practices meet students' information needs?
Are learning targets clear to students?
Will the assessment yield information that students can use to self-assess and set goals?
Are students tracking and communicating their evolving learning?

some personal communication assessment options can serve to make summative decisions about students' level of achievement.

In this chapter we examine accurate and effective use of each of the personal communication options, how to avoid possible sources of bias that can distort results, and how to use personal communication in assessment *for* learning contexts.

Chapter 8 Learning Targets

At the end of Chapter 8, you will know how to do the following:

- Frame questions to be used diagnostically to inform instruction
- Use questioning strategies to deepen students' understanding and reasoning proficiencies
- Structure class discussions for formative and summative use
- Conduct conferences, interviews, and oral examinations to obtain accurate information about student achievement
- Use student journals and logs as assessment *for* learning tools

This chapter does not entirely follow the same footprint as the three previous chapters on assessment methods. We begin in a similar fashion, examining when to use personal communication as an assessment method, but then discuss two general issues: sampling and wait time. For the remainder of the chapter, we address each personal communication option in turn, focusing on development considerations and offering suggestions for optimum use.

WHEN TO USE PERSONAL COMMUNICATION ASSESSMENT

The first consideration for using personal communication as an assessment method is the type of learning target to be assessed, as described in the target–method match section of Chapter 4. Personal communication options can assess knowledge, reasoning, and those skill targets requiring oral communication, such as speaking a foreign language and participating in group discussions. Figure 8.2 "Personal Communication Options"

FIGURE 8.2 Personal Communication Options

Format	Description	Primary Use	Target Types			
Instructional Questions and Answers	Teacher poses questions for students to answer or discuss. Students pose questions and respond to each other.	Formative	K	R		
Class Discussions	Students engage in a discussion. Can be either teacher-led or student-led.	Formative or Summative	K	R	S	
Conferences and Interviews	Teacher meets with student to talk about what students have learned and have yet to learn.	Formative	K	R		
Oral Examinations	Teacher plans and poses questions for individual students to respond to.	Summative	K	R	S	
Journals and Logs	Students write to explain, explore, and deepen their own understanding; teacher and/or other students respond.	Formative	K	R		

gives a brief summary of which option is best suited to each of the target types. We will elaborate further on the matches as we discuss each option.

Two additional conditions influence the effectiveness of personal communication as an assessment method:

- The teacher and the student must share a common language. This means a shared vocabulary and grammar as well as a common sense of the manner in which a culture shares meaning through verbal and nonverbal cues. Quiet or reserved students may not perform well in this kind of assessment context, regardless of their real achievement. To make this method work, teacher and student must connect in an open, communicative manner. This is more difficult for some students than for others. If the purpose is to gather summative evidence and personal communication is not required, you may want to plan for other options as well to ensure accuracy of results.
- Use personal communication assessment only when it is certain to generate enough information to make an adequate inference about student performance. This is a sampling issue and it affects the accuracy of both formative and summative decisions.

Sampling

In the context of personal communication, sampling has two dimensions: (1) gathering enough information for the target in question to meet the intended purpose; and (2) hearing from enough students to meet the intended purpose.

GATHERING ENOUGH INFORMATION—SAMPLING THE LEARNING. Once again with this method as with the others, the challenge is to gather enough information to lead us to a confident conclusion about student achievement without wasting time gathering too much. The sufficiency of a sample will be a function of the context within which we assess. For instance, if the target is narrow and sharply focused, as it often is during instruction, student responses to a very few questions will let us know if instruction is working for the class. Sometimes just one strategic question can tell us if a particular student is getting it and what to do if they are not. So the broader and more encompassing the learning target, the more questions we may need to pose to cover the territory, so to speak.

In this same sense, how much is enough will be a function of the decision to be made on the basis of results. The scenario implied in the previous paragraph frames a relatively low-stakes decision. We gather a bit of data, act on it, and continue to assessment to see if we made a right decision—instructional interaction. But what if the impending decision carries more profound implications, such as when we intend to grade students in part based on the quality of their contributions to a class discussion. In this case, we would want (need) to gather more instances of contribution for each to lead us to a confident conclusion. So the purpose of the assessment should influence sample size.

There are no hard and fast rules for how many questions to ask when assessing via personal communication. This is very much a part of the art of classroom assessment: the broader the target and more grave the decision, the larger must be the sample of evidence.

HEARING FROM ENOUGH STUDENTS—SAMPLING THE POPULATION. Personal communication options that involve the whole class or a group of students run the risk of oversampling the knowledge and understanding of some students and undersampling the knowledge and understanding of others. This sampling issue arises only with personal communication—with selected response, written response, and performance assessments, all students are participating in the assessment. With personal communication options such as instructional questions and class discussions, it is likely that not all students will be responding to an equal degree. The challenge here is to maximize engagement. How we do that depends on our intent for use of the process and the information.

For example, when we want to determine if students have understood a concept just taught, we might ask a few oral questions. If we only call on students who raise their hands, we will not likely obtain a representative sample from which to make an accurate generalization about the whole class's level of understanding.

Here are some suggestions that maximize the instructional value of questions by maximizing engagement, and that also maximize the accuracy of the information by maximizing the sample size:

- In a group setting, don't call on a student to answer before asking the question. Asking the question first and then inviting responses increases the chances that all students will stay engaged.
- In a group setting, call on both volunteers and nonvolunteers. There are a number of simple systems for doing this. Many teachers put students' names on Popsicle® sticks or tongue depressors, keep them in a cup, and draw out a name at random after asking the question.
- Ask students to discuss their thinking in pairs or small groups. Designate a reporter to speak on behalf of the group, ask the group to designate a reporter, or call on one person in the group randomly. You can also number the groups and draw a number at random.
- Ask all students to write a response, then collect and read them aloud. Ask students to listen for similarities and differences. Use the responses as a springboard for their further questions and discussion. You may also be able to use common misconceptions and incorrect answers as the distracters for a multiple-choice item you create to measure this learning target on a summative assessment.

- Give students a choice among different possible answers and ask them to vote on the options. Similarly, use the answers to a multiple-choice item in this fashion. Many teachers use whole-class response systems such as individual whiteboards or electronic responding devices ("clickers").
- Establish discussion norms for the class so that all contributions are treated respectfully.

Wait Time

In the traditional model of questioning in the classroom, teachers typically wait less than one second after posing a question before calling for a response. This limited amount of think time encourages responses that are brief and right-answer oriented, rather than reflective and thought out, even if the question calls for mental processing. In studying the effects of increasing wait time on science achievement at the elementary, middle school, and high school levels, researchers found that when teachers pause after asking a question, student answers reflect deeper levels of thinking (Rowe, 1972, 1987).

> Increasing the wait time from three and seven seconds results in an increase in:
>
> 1. The length of student responses
> 2. The number of unsolicited responses
> 3. The frequency of student questions
> 4. The number of responses from [lower-achieving students]
> 5. Student-student interactions
> 6. The incidence of speculative responses (Akron Global Polymer Academy, 2011, n.p.)

The benefits also occur when teachers give wait time *after* a student responds to a question, pausing before offering a response or calling on another student (Akron Global Polymer Academy, 2011).

When students first experience extended wait time, they have a tendency to respond by waiting rather than by thinking. It is a good idea to explain that the pause isn't really "wait" time in the sense that we're all waiting for a count of seven before firing off responses. Instead it is "think" time: the intent of the pause is to give each student time to ponder the question and formulate a response, which may be an answer, a question, or a comment that offers further reflection on the question.

Unless your goal is truly to get students to "popcorn" fast correct answers, pause between three and seven seconds before calling for responses. Wait time will increase the depth of thought, richness of discussion, and instructional value of your questions. Let students know what you are doing and why to help them understand what is expected of them during wait time.

PERSONAL COMMUNICATION OPTIONS: INSTRUCTIONAL QUESTIONS AND ANSWERS

With this much-used personal communication option, as instruction proceeds, we pose questions for students to answer, or we ask students to pose questions and respond to each other. Its use in the classroom is primarily formative. We ask questions to gain information about students' learning in order to plan or adjust instruction. We listen to answers, interpret them (either by means of internally held standards or a written rubric), infer students' levels of attainment or misconceptions, and act accordingly. A second, equally important formative use of questioning is to encourage thinking and deepen learning. Instructional questions and answers typically focus on *knowledge* and *reasoning* learning targets. Responses to knowledge questions are judged correct or not, while reasoning probes need to be evaluated in terms of the quality of the reasoning demonstrated (as depicted in the rubrics in Chapter 6.) While you are asking instructional questions, you won't necessarily be reading from a rubric to evaluate student responses, but it is a good idea to have the features of quality for the specific pattern of reasoning in mind. In other words, the rubric does not need to be in your hand, but it should be in your head.

Because we are so familiar with this format, it may not seem obvious to look for ways to improve it. In this section, we will look at strengthening the power of our instructional questions in assessing students' level of understanding or misconceptions, in spurring livelier discussions, and in encouraging deeper thinking.

Developing Questions to Assess Knowledge and Understanding

Instructional questions designed to assess students' levels of knowledge and understanding can be thought of as an oral version of selected response or written response assessment. There are two keys to using questions in this context:

- Plan key questions in advance of instruction to ensure they align with the target.
- Ask clear, brief questions that help students focus on a relatively narrow range of acceptable responses.

You can use the guidelines explained in Chapters 5 and 6 to assist with developing these questions. Ask them during the course of instruction using the suggestions offered previously for sampling and wait time, determine what students know and understand and what they don't, and adjust the lesson accordingly. Remember that in a group setting, instructional questions and answers are best used formatively.

Developing Questions to Assess Reasoning

Assessing reasoning through personal communication requires a well-thought-out question as well as the strategic use of wait (or "think") time, as described earlier. The guidelines in Chapters 5 and 6 can help you craft these questions. Here are three additional suggestions for success:

- Label the type of reasoning that you are looking for—comparing, analyzing, evaluating, and so forth—and include the specific reasoning verb in the question. Figure 8.3 shows key verbs and question stems targeted to elicit specific types of thinking.
- When students have difficulty responding to a question, rephrase it and ask again before offering clues to the answer.
- Invite students to elaborate. For example, say, "Please say a little more about . . ." This encourages students to develop more complex contributions.

Suggestions for Effective Formative Use of Instructional Questions

When we use personal communication as assessment *for* learning, we are using the questions themselves to teach and deepen knowledge, understanding, and reasoning proficiencies. There are a few classroom dynamics that can foster or hinder this. First, we need to make sure students feel safe in responding honestly even though they may not have confidence in the accuracy of their response. We create safe learning environments when we let students know that it is a good and desirable thing to uncover what we don't know and then go about learning it. Secondly, we need to help students understand that a response that misrepresents the truth about their achievement only gets in the way of their ultimate success as learners. Thirdly, we need to establish expectations that students will treat each others' contributions with respect as well, welcoming mistakes and misconceptions as opportunities to gain deeper understanding.

Here are some ways to maximize the learning students experience as a result of instructional questions:

1. Ask questions that elicit summaries or key points of the learning.
2. Encourage students to interact with each others' responses rather than looking to the teacher as their only responder.
3. Model the response patterns that you'd like to see from students. For example:
   - Speculate on a given topic. This encourages students to explore ideas and understand that uncertainty is a normal stage in the thinking process.
   - Reflect on topics. For example, say, "I sometimes wonder . . ." This encourages students to explore the topic rather than to seek a single quick answer.
   - Cheerfully admit when you don't have an answer and model what to do about it. Follow "I'm not sure" with "What could we do to find out?" Sometimes a class member or two will be able to answer a question you can't, in which case invite students to weigh in.
4. Teach students the question stems that elicit different patterns of reasoning for whatever content they are studying. Have them use question stems in small- or large-group discussions.

FIGURE 8.3 Verbs and Question Stems That Elicit Different Types of Thinking

Verbs that elicit recall of information:

Explain, describe, identify, tell, name, list, give examples, define, label, match, choose, recall, recognize, select

Question stems that elicit reasoning:

Analyze:

- What are the important components, parts, or ingredients of ________________?
- What is the order in which ____________ happened? What are the steps?
- What is the main idea of what you read or saw? What details support this main idea?
- What familiar pattern do you notice? (Examples include familiar story structure and numerical sequence.)
- What is this question asking?
- What kind of reasoning is being called for here?
- What information do you need to solve this problem or approach this task?

Compare/contrast:

- What are some characteristics that would help us discriminate (or distinguish) between ____________ and ____________?
- How are ____________ and ____________ alike and/or different?
- Create an analogy for ____________.
- Can you think of something else that is similar? (For example, what other stories have similar openings, characters, plots, or themes?)

Synthesize:

- What do you conclude from __________ and __________?
- How would you combine, blend, or organize __________ and __________?
- How might you adapt or modify __________ to fit __________?
- How would you describe ____________ to someone else?
- How might you formulate a response or answer to __________?

Classify:

- Find an example of __________ (a group or category).
- What is __________ an example of?
- How might you sort __________ into groups or categories?
- What characteristics of __________ tell us what group it belongs to?

Infer/deduce:

- What do you think will happen next? (predict)
- Why did the author do __________?
- What are the implications of ____________?
- What can you conclude from the evidence or pieces of information? *For example, "What does that tell us about numbers that end in five or zero?"* (generalize)

Evaluate:

- Take a position on ____________ and justify, support, defend, or prove your position.
- What is your opinion on ___________ ? What evidence do you have to support your opinion?
- Appraise, critique, judge, or evaluate ___________. Support your appraisal, critique, judgment, or evaluation with evidence.
- Dispute or judge this position. Is it defendable or not? Why or why not?
- Is this argument sound? What evidence supports your judgment?
- Is this ____________ successful? What evidence supports your opinion?
- Could __________ be better? Why or why not?
- Which is better? Why?

Johnston (2004) has collected question stems that engender open-ended assessment-*for*-learning conversations:

To help students notice and learn:

- Did anyone notice that . . . ?
- Remember how you used to . . . Now you . . . Notice the difference?
- What kind of . . . is this?
- What . . . surprised you?

To establish student control:

- How did you figure that out?
- What problems did you come across today?
- How are you planning to go about this?
- What parts are you sure (not sure) about?

To help students transfer:

- How else . . . ?
- What's that like?
- What if things changed . . . ?

To help students confirm knowing:

- How do you know we got this right?
- I hadn't thought about it that way. How did you know?
- How could we check?
- Would you agree with that? (pp. 13–59 passim)

These and similar questions can provide an excellent basis from which to encourage students to think aloud in conversation with you about their thinking and learning.

My Classroom Then and Now 8.1

Jody Petry

I used to . . .

I used to "drive through" my curriculum. When planning classroom activities and assignments, I would plan them with me (the teacher) in mind. I used my lesson plans as simply a list of things to do. Once an assignment or activity was taught, I would move on—keep driving and not look back. I was essentially the driver, with the map, and my students were in the backseat. Since I was in charge of the learning, conversations during learning were shallow. The students didn't have the knowledge of their learning to talk about.

Now I . . .

Assessment *for* learning practices have given me the tools to hand over the learning to my students, essentially putting them in charge. They are the drivers and I am in the backseat. They are holding the "map" (learning targets). My students know where their learning is headed. Learning targets have given my students the knowledge they need to have in order to talk about what they are learning and what they need to work on. Using "I can" statements, my students know what it is they are supposed to know.

Why I changed . . .

Before, students were unable to tell me what they were not understanding in relationship to a concept we were working on. I could see how they weren't sure of what they were supposed to know. After learning more about assessment *for* learning, I noticed all of the holes in my instruction. I found out how to connect my teaching with students' learning.

What I notice as a result . . .

Students can now name their learning. Using learning targets has given my students the power when it comes to their learning. They are able to tell what it is they need to know and what it is that they need to improve. My students have more in-depth conversations about learning, using rich academic vocabulary in group discussions. My students are now equipped to give focused feedback about where they are in their learning. Using a 1 through 4 scale, students can gauge their understanding of the material.

Source: Used with permission from Jody Petry, Northwest R-I School District, House Springs, MO, 2011.

Summative Use of Instructional Questions

We caution against using questions asked during group instruction as summative data about an individual student's knowledge or reasoning proficiencies. It is difficult to obtain accurate information in this context due to sampling constraints and the sources of bias that the group setting introduces. It is better to ask the questions in the one-on-one setting offered by an oral examination, as described later in this chapter.

PERSONAL COMMUNICATION OPTIONS: CLASS DISCUSSIONS

With this option, students converse with one another in a structured discussion. Class discussions can serve formative or summative purposes. Whether to use them formatively or summatively depends in part on the intended purpose and learning target. In this case, the evaluation of student contributions requires forethought about the criteria by which we judge the quality of those contributions. Typically, this requires the development of a rubric. Depending on the context, students can contribute to the development of that rubric, thus turning assessment development into an assessment *for* learning intervention.

When students participate in class discussions, their contributions can reveal a great deal about their levels of knowledge, conceptual understanding, and reasoning abilities, which can help you plan further instruction. Class discussions have the simultaneous effect of enhancing understanding and reasoning proficiency. These are both formative uses.

Discussions can be used to provide evidence of *knowledge* and *reasoning* targets for summative use as well, but there are serious limitations in terms of sampling and sources of bias to consider. Because there are better options in most cases for evaluating knowledge and reasoning targets when the intended use is summative, we recommend that you use class discussions formatively to diagnose and deepen knowledge, understanding, and reasoning.

However, if your curriculum includes a communication *skill* target, such as one specifying that students be able to participate effectively in discussions, you will need to assess it for a grade. The target may require students to demonstrate their level of achievement of discussion skills, and perhaps also their ability to employ underpinning knowledge and reasoning proficiencies.

A good example of this kind of target is a College and Career Readiness Anchor Standard (applies across grades 6–12) for Speaking and Listening from the Common Core State Standards for English/Language Arts & Literacy in History, Social Studies, Science, and Technical Subjects: "Prepare for and participate effectively in a range of conversations and collaborations with diverse partners, building on others' ideas and expressing their own clearly and persuasively" (CCSSI, 2010a, p. 48).

The grade-specific standards that flesh this target out at the eighth-grade level say this:

a. Come to discussions prepared, having read or researched material under study; explicitly draw on that preparation by referring to evidence on the topic, text, or issue to probe and reflect on ideas under discussion.

b. Follow rules for collegial discussions and decision-making, track progress toward specific goals and deadlines, and define individual roles as needed.

c. Pose questions that connect the ideas of several speakers and respond to others' questions and comments with relevant observations and ideas.

d. Acknowledge new information expressed by others and, when warranted, justify or qualify their own views in light of the evidence presented. (CCSSI, 2010a, p. 49)

As with all skill targets, assessing this standard summatively will require a scoring rubric that clearly describes each of its components at several levels of achievement. And it would be wise to engage students in practice discussions with opportunities for feedback and revision, prior to evaluating their discussion proficiencies for a grade.

Developing Class Discussion Topics and Questions

To take advantage of the strengths of this method of assessment while minimizing the impact of potential weaknesses, do the following:

- Prepare questions or discussion issues in advance to focus on the intended achievement target. Use the suggestions in Chapter 6 for developing written response questions as a springboard for crafting questions that will lead to rich discussion and also stay within the bounds of the learning the discussion is intended to focus on.
- Find, modify, or develop scoring checklists or rubrics that reflect the learning targets at the heart of the discussion task. See Chapter 7 for how to do this. If possible, work with colleagues to practice evaluating recorded student discussion sessions to ensure inter-rater reliability when judging level of achievement.
- In contexts where achievement information derived from participation in discussion will be used summatively, rely on more than your memory. Track individual student achievement with a scoring checklist or rubric and keep dependable records of performance. Also, electronic tools that can help with this function have recently come on the market and may be available in your school.

Suggestions for Effective Use of Class Discussions

Be sure students are aware of what they will be judged on, which should match the learning targets you have shared with them at the outset of instruction. Are you evaluating the *content* of students' contributions—the knowledge, understanding, or reasoning demonstrated—or the *form* of their contribution—how they communicate, or

FAQ 8.1

Keeping Track

Question:

Do we need to keep track of personal communication information?

Answer:

When the information is to be used only over a span of a few moments or hours on narrow targets, formal record keeping is usually unnecessary. When the context includes many students, complex targets, and a requirement of later use, we must absolutely keep track of results. Because there are no artifacts to refer to for later use, records of achievement must be managed carefully. This process is helped by high-quality rubrics for the reasoning or skill targets being discussed or observed. You may also want to make a video record, especially if discussion skills are the focus, if you are planning to use the information as a part of a course grade. Options for tracking formative and summative information once you have captured it are discussed in Chapter 9.

some combination of both? This focus should derive directly from the learning targets students know they are expected to master.

To increase student achievement, use Strategies 1 through 4 from the Seven Strategies of Assessment *for* Learning, as explained in Chapter 7:

1. Introduce the language and concepts of the rubric.
2. Use strong and weak examples.
3. Offer feedback focused on one aspect of quality at a time. Teach students to give each other feedback based on the rubric.
4. Teach students to self-assess and set goals with the rubric.

For Example 8.1

Line-up

A line-up is an activity that structures a class discussion so that students talk to each other to investigate a question or argument. The line-up teaches students to examine both sides of an issue or argument before committing to one side. It also helps correct the misconception that opinions can be effectively supported with further opinions, or that the volume with which an opinion is expressed constitutes support.

In the example used, students are learning to develop arguments for and against a position.

1. The teacher identifies a statement that could be argued reasonably for or against. This works best if there is no "right" or "wrong" side. For example, after reading a short story about a boy who lies to cover up the fact that he didn't get into the highly competitive school his father attended, the teacher may post the statement, "Parents should push their children."
2. The teacher and students clear a space so that students are able to form two lines facing each other. The teacher posts the statement on the wall at one end of the cleared space, also posting two signs, "Yes" and "No," one on each side of the statement.
3. Students form two lines facing each other, one line extending from the "Yes" sign and the other extending from the "No" sign. The teacher can let students choose which side reflects their own position or can number students by twos and assign them a position.
4. The discussion begins, following these rules:

   One person talks at a time.

   After one person from one side has talked, it is the other side's turn. The comment may be a counterargument, a question, or a new argument.

   Share the talking time fairly. A goal is to hear as many diverse arguments as possible.

   Talk to those in the other line, not to the teacher.

   The teacher doesn't talk, except to remind of the rules.

   Comments should explain reasons for the position, for or against.

   The same comment should not be repeated. Once a reason has been shared, if a person wants to share it again, the new comment must include an elaboration.

   Stating a comment at a louder volume does not make it a stronger reason.

5. If a person wants to make a comment in support of the other line's position, he or she walks over to the other line and makes it. (When students do this, it may require a little norming about turn-taking while talking.)
6. To debrief this activity, students identify the strongest arguments for and against in small groups and then share their thoughts in the large group. They may then be asked to take a position and defend it in writing.

As a variation, students can line up according to the intensity of their commitment to the side they have chosen. At first this may produce the two lines forming a "U" shape, with lots of students on the fence—the bottom of the "U." Consider not offering this option until they have participated in a line-up a few times and have become more comfortable taking a position in public.

PERSONAL COMMUNICATION OPTIONS: CONFERENCES AND INTERVIEWS

With this personal communication option, we meet with students individually to talk about what they have learned and have yet to learn. We tend to use these formatively to provide insights that both we and the student may use to guide further learning. In the context of a conference or interview, we can assess students' grasp of *knowledge* targets and proficiency with *reasoning* targets. Conferring individually with students is a powerful assessment *for* learning tool when we ask carefully thought-out followup questions to uncover strengths and misconceptions or misunderstandings.

In addition, we can probe whether students have the underlying knowledge, conceptual understanding, and reasoning proficiencies necessary for successful demonstration of skill and product targets. Although the conversation itself will not provide sufficient evidence to judge level of attainment of skill and product targets, it can be used to diagnose underlying instructional needs and plan for interventions.

Conferences and interviews need not be standardized or conducted with every pupil. We might meet with only one student or vary the focus of the conference with students who have different needs.

Developing Questions and Topics for Conferences and Interviews

The goal of a conference or interview is to establish a deeper understanding of the student as a learner, so you will want to create questions that cause the student to do most of the talking. Here are some keys to developing a question framework to guide the discussion:

- Carefully think out and plan questions in advance.
- Avoid asking "yes" or "no" questions.
- Develop questions that focus attention on the student's progress toward preestablished learning targets.
- Have samples of student work available to add specificity to the discussion. Make sure the student understands which learning targets the samples provide evidence of. Also have available the rubrics used to evaluate them, as appropriate.

In Chapter 11 we offer suggestions for a variety of ways to collect student work into portfolios that can become the basis for the conference discussion. That chapter also includes lists of questions that initiate student self-analysis of learning strategies, skills, and processes. In Chapter 12 we offer more in-depth information about kinds of conferences and options for conducting them.

Suggestions for Effective Use of Conferences and Interviews

One important advantage of the conference or interview as a mode of assessment lies in the impact it can have on our relationships with students. When students understand the achievement target and the formative intent of the discussion, this form of assessment becomes "sitting beside" in truth, with both teacher and student working together for the individual student's good. In addition, an effective conference or interview sets students up to take more ownership of their learning progress.

The following are keys to successful use of conference and interview assessment formats:

- Let students know in advance the purpose and the focus for the conference or interview to minimize the chance that they will think they are "in trouble" because they have to talk to the teacher.
- Give students an opportunity to prepare for the conference or interview. What questions might they have? What materials might they want to bring?
- Plan for enough uninterrupted time to complete the discussion. Prioritize your questions if you are concerned about running out of time.
- Give students plenty of responding time. Listen carefully to what they say. Feeling "heard" helps students trust that the purpose of the conference or interview is to engender mutual understanding of the student's learning strengths and needs. Anne Davies (Davies & Stiggins, 1996) suggests sitting on your left hand to remind yourself to listen.
- Conclude each meeting with a summary of the lessons learned and their implications for future actions. Let the student do the summarizing orally or in writing, as appropriate.

PERSONAL COMMUNICATION OPTIONS: ORAL EXAMINATIONS

When personal communication takes the form of an oral examination, we plan and pose questions for students, who reflect and provide oral responses. We listen to and interpret the responses, evaluating quality and inferring levels of achievement using scoring guides like those of the written response exam or a performance assessment. Oral examinations are generally used summatively. They can reliably measure *knowledge* and *reasoning* targets and can also measure *skill* targets that require one-to-one communication, such as correct pronunciation in a foreign language. Oral examination questions are structured similarly to selected response questions, short-answer and extended written response items, and performance assessments, but they have the added benefit of allowing us to ask followup questions to attain greater accuracy of results.

Developing Questions for Oral Examinations

Quality control guidelines for oral examinations include those listed in Chapters 5 and 6 for selected response and written response assessments as well as some guidelines particular to this form of assessment, as follows:

- Develop questions that focus on the desired learning target(s).
- Ask questions using the easiest possible vocabulary and grammatical construction. Don't let language get in the way of allowing students to show what they know.

- If the question is to be used to assess mastery of a combination of knowledge and reasoning targets, use the formula explained in Chapter 6: Identify the knowledge to be brought to bear, specify the kind of reasoning students are to use, and identify the standards you will apply in evaluating responses.
- Present one set of questions to all students; don't offer choices of questions to answer.
- Develop scoring checklists or rubrics that describe levels of quality in a response in advance of the assessment. Be sure that qualified experts in the field would agree with the features of a sound response. See Chapters 6 and 7 for guidance on how to do this.
- Your scoring checklists or rubrics should allow you to separate achievement on knowledge and reasoning targets from facility with verbal expression so that students aren't able to do well on the exam without having mastered the targets.
- Prepare in advance to accommodate the needs of any students who may confront language proficiency barriers.
- Have a method of recording results ready to use at the time of the assessment.
- If necessary, audiotape responses for later reevaluation.

Suggestions for Effective Use of Oral Examinations

Just as with selected response, written response, and performance assessments, students will benefit from an opportunity to practice demonstrating their learning in this format, with feedback prior to sitting for an oral examination that will be used as a part of their grade. For an example of how an oral examination might be used both for practice and to contribute to a final grade, consider the test developed by a foreign language teacher for her first-year students. One of the important learning targets for the term was to engage in short social conversations with a range of vocabulary and sentence constructions. The teacher identified the contexts in which students were to learn to converse (e.g., meeting someone for the first time, talking about your school, talking about your family, asking directions), and students practiced the discussions with each other over the course of the term. As part of the final exam, the teacher drew one of the topics at random for each student, who then was responsible for conducting the conversation.

PERSONAL COMMUNICATION OPTIONS: JOURNALS AND LOGS

Sometimes personal communication takes a written form: students write to explain, explore, or deepen their own knowledge and understanding and the teacher or another student responds. Journals and logs are used for a variety of reasons in the classroom. This section addresses their use as a structured interaction with the teacher or another student, where students describe their views, experiences, reactions, insights, understandings, confusions, and misunderstandings related to specific learning targets. Thus, their primary use as an assessment option is formative (Figure 8.4). As assessment tools, journals and logs are especially well suited to focusing on knowledge and reasoning learning targets. In this section we will discuss four types of journals and logs: *response journals*, *dialogue journals*, *personal journals*, and *learning logs*.

Response Journals

Response journals are most often used in situations where we ask students to read and construct meaning from text, such as in the context of reading and English language arts. In any subject, students can record responses to ideas in a text, to an experience, to what they are viewing, or to what they are listening to. Typically, we provide structured assignments to guide their responses.

Here are some examples from English language arts:

- Describe characters in terms of key attributes or contribution to the story.
- Trace an evolving story line, plot, or story events.
- Note the questions that come to you as you are reading.
- Compare one character to another.
- Anticipate or predict upcoming events.
- Evaluate either the piece as whole or specific parts in terms of appropriate criteria.
- Suggest ways to change or improve character, plot, or setting. Give reasons for your suggestions.

FIGURE 8.4 Written Forms of Personal Communication

Students write to explain, explore, or deepen their knowledge and understanding. The teacher or another student responds.

Response Journals

Students record their responses to ideas in a text, in what they are viewing, listening to, or experiencing.

Dialogue Journals

Students write messages conveying thoughts and ideas about what they are learning. Teachers respond. Students may reply to the response.

Personal Journals

Students write regularly in a journal to reflect on ideas, on their learning, or on themselves as learners.

Learning Logs

Students keep ongoing records to document learning, progress made, and processes used.

ASSESSMENT *FOR* LEARNING WITH RESPONSE JOURNALS. One interesting example of the use of a response journal to help students learn more deeply comes from Janice Knight: "Most students' initial efforts at writing journal entries were lengthy, literal accounts about what was read. These boring responses, displaying a lack of critical thinking, filled page after page in their journals. It seemed that demonstration lessons on how to [think more deeply] were needed" (1990, p. 42). So she taught students how to use a system for coding their journal entries for the types of thinking displayed. She taught the codes one at a time, first modeling and then having students practice writing about what they read, coding for that type of thinking. By doing this, she saw a dramatic increase in the depth of thinking displayed in journal entries. "(N)ot only does the teacher have a record of the type of thinking that went into their creation, so do the students. They can readily self-evaluate and work independently towards improving their responses. The students are also more motivated to include different kinds of thinking in their entries" (1990, p. 42).

Dialogue Journals

Dialogue journals capture conversations between students and teachers in writing. As teaching and learning proceed, students write messages to us conveying thoughts and ideas about the achievement expected, self-evaluations of progress, points of confusion, or important new insights. Periodically, they turn the journals in and we read them and reply, responding to an idea, asking a question, clarifying or amplifying a key point. Students read what we have written, sometimes responding, and other times moving on to a new topic. This process links us with each student in a supportive communication partnership.

Personal Journals

Personal journals represent the least structured of the journal options. In this case, we give students time during each day (or week) to write in their journals. It is important to establish a clear purpose and audience for personal journals at the outset. They can either be used to help us understand each student's level of understanding or to give students an opportunity to respond to or reflect on the day's (or week's) learning.

When the purpose is to give the teacher insight into student level of understanding, we specify the topic and read what they have written to determine what instruction they need next. We may or may not comment in the journal, depending on what we decide to do with the information given. If only a few students exhibit a misunderstanding and a remark, question, or reminder will clear it up, we may choose to comment. If students' personal journals exhibit strong understanding, we may choose to note that. If, based on what we read, we decide to reteach, a comment may not be necessary.

On the other hand, when the writing is solely for the student's use—to question, track, or reflect—then if we read the journals we comment only at the invitation of the student.

Learning Logs

Learning logs ask students to keep ongoing written records of the following aspects of their studies:

- Achievement targets they have mastered
- Learning targets they have found useful and important
- Learning targets they are having difficulty mastering
- Learning experiences or instructional strategies that worked particularly well for them
- Learning experiences or instructional strategies that were confusing or difficult for them
- Processes they are trying, including problems and successes
- Questions that have come up along the way that they want help with
- Ideas for important study topics or learning strategies that they might like to try in the future

The goal in the case of learning logs is to have students reflect on, analyze, describe, and evaluate their learning experiences, successes, and challenges, communicating the conclusions they are in the process of drawing about the learning and about themselves as learners. This is the heart of assessment *for* learning as we describe it.

POSSIBLE SOURCES OF BIAS THAT CAN DISTORT RESULTS

There are several potential sources of bias that might distort the results of personal communication assessment. Some have to do with the quality of the ingredients that make up the assessment, while others can arise from the inherently subjective nature of the scoring process. We prevent the first kind of problem with careful development or selection of probes. We avoid the second through the development of high-quality scoring guides and careful preparation to apply them dependably.

Since personal communication overlaps with performance assessment, when assessing oral skills such as group discussion skills and second-language fluency, this method can fall prey to the same sorts of problems as performance assessment—tasks that don't elicit the needed performance, poor or nonexistent performance criteria and rubrics, and lack of consistency in using rubrics.

Also, because personal communication overlaps with selected response and written response assessment, when focused on knowledge and reasoning targets, it can fall into the same traps, such as unclear questions, poor or nonexistent scoring guides and rubrics, lack of the English skills needed to demonstrate learning, and questions that don't make clear the knowledge to be brought to bear, the kind of reasoning to use, or the standards to be used in evaluating responses.

Adhering to standards of assessment quality for selected response, written response, and performance assessment will help minimize or avoid these sources of bias (Figure 8.5).

FIGURE 8.5 Sources of Bias with Personal Communication

Problems with the context

Insufficient wait time
Students not understanding what to do with wait time
Lack of student's English language skills

Problems with the question or task

Questions are not aligned with the intended learning
Unclear questions
Unclear directions
Unclear expectations
Task doesn't elicit the intended performance
Task is poorly constructed

Problems with interpreting levels of student performance

Poor or nonexistent scoring guides and rubrics
Lack of consistency in using scoring rubrics

Problems with using the information

Insufficient sample size to support intended use
Lack of accurate and efficient record-keeping system

Reminder of Problems and Solutions

Here are some of the problems that can arise from the subjectivity of personal communication methods.

Problem: Trying to remember everything without writing it down is a recipe for mismeasurement if there is an extended time between assessment and ultimate evaluation as in the case of report card grading.

Solution: Keeping good written records is essential if you are planning to use the information beyond the immediate context.

Problem: Unconscious personal and professional filters, developed over years of experience, through which we hear and process student responses also can contribute to mismeasurement. We develop such filters as efficient ways to process large quantities of information, but sometimes they backfire. For example, if we have come to expect excellent work from a student, we might overlook a lapse in understanding by inferring that the student actually had the understanding but unintentionally left the information out of an explanation. These same filters may cause us to provide more clues to some students than to others without realizing it, thereby causing the assessment task to vary in level of difficulty unintentionally.

Solution: A good scoring rubric and attention to record keeping can help overcome these problems.

Problem: Unexamined stereotypes might come into play, distorting results. If we're not expecting a person to be good at spatial reasoning, we might underrate what we actually hear. If a student appears defiant, we might unintentionally shade our judgment of the quality of the student's contribution to a group discussion.

Solution: A good scoring rubric and attention to record keeping can help overcome these problems.

Problem: Group discussion can also fall prey to sources of bias due to student characteristics. A quiet person who knows the material might be too uncomfortable or otherwise unwilling to speak up in a group. If the goal of the discussion is to assess understanding of the material, we may make an incorrect inference about that student's level of achievement.

Solution: Keep in mind that the public display of achievement or lack thereof is risky for some students. Provide those students with other, more private means of demonstrating their level of achievement if you are unable to get accurate achievement information in a group discussion context.

Problem: Assessing achievement during a group discussion can result in inaccurate results due to inadequacies in sampling. Even though we are observing the group, we might miss a student's finest moment or not see typical performance because there are too many students to watch or too many things to watch for. Or the discussion time may be too limited, rendering our sample too small to make a good inference about student achievement.

Solution: We must attend carefully to sampling issues when planning to use data obtained from observation of group discussion.

Summary

Personal communication assessment is an efficient and effective way to both gather information about students to plan your next instructional steps, and to involve students in their own assessment. Personal communication can be used to collect information about knowledge, reasoning, and level of certain skills such as ability to speak a foreign language.

There are several different ways to collect information through interpersonal communication—instructional questions and answers, conferences and interviews, classroom discussions, oral examinations, and journals and logs. Some of these are oral and some are written.

Personal communication forms of assessment must adhere to standards of sound assessment practice. Teachers must base them on a clear idea of which learning targets are to be the focus, have a clear purpose for gathering the information, and attend to possible sources of bias that could lead to misinterpretation of student learning.

As with other forms of assessment, personal communication can be used as a platform for formative assessment and student involvement. Because of the similarities between short oral answers and selected response written questions, extended oral responses and extended written response, and personal communication and performance assessment, strategies for student involvement outlined in Chapters 5, 6, and 7 can also be used with personal communication. In this chapter we provided activities to involve students in the oral questioning of each other, using journal icons to deepen thinking, and using a group discussion rubric to promote better group discussions.

CHAPTER 8 ACTIVITIES

End-of-chapter activities are intended to help you master the chapter's learning targets. They are designed to deepen your understanding of the chapter content, provide discussion topics for learning team meetings, and guide implementation of the practices taught in the chapter.

Forms for completing each activity appear in editable Microsoft Word format in the Chapter 8 CD file. Documents on the CD are marked with this symbol:

Chapter 8 Learning Targets

At the end of Chapter 8, you will know how to do the following:

1. Frame questions to be used diagnostically to inform instruction.
2. Use questioning strategies to deepen students' understanding and reasoning proficiencies.
3. Structure class discussions for formative and summative use.
4. Conduct conferences, interviews, and oral examinations to obtain accurate information about student achievement.
5. Use student journals and logs as assessment *for* learning tools.

Activity 8.1 Keep a Reflective Journal
Activity 8.2 Frame Diagnostic Questions
Activity 8.3 Use Questioning Strategies to Deepen Understanding
Activity 8.4 Develop and Use a Class Discussion Rubric
Activity 8.5 Conduct a Line-up Discussion
Activity 8.6 Develop Oral Examination Questions
Activity 8.7 Use Journals or Logs in the Classroom
Activity 8.8 Reflect on Your Own Learning
Activity 8.9 Select Portfolio Artifacts

Activity 8.1

Keep a Reflective Journal

Keep a record of your thoughts, questions, and any implementation activities you tried while reading Chapter 8.

Reflective Journal Form

Activity 8.2

Frame Diagnostic Questions

Work independently, with a partner, or with a team to carry out the following activity.

1. After reading the section titled "Personal Communication Options: Instructional Questions and Answers," select a learning target or cluster of learning targets that you will be teaching shortly.
2. Think of (or discuss with your team) misunderstandings and misconceptions students typically begin with when studying this learning target. List them.
3. Create several questions you could ask to determine students' preexisting knowledge and uncover misconceptions.
4. Use the guidelines for item quality in Chapters 5 and 6 as needed to refine the questions.
5. Plan lesson options to address the misconceptions, as needed.
6. Ask the questions during the course of instruction using the suggestions offered for sampling and wait time. Note which ones gave you the most usable information and which ones were less productive.
7. Discuss the results with your learning team. Revise the questions that weren't productive and keep them for future use.

Frame Diagnostic Questions

Activity 8.3

Use Instructional Questions to Deepen Understanding

Work independently, with a partner, or with a team to carry out the following activity.

1. After reading the sections titled "Developing Questions to Assess Reasoning" and "Suggestions for Effective Formative Use of Instructional Questions," select a learning target or cluster of learning targets that you will be teaching shortly.
2. Make a checklist of the questioning strategies you want to practice in the classroom. Consider use of wait time and other ways to maximize student participation as well as the suggestions from the sections "Developing Questions to Assess Reasoning" and "Suggestions for Effective Formative Use of Instructional Questions."
3. Working with a partner, videotape or watch each other while you practice using the strategies on your checklist in the classroom. Analyze the videotapes or your notes for instances of successful use. Also note any improvements you would like to make.
4. Repeat the process as time allows.
5. This activity can be expanded to include students as questioners and as observers and evaluators of questioning strategies, if appropriate to your learning targets.
6. Reflect individually, with a partner, or with your team. What effect did the questioning strategies have on your instruction? What effects did you notice on student engagement and learning?

 Use Instructional Questions to Deepen Understanding

Activity 8.4

Develop and Use a Class Discussion Rubric

This activity has two parts—the development of a suitable rubric and the effective use of the rubric with students. Work with a partner or with a team to carry out the activity.

Part A: Developing the Rubric

1. Gather samples of class discussion checklists and rubrics you have used or are familiar with. One example, "Seminar Discussion Rubric," is offered on the Chapter 8 CD file.
2. To ensure that the rubric you develop meets standards of quality, follow the instructions for rubric development given in Chapter 7.
3. Evaluate your rubric with the Rubric for Rubrics (see Figure 7.10). Make any revisions needed.

Part B: Teaching with the Rubric

1. Introduce the rubric to students by following the protocol explained in Strategy 1 of the Seven Strategies of Assessment *for* Learning in Chapter 7.
2. Let students engage in a practice discussion in small groups. Offer them individual feedback with the rubric, as needed (a variation of Strategy 3 explained in Chapter 7). As appropriate, let students give each other feedback in partners, as well.
3. Videotape groups of students engaged in a discussion. Let them view the tape to self-assess and set goals for improvement (a variation of Strategy 4 explained in Chapter 7).
4. Discuss the impact of these strategies with your partner or team. What effects did you notice on student motivation and achievement? What were the effects on your instruction? What was difficult for students? What would you do differently next time?

Seminar Discussion Rubric

Rubric Development Template

Rubric for Rubrics

Rubric Evaluation Form

Debrief Use of Class Discussion Rubric

Activity 8.5

Conduct a Line-up Discussion

After reading the description of a "line-up" discussion in For Example 8.1, work independently, with a partner, or with a team to plan and conduct a line-up with your students.

Prepare

1. Review the learning targets in your curriculum that call for this type of reasoning or discussion skill. Identify the learning target(s) that will be the focus of the activity.
2. Select a context suited to students' exploration of multiple perspectives.
3. Generate several options for your "line-up" statement. These are statements that a reasonable person could support or disagree with. Test them out with a partner or team, if possible. Can you think of good arguments for both sides? Select the one that provides the richest discussion fodder. Write it on a piece of construction paper in big enough letters to be read from across the room.
4. Make a "Yes" sign and a "No" sign (or "Agree" and "Disagree" signs).
5. Plan for how you will debrief the activity. Make sure the debriefing process brings attention back to the intended learning that caused you to conduct the line-up. Also plan for any followup assignments you may wish to give to capitalize on the thought generated during the activity.
6. Clear a space in your room big enough to accommodate the students in your class standing in two rows facing each other. Remember that for a number of statements the class will divide unevenly. If you anticipate a grossly uneven division, consider numbering the students by twos and assigning them involuntarily to the "yes" and "no" lines. This helps those who are in the "wrong" line think of counterarguments to their own position.
7. Post the "line-up" statement on a wall centered in the cleared space. Post the "Yes" and "No" signs three to five feet on either side of the line-up statement.

Conduct

8. Explain to students the purpose of the line-up, the intended learning, and the directions.
9. Have students line up and share reasons that support the position of their line.
10. Make sure you don't reinforce or contradict anyone's comments. Speak only to re-establish the rules. When students attempt to convince you, rather than their peers, nonverbally direct them to talk to "the line."

Debrief

11. Have students form small groups and discuss what they thought were the strongest arguments for and against the line-up statement. Then have them

engage in an activity that connects the discussion to the intended learning. Last, you may want to give them an assignment directed at the learning target that applies the thoughts they generated during the line-up.

12. Discuss the classroom experience with a partner or a team. What learning target was the focus of the line-up activity? What question did you use? How did the question work? What were the students' responses to the activity? Did it deepen thought and broaden engagement? What did you do with students to debrief it? Would you make changes to the question, the protocol, or the debriefing process as a result of this experience? Would you do it another time with a different question? What learning targets will these discussions address?

Student Directions for the Line-up

Activity 8.6

Develop Oral Examination Questions

Work independently, with a partner, or with a team to carry out the following activity.

1. After reading the section titled "Personal Communication Options: Oral Examinations," select a learning target or cluster of learning targets that is suited to assessment via oral examination.
2. Determine whether you will use the information generated from the examination formatively or summatively.
3. Create a test blueprint using one of the two forms explained in Chapter 4 (or a version of one of them).
4. Use the assessment development guidelines from Chapters 5, 6, and/or 7 to create questions and/or prompts for your oral examination. Which chapter's information you use is determined by the kind of learning target(s) you will be assessing. If the oral examination will include answers that go beyond the range of right or wrong, also develop a scoring checklist or rubric as described in Chapters 6 and 7.
5. Determine how you will record your judgments of student achievement. Plan for how you will share the results with students.
6. Administer the assessment, attending to relevant sources of bias.
7. Keep track of any problems you noticed with the assessment itself, problems students had in responding, or problems with recording and communicating results.
8. Debrief the assessment experience with a partner or with your team. Were the results of the oral examination to be used formatively or summatively? What learning targets were the focus of the examination? What questions did you ask? How did you evaluate responses? What records did you keep? What worked well? What would you revise for future use?

Test Blueprint Form A

Template for Oral Examination Questions and Scoring Guides

Test Blueprint Form B

Debrief the Oral Examination

Activity 8.7

Use Journals or Logs in the Classroom

Work independently, with a partner, or with a team to carry out the following activity.

1. After reading the section titled "Personal Communication Options: Journals and Logs," select a learning target or a collection of learning targets, such as those from a unit of study as the focus for the journal or log.
2. Determine your rationale for asking students to keep a journal or log.
3. Determine which written communication format is best suited to your students, your intended use of the communication, and the learning target(s): response journals, dialogue journals, personal journals, or learning logs. (For descriptions of each format, refer to Figure 8.4.)
4. Read through Chapter 11 to get a sense of the options for prompts and instructions you might give to students for their entries.
5. Think about how much individuality, freedom, and choice students might be able to exercise and still accomplish the desired outcome of journal or log keeping. Build in as much student ownership in as the learning targets and your goals for doing this allow.
6. Decide what form their journals or logs will take—notebook, spiral-bound booklet, personally created booklet, folder of loose pages, computer file, other? Assemble any materials needed.
7. Estimate how often students will be asked to make entries. Determine who will respond and approximately how often. Possible audiences are you, other students, and parents as well, again depending on the intent of the communication.
8. Write the instructions you will give to students to guide their entries. Include the following:
    - The intended learning targets and the rationale for keeping a journal or log
    - The types of entries you will ask them to make and how often
    - Who will read them and how often
    - How you and other readers will respond
    - What you will do with the information they share
    - Any other guidance your students will need to maximize their success at this communication project
9. At the conclusion of the journal/log project, reflect on its impact on student learning. What did you notice happening with students as a result? What information did this type of personal communication give you that you might otherwise not have had? What worked well for you? What would you change? Make a note of these insights for future use if you intend to use journals or logs again.

 Decisions about Using Journals or Logs

 Debrief Use of Journals or Logs in the Classroom

Activity 8.8

Reflect on Your Own Learning

Review the Chapter 8 learning targets and select one or more that represented new learning for you or struck you as most significant from this chapter. If you are working individually, write a short reflection that captures your current understanding. If you are working with a partner or a team, either discuss what you have written or use this as a discussion prompt for a team meeting.

 Reflect on Chapter 8 Learning

Activity 8.9

Select Portfolio Artifacts

Any of the activities from this chapter can be used as portfolio entries. Select activities you have completed or artifacts you have created that will illustrate your competence at the Chapter 8 learning targets:

1. Frame questions to be used diagnostically to inform instruction.
2. Use questioning strategies to deepen students' understanding and reasoning proficiencies.
3. Structure class discussions for formative and summative use.
4. Conduct conferences, interviews, and oral exams to obtain accurate information about student achievement.
5. Use student journals and logs as assessment *for* learning tools.

If you are keeping a reflective journal, you may want to include Chapter 8's entry in your portfolio.

Chapter 8 Portfolio Entry Cover Sheet

CHAPTER

9

Record Keeping: Tracking Student Learning

I'm doomed in this class. All of my mistakes count against me.

—CLAIRE, 9TH-GRADE STUDENT

In a class where everything students produce—homework, practice activities, projects, papers, labs, quizzes, and tests—results in a score that contributes to the final grade, all assessments become summative assessments *of* learning, with associated motivational effects, whether or not we have intended them to be. Claire's worry—that nothing is for practice, that all work counts toward the grade—may or may not be an accurate read of the teacher's plan, but it does point to the importance of giving students opportunities to improve before the graded event, a hallmark of effective formative assessment. It also points to the importance of including students in the record-keeping process, to help them notice their growth over time and keep them engaged in trying.

If you have been using assessment information formatively, you may have found yourself rethinking traditional record-keeping practices. You may also have wrestled with the question of what formative assessment information to keep track of. Formative assessment information comes in many forms: it can include practice work and any other evidence of student achievement used diagnostically to inform your instructional decisions, but it can also include assessment information used as feedback to students to inform their own decisions about next steps to take. In addition, students may be using assessment information to self-assess and set goals. All of these activities require access to organized assessment information, some of which it makes sense for the teacher to track and some of which it makes more sense for the student to track.

You may have also noticed that traditional record-keeping practices used for summative information are not always a good fit for the more focused reporting

FIGURE 9.1 Keys to Quality Classroom Assessment

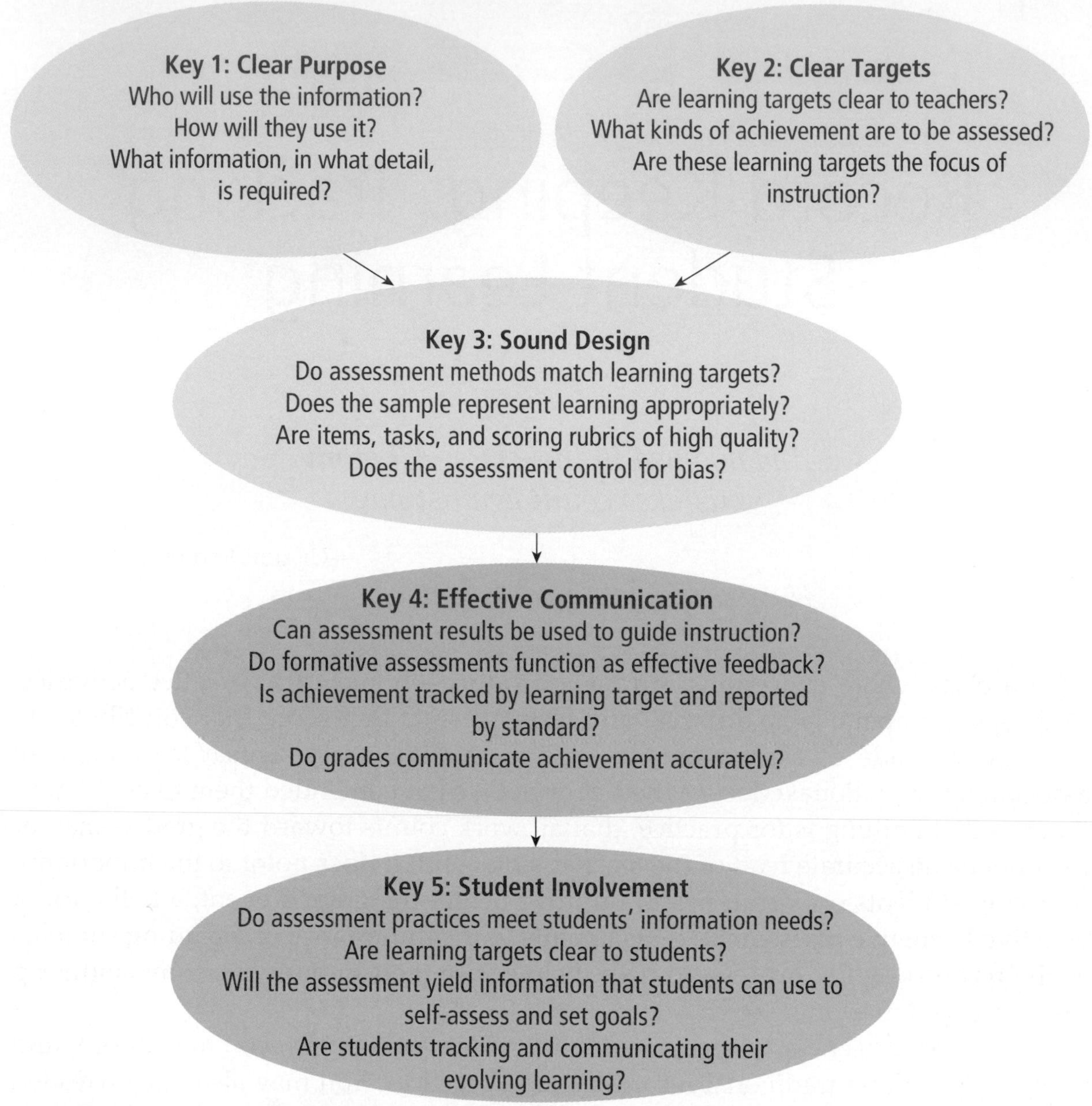

Key 1: Clear Purpose
Who will use the information?
How will they use it?
What information, in what detail, is required?

Key 2: Clear Targets
Are learning targets clear to teachers?
What kinds of achievement are to be assessed?
Are these learning targets the focus of instruction?

Key 3: Sound Design
Do assessment methods match learning targets?
Does the sample represent learning appropriately?
Are items, tasks, and scoring rubrics of high quality?
Does the assessment control for bias?

Key 4: Effective Communication
Can assessment results be used to guide instruction?
Do formative assessments function as effective feedback?
Is achievement tracked by learning target and reported by standard?
Do grades communicate achievement accurately?

Key 5: Student Involvement
Do assessment practices meet students' information needs?
Are learning targets clear to students?
Will the assessment yield information that students can use to self-assess and set goals?
Are students tracking and communicating their evolving learning?

needs of the standards-based classroom. Many grade reports now are organized by content standard clusters—the old way of recording grades on individual assignments makes it very difficult to fill in the categories. With an outdated record-keeping system, completing standards-based report cards is a lot like fitting a square peg into a round hole.

In this chapter, we will offer guidelines for tracking both formative and summative information so each can easily be used for its intended purposes, guidelines that lay the foundation for increased student achievement as well as sound grading and reporting practices.

Chapter 9 Learning Targets

At the end of Chapter 9, you will know how to do the following:

- Separate formative from summative assessment information
- Identify which formative assessment information to track
- Select one or more physical locations for the information
- Set up labels and categories to represent the learning assessed
- Identify what work habits and social skills to track; track them separately from achievement information
- Record achievement information by raw score
- Create a system for students to keep track of their own learning

PRELIMINARY DECISIONS

Tracking formative and summative information involves several preliminary decisions that are at your discretion. Of all of the kinds of evidence that students give you each day, which will be used formatively? Which will be used summatively? Of the formative evidence, what do you need or want to keep track of? Where, physically, will you keep the information? Will students also be involved in tracking their progress? Of the summative evidence, what will figure into the grade? What evidence will be reported separately? Figure 9.2 provides an example of the kinds of information we typically gather, sorted into categories for tracking purposes.

Differentiating Information for Formative or Summative Use

First, let's review sources of evidence of student achievement. In the "methods" chapters (Chapters 5 through 8), we have discussed how to create and use selected response assessments, written response assessments, performance assessments, and personal communication modes of assessment. Even though these are described as *assessment* methods, their use is not limited to testing. They can be used to generate diagnostic information or to provide practice experiences. They can take the form of questions, discussions, exercises, problems, teaching tasks, quizzes, projects, and performances. So, when we refer to *evidence of student achievement*, we can be referring to information coming from any of these sources, regardless of intended use of the resulting information. In this chapter, we will use the term *assessment events* to describe them all.

When you plan a unit or module of instruction, you will plan for some assessment events that you and/or your students will use *formatively*, during the learning, to decide what comes next in that learning. Recall that this is part of the planning

FIGURE 9.2 Deciding What to Keep Track of, What to Report, and How to Report It

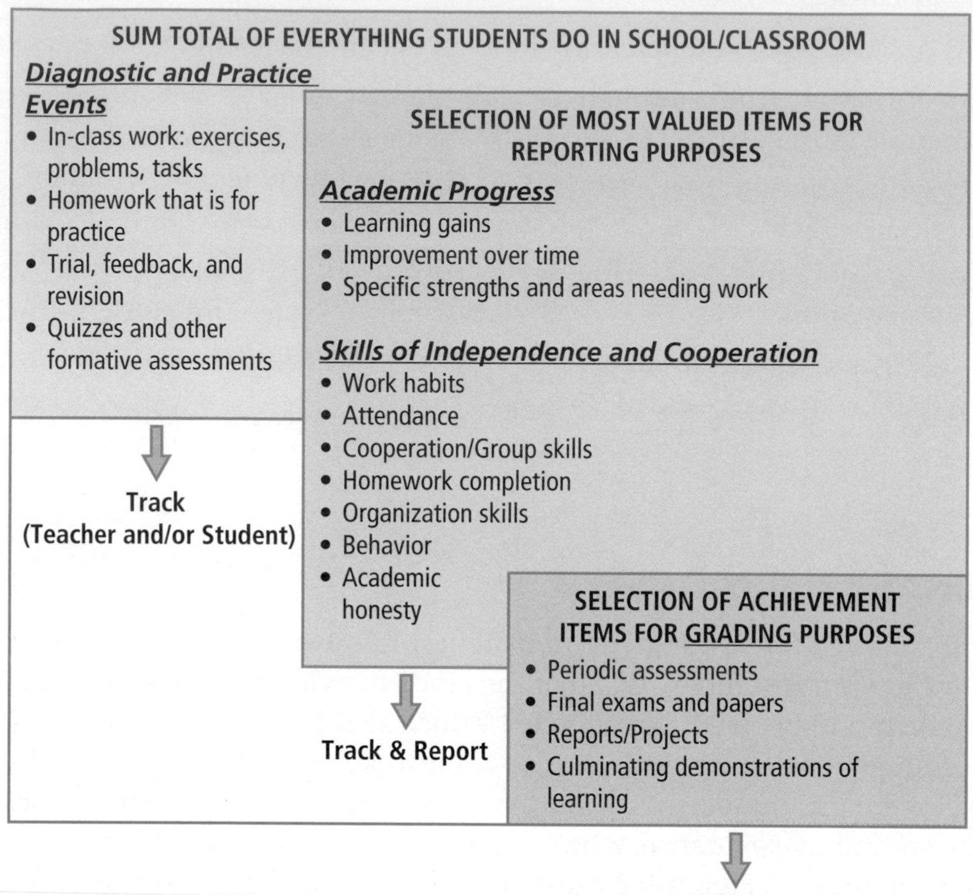

Source: Adapted from Ken O'Connor, unpublished workshop materials, 2001. Adapted by permission.

stage of assessment design described in Chapter 4. Formative assessment events can look like any of the following:

- Work students do for practice
- Evidence of current status of learning or understanding collected with the intent of grouping students for instruction and/or reteaching
- Work students turn in for feedback from you or from other students
- Evidence students use for self-assessment and goal setting (determining what they have mastered and what they still need to work on)

You will plan other assessment events to be used *summatively* during or at the end of a unit or module, *after* the learning is to have taken place, to report out level of achievement. This information usually takes the form of a summary number, symbol, phrase, or grade.

So your first decision in preparing to track student learning is what of the assessment information you gather will be used formatively, and what will be used summatively. For Example 9.1 shows a student tracking form created by 7th-grade language arts teacher Elizabeth Schroeder that clearly divides the formative and summative events for a unit of instruction.

For Example 9.1

Who Am I? Tracking Sheet

Who Am I? Tracking Sheet

Name ______________________________ Class Period # ______________
7th Grade Reading/Mrs. Schroeder Grading Period: 2nd Trimester

ALL learning is standards based—Begin with a goal and then practice, practice, practice until you are proficient. The formative work assigned to you is the "practice" towards the mastery of the standard. It may take a few times before you are ready, but you need to be prepared before testing on your goal. You need to feel confident about what you know! Although you are not given a grade for the practice work, you must correctly complete each assignment before you can take the summative. As each formative is completed, you and I will update this form to track your progress. Please place ALL work behind your tracking sheet in your binder. Work hard! I know you can do this!

READING PROCESS:

________ **1.** 7.LA.1.8.2 I can clarify word meanings by using definitions, examples, graphic features, and the use of denotative and connotative meanings.

Formative Assessment: ______ Mischief Mouse/ Denotative, Connotative w/exit ticket

Formative Assessment: ______ NFL Worksheet for Denotative, Connotative

Formative Assessment: ______ Bloom's Vocabulary Cards: Denotative/ Connotative, Fact/Opinion, Compare/ Contrast, Autobiography/Biography

READING COMPREHENSION:

________ **2.** 7.LA.2.1.3 I can draw conclusions and form opinions based on information that I get from the text and I can prove what I know by showing evidence from the passage.

Formative Assessment: Fact and Opinion Contract (Bloom's shapes)
_____Circle _____Octagon _____ Square

________ **3.** 7.LA.2.2.1 I can analyze expository text to broaden my comprehension by comparing and contrasting ideas from the passage.

Formative Assessment: _____ Compare and contrast Barrio Boy and Names/Nombres

Formative Assessment: _____ Practice recognizing similarities and differences in reading passages

________ **4.** 7.LA.2.3.1 I can read and respond to literature from a variety of genres

Formative Assessment: _____ Autobiography writing assignment

Formative Assessment: _____ Practice recognizing Autobiography clues in reading passages

________ **5. SUMMATIVE ASSESSMENT:**

7.LA.1.8.2 I can clarify word meanings by using definitions, examples, graphic features, and the use of denotative and connotative meanings.

_______ / 25 pts.

7.LA.2.1.3 I can draw conclusions and form opinions based on information that I get from the text and I can prove what I know by showing evidence from the passage.

_______ / 25 pts.

7.LA.2.2.1 I can analyze expository text to broaden my comprehension by comparing and contrasting ideas from the passage.

_______ / 25 pts.

7.LA.2.3.1 I can read and respond to literature from a variety of genres.

_______ / 25 pts.

Source: Used with permission from Elizabeth Schroeder, unpublished classroom materials, Jerome School District, Jerome, ID, 2011.

Second, determine what formative assessment information to keep track of. You will be able to use much of the formative information you gather, such as answers to instructional questions or in-class practice exercises, to make the necessary instructional decisions without writing anything down. Other information, such as results from formative quizzes, is useful in monitoring student progress or determining instructional groups for reteaching and therefore it would be helpful to have it as a part of a written record. So your second decision is what types of formative assessment information it makes sense to record.

Third, begin thinking about what information *students* would benefit from tracking. The more involved students are in keeping track of achievement, the more in touch they are with their own progress, which has positive motivational benefits. "How'm I doing?" ought to be a question they can answer themselves at any point in their learning. On the formative side, it may be more beneficial for them to keep records of feedback, self-assessment, and goal-setting information than it would be for you to track those things separately. When their records are available to you, you still have access to the information. So, as your third decision, consider what formative and summative assessment information it makes sense for students to record.

My Classroom Then and Now 9.1

Sierra Swanson

I used to . . .

In past years of my teaching I have always had the day's learning target posted somewhere in my room. I would go over it at the beginning and sometimes the end of my lesson so all students knew exactly what it is we were learning for the day. I didn't put too much emphasis on the targets and I did not really focus much attention on students' understandings of the targets. I would tell everyone what the target was, then continue on with my lesson. I never used the students' understandings of those targets to change the pace of my lesson or the whole unit.

Now I . . .

This year I have been passing out an organized list of the learning targets that each student can use to track their understanding. The list has four columns. The first is the target, then the next three are for the student to rank where they feel about their understanding of that target. We put the date in the boxes so students can see how much they learned over the course of the unit. When the student feels that they have a good understanding of the topic, they can bring their checklist to me and I give them a learning link with a problem for them to demonstrate their understanding. When they get that correct, they can put their name on the link and add it to the class learning chain.

Why I changed . . .

I tried the new method for a couple of reasons. First, I feel that it allows everyone to see where their understanding is of the topics at any time. It can also show them how much they have learned over the unit, by how they have moved columns over time. It helps the students see the pace of the whole unit and keep track of what we have already done, and what we are still planning on doing. Students can also look at their objective list to see what topics they may want to get more help on or practice more before a test or a quiz to help maximize their study time. On top of the benefits for students, it also is a quick and easy way for me to track where students are. We have it on our desks every day so I can walk around and see who feels they have it and which students may need more one on one time to help master the content. It is a quick spot check for me to see how to differentiate a lesson to help all students achieve.

What I notice as a result . . .

I have noticed that my students are taking more responsibility for their work in class and have an overall better understanding of what we are doing and where we are going with the content. I as the teacher find it easier to differentiate and monitor to help all students at their levels.

Source: Used with permission from Sierra Swanson, 4th-grade science and mathematics teacher, Olmsted Falls School District, Olmstead Falls, OH, 2011.

WHEN ASSESSMENTS *FOR* AND *OF* LEARNING OVERLAP. We can plan assessments *for* and *of* learning so formative assessment information is never used summatively and summative assessment information is never used formatively. Or, under certain circumstances, we can and should use for one purpose assessments originally intended for the other.

When we design separate assessments *for* and *of* learning, we can structure some assessments to fulfill one or more formative uses: practice, diagnosis, feedback, or self-assessment; and others to contribute to a summative judgment of level of achievement, such as a chapter or unit test, a midterm examination, or a culminating performance or project. In this case we designate some of the work students do as formative and identify which formative use each will fulfill (as described in the Assessment Planning Cycle in Chapter 4). We designate other assessments to function summatively, using the information they generate to document levels of individual student achievement for reporting purposes. Summative assessments may be planned so that each one covers a different set of learning targets, with the final grade calculated by combining information across assessments. Or periodic summative assessments may be planned so that later tests include learning targets from earlier assessments. If students demonstrate a higher level of mastery of earlier concepts, summative judgments of level of achievement can be updated. The advantage here is that the more current information can and should replace the out-of-date information.

Sometimes complete separation of assessments *for* and *of* learning isn't necessary or practical. For example, in English language arts classes, where students engage in the writing process (prewriting, drafting, revising, editing, and publishing), students may prepare several drafts of a piece of writing. The earlier drafts are used formatively—teachers and/or other students provide feedback and students act on it to revise their writing. They may also self-assess their later drafts using a scoring rubric. With each revision, the goal is to practice and improve. At some point, students may turn a final draft as evidence of their level of achievement in writing, to be graded (the publishing stage of the writing process). In this instance, the same assignment has been used first formatively, perhaps several times as the work moves through multiple drafts, and then summatively when it becomes a final draft.

Or teachers (and sometimes students) might select from a collection of work those pieces that provide the best evidence to be used summatively to determine level of achievement. For example, in the primary grades, some school districts use developmental continua for assessing reading and writing learning targets. These continua track student achievement through a series of levels designed to span several grades. Each stage in each continuum is defined and illustrated with samples of student work. Teachers can select work at predetermined times during the school year to reflect each student's current level of achievement. This evidence can be used to report progress to parents and to summarize student standing for the district without requiring a separate summative assessment event.

Any learning target at any grade level where proficiency develops over time is a potential candidate for intentional movement from assessment *for* learning to assessment *of* learning. These include reasoning, skill, and product targets—e.g., problem solving or communication in mathematics, creating research reports, displaying data, giving oral presentations, planning and carrying out experiments, or playing a musical instrument. Reasoning, skill, and product targets tend to be taught throughout content units; they generally require repeated opportunities to practice with feedback in order to develop over time. In some of these instances we assign tasks that are repeated as formative and then summative assessment events.

On the flip side, as we have seen in Chapters 5 through 8, summative assessments can and should sometimes be used formatively. When students analyze the results of a summative test to see which targets they have mastered and which they haven't, and then are provided an opportunity to retest and receive credit for their higher level of achievement, we are using a test whose primary purpose is assessment *of* learning as an instance of assessment *for* learning, thereby *increasing what students have learned.* Or, when we plan a test as a summative event and notice from the results that many students had difficulty with one or more learning targets, we might decide to reteach and retest those targets. This is another instance of an assessment *of* learning being used as assessment *for* learning, again increasing what students have learned.

Figure 9.3 shows a form you can use plan for both formative and summative assessment events throughout a unit or module of study.

FIGURE 9.3 Formative and Summative Assessment Plan

Chapter/Topic(s)/Unit of Study: ______________________________

Time Frame: ______________________________

Learning Target	Assignments & Assessments		
	Date	Type	Description

Type:
S = Summative
FC = Check for learning (formative)
P = Practice (formative)
O = Other (formative)

DECIDING WHERE YOU WILL KEEP THE INFORMATION

Historically, our tracking system has taken the form of a *gradebook*, whether we keep it in hard copy or electronically. That is a bit of a misnomer these days, because we need to record information beyond summative grades. When we broaden the uses of assessment information to include formative applications, we may also need to consider different record book options.

The first choice is the physical location(s) for your evidence—on paper or in a computer program. Will you write information by hand in a gradebook? Will you keep records by hand on a form you design yourself? Will you design a record-keeping system on your computer? Will you use a commercially developed electronic gradebook program? Will you use some combination of these options or something else?

To help you decide, remember that you will need to be able to differentiate formative and summative data. Hardcopy options include the following:

- Formative and summative data clearly labeled and recorded together
- Formative and summative data recorded separately

Figures 9.4 and 9.5 show examples of formative and summative data recorded together. In Figure 9.4, each column is marked either "F" for "formative" or "S" for "summative." There is also a column marked "test" for data from a cumulative assessment following each mathematics strand. Some teachers prefer a less formal system for differentiating entries—they enter formative data in pencil and summative data in pen or devise some other color or marking code.

Figure 9.5 shows an English language arts example where students are assigned three writing tasks for the quarter, each of which goes through two revisions with feedback and one edit with feedback before being evaluated for a grade. Each writing assignment begins as a formative assessment and ends as a summative assessment. In this example, for the two criteria of *Ideas and Content* and *Organization*, the formative data for each assignment is labeled as "draft" and the summative data is labeled as "final." For the criterion of *Conventions*, the formative data is labeled as "edit" and the summative data is labeled as "final."

You can also keep the data in separate sections on the same page, on different pages of the record book, or in different books. Figure 9.6 shows an example of formative and summative data recorded separately on the same page, where all entries except those labeled "Test" are formative.

Electronic options may be limited by the program you are using but most will allow you to create separate categories weighted differently, which you can use as "bins" for formative and summative data, as shown in Figure 9.7.

If you are keeping hardcopy records, you will also have the choice of how you organize each student's data. Some teachers, especially at the elementary level, like to have a separate page or section for each student, but for many teachers it makes most sense to have all students on the same page.

It is also possible to supplement records with collections of student work, which can provide more detailed assessment information to be used formatively or summatively. We describe ways to do this in Chapter 11.

In sorting through the options, although there is no one best choice, it is helpful to keep the rule *form follows function* in mind: how you want to use the information should drive your decision about how to organize it. For example, you may keep the summative information in an electronic gradebook because the final grade will be calculated from these electronic records, and record formative information by hand in a log because you want to be able to access it quickly and revise it while moving around the classroom.

FIGURE 9.4 Formative and Summative Data Recorded Together—Mathematics Example

	Number Sense					TEST	Measurement					TEST	Algebraic Sense					TEST	Solves Problems & Reasons					TEST	Communicates Reasoning					TEST
Learning Target #																														
Date																														
Task																														
F/S																														
Students																														
1.																														
2.																														
3.																														
4.																														
5.																														
6.																														
7.																														
8.																														
9.																														
10.																														
11.																														
12.																														
13.																														

F/S: F = Formative; S = Summative

Source: Adapted from the work of Ken O'Connor, Scarborough, Ontario. Personal communication, June 1, 2004. Adapted by permission.

FIGURE 9.5 Formative and Summative Data Recorded Together: Writing Example

Writing		Ideas and Content									Organization									Conventions					
Last	First	Draft 1	Draft 2	1. Final	Draft 1	Draft 2	2. Final	Draft 1	Draft 2	3. Final	Draft 1	Draft 2	1. Final	Draft 1	Draft 2	2. Final	Draft 1	Draft 2	3. Final	1. Edit	1. Final	2. Edit	2. Final	3. Edit	3. Final

FIGURE 9.6 Formative and Summative Data Recorded in Separate Sections: Reading Example

Reading		Applies Skills & Strategies to Read									Understands What Is Read									Test: Skills & Strategies			Test: Understands		
Assignment		1 Syn/Ant	2 Syn/Ant	3 Syn/Ant	4 Pre/Suf	5 Pre/Suf	6 Pre/Suf	7 Fluency	8 Fluency	9 Fluency	1 Inference	2 Inference	3 Inference	4 Summary	5 Summary	6 Summary	7 Comp/Cont	8 Comp/Cont	9 Comp/Cont	Syn/Ant	Pre/Suf	Fluency	Inference	Summary	Comp/Cont
Last	First																								

Source: Adapted from Kim Backlund, 2004, Jackson Park Elementary School, Central Kitsap School District, Silverdale, Washington. Adapted by permission.

FIGURE 9.7 Electronic Gradebook Page

PowerTeacher Gradebook: Mark Adams - Apple Grove High School 2

Scoresheet | Assignments | Student Info | Grade Setup | Class Content | Reports

Reporting Term: S2 Mode: Assignments | Final Grades | Student View

Anderson, Cody

Asmts | Terms | Cmnts | S2

Assignments (20)	Scores	MATH Danny's Numeri... NUM	Explains rea... Numeric Scale NUM	Collects, org... Danny's Num... NUM	Explores mu... Danny's Num... NUM	Recognizes ... Danny's Num... NUM	SCIENCE Elementary Rati... LTR	Understands... Elementary R... LTR
Classwork #1	Ta...	4						S
Letter Recognition: A-G	F	4						S
Letter Recognition: H-N	C-	4					Ex	
Project 1	A-	4					S	
Unit 1 - Quiz	B-	4		3	3	2		E
Classwork #2	✔	4	2	3	3			E
Learning Project	A	3	2	3		1		E
Review	Ex	3	2	3	3	1		S
Special Project		INC	2					
Unit 1 - Quiz 2	F	3	3	4	3	1		E
Test 10	INC	4	2	4				
Unit Test 11	A	4	2	4				
Unit Test	INC	4	2	4	3	1		E
Final Score - most recent - 3	B-	4	2	4	3	1	S	E
mean	C	3.7	2.3	2.8	2.8	1.2	S	E
weighted mean	C ..	3.7	2.4	2.9	2.7	1.2	S	E
median	B-	4	2	3	3	1	S	E
mode	B-	4	2		3	1	S	E
highest	A ..	4	4	4	4	2	S	E
most recent - 3	C ..	4	2	4	3	1	S	E
times assessed	8	15	15	13	11	9	1	8

Explains reasoning when problem solving
ID: W1.2.3
Grade Scale: Numeric Scale

Summary

points earned:82.5/100 percentage:82.500% grade:B-

NCS Pearson. (2007–2011). PowerTeacher 2.3 [computer software]. Minneapolis, MN: NCS Pearson.

RECORD-KEEPING GUIDELINES

After you have made initial decisions about what will be formative and what will be summative, where you want to keep the information, and what information students will track, you are ready to set up the tracking system. We suggest three record-keeping guidelines that apply to both formative and summative information to indicate the learning targets represented by your data and to maximize the usefulness of your entries:

1. Organize entries by learning target.
2. Track information about work habits and social skills separately.
3. Record achievement information by raw score, if practical.

Guideline 1: Organize Entries by Learning Represented

The first guideline governs the labels and categories in your recording system. When both instruction and assessments have focused on specific learning targets, it is an easy transition to record the resulting information according to the learning target being assessed. And when your report card format is standards based, recording data by learning target makes it easy to merge your data into that template. Organizing a record book this way also can help you track student progress by learning target, diagnose and remediate difficulties, and speak knowledgeably about the state of student learning during conferences.

Traditionally, we have categorized summative assessment information by the type of evidence—homework, quiz, lab, test, homework, and so on—rather than by the learning represented. With a system in place to differentiate formative from summative data, categories for types of evidence become less useful while categories that indicate the learning represented become more useful.

To use the results of assessments to provide descriptive feedback, to plan instruction, and to track student progress toward important content standards, we must organize the information by learning target or by target clusters. How much detail to record is up to you. What do you want to do with the information? With formative records, we generally benefit from capturing more detail rather than less about specific learning targets, whereas with summative records we can combine separate learning target information into the content standards they contribute to, or even into strands representing several content standards when our purpose is to report out an overall level of achievement.

For example, Figure 9.8 shows a record for a third-grade mathematics class. It is organized so that the entries are grouped by the individual learning targets this teacher is focusing on during the grading period. Each set of learning targets is identified by content strand. This example illustrates what this looks like for two content strands, *Number Sense* and *Computation*. This teacher's report card requires that students receive a grade for each content strand, so he will be able to aggregate the summative data for each learning target to calculate the grade. He will also be able to review the formative data to determine who needs further instruction and on what, prior to administering the summative assessment.

Figure 9.4 also shows data organized by strand. In this example, the specific learning targets addressed during the grading period are numbered and the record book identifies the learning target by its number. In Figure 9.5, the categories *Ideas and Content*, *Organization*, and *Conventions* represent learning target clusters. Each target cluster has an associated list of learning targets that also correspond to the rubric used to assess the learning targets. For example, *Ideas and Content* at the middle school level includes learning targets related to *focus* and *supporting details*. The rubric for *Ideas and Content* provides descriptive detail for each of these two learning targets at various levels of achievement, from high to low. So a rubric score could be used formatively because it is attached to a stable description representing each of these two learning targets. A teacher might want to separate those two learning targets and teach to them separately, in which case, she may want to revise this record book to allow for data entry on each of those two learning targets.

FIGURE 9.8 Records Arranged by Learning Target

Number Sense

Identifies place value to 10,000s	Reads whole numbers through 4 digits	Writes whole numbers through 4	Orders and compares whole numbers
Date Task F/S Student 1. 2. 3.			

Computation

	Addition	Subraction	Multiplication		Division		Uses calculator to + or -4 or more digits	Estimation skills
	+ with 3 or more digits	-with or more digits	Facts to 10	Fact families	Facts to 10	Fact families		
Date Task F/S Student 1. 2. 3.								

F/S: F = Formative; S = Summative

Source: Adapted from the work of Ken O'Connor, Scarborough, Ontario. Personal communication, June 1, 2004. Adapted by permission.

Figure 9.6 shows both content strands and individual learning targets. It uses shorthand for the learning targets. For example, *Syn/Ant* refers to the learning target "Identify synonyms and antonyms," *Pre/Suf* refers to the learning target "Identify the meanings of prefixes and suffixes," and *Fluency* refers to the learning target "Reads aloud with fluency." The content strands "Applies skills and strategies to read" and "Understands what is read" are two of the report card categories that this teacher will report on separately under the umbrella of "Reading."

Notice that in Figures 9.4 through 9.8 there is a place to keep track of the assignment, even though it is not the major organizer of information. In Figures 9.4

and 9.8, assignment information goes into the column labeled "Task." This is where you can record the page number or other identifying details about the specific assignment. In Figure 9.6, it is labeled "Assignment." In Figure 9.5, the writing assignments are numbered 1, 2, and 3 to indicate the writing assignment. Instead of numbering the assignments, you could name them if you wanted to and had the space.

Guideline 2: Track Information about Work Habits and Social Skills Separately

To use the summative information to calculate a standards-based grade, we will need to track information about achievement level separately from information about work habits and social skills. Student characteristics such as class participation, compliance with rules, academic honesty, attitude, neatness, timeliness of work turned in, attendance, cooperation with classmates, and level of classroom attention all contribute to learning. So it's fine to identify the work habits and social skills you want to track and report. If the categories you identify are broad, such as "effort" or "work habits," you will need to define the actions that underlie them. What do we mean by *effort*? Work turned in on time? Class participation? Neatness? Regular attendance? This work is best done as a team—department, grade level, school, or district—so that students experience consistency of stated expectations. And you will need to devise ways of assessing these things to provide dependable evidence for all students.

In that regard, all that we have said about the need for clear academic learning targets accurately assessed and reported applies to behavioral expectations as well as achievement. Remember that you must get an accurate and fair estimate for reporting purposes. This requires that you know what you are looking for, gather accurate evidence, track the same characteristics consistently over time, and that you transform (summarize) evidence appropriately for reporting. All students must know what characteristics contribute to that evaluation, as this helps them to be clear about the behaviors you expect, will be tracking, and will be reporting. Further, when there is a problem, the diagnosis can be specific, which helps in communicating the problem to students and parents and in devising a solution.

After you have defined these expectations, set up a system for tracking them that works for you, keeping in mind how you want to use the information. Keeping these valuable pieces of information separate facilitates instructional planning, diagnosing problems, communicating about them, and devising solutions to remedy them. If we don't record academic achievement separately from work habits and social skills, raising or lowering the grade stands as the only solution to a disparate range of learning problems. It is clear that the punishment and reward system grades have evolved into does not work to solve these problems for a whole host of students (see Stiggins & Chappuis, 2011).

EXTRA CREDIT WORK. Does extra credit work provide evidence of effort or achievement? Is it an avenue to a higher grade or a way to engage in and demonstrate further learning? When it is used as a means to raise a grade, often all that gets recorded is points for completion. When it is used as a way to engage in and demonstrate further learning, we evaluate the work and record the score in the same way that we evaluate and record any other evidence of achievement.

"Grades are broken when they do not accurately communicate achievement. The fix for this is to make grades as pure a measure as possible of student achievement: that is, make them reflect only *student performance in mastering the public, published learning goals . . ." (O'Connor, 2011, p. 16)*

Simply awarding completion points for extra credit work has two problems. First, the points may not represent evidence of achievement—they tend to be "effort" points. Even though we might hope the extra credit work takes the student further, without an evaluation of the quality of what the student submits, we have no way of knowing. Second, introducing "effort" points into the record of academic achievement will artificially inflate the grade when it comes time to calculate one (O'Connor, 2011), and it will no longer accurately represent level of achievement.

So do not use extra credit work to add "effort" points to the grade. Think of extra credit work as an opportunity for students to engage in and demonstrate further learning. Base any points awarded on the quality of the work as it relates to the learning targets students are in the process of mastering. When the work has caused an increase in learning, the points can function accurately as further evidence of achievement.

This assumes that the extra credit work relates directly to the learning targets students are working on. If it doesn't, as is the case when students earn extra credit for bringing in boxes of tissue, then there is no defensible basis for awarding points toward a grade for the "work."

MISSING OR LATE WORK AND CHEATING. What about the issues of poor work habits or academic dishonesty? How should that evidence be recorded? It is tempting to record a lowered grade or a zero when student work is accompanied with problems such as these. However, we advise for several reasons that you look for another way to track, correct, and/or punish such problems. First, lowered scores and zeroes are not accurate representations of the student's current level of achievement. Regardless of the other problems the student has, we should not take their evidence of learning away from them, either as a preventative measure or as a punishment. Second, it does not work to change the behavior of students who have made themselves indifferent to lowered grades. They are more willing to risk the consequences than to do the work, for a variety of reasons. Yet these are the very students who, if they would just do the work and learn from it, would be succeeding at higher levels because they would be learning more and not just because they would have more points. Third, lowering scores and assigning zeroes keeps us

No grade ever recovers fully from the effect of a zero, for whatever reason it is assigned.

from addressing the underlying problems. Especially at the secondary level, it can be difficult to take the time with any one student to understand why the work is not coming in or why they felt pressured to cheat. Yet, these students are developing behaviors that will not serve them well as adults and if we can identify the students and their problems while they are with us, we have a responsibility to retrain them within the system in more productive approaches to learning.

If we wish to provide solutions or consequences for unproductive behavior, those actions or punishments must take a form that does not distort the student's actual record of academic achievement. That record is too important for informing subsequent instructional decisions in a standards-driven environment to permit its distortion. We encourage you to work with your colleagues and your school to identify other solutions to and consequences for the problems for which lowered grades and zeroes have been the consequence in the past.

For example, a team of teachers from Orange Middle School in Lewis Center, Ohio, has created a "grade-free" way of dealing with late work—students fill out a sheet, shown in Example 9.2, and attach it to any late work. Non–grade-related solutions and consequences progress with the number of instances of late work. As team member Jessica Cynkar explains: "My team prints the sheets on brightly colored paper and we make students fill them out to submit late work. Students don't like filling the sheets out because it is a lot of work. I also have a record to talk to parents about (kids are typically pretty honest in their responses) when I have a concern or at conferences" (personal communication).

They report a significant decrease in missing or late work as a result.

Guideline 3: Record Achievement Information by Raw Score, if Practical

In Chapter 10, we will look at the procedure for converting achievement data into a summary grade. Until then, we retain the most options for accurate use of information if we keep raw scores—the number of points awarded in relation to the number possible; e.g., 4/5 or 32/38. Raw scores give instant access to the sample size. When we only record a percent or a summative mark, the detail is lost. For example, if a student gets 2 out of 3 points correct on an assignment, you could record it as 2/3, as 67 percent, or as a D. On a different task the student could get a score of 12 out of 18, which you could record as 12/18, as 67 percent, or as a D. If each of these tasks covers the same learning target, which provides the more stable estimate of student achievement? Having access to raw scores will also help with weighting decisions when combining information to calculate a final grade.

For Example 9.2

We Get It . . . You Were Busy

I (name)______________________________ am submitting "Absent" work and/or "Late" work for credit.

I understand that this slip is to accompany any work that is being turned in late and that I can use ONLY one (1) slip per assignment.

Today's date: __________________ I was absent on this date: __________________

Assignment title: __________________ Assignment due date: __________________

My assignment was late __________ days because:

- ❑ A hurricane snatched it from my hands.
- ❑ I was sooooo sick, I couldn't get out of bed.
- ❑ My dog/cat ate it.
- ❑ I was ____ and homework was not exactly the most important thing on my list of things to do that night.
- ❑ Other (please specify and be honest): ______________________________

  - *Upon returning to school following an absence, it is a student's responsibility to contact the teacher to request make-up work. The contact should be made on the day the student returns to school.*

This is my...

First Second.... Third....Fourth....Fifth....Sixth.... Seventh late assignment

(1st and 2nd) Student Signature: ____

(3rd, 4th, 5th, & 6th) Parent Signature ________________________ Date __________

(7th) Administrator's signature ____

In order to receive credit, you must turn in this form stapled to your completed assignment.

Source: From Jessica Cynkar, unpublished classroom materials, Olentangy Local School District, Lewis Center, OH, 2011. Reprinted by permission.

If we are recording rubric scores for summative use, it is essential to use the raw score. Accurately calculating a final grade from a mixture of rubric scores and other data requires that we record the rubric score in its original form. In Chapter 10, we will also look at how to convert rubric scores to grades once they are recorded.

When the intended use is formative, whether the information is number correct out of number possible, number of points earned out of number possible, a rubric score, or some other mark, a raw score gives more detail. This helps in planning instruction and in keeping track of progress on each achievement target.

Sometimes it is useful to have access to more than just a number—we may want to keep samples of student work in a working folder or portfolio. We discuss folder and portfolio options in Chapter 11. In the case of evidence gathered through personal communication, you may have created anecdotal records keyed to learning targets or standards of quality represented on a rubric, which you may also keep in a file on your computer or in a folder or notebook.

OPTIONS FOR STUDENT RECORD KEEPING

The benefits of student-involved record keeping far outweigh the initial effort it takes to get a system going. First, tracking their progress toward a learning target and identifying when they have mastered it helps students understand the impact of effort. Second, when students experience positive growth, the process of tracking itself can be motivating. Third, having a record of achievement at hand helps students engage in self-reflection activities and discuss their progress meaningfully with others.

These are prerequisites to student-involved record keeping:

- Assignments and assessments align directly with the intended learning target(s).
- Students know which learning target is represented by each piece of assignment or assessment information.
- The learning targets are clear to students.

Student tracking systems can take a number of forms. For example, students can record progress by assignment, as shown in Figure 9.9. In this example, the students write the following:

- Information to identify the assignment (e.g., page number, title, project name)
- Date of assignment
- Learning target or learning target number (referenced to a list)
- The score received (e.g., points earned/points possible)
- Whether the assignment was formative (for practice) or summative (for a mark or grade)
- Their strengths related to the learning target and areas for improvement or next steps related to the learning target

FIGURE 9.9 Students Tracking Progress by Assignment

Assignment	Date	Target	Score	F/S	★ (stairs)

Source: Adapted from *Seven Strategies of Assessment* for *Learning* (p. 153), by J. Chappuis, 2009, Upper Saddle River, NJ: Pearson Education. Adapted by permission.

In the "stars and stairs" column, students are copying or paraphrasing the feedback the teacher has offered or they are interpreting the evaluative information on the assignment to self-assess and set a target for further learning.

Or students can graph their results on both practice activities and tests. Figure 9.10 shows an example of a tracking form where students graph results on reading targets with both right/wrong data and rubric score data. Two of the learning targets, "Identifies synonyms and antonyms" and "Understands the meaning of prefixes and suffixes," are knowledge targets practiced and assessed with selected response questions. The third target, "Reads aloud with fluency," is a skill target practiced and assessed with a five-point rubric. In this example, students have three practice events for each learning target. The first two learning targets have 10 problems and the third learning target is awarded a maximum of 5 points, corresponding to the rubric score points. After each practice assignment, students graph their results by learning target. When they take the test, they also graph their results by learning target. This record enables students to notice where they are improving and where they are having difficulty. Rather than conclude she is not good at reading, a student is able to say, "I am good at synonyms and antonyms and at prefixes and suffixes, but I need to work on fluency."

Another tracking option is to have students record their scores as well as notes about strengths and areas needing work by learning target, as shown in Figure 9.11. This example is set up to be used with selected response or written response information. As with the other examples, information is organized by learning target, but with this form you may have a separate page or half-sheet for each learning target, especially if students are also collecting samples of their work for use in a portfolio. That way, they can collect their work samples by learning target and their records of achievement can also be grouped by learning target.

This last example, shown in Figure 9.12, is a variation from an activity described in Chapter 5, where students analyze their quiz or test results, identifying which problems they got right, which they got wrong due to a simple mistake, and which

FIGURE 9.10 Students Graphing Progress by Assignment

	PRACTICE									TEST		
	Synonym/Antonym			Prefix/Suffix			Oral Fluency					
	(Assignment)	(Assignment)	(Assignment)	(Assignment)	(Assignment)	(Assignment)	(Assignment)	(Assignment)	(Assignment)	Synonym/Antonym	Prefix/Suffix	Oral Fluency
10												
9												
8												
7												
6												
5												
4												
3												
2												
1												
Date												

Learning targets: I can identify synonyms and antonyms.
I can tell the meaning of prefixes and suffixes.
I can read aloud with fluency.

Source: Adapted from *Seven Strategies of Assessment* for *Learning* (p. 155), by J. Chappuis, 2009, Upper Saddle River, NJ: Pearson Education. Adapted by permission.

they got wrong because they don't yet understand it. Students then translate that information into a generalization about which learning targets they have mastered, which learning targets they need to keep focusing on, and which they need to fine tune. A record sheet such as this one can help them self-assess and set goals for continued learning and can become a part of a portfolio shared during a conference as well.

FIGURE 9.11 Students Tracking Progress by Learning Target

Learning Target	Date	What I did well	What I need to work on
1. I can explain the constitutional structure of our government.			
2. I can describe the processes that have been used to create, amend, and repeal laws.			

or

Learning Target 1: *I can explain the constitutional structure of our government.*				
Assignment	Date	Score	What I did well	What I need to work on

Learning Target 2: *I can describe the processes that have been used to create, amend and repeal laws.*				
Assignment	Date	Score	What I did well	What I need to work on

Source: Adapted from *Seven Strategies of Assessment* for *Learning* (p. 155), by J. Chappuis, 2009, Upper Saddle River, NJ: Pearson Education. Adapted by permission.

FIGURE 9.12 Students Tracking Quiz or Test Results

Assessment:

Date:

Learning targets I have mastered:
Learning targets I need to keep working on:
Mistakes I need to pay attention to:

My Classroom Then and Now 9.2

Elizabeth Schroeder

I used to . . .

First, I used to grade every piece of work that my students completed. I was of the mindset that work is not valued unless it is acknowledged . . . and I thought that acknowledgement was a letter grade. Second, I used to use what I call a "tracking sheet" that students could use to follow their progress on learning targets, formatives, and summative—an organizer to remind them of the goals, take part in their own learning, and give them a way to evaluate their own work and progress (see For Example 9.1). However, it was "hit or miss" with the tracking sheet and it was hard to keep it up to date and was eventually placed in their binder unfinished. Lastly, I used to let everyone take the summative test at the end of the unit, regardless of their completion or understanding of their practice work. This procedure resulted in many incomplete assignments and lower scores on the summative exam.

Now I . . .

I still acknowledge every piece of work that my students complete. However, I have developed a new way to look at standards, learning, and grading. I began educating students, parents, and ME that everything does not need to be given a letter grade. I now show formative work as "collected" in the grade book. I still check their assignments to make sure that they understand the learning goal before moving on; but I check student work with them, individually, giving them direct feedback—as they do the work and while it is fresh in their mind instead of by me on my sofa at home. The value is now my time instead of a grade.

The next thing I changed was the unit tracking sheet. I kept the main portions of the document to gauge their learning, tweaking a few words here and there; but the major change came in the use of the page. The students now refer to it every day, bringing it with them as we check their practice work. I make initials on the work they complete and then at the end of the summative exam they evaluate their progress, charting their course of work.

The last thing I changed was the requirements to take the summative exam. Previously, I would allow students to take the test if some of their formative work was not turned in. I had a certain day that it was scheduled and everybody took it. Now, I have a "test day", but only the students who have successfully completed the formative work are allowed to take it. If a student does not get to take the test that day, it is their responsibility to finish their practice work and then take the test on their own time.

Why I changed . . .

I knew the pieces were not working right. I learned a new way of making it happen as I envisioned it through reading the book *Classroom Assessment* for *Student Learning*.

What I notice as a result . . .

WOW! So many things to report as change! My students are more engaged in their learning. They enjoy showing me their work instead of placing it in a box for a grade. They put more effort in their practice, knowing that I will be reviewing it with them, and they enjoy the one-on-one attention. Secondly, I now have a tracking sheet that is used as a personal assessment piece, a quick look for a parent/conference meeting, and a gauge for standards-based learning. Lastly, my students WANT to complete their practice—because lack of effort or incomplete means NO GRADE in my class. And the biggest change has been the numbers of "incomplete work" to report. **It is now nonexistent.**

Source: Used with permission from Elizabeth Schroeder, 7th-grade English language arts teacher, Jerome School District, Jerome, ID, 2011.

Summary

Both assessments *for* and *of* learning play a crucial role in determining and communicating levels of student learning. We can develop a variety of protocols to maintain accurate records that allow us to use each source of information in the ways we intend.

We begin with preliminary decisions regarding which information will be used formatively and which will be used summatively, keeping in mind that sometimes the uses overlap. We decide what formative assessment information it makes sense to record. And we think about what formative assessment information students might keep track of.

Next we move to options for the physical location and layout of the information. This is where we keep in mind that *form follows function*: our choices should be guided by the intended use of the data. Options include hardcopy and electronic gradebooks, formative and summative data kept in the same or different places, students' information kept together or separate, and methods for differentiating formative from summative data.

We explain three guidelines for record keeping so that the data can always be traced back to the learning it represents and so that you can maximize the usefulness of your entries. The first is to organize the entries by the learning represented. The second is to keep track of information about work habits and social skills separate from academic achievement information. This also has implications for what we do with extra credit work, with missing or late work, and with work displaying evidence of academic dishonesty. The third guideline is to record achievement information by raw score when practical, rather than by percent or symbol, to retain the most options for accurate use of the data.

Last, we offer suggestions for how students might track their achievement with both formative and summative assessment information, helping them stay in touch with their own progress as learners.

With a protocol in place, tracking assessments *for* and *of* learning in the classroom does not need to consume a lot of time. If our classroom assessments are of high quality, we will be able to calculate a justifiable grade with fewer assessment scores than may be in place in many gradebooks now.

CHAPTER 9 ACTIVITIES

End-of-chapter activities are intended to help you master the chapter's learning targets. They are designed to deepen your understanding of the chapter content, provide discussion topics for learning team meetings, and guide implementation of the practices taught in the chapter.

Forms for completing each activity appear in editable Microsoft Word format in the Chapter 9 CD file. Documents on the CD are marked with this symbol:

Chapter 9 Learning Targets

At the end of Chapter 9, you will know how to do the following:

1. Separate formative from summative assessment information.
2. Identify which formative assessment information to track.
3. Select one or more physical locations for the information.
4. Set up labels and categories to represent the learning assessed.
5. Identify what work habits and social skills to track; track them separately from achievement information.
6. Record achievement information by raw score.
7. Create a system for students to keep track of their own learning.

Activity 9.1 Keep a Reflective Journal
Activity 9.2 Plan Formative and Summative Assessment Events
Activity 9.3 Organize Your Recording System
Activity 9.4 Track Work Habits and Social Skills
Activity 9.5 Develop Student Record-keeping Forms
Activity 9.6 Reflect on Your Own Learning
Activity 9.7 Select Portfolio Artifacts

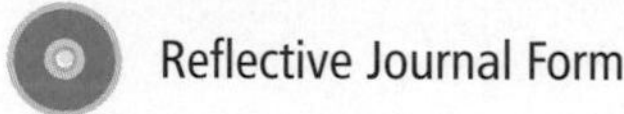

Activity 9.1

Keep a Reflective Journal

Keep a record of your thoughts, questions, and any implementation activities you tried while reading Chapter 9.

Reflective Journal Form

Activity 9.2

Plan Formative and Summative Assessment Events

After reading the section titled "Differentiating Information for Formative or Summative Use," select an upcoming unit of study to use in mapping out formative and summative assessment events. Work independently, with a partner, or with a team to carry out the following activity.

1. Copy the form "Formative and Summative Assessment Plan" (Figure 9.3), or create an adapted form to fit your context.
2. Identify the unit of study and how many days or weeks it will cover.
3. List the learning targets that will be the focus of instruction during the unit in the order you will teach them.
4. Describe the assignments and assessments that will serve a summative purpose for each learning target. Descriptions can take the form of page numbers, assignment or assessment titles or numbers, or any other information that works for you. Note the approximate date for each and mark it with the letter "S" for "Summative" in the column labeled "Type."
5. Describe any pretests, checks for understanding, or quizzes you plan to administer to guide further instruction. Descriptions can take the form of page numbers, assignment or assessment titles or numbers, or any other information that works for you. Note the approximate date for each and mark it with the letter "C" for "Check for learning" in the column labeled "Type."
6. Describe the practice event or events that students will engage in for each learning target. Descriptions can take the form of page numbers, assignment titles, or any other information that works for you. Note the approximate date for each and mark it with the letter "P" for "Practice" in the column labeled "Type."
7. Describe any other formative assessment events that students will engage in, along with the approximate date.
8. Follow the plan. Note any adjustments needed. Revise the plan for future use.
9. Share your plan with a partner or your team. Described what worked well and what you will revise.

Formative and Summative Assessment Plan

Activity 9.3

Organize Your Recording System

After reading the section titled "Deciding Where You Will Keep the Information," work independently, with a partner, or with a team to make the following decisions.

1. Physical location—where will you keep the summative information? Where will you keep the formative information?
2. If you keep them in the same place, how will you differentiate formative from summative information? Review Figures 9.4 through 9.7 for ideas. Select an option, modify an option, or create your own.
3. What information does it make sense for students also to track?

After reading the section titled "Guideline 1: Organize Entries by Learning Represented," work independently, with a partner, or with your team to make the following decisions. You may also want to review Figures 9.4 through 9.8 for ideas.

1. How will you identify the learning represented by each formative entry? How much detail will you want in the heading of each column? What kinds of headings will you use?
2. How will you identify the learning represented by each summative entry? How much detail will you want in the heading of each column? What kinds of headings will you use?
3. After making these decisions, revise your recording system and try it out for a few weeks.
4. Share with a partner or your team the structure of your recording system, the adjustments you have made, and what you may need yet to refine.

 Organize Your Recording System

Activity 9.4

Track Work Habits and Social Skills

Work independently, with a partner, or with a team to complete the following activity.

1. After reading the section titled "Guideline 2: Track Information about Work Habits and Social Skills Separately," make the following decisions:
   - What work habits and/or social skills do you want to keep track of?
   - What actions define competence?
2. To clarify them, discuss them with colleagues and come to consensus on the actions that will represent attainment of each.
3. Next, determine how you will assess and judge level of attainment of each.
4. Decide on a system for tracking this information.
5. Determine how you will summarize and report student attainment of work habits and social skills.
6. Last, plan for how you will make clear to students the work habits and social skills they are expected to demonstrate and how you will help them understand the ways in which you will assess and report their performance.
7. Use the system for the duration of a grading period. Note any adjustments needed.
8. Share with a partner or your team the system you have set up, what is working well and what you intend to revise. Also share the impact it has had on student achievement and motivation and what, if any, interventions or consequences you put in place to encourage work completion.

Track Work Habits and Social Skills

Debrief Tracking and Reporting Work Habits and Social Skills

Activity 9.5

Develop Student Record-keeping Forms

After reading the section titled "Options for Student Record Keeping," work independently, with a partner, or with a team to carry out the following activity.

1. Make sure the prerequisites listed in the section are in place.
2. Determine what students will track.
3. Determine the time frame.
4. Select or modify an option described in the section and create the forms students will use. (Further suggestions can be found in Chapter 6 of *Seven Strategies of Assessment* for *Learning* [Chappuis, 2009].)
5. Plan for who will keep track of the forms and where they will be kept. (In Chapter 11 we offer guidance on managing student record-keeping forms.)
6. Introduce the tracking system to your students. Periodically ask for their feedback.
7. Also make notes of your own observations regarding the system's strengths and problems. Make revisions as needed.
8. Share your students' and your own reflections with a partner or your team.

Activity 9.6

Reflect on Your Own Learning

Review the Chapter 9 learning targets and select one or more that represented new learning for you or struck you as most significant from this chapter. If you are working individually, write a short reflection that captures your current understanding. If you are working with a partner or a team, either discuss what you have written or use this as a discussion prompt for a team meeting.

Reflect on Chapter 9 Learning

Activity 9.7

Select Portfolio Artifacts

Any of the activities from this chapter can be used as portfolio entries. Select activities you have completed or artifacts you have created that will illustrate your competence at the Chapter 9 learning targets:

1. Separate formative from summative assessment information.
2. Identify which formative assessment information to track.
3. Select one or more physical locations for the information.
4. Set up labels and categories to represent the learning assessed.
5. Identify what work habits and social skills to track; track them separately from achievement information.
6. Record achievement information by raw score.
7. Create a system for students to keep track of their own learning.

If you are keeping a reflective journal, you may want to include Chapter 9's entry in your portfolio.

Chapter 9 Portfolio Entry Cover Sheet

CHAPTER

10

Converting Summative Assessment Information into Grades

The academic grade a student earns in a class should be determined by evidence of that student's achievement alone.

Teaching and learning have been a part of our experiences for as long as we have been in existence. Both can and do take place just fine without grades. As we have seen, student learning benefits from a number of instructional uses of assessment information, including effective feedback, but it seldom benefits directly from grading practices.

So why do we grade? The obvious reason is that others want and need the information to make decisions about students. Parents consistently want to see the familiar, periodic report card grades they knew as students so they know how their children are doing. Employers, other schools, athletic coaches and school advisors, scholarship committees, automobile insurance companies—the list goes on—want learning summarized in the shorthand that grades afford to make decisions that affect students' future well-being—course or program eligibility, scholarship awards, and good driver discounts among them. Few of these uses are within the teacher's control. Once a summary grade is assigned it must be able to stand alone as an accurate representation of student achievement.

Grades are gatekeepers and too often they shut students out of further learning, even when that is not our intent. In this chapter we build on the recommendations for formative and summative uses of assessment information taught in all previous chapters to ensure that our grading practices support learning to the extent possible. We also build directly on the record-keeping practices taught in Chapter 9.

We first explore challenges inherent in assigning report card grades. Next we describe in detail three grading guidelines that will lead us to fair and accurate standards-based report card grades. Following that, we explain "number-crunching" options, including how to convert rubric scores to grades, that also affect accuracy. We then summarize all grading recommendations from Chapters 9 and 10 in a six-step process. Finally, but importantly for individual or organization professional growth, we offer a rubric for reviewing current grading practices.

FIGURE 10.1 Keys to Quality Classroom Assessment

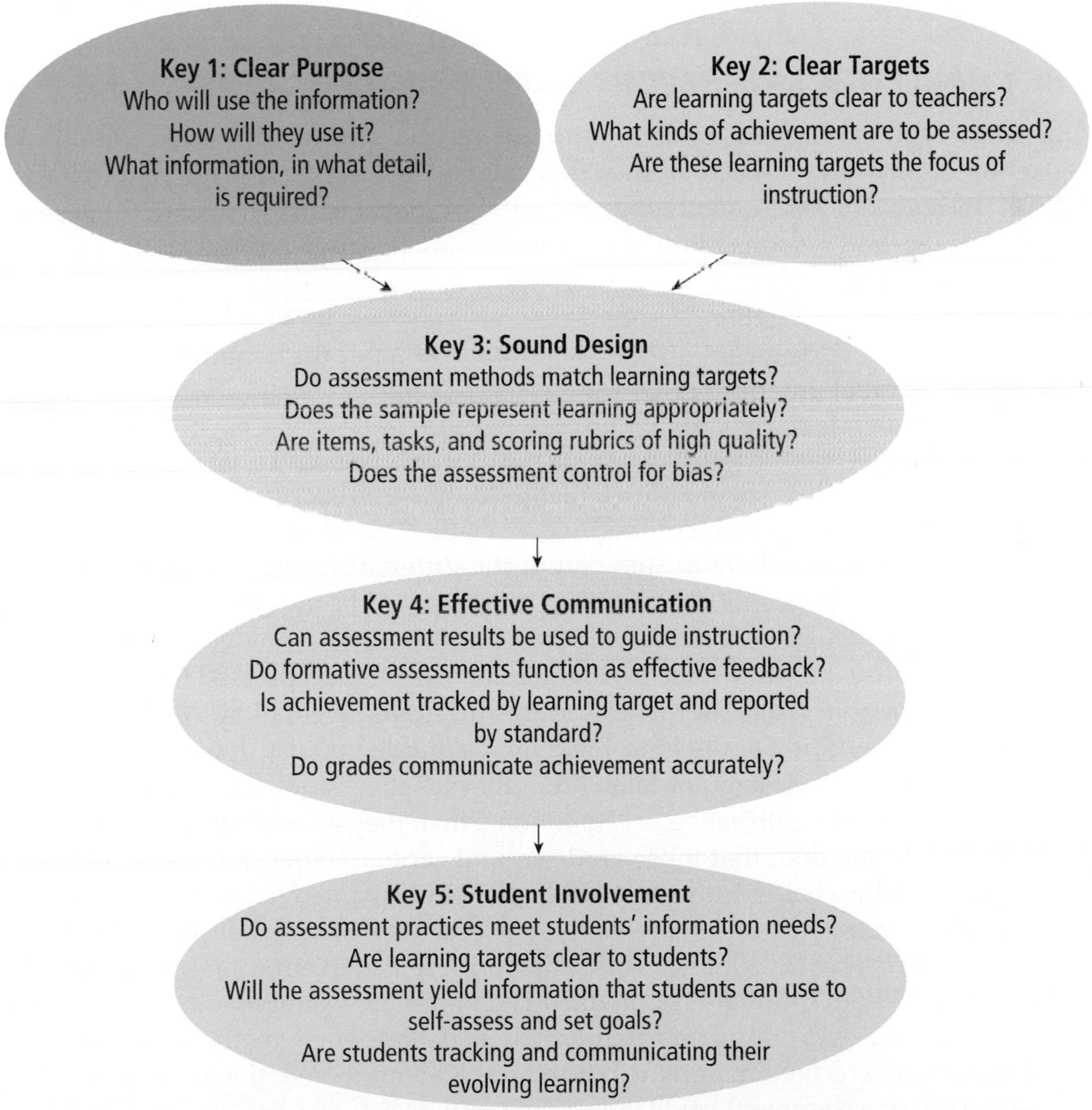

Key 1: Clear Purpose
Who will use the information?
How will they use it?
What information, in what detail, is required?

Key 2: Clear Targets
Are learning targets clear to teachers?
What kinds of achievement are to be assessed?
Are these learning targets the focus of instruction?

Key 3: Sound Design
Do assessment methods match learning targets?
Does the sample represent learning appropriately?
Are items, tasks, and scoring rubrics of high quality?
Does the assessment control for bias?

Key 4: Effective Communication
Can assessment results be used to guide instruction?
Do formative assessments function as effective feedback?
Is achievement tracked by learning target and reported by standard?
Do grades communicate achievement accurately?

Key 5: Student Involvement
Do assessment practices meet students' information needs?
Are learning targets clear to students?
Will the assessment yield information that students can use to self-assess and set goals?
Are students tracking and communicating their evolving learning?

Chapter 10 Learning Targets

At the end of Chapter 10 you will know how to do the following:

- Identify the special challenges associated with effective communication using grades.
- Follow a series of guidelines for effective grading.
- Summarize evidence gathered over time into a meaningful grade.
- Convert rubric scores into grades.
- Evaluate and refine your own grading practices using the Rubric for Sound Grading Practices.

THE CHALLENGES OF REPORT CARD GRADING

Our first responsibility as teachers is to ensure that grades provide an accurate reflection of all students' actual level of academic achievement. This requires that grades derive from assessments that accurately reflect clearly articulated learning targets. Our second responsibility is to minimize any negative impacts of the grading process on learning.

To start our investigation of sound grading practices, let's look at one teacher's experience in the early years of her career. As you read, think about whether her experiences parallel any of your own experiences with grading, or what you might know and do in your classroom that this teacher did not.

> As a young teacher, I never had a student or parent seriously question a report card grade that I assigned. As a result, I never really had to open my gradebook to others to show all of the different colored symbols and markings, numbers and letter grades, comments, and codes that I somehow massaged (calculated is too strong a description) into a final grade. I was lucky, because had they done so, I would have been hard pressed to explain or defend a nonsystem, or my procedures for grade calculation. Although I didn't realize it fully at the time, I had no real guide for ensuring my grades were accurate, consistent, or fair, and in the end the grades I assigned were far more intuitive, subjective, and emotional than they were rational. It never occurred to me then that those grades might serve to either hinder or help someone to be a better learner. So although I never wanted to have grades be harmful, I frequently and subjectively included in the final grade all kinds of things—perpetual tardiness, good behavior, or a lack of effort on the part of a student whom I thought should be doing better, for example.
>
> Further, everything, no matter when it happened in the semester, counted toward the final grade. I didn't think about the relative importance of the test or assignment, and I didn't differentiate between practice and final

> exercises or assignments. In my mind grading was divorced entirely from teaching and learning so it didn't bother me in the slightest that a student aide evaluated a large portion of student work, entered the data, and helped in figuring the grades.

Like far too many of us, this teacher did not have the opportunity to learn what are known as *sound grading practices* prior to beginning her career. With no external standards of quality or fairness to guide her, she was left to develop her own system for arriving at report card grades. Like her, many of us calculate grades by adhering to our own unique procedures and formulae. Some of us have no articulated process other than to record, average, and convert to a grade, while others use more elaborate mathematical systems to "crunch" the grade. Some electronic gradebook programs offer optional guidance in using their features to ensure fairness and accuracy, but we may not know what options are best to choose. Even with school and district policies in place, there can be as many different grading systems in a school as there are teachers.

And yet, of all the things we do as teachers, few have the potential for creating more conflict and communication problems than grading. All it takes to realize this is to be the teacher on the explaining end in a conference with a parent who is questioning her child's surprisingly low grade. We can experience friction at report card preparation time as we calculate the grades of students who worked hard during the semester, but who achieved at a low level, resulting in what is sure to be a disappointing grade. At times like this we can be emotionally torn, worried about the impact of a low grade on the student's morale, and drawn to a subjective compromise that considers the student's individual circumstances while decreasing objectivity and accuracy.

Adopting the sound grading practices recommended in this chapter allows us to create accurate grades that communicate what they are intended to, that are fair to students, and that do not harm motivation or achievement.

On top of this, there is the grading challenge of finding the time to manage the wealth of information we collect daily in the classroom. We may sort through it, prioritize it, and assign weights to it, guided by sound grading principles. Or, like the teacher in our example, we may funnel the information through a process of our own making.

And finally, we face the relatively new challenge of altering reporting systems to reflect standards-based teaching and learning. In a standards-driven environment, the goal of grading is to provide students and their parents the information that communicates specifically about student success in mastering relevant standards. Yet, even with individual state or provincial standards and the Common Core State Standards, many schools' grading systems continue to report student learning using letters or numbers that do not accurately summarize achievement of content area academic standards.

THREE GRADING GUIDELINES

Everyone who uses grades to make decisions about students counts on them to be accurate—our responsibility to them and to our students is to provide as accurate a picture of learning as possible. This requires that we carefully answer three questions: "What is our purpose for grading?"; "What factors should we include in the grade?"; and "How do we combine those factors to give the truest picture possible of student achievement?"

We offer answers to those questions in the form of three *grading guidelines*—three statements that serve as the foundation for an accurate and defensible grading system.

Guideline 1: Use Grades to Communicate, Not to Motivate

Going back to why we grade—because others need the information to make decisions about students—we may all agree that we grade to communicate about student learning. But we are also familiar with grading practices designed to motivate students toward desirable learning habits and responsible behaviors and away from undesirable ones. While it is unarguable that many students need help with their habits and behaviors, it is arguable that factoring their presence or absence into the academic grade is a satisfactory remedy.

Consider these three scenarios:

John is a very capable student who in the teacher's opinion is not performing at the level he should. His end-of-term grade is a borderline B/C. His teacher gives John a C to help him recognize that he needs to put forth more effort; in effect punishing him for not doing more, with the intent of waking him up and causing him to work harder.

Sarah is a hardworking student and she always turns everything in. Her end-of-term grade is a borderline C/D. Her teacher raises her grade to a C to keep up her morale; in effect rewarding her for her hard work, with the intent of keeping her from being discouraged.

Your daughter has earned As and Bs on all projects, reports, and tests in one of her classes, yet receives a C as her end-of-term grade because her last report was one week late. Her teacher's policy is to subtract 10 points for each day an assignment is late as a deterrent to late work. Had your daughter's report been turned in on time, her final grade would have been a low A.

In these examples considerations other than achievement are included in the grade with the intent of influencing behavior. When we do this, we are on shaky

FIGURE 10.2 Three Grading Guidelines

1. Use grades to communicate, not to motivate.
2. Report achievement and other factors separately.
3. Reflect only current level of achievement in the academic grade.

ground, for three significant reasons: (1) grades don't work well enough as motivators, (2) this practice often masks the problem rather than solving it, and (3) it interferes with the grade's ability to serve its communicative purpose. This is not to say that grades don't motivate some students—they do. The points here are these:

- We should not manipulate grades with the intent of changing behavior.
- Some of our attempted motivational uses of grades, while well-intentioned, harm students.

IT DOESN'T WORK WELL ENOUGH. Tinkering with grades to cause a change in behavior is not a reliable way to effect the desired change. Educators have done everything imaginable to make grades work as motivators and yet far too many students still are not putting forth the effort needed to succeed. We have no way of knowing whether students even get the message behind the manipulation of the grade. Further, no studies find that reducing grades as punishment increases effort. Instead of prompting stepped-up engagement, lowering grades more often causes students to withdraw from further learning (Guskey & Bailey, 2001). And far too many students are willing to take the lower grade rather than change their habits or behaviors.

Rank in class is another attempt to use grades as motivators. Instill a sense of competition, some believe, even with an artificial creation of winners and losers, and students will work harder and learn more. If that works at all, it only motivates the few who are at the top. And those generally aren't the ones who need it. In a learning environment that aspires to helping all students master essential competencies for success in college and the work place, we can't have major portions of our student population considering themselves losers.

What should we do instead? As we have described throughout this book, we can increase students' willingness to work harder in an intellectually healthy, learning-centered way through assessment *for* learning practices. Even when motivation appears to have evaporated, changing our assessment practices works far better to increase engagement than promising As or threatening Fs.

IT MASKS THE PROBLEM. Raising an academic grade for reasons unrelated to achievement to compensate for low scores does nothing to uncover the reasons behind the lack of sufficient progress. Why is Sarah's effort not resulting in adequate achievement? This should be a red flag, pointing to the need for investigation. When the underlying problem has not been identified and addressed, Sarah's potential for future achievement is compromised.

Lowering John's grade because of his perceived lack of attention to the quality of his work is not an instructional solution to the problem. He may not even be aware that he incurred this punishment. If we want to help students with these kinds of problems, they should be addressed directly during the learning, assignment by assignment, well in advance of report card grading time.

In general, lowering any academic grade for problems with work completion, attendance, effort, participation, or lack of academic honesty, while serving as a deterrent to some, does not tend to remediate repeat offenders.

What should we do instead? Address the real problems during the learning. Treat each of the desired habits and responsible behaviors as learning targets. Work as a team in your school to define each, communicate them as expectations, identify students experiencing difficulty, and develop appropriate remediation for each as well as deterring consequences that don't involve manipulating the grade.

IT INTERFERES WITH COMMUNICATION. Because key decisions hinge on them in the student's future, the purpose of grades must be to communicate. *Accurate, fair, and defensible academic grades communicate about student learning. Period.* The practice of assigning or altering academic grades to shape behavior results in the miscommunication of students' real levels of achievement. John, Sarah, and your daughter all *received* Cs, but each *earned* a different grade because they all showed evidence of different levels of achievement. Any motivation effect is fleeting, if it exists at all, yet the record is permanent. When we allow motivational intent to influence academic grades, we cripple the grade's ability to communicate.

Using grades as motivators to reward and punish or deter behavior is not consistent with a rigorous standards-based educational system such as that envisioned as the result of implementing the Common Core State Standards. It won't offer a distortion-free picture of level of achievement. Neither will it communicate about any of the hidden factors that may have contributed to or prevented learning. Any practice that distorts the meaning of the grade renders it meaningless as a communication tool.

What should we do instead? As O'Connor (2011) points out: "Grades are broken when they mix achievement and nonachievement elements. The fix is to report variables such as behaviors separately from achievement, thereby ensuring that grades reflect student achievement as accurately as possible" (p. 22).

FAQ 10.1

Zeroes

Question:

Why do you recommend never assigning zeroes?

Answer:

Averaging zeroes with other scores to calculate a midterm or quarter grade skews the grade in a way from which it can never recover, making the final grade a completely inaccurate picture of student achievement. Consider the case of a student who has taken three of four tests and attained scores of 100, 90, and 95 percent. The student missed one test and the score was entered as a zero, due to an unexcused absence. Her average is 71 percent, usually a C but sometimes a D. This grade clearly does not reflect her level of achievement. A more fair solution to the problem of missing work is to gather or use other information about student learning to fill in the gap. This student could, for instance, take the test before or after school. If we can't get other information in time, we may have to use an "Incomplete" to stand in for the grade until we can get enough information to make a stable generalization about the student's level of achievement on the course learning targets.

My Classroom Then and Now 10.1

Sara Poeppelman

I used to ...

Like many teachers, I used to give summative quizzes and tests and assignments that may or may not have assessed the most important aspects of what the students were supposed to have learned as a result of the instruction that was taking place in my classroom. If the students scored well, that was wonderful for them and if the students did not score well, too bad, and we went on with content that needed to be covered by the end of the year. Breaking down standards into meaningful targets that were useful to the students and myself rarely occurred. Formative assessment? I did not have a clue what that was either and how it could be any more useful than the summative assessments that I was already utilizing.

Grades generally reflected and favored those students who turned in assignments on time and did not really assess students' knowledge and understanding of key science concepts.

Now I ...

Daily, students and I utilize learning targets to move the class toward the critical learning that will result from that day's instruction. Formative assessment is regular and ongoing. Instruction is modified as a result of formative assessments, sometimes for the whole class and sometimes differentiated for groups with specific challenges related to the formative assessment results. Feedback is now king. Students receive frequent feedback and utilize the feedback to make improvements on their work. Grades focus predominantly on student knowledge, skills, and understanding related to the learning targets, rather than being predominantly a measure of which students "played school well."

Why I changed ...

I was at my first training on formative assessment practices, and this just made so much more sense than the way that I had been practicing the art and science of teaching up to that point, especially the importance of feedback rather than "grades." Up to this point in my career, one of the things that really bothered me was that students were often too concerned about their grade rather than what they were learning. As a teacher my philosophy has always been to focus on the learning, but I realized that my assessment practices were not promoting learning and it seemed that use of formative assessment and feedback would be a practical method to promote learning rather than a grade-driven focus.

What I notice as a result ...

As a result of changing my assessment practices (what I assess, how I assess it, what my students or myself do as a result), I have noticed more students are engaged in the process of learning without the focus on the grade. By focusing in on the critical content and skills that I assess and reporting those to derive a final grade, rather than habits, such as turning homework in, I have significantly fewer students who have to be retained. Providing specific feedback with students on the other end attending to that feedback has helped motivate students to attempt to do better on assessments and other challenges in the future. I feel that I am now helping to develop learners who have the skills and confidence to take on challenges with intrinsic motivation rather that students who focus on the "once and done," grade and extrinsic motivation.

Source: Used with permission from Sara Poeppelman, high school science teacher, Lewis County Schools, Vanceburg, KY, 2011.

Guideline 2: Report Achievement and Other Factors Separately

Once we have determined that academic grades are to be calculated and assigned for the purpose of communicating level of achievement on learning targets we have been teaching, we can examine other factors we may want to track, assess, and report.

EFFORT. Effort is highly valued both in and beyond school because it is a necessary ingredient in learning or doing anything difficult. When students are trying hard to learn, our jobs as teachers are much easier because the students are meeting us at least halfway. Also, employers value people who work hard, who demonstrate persistence, who take initiative, and who go beyond what is required of them to make the business successful.

However, John's and Sarah's Cs tell us nothing about their very different levels of effort. If information about their effort would assist us in interpreting the grade they were assigned, then evidence of that effort should be reported separately from the academic grade. Rarely are there explicit criteria available to judge effort. The task is made harder by the fact that students, through physical appearance or behavior, may appear either to be engaged or totally out of it, when in fact, the opposite may be true (Brookhart, 2004). Further muddying the waters, effort isn't one thing—it is a collection of behaviors and attitudes. It doesn't look the same to all teachers—different teachers may describe it differently and look for different evidence of it.

The keys to assessment quality apply here just as they do with achievement: If we wish to communicate about level of effort, we will need to define what behaviors and attitudes comprise our definition, determine how best to evaluate them accurately, determine what symbols we will use to communicate and what they will mean, and then create a separate space on the report card for our judgment.

Define it, diagnose it, teach it, remediate it, assess it, and report it separately.

OTHER FACTORS. And so it is for all other factors we might wish to take into account in figuring final grades—attendance, work completion, turning work in on time, group participation, skills of cooperation, academic honesty, or any other valued habit or behavior. If we decide that factors beyond level of achievement are important to report, we must define them, communicate our expectations to students, decide what data to collect, then collect and report it separately. Admittedly this process is initially more time consuming than lowering grades, but if factors other than achievement are import to develop in students and to report out, we can see no other way to make meaning clear.

We recommend Ken O'Connor's *A Repair Kit for Grading: 15 Fixes for Broken Grades* (O'Connor, 2011) for an in-depth treatment of how to address problems with habits and behaviors without using grades as rewards, deterrents, or punishments.

Guideline 3: Reflect Only Current Level of Achievement in the Academic Grade

In a standards-based environment, grade reports must reflect our best measure of student achievement at the time they are assigned. If more recent information about student achievement shows a higher level of learning on a given content standard or learning target, then the grade should be based on the newer evidence. Averaging the new information with the old, outdated information has the effect of lowering the grade for students who had the farthest to come and did so. It provides an incorrect picture of student achievement at that point in time and can lead to ill-informed instructional and support decisions. It also reinforces in students the notion that it's better to already know than to learn. O'Connor (2011) reminds us it's not where a student starts on a given learning target that matters, but where the student finishes.

We can also think of formative and summative assessment information in this light. The formative assessment information is data gathered about level of achievement during learning—practice, trial and error, and so forth. So we use assessments *for* learning to diagnose problems, plan further instruction, provide students with feedback, and to help them improve. Periodically, we ask them to demonstrate their level of achievement by means of summative assessments *of* learning, which are a culmination of what they have learned and comprise the most recent evidence of achievement.

The recommendation to base grades on the most current evidence of the student's level of achievement on the intended learning targets does not mean that only grades from the end of the marking period should figure into the final grade. For example, if we divide the learning targets for a social studies course into several equal segments each lasting about two weeks, we might give a summative assessment at the end of each segment. Because each summative assessment provides information on different learning targets and no content has been repeated, every summative assessment score represents the most current information on the targets covered.

SUMMARIZING INFORMATION

This process picks up where we left off in Chapter 9. As you recall, we recommended that you first decide what information will be used summatively and what will be used formatively. We discussed systems that you can use to differentiate the two in your record book. Then we presented three record-keeping guidelines: (1) Organize entries by learning represented, (2) Track information about work habits and social skills separately, and (3) Record achievement information by raw score. By following the recommendations in Chapter 9, your data will be organized so that you can easily convert them to a common scale, weight them as desired, and combine them to arrive at one overall number.

Verify Accuracy of Data

Before we go through those steps, however, it is a good idea to review your summative data for accuracy. Discard any inaccurate information from grading records. Do not include outdated information in your grade calculations. No one has yet developed an information management and communication system that can convert inaccurate information—misinformation about a student's achievement—into an accurate grade. Chapters 1 through 8 offer the guidance you need to ensure that accuracy.

FIGURE 10.3 Process for Summarizing Information

- Verify accuracy of summative data.
- Convert record book entries to a common scale.
- Weight information as needed.
- Combine information thoughtfully.

Convert Entries to a Common Scale

Once you have identified which information you will use, you will need to convert each score to a common scale. You may have recorded summative information in a variety of forms: raw scores, percentages, rubric scores, letters, and/or other evaluative symbols.

If your entries are in the form of raw scores (number correct out of number possible) and percentages (percent correct), we recommend two traditional combination procedures. You can convert all scores to percentages or you can convert all entries to raw scores. In either case, remember to use only the most current body of information and to make sure you have enough evidence to sample the learning targets adequately.

If you have rubric scores in the mix, you will need to follow an additional procedure, explained in the section "Converting Rubric Scores to Grades" later in the chapter.

If you have letters or other symbols as summative data, you will need to go back to the underlying assessments and replace the letters or symbols with raw scores, percentages, or rubric scores.

Weight Information as Needed

If you wish to give greater weight to some assessment results than to others, you can accomplish this by multiplying those scores by a weighting factor. For instance, if one score is to count twice as much as others, the weighting factor for that score is 2. Simply multiply the score by two before moving on to the next step of combining information.

An additional consideration in applying weights to grade is the structure of the grade report. Will you figure one grade to cover all of the learning targets you taught in a subject or does your report card have separate categories within the subject? You may have set your record book so your data are tracked according to those categories, but if not, now is the time to separate them.

If you will be reporting in several categories, first apply weighting factors as desired for the data within each category. If, in addition, you must combine those grades or marks into a single summary grade, determine if and how the categories will be weighted.

Combine Information Thoughtfully

Combine information from assessments into a final grade using the appropriate measure of central tendency—mean or median—for the type of data. (Figure 10.4 provides definitions and examples of mean and median.) We traditionally combine individual pieces of achievement evidence into a final summary by calculating the mean. When data are consistent—that is, when they fall within a narrow score

FIGURE 10.4 Measures of Central Tendency

Here is a set of numbers from a precalculus student's quarter grade report. Notice how the summary score derived changes according to the measure of central tendency.

55, 80, 42, 89, 83, 85, 91, 70, 91

Term	Definition	Result
Mean	The average score	76.2
Median	The middle score	83

range—the mean will yield an accurate representation of level of achievement. But when data include extreme scores—when they span a range of score points—calculating the mean will skew the resulting score, as shown in Figure 10.4. To counter this problem, many grading experts advocate using median scores rather than mean scores to summarize achievement. O'Connor (2011) encourages us to think of this process as *determining* a grade rather than *calculating* it because the measure of central tendency must be chosen to suit the data at hand:

> Grades are frequently broken (inaccurate) when they result only from the calculation of the mean in contexts where extreme scores distort; they can be repaired by considering other measures of central tendency and using professional judgment. Thus we should think and talk not about the calculation but the *determination* of grades. (p. 93)

FAQ 10.2

Norm-Referenced Grading

Question:

Is it ever okay to grade on a curve?

Answer:

Assessments, grades, and report cards should reflect student attainment of established achievement targets, rather than the students' place in the rank order of the class. If a student receives a grade of B, the interpreter must understand that the B reflects attainment of a certain level of mastery of the learning targets for that subject.

Guskey (1996) advises against normative grading with the following argument: "Grading on a curve makes learning a highly competitive activity in which students compete against one another for the few scarce rewards (high grades) distributed by the teacher. Under these conditions, students readily see that helping others become successful threatens their own chances for success. As a result, learning becomes a game of winners and losers; and because the number of rewards is kept arbitrarily small, most students are forced to be losers" (p. 21). All students could get an A, or "Exceeds the standard," if they prove that they have learned the material at the corresponding level of mastery.

In some classrooms, grades are "curved" to spread students out along a continuum of achievement, creating an artificial and inaccurate report of actual learning. If report card grades are manipulated for motivational effect, who can possibly interpret their true meaning in terms of student achievement?

CONVERTING RUBRIC SCORES TO GRADES

In Chapter 7 we established that rubrics are useful as formative assessment tools to help students understand and master complex learning targets. They can also be used summatively to assign a grade or determine level of student mastery of key standards. In this section we describe how to convert ratings from rubrics to grades or mastery levels.

To begin with, any rubrics to be used to evaluate student work for grading (summative) purposes need to satisfy the quality criteria described in detail in Chapter 7 on performance assessment. If those standards of quality are not met, then the resulting grade is not likely to provide an accurate reflection of the student's achievement.

The transformation of rubric ratings into grades, like so much of the classroom assessment process, involves a major helping of professional judgment. The challenge is to turn a profile of several ratings for each student into a single grade in a consistent manner that ensures accuracy and complete understanding by the grade recipient. There are two ways to do this. One relies on average ratings and the other on defining patterns of ratings.

Note at the outset that these processes can be applied either in assigning a grade to (1) a summative assessment during the grading period that will later be combined with other evidence to feed into the determination of a final grade or (2) a "final exam" assessment that is the culminating demonstration of proficiency that the final grade will be based on.

FAQ 10.3

Counting Rubric Levels as Points

Question:

Why can't I just add up the rubric points and divide the total by the number of points possible to calculate a grade?

Answer:

This will usually result in an inaccurate depiction of student achievement because numbers in a rubric are *labels for levels*, not points earned. Calculating *percentage of points earned* doesn't accurately represent student achievement because there are too few points possible and the resulting grade won't match the description of that level on the rubric. For example, on a 5-point scale the only choices are

5/5 = 100% = A
4/5 = 80% = B or C
3/5 = 60% = F
2/5 = 40% = F
1/5 = 20% = F

The description in the rubric for 1-level work might indicate a failing level of quality, but the descriptions for 2- and 3-level work probably don't.

Likewise, on a 4-point scale the only choices are

4/4 = 100% = A
3/4 = 75% = C
2/4 = 50% = F
1/4 = 25% = F

You may wonder why even a single point is given for the work described at the lowest level of a rubric. Once again, the reason is that it's not a point earned; it's a *label* (as are *novice and beginning*) for a set of statements that describes novice or weak performance.

Average Ratings

For each student, calculate the average rating across the profile of scales within the rubric. The *average rating* is the total of the ratings a student received divided by the total number of ratings. What we're doing here is figuring out the typical rating by calculating an average. We want to know what the ratings tell us about how well, in general, a student performs. For grading purposes, use only the scores from work toward the end of the grading period to determine a grade for a given content

FIGURE 10.5 Logical Grade Conversion Table for Average Ratings

Rubric Rating Average	*Logical Grade* Conversion	*Logical Percentage* Conversion
3.5–4.0	A	95%
2.9–3.4	B	85%
2.3–2.8	C	75%
1.7–2.2	D	65%
1.6 and below	F	55%

standard because the later scores will be more representative of the student's current achievement level.

Look at the rubric and decide logically what range of average ratings would match to each grade or level of mastery. We recommend that you work with colleagues on this to make sure everyone agrees. Create a conversion table that stipulates the range for each grade. Use this table to determine the appropriate grade for each student. Figure 10.5 illustrates one way to convert *average ratings* from a four-point rubric into a summary grade and then into a percentage. (If you need to combine rubric scores with other kinds of assessment information, you will need the percentage information, as explained in the following section.)

Pattern of Ratings

The second option is to work with colleagues to fashion a means for converting profiles of ratings on each particular assessment into grades. First, for example, we decide that, to get an *A*, the preponderance of student work has to be at the highest level of ratings. So, we decide that at least 50 percent of the ratings must be 4 on a set of 4-point rubrics. From here, the team establishes the pattern of ratings needed for each of the other grades, creating a conversion table to be used consistently in assigning grades. Figure 10.6 illustrates one way to use the *pattern of ratings* option to create a conversion table for linking student scores to grades.

You will notice in both of these conversion charts that the percentages are a somewhat simplified representation of the range of scores that each grade represents. When using or reporting percentages rather than grades, we recommend that you create a more precise equation table, such as that shown in Figure 10.7. Note that the grade-to-percentage conversions in Figures 10.5, 10.6, and 10.7 are intended as examples. We encourage you to work with colleagues to devise conversions that match your expectations. These become the preset standards you can share with students and parents to help them understand how the numbers on individual summative assessments will be used to calculate a final grade.

FIGURE 10.6 Logical Conversion Table for Patterns of Averages

If the student's pattern of ratings is:	The *logical grade* is:	The *logical percentage* is:
At least 50% of the ratings are 4, and not more than 5% are lower than 3	A	95%
75% of the ratings are 3 or better, and no more than 5% are lower than 2	B	85%
40% of the ratings are 2 or better and no more than 5% are lower than 2	C	75%
40% of the ratings are 2 or better and no more than 50% are lower than 2	D	65%
More than 50% of the ratings are lower than 2	F	50%

To set this up appropriately and apply it consistently, obviously, the underlying ratings need to provide an accurate reflection of the student's achievement and the conversion must be done consistently. This requires that each teacher possess sufficient knowledge of levels of quality represented in the rubric to assign scores accurately and consistently with other teachers.

Combining Rubric Ratings with Other Assessment Information to Get a Final Grade

To illustrate this straightforward four-step process, we'll use the scores of one student, Desmond.

Step 1: Use the logical conversion tables you have created to convert the rubric scores to a logical percentage. Let's say you have done that for Desmond's rubric scores and his logical percentage is 85 percent.

Step 2: For the "non-rubric" portion of the grade, compute one final percentage that represents the assessment information from other sources. Let's say you gave several selected response tests that each yielded a percent correct score. You have combined these percentages using the measure of central tendency that best fits the data and Desmond's resulting score is 93 percent.

FIGURE 10.7 Grade to Percentage Conversion Table for a Four-level Rubric

Rubric Rating Average	*Logical Grade* Conversion	*Logical Percentage* Conversion
3.9–4.0	A+	99
3.7–3.8	A	95
3.5–3.6	A−	91
3.3–3.4	B+	88
3.1–3.2	B	85
2.9–3.0	B−	81
2.7–2.8	C+	78
2.5–2.6	C	75
2.3–2.4	C−	71
2.1–2.2	D+	68
1.9–2.0	D	65
1.7–1.8	D−	61
1.5 1.6	F	55
1.3–1.4	F	48
1.0–1.2	F	40

Step 3: Decide if the rubric percentage (from Step 1) will have the same weight as the non-rubric percentage (from Step 2). More? Less? Assign a weighting factor, as appropriate. Assume for Desmond's class that you want the rubric percentage to count twice as much as the non-rubric percentage. So the weighting factor for the rubric percentage is 2.

Step 4: Use the weighting factor to combine the rubric percentage with the non-rubric percentage. Combine the weighted percentages to calculate a final average. In Desmond's case, it would look like this: (We'll add 85 twice because it counts twice as much.)

$$(85 + 85 + 93) \div 3 = 263$$
$$263 \div 3 = 88\%$$

Desmond's combined final score is 88 percent.

Figure 10.8 summarizes the recommendations for converting rubric scores to grades.

FIGURE 10.8 Recommendations for Converting Rubric Scores to Grades

1. *Don't convert rubric scores to letter grades at all if you can help it.* The descriptions associated with each score point give a clearer picture of students' level of achievement.
2. *Use a decision rule to convert a set of rubric scores to a final grade.* Look at the rubric and decide what level on the rubric describes "excellent work," "good work," "fair work," and "poor work." Then come up with a decision rule for combining the rubric scores.
3. *Replace out-of-date evidence with more recent evidence.* Keep in mind, however, that you still need a large enough sample of work to provide a stable estimate of achievement.
4. *Be careful when combining rubric scores with percentage information to form a final grade.* Decide how much weight the percentage and rating portions of the grade will get. Combine letter grades directly using these weights. Or use a decision rule to convert the resulting rubric grade back to a percentage and then combine the percentage with other percentage scores using your weighting scheme.

REPORTING THE FINAL GRADE

Reporting the final percentage score on the report card has the benefit of preserving some detail about a student's level of achievement. But most districts require teachers to convert the academic achievement summary score to a letter or number grade or a proficiency scale.

Standards for setting cutoffs vary from district to district, school to school, and sometimes teacher to teacher. The range for an A in some places may be 94 to 100 percent, for example, and in others it may be 89 to 100 percent.

Although these differences cannot be eliminated, we can acknowledge the lack of precision they carry and work to ensure consistency in our own organizations. It is also important communicate to parents in commonsense terms the level of achievement represented by each of our report card symbols. For Example 10.1 shows a common rule for converting percentages to letter grades. You should have an agreed-on conversion rule that allows all teachers to translate summary numbers into your report card's symbols with consistency.

Keep the Link to Learning Targets

Beyond this, keep the big communication picture in mind as you think about reporting. We began by articulating a set of achievement expectations in the form of clear learning targets; that is, by specifying the things you will need and want to communicate about. We then carefully translated these standards into high-quality assessments capable of informing you about how well each student mastered each standard. We recommended keeping achievement records by learning target. Finally we discussed summarizing the evidence of learning across assessments to determine

For Example 10.1

Rule for Converting Percentages to Letter Grades

A+	= 97–100%	C	= 73–76%
A	= 93–96%	C−	= 70–72%
A−	= 90–92%	D+	= 67–69%
B+	= 87–89%	D	= 63–66%
B	= 83–86%	D−	= 60–62%
B−	= 80–82%	F	= 59% and below
C+	= 77–79%		

a summary grade. But that grade isn't merely a summary of scores. It also is a summary of student success in mastering the underlying standards reflected in your assessments. For this reason and given the records kept, we strongly recommend that, whenever you report a grade, that report be accompanied by a listing of these standards, indicating which ones the recipient of the grade did and did not master. This link brings the reporting process full circle from expectations to achievements in very specific terms.

FAQ 10.4

Proficiency-based Grading

Question:

We use proficiency-based grading and we mark each assignment with a level of proficiency. That is the data we keep in our record books. How do we average levels to come up with one overall level?

Answer:

Consider keeping raw scores or percentages instead of proficiency levels on individual pieces of work. Create and use a conversion table to translate the raw scores or percentages into a proficiency level for the report card.

Making a rule to translate aggregations of proficiency levels into one "uber-proficiency" level for the report card is problematic from an accuracy perspective, for the following reason. When you assign a proficiency level to each piece of evidence you will use for the summary report, you are making a subjective and perhaps arbitrary interpretation of each piece of evidence. Even if your judgments are consistent, a decision about proficiency based on one sample is likely to lead to an inaccurate conclusion. Instead, we would recommend that levels of proficiency be judged from a collection of work because such decisions benefit from a larger sample size.

Make Modifications with Care for Special Needs Students

Part of our responsibility and challenge in standards-based schools is to expose all students to an appropriate and rigorous curriculum. How we determine a final grade for students with special needs should reflect their individual progress toward the standards as specified in their individualized instructional plan (IEP) (Munk & Bursuck, 2003). For these students, as with all students, we need to make final grades criterion referenced, and have the grade indicate the level of learning attained relative to the learning goals documented in the IEP. In this context, report card grades should be accompanied by some narrative description or rating system that clearly communicates student progress toward the IEP goals (O'Connor, 2002). When such modified learning targets are the basis of grades, ensure this is clear to all parties and is incorporated into the IEP. A special needs student can receive an A for attainment of different learning targets than other students in the same classroom, if such targets are specified in advance through an IEP. We simply must be sure that everyone understands that either the learning targets have been modified or a specialized grading plan within the IEP is being applied (Brookhart, 2004).

Decide Borderline Cases with Extra Evidence

In those instances when a student's summary score lies right on the borderline between two grades, we recommend that the decision about which way to go *not* be based on consideration of nonachievement factors such as effort, but on additional evidence of learning. Some teachers keep one assessment or assignment reflective of important learning in reserve to administer for such instances. Others review the record to determine how the student performed on some of the most important assessments. Others offer extra credit that provides additional evidence of learning. Whatever you do, base your judgment on the most current evidence of achievement you have.

FAQ 10.5

Aptitude

Question:

What about aptitude? If a student is not capable of doing grade-level work, but we assign it anyway, should we not adjust the grading scale to take into account our estimation of that student's reduced ability? Conversely, if the work assigned is too easy for a student's ability, should we lower the grade to reflect the difference between the quality of work and what the student is capable of?

Answer:

Cizek, Fitzgerald, and Rachor (1996) report that 51 percent of teachers factor ability into their grade. Although this is a common practice, the answer has to be *no*, for two reasons.

First, there is great debate in the fields of psychology and measurement about what constitutes *intelligence* and how to gauge it. In the classroom we are not equipped with the kinds of background or tests needed to be accurate in our judgments of intelligence. We can do students great harm if we act on an inaccurate perception of their ability. But, in fact, we don't determine students' instructional needs on the basis of evidence of intelligence. Instead, we use evidence of past performance as a guide in determining which learning targets are most appropriate for a given student, and then we adjust the targets, if needed, so that the student encounters work at the right level of difficulty. If we were simply to adjust the grading scale, we would mask not only the student's true level of achievement but also a learning problem that we should address.

The second reason for not adjusting the grading scale for aptitude is that it confuses the meaning of the grade. As with effort, when a teacher raises or lowers a grade based on any information other than achievement data, the grade becomes uninterpretable. It cannot stand alone as a communicator about student learning.

Involve Students

At any time during the grading period, be sure students know how their current level of achievement compares to the standards they are expected to master.

Whenever students interpret their performance to be below what they want in their record of achievement, they can be given the opportunity to study more, learn more, and retake that assessment. This is especially crucial when the material in question is prerequisite for later learning. If the objective is to bring all students to appropriate levels of mastery of standards, anything we can do to keep students learning and wanting to succeed is worth doing.

FIGURE 10.9 Steps in Report Card Grading

1. Create a list of the learning targets you will assess during the quarter.
2. Make an assessment plan for summative and formative events.
3. Create, choose, and/or modify assessments.
4. Record information from assessments as you give them.
5. Summarize the achievement information into one score.
6. Translate the summary score into the report card symbol.

SIX STEPS TO ACCURATE, FAIR, AND DEFENSIBLE REPORT CARD GRADES

To put the grading guidelines into practice and to obtain accurate, justifiable grades, we suggest following the six steps (also shown in Figure 10.9).

Step 1: Start with learning targets. Create a list of the learning targets you will assess for grading purposes during the quarter, as described in Chapter 9.

Step 2: Make an assessment plan to include both formative and summative assessment events for each unit of study, as described in Chapter 9.

Step 3: Create, choose, and/or modify assessments, either in advance of instruction or along the way, as instruction unfolds. Verify assessments for quality, using procedures explained in Chapters 5 through 8.

Step 4: Record information from assessments as you give them. Record scores according to the learning target(s) they represent. Keep raw scores, if possible, as explained in Chapter 9. Keep rubric scores intact in the record book, as explained in this chapter.

Step 5: Summarize the achievement information into one score. Select a representative sample of most recent information for each learning target. Convert each score to a common scale, multiply any scores to be weighted by their weighting factor, and then apply the appropriate measure of central tendency to get one summary score.

Step 6: Translate the summary score into the symbol used on your report card using preset criterion-based standards rather than norm-referenced standards.

RUBRIC TO EVALUATE GRADING PRACTICES

Figure 10.10 presents a rubric showing each of the previous recommendations as a performance continuum that you can use to think about your own grading beliefs and practices. Instructions for using it to evaluate your own grading practices are found in Activity 10.5 at the end of this chapter.

FIGURE 10.10 Rubric for Evaluating Grading Practices

Criterion	Proficient	Developing	Beginning
1. Organizing the record book	Scores are organized by reporting categories from the report card. Scores are recorded according to the learning represented. Summative and formative data are differentiated. Summative data are entered as raw scores or percentages. Formative data are entered with numbers or symbols chosen to convey meaning suited to intended use.	Scores are organized by reporting categories from the report card. Scores are recorded according to assignment. Summative and formative data are differentiated. Some summative data are entered as raw scores or percentages; others are entered as symbols. Formative data are entered with numbers or symbols, but some may not convey meaning as needed.	Scores are not organized by reporting categories, even though the report card requires reporting out in categories. Scores are recorded according to assignment. Summative and formative data are undifferentiated. Data are entered as symbols that are difficult to interpret or use for intended purpose.
2. Keeping achievement data separate from other factors	Academic grades are based on achievement only. Extra credit work, if offered, links directly to learning targets, is evaluated for quality, and is only used to provide extra evidence of learning. Habits and behaviors such as turning in work late, not turning in work, and academic dishonesty are tracked separately.	Academic grades are based mostly on achievement, but one or two other factors may also make a small contribution to the grade. Extra credit work, if offered, links directly to learning targets, but may be awarded credit for completion. Habits and behaviors such as turning in work late, not turning in work, and academic dishonesty are tracked separately.	Academic grades are based on a mix of achievement and other factors; other factors have a major impact on the grade. Extra credit work, if offered, does not link directly to learning. Habits and behaviors such as turning in work late, not turning in work, and academic dishonesty are not tracked separately.

(continued)

FIGURE 10.10 (*continued*)

Criterion	Proficient	Developing	Beginning
	The affected work is recorded as "incomplete" or "not enough information" rather than as zero. There is an opportunity to replace an "incomplete" with a score without academic penalty. Grades in borderline cases are determined by additional achievement evidence.	They are penalized with a lower grade, but students have opportunity to replace the lower grade with satisfactorily completed work. Grades in borderline cases are determined by a combination of additional achievement evidence and evidence of other factors such as effort.	They are penalized with a radically lower score or a zero. Students have no opportunity to submit or resubmit the work. Borderline grade cases are handled by considering nonachievement factors.
3. Using most recent information	More recent evidence replaces earlier evidence on the same learning target. Evidence used to figure the grade constitutes a representative sample size. Formative assessment information is not figured into the grade when later summative data are available.	Sometimes more recent evidence replaces earlier evidence on the same learning target. Sometimes earlier evidence is included as well to meet sample size requirements. Some practice work contributes to the grade.	All data in the record book are used to determine a grade. No consideration is given to identifying or using the most current information. All student work contributes to the final grade. There is no distinction between scores on practice work and scores on work to demonstrate level of achievement.
4. Summarizing information	Record book entries are converted to a common scale before being weighted and combined. Scores are weighted and combined appropriately to represent learning accurately. Rubric scores are combined appropriately with other data or are converted to a score using a decision rule that results in an accurate depiction of the level of achievement.	Record book entries are converted to a common scale before being weighted and combined. Some weighting is not justified by the learning it represents. Some type of decision rule is used to convert rubric scores to grades, but in combination with other information, the resulting score may not accurately depict level of achievement.	Record book entries are not converted to a common scale before being weighted and combined. Weighting, if done, misrepresents the learning and distorts the grade. Rubric scores are recorded as grades, treated as raw scores or converted to percentages inappropriately.

Criterion	Proficient	Developing	Beginning
	The most appropriate measure of central tendency is used to arrive at a summary score.	The mean is the only measure of central tendency used to arrive at a summary score, even when the median would provide a more representative summary score.	Combining information is done subjectively or informally, by "feel," rather than by applying a measure of central tendency.
5. Determining the grade	Summary scores representing achievement data are translated into the grades or symbols used on the report card by means of preset criterion-referenced standards. There are clear descriptions of how to apply the preset standards and what each grade or symbol means.	Summary scores representing achievement data are translated into the symbols used on the report card by means of preset criterion-referenced standards. There may not be sufficient information available to guide accurate or consistent translation of summary scores to report card grades or symbols.	Summary scores representing achievement data are plotted on a normal curve to determine report card grades.
6. Verifying assessment quality	Summative data are reviewed for accuracy. Inaccurate or incomplete data are not used. Assessments modified for special needs students to conform to IEP requirements yield accurate information.	Summative data are reviewed for accuracy, but some inaccurate or incomplete data goes unrecognized. There is an attempt to modify assessments for special needs students to conform to IEP requirements, but they may not be carried out correctly.	Summative data are not reviewed for accuracy, or there is no understanding of what to look for. There is no attempt to modify assessments for special needs students to conform to IEP requirements, or no awareness of the IEP requirements.
7. Involving students	Summative assessment information and report card grades do not come as a surprise to students. Students have opportunities to demonstrate higher achievement on previously evaluated learning targets.	Summative assessment information and report card grades come as a surprise to some students. Students have limited opportunities to demonstrate higher achievement on previously evaluated learning targets.	Summative assessment information and report card grades come as a surprise to most students. Students have no opportunities to demonstrate higher achievement on previously evaluated learning targets.

Summary

We think at times that the pursuit of grades dominates the lives of far too many students, and that the focus on grades still adversely affects the environment of too many classrooms. However grades are used once they are given, we must be dedicated to ensuring that they communicate as clearly and accurately as possible when we create them. The issue is not whether something needs to be done about grades; the issue is what to do. The grading recommendations in this chapter reflect what we think grading practices should look like if they are to be accurate and have a chance of promoting learning.

We also believe that there is a role for professional judgment in grading. In fact, it is impossible in any grading context to leave professional judgment out of the equation. Each teacher brings to their grading practices specific knowledge about individual students and their progress toward the standards. We exercise professional judgment when deciding what content to test. We exercise professional judgment when deciding how best to convert rubric scores to grades. The goal of the recommendations in this chapter is to make an essentially subjective system as objective and defensible as possible.

One of our messages throughout this book is about the power of a classroom with an aligned system of curriculum, instruction, assessment, and reporting. By now you know it begins with clear curriculum targets aligned to standards. Teachers then clarify those targets for students and transform them into accurate assessments. Along the way students are involved in their own assessment, record keeping, and communication about their progress toward those targets, and student learning is documented and organized in record books according to learning target and standard. Finally, student achievement is reported to parents and students relative to those same standards.

This chapter has focused largely on assigning report card grades by subject in a traditional letter- or number-based system. Often parents expect, if not demand, this form of reporting, and yet they also value the specific information that can be provided through a standards-based reporting form (Guskey, 2002). We have established here that the purpose of grades is to communicate about student achievement. The next two chapters will explore other forms of communication. As you proceed, keep the goal of standards-based education in mind: to teach, assess, improve, and communicate about student learning in relation to academic learning standards. We can focus less of our time on providing subject area grades and still accomplish our goal if we move toward the use of rich, descriptive performance standards that provide specific information about where the student is relative to each standard. In the chapters that follow, we will provide more detail about how to gather and communicate that detail. When we do it well, the payoff is worth it for us and for our students.

CHAPTER 10 ACTIVITIES

End-of-chapter activities are intended to help you master the chapter's learning targets. They are designed to deepen your understanding of the chapter content, provide discussion topics for learning team meetings, and guide implementation of the practices taught in the chapter.

Forms for completing each activity appear in editable Microsoft Word format in the Chapter 10 CD file. Documents on the CD are marked with this symbol:

Chapter 10 Learning Targets

At the conclusion of Chapter 10 you will know how to do the following:

1. Identify the special challenges associated with effective communication using grades.
2. Follow a series of guidelines for effective grading.
3. Summarize evidence gathered over time into a meaningful grade.
4. Convert rubric scores into grades.
5. Evaluate and refine your own grading practices using the Rubric for Sound Grading Practices.

Activity 10.1 Keep a Reflective Journal
Activity 10.2 Develop Solutions Other Than Grades
Activity 10.3 Analyze Steps in Your Grading Process
Activity 10.4 Revisit How You Convert Rubric Scores to Grades
Activity 10.5 Evaluate Your Grading Practices
Activity 10.6 Reflect on Your Own Learning
Activity 10.7 Select Portfolio Artifacts

Activity 10.1

Keep a Reflective Journal

Keep a record of your thoughts, questions, and any implementation activities you tried while reading Chapter 10.

Reflective Journal Form

Activity 10.2

Develop Solutions Other than Grades

After reading the descriptions of each grading guideline in the section, "Three Grading Guidelines," turn back to Chapter 9 and reread the section, "Guideline 2: Track Information about Work Habits and Social Skills Separately." Work with a partner or your team to carry out the following activity.

1. Select one problem to focus on: missing work, late work, cheating, or attendance.
2. List the interventions and consequences currently in place in your school for the problem.
3. Identify which consequences, if any, involve lowering the grade.
4. If you were to remove the "lowered-grade" consequence for the problem, what other consequences might you institute to deter students from engaging in the problem behavior? What support system might you set up to help students who have the problem? Discuss with a partner or your team. (You may also want to refer to Fixes 1, 2, 4, and 5 in O'Connor [2011].)
5. Draft a classroom policy that reflects a solution to the problem other than lowering the grade.
6. If your building policy allows it, introduce your draft policy to students.
7. Track either informally or formally any changes in student behavior that you believe are due to the new policy.
8. Share your observations with a partner or with your team.

Develop Solutions Other Than Grades

Activity 10.3

Analyze Steps in Your Grading Process

After reading the section, "Six Steps to Accurate, Fair, and Defensible Report Card Grades," work independently, with a partner, or with your team to complete the following activity.

1. Imagine it is the beginning of a grading period—you are going to send home grades in X number of weeks. Right now, your record book is blank. What are the steps you usually take to go from no data to a final grade? List the steps in your process.
2. Mark each step to indicate your level of satisfaction with it:

    + = Works fine

    > = Could be refined

    # = Needs major work or unsure what to do

3. Compare your process to the one outlined in Figure 10.9. Where does your practice align? Where does it diverge?
4. Revise your process as needed.
5. Use it for the next grading period. Keep track of how well it works for you.
6. Share with a partner or your team your observations about the impact the changes have made.

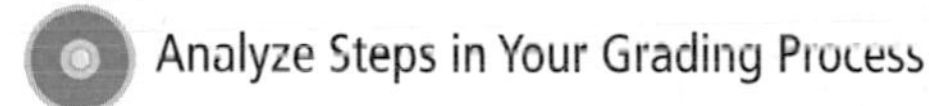
Analyze Steps in Your Grading Process

Compare to Steps in Report Card Grading

Activity 10.4

Revisit How You Convert Rubric Scores to Grades

After reading the section, "Converting Rubric Scores to Grades," work independently, with a partner, or with your team to complete the following activity.

1. Decide whether you will determine the grade using the *average ratings* process or *pattern of ratings* process.
2. If you are using the *average ratings* process, follow the instructions in the subsection titled "Average Ratings."
3. If you are using the *pattern of ratings* process, follow the instructions in the subsection titled "Pattern of Ratings."
4. Discuss the following questions with a partner or your team: How does this process differ from the one you have traditionally used? What are the advantages to converting rubric scores to grades using the process you selected? Would you prefer to try the other process?

none

Activity 10.5

Evaluate Your Grading Practices

Review the Rubric for Evaluating Grading Practices (Figure 10.10). Work independently, with a partner, or with your team to complete the following activity. You will need your record book or access to your electronic grade reports.

1. Use the rubric to evaluate your practices for each of the seven criteria. You can either record your judgments on the evaluation form or highlight the phrases in each criterion on the rubric that most closely describe your grading practices.
2. Discuss both the rubric and your self-ratings with a partner or your learning team. What changes, if any, might you want to make based on the evaluation? What might be your highest priority adjustment? What might be difficult to do? What, if any, other changes would need to occur first?

Rubric for Evaluating Grading Practices

Debrief Evaluating Your Grading Practices

Grading Practices Evaluation Form

Activity 10.6

Reflect on Your Own Learning

Review the Chapter 10 learning targets and select one or more that represented new learning for you or struck you as most significant from this chapter. If you are working individually, write a short reflection that captures your current understanding. If you are working with a partner or a team, either discuss what you have written or use this as a discussion prompt for a team meeting.

Reflect on Chapter 10 Learning

Activity 10.7

Select Portfolio Artifacts

Any of the activities from this chapter can be used as portfolio entries. Select any activity you have completed or artifacts you have created that will illustrate your competence at the Chapter 10 learning targets:

1. Identify the special challenges associated with effective communication using grades.
2. Follow a series of guidelines for effective grading.
3. Summarize evidence gathered over time into a meaningful grade.
4. Convert rubric scores into grades.
5. Evaluate and refine your own grading practices using the Rubric for Sound Grading Practices.

If you are keeping a reflective journal, you may want to include Chapter 10's entry in your portfolio.

Chapter 10 Portfolio Entry Cover Sheet

CHAPTER

11

Portfolios

We need a more robust display of evidence than a collection of grades can provide to tell the full story of student achievement and of their journey toward competence. More importantly, so do students.

Portfolios have at their heart the desire to capture and communicate depth of student learning. A *portfolio* is a collection of artifacts put together to tell a story. We often associate portfolios with artists, who use them to communicate visually about their talent, style, and range of work; or with writers, who put them together to illustrate their writing capabilities. The contents are selected to offer a rich and detailed view of their subject's characteristics or qualities.

Beyond their potential as a rich source of information, in the classroom portfolios can play a significant role in learning. Many times the responsibility for collecting, interpreting, and sharing portfolio contents falls to the teacher. However, we overlook a powerful learning opportunity when the *subject* of the portfolio—the student—is not also the *creator*. Collecting, organizing, and reflecting on their own work builds students' understanding of themselves as learners and nurtures a sense of accomplishment. Becoming reflective learners, developing an internal feedback loop, learning to set goals, and noticing new competencies and new challenges are all habits of thought we can cultivate in students through the use of portfolios.

Portfolios can tell lots of different stories. The keys to effective and efficient portfolio use lie in knowing which story you want to tell, maximizing the students' role, and managing the variables accordingly. In this chapter we will explore the kinds of portfolios commonly used today and purposes for each, student and teacher roles in preparing portfolios, sharing options, and keys to their successful use.

Chapter 11 addresses the shaded portions of Figure 11.1. Figure 11.2 summarizes the portfolio decisions we will address.

Chapter 11 Learning Targets

At the end of Chapter 11, you will know how to do the following:

- Select the kind of portfolio best suited to your context.
- Determine the learning targets that will be the focus of the portfolio.
- Engage students in selecting artifacts to include.
- Prepare students to annotate entries and reflect on the portfolio contents.
- Plan for sharing options.
- Manage the process and minimize the mess.

FIGURE 11.1 Keys to Quality Classroom Assessment

Key 1: Clear Purpose
Who will use the information?
How will they use it?
What information, in what detail, is required?

Key 2: Clear Targets
Are learning targets clear to teachers?
What kinds of achievement are to be assessed?
Are these learning targets the focus of instruction?

Key 3: Sound Design
Do assessment methods match learning targets?
Does the sample represent learning appropriately?
Are items, tasks, and scoring rubrics of high quality?
Does the assessment control for bias?

Key 4: Effective Communication
Can assessment results be used to guide instruction?
Do formative assessments function as effective feedback?
Is achievement tracked by learning target and reported by standard?
Do grades communicate achievement accurately?

Key 5: Student Involvement
Do assessment practices meet students' information needs?
Are learning targets clear to students?
Will the assessment yield information that students can use to self-assess and set goals?
Are students tracking and communicating their evolving learning?

FIGURE 11.2 Portfolio Decision Flow

1. What kind(s) of portfolios will we assemble? What story do we want to tell?
2. Which learning target(s) will be the focus of our portfolios?
3. Based on purpose and target(s), which pieces of evidence will we include? What are our guidelines for inclusion? How will we ensure a representative sample of student work?
4. What kinds of annotations will students make on each piece?
5. What kinds of reflection on the overall contents will students engage in?
6. When and with whom will we share the portfolios?
7. How will we organize the materials?

KINDS OF PORTFOLIOS—FOCUS ON *PURPOSE*

As a collection of evidence, the portfolio itself is only an organizing tool. The *artifacts*—the individual items—in an artist's, an author's, or your own assessment portfolio require more than placement in a folder to hang together. The portfolio story, like all other stories, needs a theme to guide the selection of ingredients.

The purpose of a portfolio is essentially the theme of the story it is designed to tell. In this section, we will look at five basic purposes for portfolios: growth, project documentation, achievement, competence, and celebration (Figure 11.3). After choosing the purpose that fits your context best, you will be in a position to make logical decisions about artifacts to select, student commentary to include, and options for sharing the contents with others.

Growth Portfolios

Growth portfolios show progress toward competence on one or more learning targets. They document increasing levels of achievement. Students select evidence related to a given learning target at two or more points in time and their annotations explain the level of achievement each artifact represents. Each selection may represent best work as a point in time or typical work. The sampling challenge is to ensure that the samples chosen really do represent best *or* typical work, and not anomalous work from which to judge growth (e.g., selecting a piece of poor quality at the beginning that underrepresents the student's true level of achievement at that time). The student writes a self-reflection to summarize growth: "Here's how far I've come and here's what I know and can do now that I couldn't do before" or "I used to . . , but now I . . ."

Project Portfolios

Project portfolios are, as the name suggests, focused on the work from an individual project. Their purpose is to document the steps taken, often to show evidence of having satisfactorily completed intermediary steps along the way to the finished product. Sometimes their purpose is to show competence, such as with writing processes or scientific processes. They also can document such things as time management capabilities.

Artifacts are chosen to provide evidence suited to the project to be documented. In the case of a research paper, students might show their progression of work from initial question to finished product, including those pieces of evidence that best illustrate the major steps they took. Each piece of evidence is accompanied by an explanation of what step or steps it is intended to show and how it does that. Students may write a comprehensive "process paper" or they may annotate each artifact. In either case, students will learn more from the process and remember it better if they also write a reflection on what they learned from completing the steps involved in the project.

Achievement Portfolios

Achievement portfolios document the level of student achievement at a point in time. They are comprised of best, most recent work organized by the learning target each represents. In the case of achievement portfolios, it is important to attend to the number of samples collected. Certain learning targets will call for multiple samples to demonstrate level of achievement while other achievement targets may need only one. Student annotations refer to the learning target and level of competence each sample shows. These are often used as the basis for discussion and goal setting at conference time.

Competence Portfolios

Competence portfolios offer evidence in support of a claim to have attained an acceptable or exemplary level of achievement. They sometimes take the form of "exhibition of mastery" portfolios or "school-to-work" portfolios. As with achievement portfolios, competence portfolios require that we attend to sampling issues. It is crucial to their success to determine in advance the number of pieces of evidence needed to support an assertion of competence for each learning target addressed. We want to show that a high level of achievement has been sustained and is not just the result of chance.

Celebration Portfolios

Celebration portfolios give students the opportunity to decide what accomplishments or achievement they are most proud of. In this case, students decide what to put in and why, and sampling is not an issue. The elementary teacher may choose to leave the subject of the celebration open ended—"anything you're proud of"—or focus it more

FIGURE 11.3 Kinds of Portfolios

Type of Portfolio	Purpose	Artifacts to Collect
Growth	To show progress toward one or more learning goals	Artifacts from before, during, and after learning
Project	To document the trajectory of a project	All drafts of work during the creation of the product or performance
Achievement	To demonstrate current level of achievement over a collection of learning targets	Artifacts comprising a representative sample of achievement
Competence	To provide evidence of having attained competence in one or more areas	Artifacts representing highest level of achievement
Celebration	To showcase best work or what the student is most proud of	Student choice based on quality of work or preference

Source: Reprinted from *Seven Strategies of Assessment* for *Learning* (p. 157), by J. Chappuis, 2009, Upper Saddle River, NJ: Pearson Education. Reprinted by permission.

narrowly—"your work in science" or "things that show you are a reader." Secondary teachers using celebration portfolios generally narrow the focus to some aspect of the subject they teach.

Working Folders

Working folders are not portfolios. They function as holding bins, sometimes for every scrap of paper related to a project, sometimes as an idea "seed bed," sometimes as a collection of works in progress, and other times as an undifferentiated collection of finished pieces. Working folders are often used as the place to go to review work that might be included in the portfolio, the collection of all possible artifacts from which to make selections. Portfolios serving more than one purpose can be developed from a single working folder. Similarly, the same piece of student work can be selected for portfolios having different purposes.

PORTFOLIO CONTENTS—FOCUS ON *LEARNING TARGETS*

What goes into a portfolio? All of a student's work? Only the best? "Before" and "after" samples? Whatever the student selects? Artifact selection is first governed by the purpose. As we saw in the previous section, different portfolios require different artifacts to tell their stories.

Although portfolios lend themselves naturally to artifacts created by performance assessments, we are not limited to the evidence produced by that one assessment method. All five kinds of learning targets—knowledge, reasoning, skill, product, and disposition—can be the focus of evidence gathering for portfolios. Thus, all forms of assignments and assessments, both formative and summative, can be included, as suited to the intended purpose of the portfolio.

Contents can reflect a single learning target, a series of learning targets, or all learning targets in a given subject. They can also reflect learning targets that cross subject areas. For example, a middle school portfolio project may require students to demonstrate their achievement of research skills in English, social studies, and science.

Artifact Selection

The artifacts in a portfolio should not consist simply as proof of direction following, as when the only instructions students receive are to include three samples from September, three samples from October, and three samples from November. They must be aimed at telling a story about specific, intended learning. It might seem to be a simple point, but it bears emphasizing: Clearly identify in advance the learning targets about which the portfolio is intended to communicate. *Do not skip this step.* Much portfolio chaos can be avoided entirely right here. You have identified the purpose (to document project work, growth, achievement, or competence, or to celebrate), and now you must identify what learning targets are the appropriate focus of the examination of growth, project work, achievement, competence, or celebration.

Let's say your students will assemble a project portfolio. The project consists of a task: to design and conduct a scientific investigation, to document the work and the results, and to prepare a written report. What learning targets are at the heart of this project? What aspects of the learning will the portfolio document? You may be focusing on the learning target "designs and conducts a scientific investigation." So you might choose to have the students document the steps of their investigations. Therefore the artifacts they will collect should show how they formulated the question, how they came up with the investigation design, what they did at each step, the thinking behind their data interpretation, and the options they considered in settling on an explanation. This list sounds like it could be accomplished through a written report—it includes the question, a description of the investigation, presentation of data, and conclusions. The difference between the collection of artifacts and a written report is this: the portfolio contents are chosen to *illustrate the thinking behind the steps* of a scientific investigation, not just to document that they were done. The goal of this kind of portfolio is *not* to show that students completed each step—the report can do that—but to show how they thought through and implemented each step.

Suggestions for types of artifacts suited to each kind of portfolio were offered in the previous section and are summarized in Figure 11.3.

ASSESSMENT OF INDIVIDUAL ARTIFACTS. For growth, achievement, and competence portfolios, artifacts should have been assessed by the teacher or student either formatively or summatively, before or during selection. A piece of evidence with no form of assessment attached is of limited use in illustrating growth, achievement, or competence. Often the piece has been assessed previously; other times, the annotation serves as the assessment.

For project portfolios, the artifacts do not need to have been assessed. The annotations and reflection function as a kind of assessment: "I chose this to illustrate . . ." If students write a process paper as their reflection, you may wish to assess it. Just make sure the assessment criteria are based on learning targets as described in Chapter 7.

For celebration portfolios, almost anything goes. The value in them is that students are creating their own criteria for selecting artifacts. Their annotations and reflections become the only assessment needed to accomplish the purpose of this type of portfolio.

SAMPLING. Sampling is an important issue for achievement and competence portfolios. For example, if the portfolio's purpose is to demonstrate level of achievement in a student-led conference and the target is mathematics problem solving, we will have to think about how much evidence is enough to show level of achievement. How many and what types of artifacts would need to be included in the portfolio to be sure that any inference we make about overall student problem-solving competence is accurate? We might need 10 examples from a variety of content strands, some of which may include real-life applications. Therefore, to ensure that students are selecting a broad enough sample of accurate information to share with their parents, we might specify how many and what types of items must be included, and which learning targets are to be represented. The size of the sample, as always, depends on the intended use and the type of learning target at the focus of the achievement.

WHO DECIDES? Usually the teacher decides on the type of portfolio. Depending on the age of the students and the type of portfolio, either the teacher or students (or both) will select the targets to illustrate. When sampling is a consideration, the teacher generally crafts guidelines to ensure selection of a sufficient number of artifacts. However, to the extent possible, choice of the artifacts themselves should be within the student's control.

When students participate in assembling the portfolio, reflect on what the evidence says, and prepare to share, they become more invested in the process and the outcome. Inviting students to help determine what will go into the portfolio offers them an opportunity to practice thinking about what constitutes evidence in a given context. Help them think through the criteria for the selections they will be making—you may also want to engage them in the same kind of thinking you had to do about purpose and learning targets. To the extent that your students are able to do it (and even young

FIGURE 11.4 Who Decides?

The teacher generally decides on the kind of portfolio to use. Either the teacher, the students, or both make the rest of the decisions.

Decision	Project	Growth	Achievement	Competence	Celebration
Learning Target(s)	Teacher or both	Teacher or both	Teacher or both	Teacher	Student or both
Number and Kind of Entries	Student or both	Teacher or both	Teacher or both	Teacher or both	Student
Artifact Selection	Student or both	Student or both	Student or both	Student or both	Student
Kind of Annotations	Teacher or both	Teacher or both	Teacher or both	Teacher or both	Student or both
Kind of Reflections	Teacher or both	Teacher or both	Teacher or both	Teacher or both	Student or both
Audience	Teacher or student	Teacher or student	Teacher or student	Teacher or student	Teacher or student

ones can complete much of this), let the majority of work shift from you to them, where the ownership belongs. Figure 11.4 summarizes the extent to which teachers and students can make various decisions for each kind of portfolio.

Work Sample Annotations

If a portfolio's contents consist solely of samples of student work, no matter who collects them, it will not function effectively either as a communication tool or as an enhancement to learning. It can be an awkward experience for the student, parent, and teacher to engage in a conference where the student opens up a folder and says "Here is my social studies work," with nothing else to do but flip through pages of assignments, projects, and tests. More thought on the student's part is needed to bring the story to life and to be the catalyst for increased achievement.

Work sample annotations are comments students or teachers make about each piece of evidence selected for the portfolio. Generally, they link the work to the intended learning in some way. Creating these comments helps portfolio creators be clear about why they are choosing each artifact and what it shows. They also help the portfolio's audience know what to notice; without some form of explanation for each artifact included, the audience will most likely not make a link to the learning. If students prepare annotations when selecting their artifacts, when the time comes to share their portfolios with others, nervousness or other distractions will not cause them to forget *how* this particular entry demonstrates their learning.

An unstructured form of annotation is the "pause and think" comment. Students use a work sample to reflect in an open-ended way about what they are learning, such as in the following:

- Why the learning is important to them
- Something they notice about themselves as learners
- A key point they have learned from doing the assignment

Annotations can also take the form of statements of the learning target each artifact represents, along with an explanation of how this artifact demonstrates achievement. ("I can summarize stories. I have included the biggest events and main characters. I have left out the details. I have put things in the right order and used my own words.")

Another form of annotation consists of student self-assessment against established criteria. For growth and achievement portfolios, students can point out features of the work that match phrases in the criteria and draw conclusions about level of quality, strengths, and areas for improvement. For competence portfolios, students can explain why a particular artifact constitutes proof of proficiency, showing how it meets established criteria. ("This work is an example of level _________ on the ________ criteria because it __________.")

Frequently, annotations are written on a cover sheet. For Example 11.1 shows two versions of a portfolio entry cover sheet.

Student Self-reflection

Portfolios also offer an opportunity for student self-reflection. It can be tempting to pass over having students reflect on what the portfolio as a whole means to them. But, if we pull up here, we have stopped just short of increased learning.

Self-reflection is somewhat different from the self-assessment students may have engaged in for each artifact. With self-reflection, students revisit their experiences, looking back over a body of evidence to make statements about what they have learned, how they have learned it, what worked and what didn't work, and what they would do differently, or how far they have come (Chappuis, 2009, p. 159). While success at self-reflection may seem serendipitous at first, we can nurture learning beyond the bounds of our targets if we allow students to think about themselves as learners and provide opportunities for them to dig a little deeper into what the learning means to them. When they have selected and annotated artifacts, they are primed to uncover insights into themselves. Insight requires time to reflect and something to reflect on, which is what this part of the portfolio process provides.

If students have not done reflective thinking before—open-ended, who-am-I-as-a-learner thinking—be prepared to devote a little class time to practicing. Figure 11.5 offers prompts to stimulate self-reflection. Choose one, or create your own, explain the task, model it, let students discuss it, then give them time to try it out. Let volunteers

For Example 11.1

Portfolio Entry Cover Sheets

(Form A)

Date: ______________________ Title of Selection: ________________________

Learning target(s) this selection addresses:

What this selection illustrates about my learning:

Why I chose this selection:

(Form B)

Date: ______________________ Name of Assignment: ____________________

What this shows I am good at/have learned/know how to do:

What this shows I need to work on:

Source: Reprinted from *Seven Strategies of Assessment* for *Learning* (pp. 246 & 247), by J. Chappuis, 2009, Upper Saddle River, NJ: Pearson Education. Reprinted by permission.

share their self-reflections and ask them what doing this has taught them. After they know what is required in this kind of thinking, self-reflection makes a good homework assignment, especially if students discuss their thoughts with their parents before, during, or after writing.

FIGURE 11.5 Prompts to Stimulate Self-reflection

Reflect on . . .	Prompts
Growth	I have become better at ____. I used to ____, but now I ____. I have developed a better understanding of ____ through ____. What helps me as a learner? What did I learn about myself as a learner? What gets in my way as a learner? What things are difficult for me as a learner? What used to be difficult that is easier now? How did that happen/What did I do to make that happen? What are my next questions? Here are "before" and "after" pictures of my learning.
Project	What did I learn about myself as a learner by doing this project? What skills did I develop? What skills would I like to develop as a result of doing this project? What did I like most/least about this project? Why? How did my thinking about ________ change as a result of doing this project? What impact has doing this project had on my interests regarding __________?
Achievement	What did I learn? How did I learn it? What learning targets have I mastered? What are my strengths (in this subject/on these learning targets)? What do I still need to work on? What learning targets have I not yet mastered? What would I change about what I did?
Competence	Here is what doing ________ taught me about myself as a learner: __________. What does my evidence show that I have mastered? How does it show that?
Celebration	What am I proudest of/happiest with? What did I enjoy doing the most? What does my portfolio say about me? What impact has putting together this portfolio had on my interests, attitudes, and views of ________ (content or process)?

Source: Adapted from *Seven Strategies of Assessment for Learning* (pp. 159–166), by J. Chappuis, 2009, Upper Saddle River, NJ: Pearson Education. Adapted by permission.

FIGURE 11.6 Creating Specific and Challenging Goals

Creating Specific and Challenging Goals

Specific and challenging goals include the following key elements:

- A clear statement of the intended learning: "What do I need to get better at?"
- A description of current status: "Where am I now with respect to my goal?"
- An action plan: "How will I do this?"
  - My actions: "What steps will I take?"
  - Assistance: "Who can I work with? What materials will I need?"
  - Time frame: "When will I accomplish my goal?"
- Evidence of accomplishment: "What will I use as my 'before' and 'after' pictures?"

Source: Reprinted from *Seven Strategies of Assessment for Learning* (p. 124), by J. Chappuis, 2009, Upper Saddle River, NJ: Pearson Education. Reprinted by permission.

Goal Setting

A good strategy for establishing an "I can do it" mindset toward learning is for students to show themselves and others that they are accomplishing goals. In one form of goal setting, the student's annotation for each artifact includes an area or learning target to work on, based on analysis of the artifact's strengths and weaknesses. In another form, students set goals after reviewing the whole portfolio.

Goals that have the greatest impact on achievement are specific—they identify the intended learning, describe the current status, and outline a plan of action. Figure 11.6 offers a formula for creating specific and challenging goals most likely to lead to further learning. (For a more in-depth treatment of self-assessment, self-reflection, and goal setting, see Chappuis, 2009, Chapters 4 and 7.)

SHARING OPTIONS

We determine the audience for a portfolio by thinking about the story it has to tell. Who might be interested in this story? Audiences for portfolio sharing include parents, other students, teachers, the principal, central office staff, community members, grandparents, friends, businesses, review committees, and potential employers. Student-involved conferences often rely on portfolios to focus or augment the discussion.

The audience for a portfolio can also be its creator. After assembling your own classroom assessment portfolio, you may be the only one who sees it. If so, is it a waste of time? We believe not. However, for most students, sharing their work with an interested audience can generate additional learning and insight into themselves as learners, as well as increased motivation to keep working. See Chapter 12 for guidance on how to plan for and conduct portfolio-based conversations.

KEYS TO SUCCESSFUL USE

We offer a few reminders and suggestions for effectively implementing portfolios, related to four keys to success: ensuring accuracy, keeping track of evidence, investing time up front, and making the portfolio experience safe for students.

1. Ensure Accuracy of the Evidence

A portfolio as a reflection and communication device is only as good as its contents. Each piece must provide credible evidence. Each entry is only as good as the assignment given: The underlying assignment must provide accurate evidence of the intended learning target, or the evidence will not be useful. It is a good idea to verify that it shows what you and the student think it shows prior to sharing the portfolio with others.

2. Keep Track of the Evidence

Keeping track of artifacts has been a personal Waterloo for more than one teacher. The following guidelines should help you institute a system to avoid the nightmare of thousands of papers spilling out of folders and milk crates. One key to success is to find a system that fits your natural (or learned) organizational style.

- *Identify the type of artifacts you will be keeping.* Will they include the physical product itself, a photograph of articles or projects that do not lend themselves to storage, a videotape, an audiotape, the artifact on a computer hard drive or disc, or something else?
- *Organize the artifacts.* How you choose to do this depends on what type of artifacts you will be collecting. Options include notebooks, file folders, accordion folders, hanging files in a file drawer, clear-view binders, 11 × 17 paper folded in half as dividers (especially for growth portfolios—artifacts can be pasted on each facing page, with flip-up annotations), binders with categories, and binders with envelopes for computer discs.
- *Store the collections.* Options include magazine file boxes, cereal boxes, laundry detergent boxes, plastic crates, or file cabinet drawers (with collections organized by period at the secondary level and by table group, row, or subject at the elementary level). If choosing to store artifacts in a computer program, remember that the software is only a place to keep artifacts. Computer programs won't automatically create quality portfolios; you still have to make all of the decisions outlined in this chapter.
- *Schedule time throughout the process.* Periodically schedule time for students to select, date (this is crucial), and annotate artifacts while they are collecting them. Don't wait to do this until it is time to share or publish the portfolio.

3. Invest Time Up Front

Dedicate time at the beginning of a portfolio project to save time later. Teach students the purpose and process for portfolios, the criteria for selecting individual entries and annotating them, and strategies for self-reflection. Turn responsibility over to students as soon as possible. In our opinion, portfolios are not worth the time and effort they take if teachers do all the work.

4. Make the Experience Safe

Although it might not appear so on the surface, creating and sharing a portfolio can be a risky business. We are asking students to publicly share what they have accomplished and who they are as learners. To students, the risks include these:

- Someone else's artifacts will be better than mine.
- Mine will be better than everyone else's.
- Mine will be better (or worse) than my friend's.
- I will look clueless.
- I will come off as smug.

From your own experiences, you may be able to add to the list. We reduce the risk factor for students by what we model and what we allow, by how we treat each student and how we allow each student to treat others. Set norms for your students that make them comfortable with the whole portfolio process.

Summary

Portfolios serve two functions: to improve communication about complex student learning targets; and to promote student learning.

All decisions regarding portfolios, from selecting content to determining the amount of student involvement, depend on the purpose of the portfolio. We examined five types of portfolios—growth, project, achievement, certifying competence, and celebration—and the effect of these purposes on portfolio design decisions. We offered suggestions for maximizing success in four areas: ensuring accuracy of results; keeping track of the evidence; investing time up front; and making the experience safe.

In this chapter, we have encouraged you to involve students in preparing and maintaining portfolios. They are too much work to be used solely by the teacher as backup evidence for a grade. No matter what kind of portfolio you have, to be worth the investment of time as a learning and communication tool, include three elements:

- Student involvement in content selection
- Student commentary on the contents—why they were selected and what they represent
- Self-reflection about what they learned

Portfolios are a means to an end, not the end itself. They provide a direct route to students thinking more deeply about their learning and retaining it longer. They are a medium in which students can take responsibility for their own learning and engage in the critical thinking needed for self-assessment and self-reflection. They foster richer conversations with others about complex student achievement. And if students are the ones talking, so much the better.

CHAPTER 11 ACTIVITIES

End-of-chapter activities are intended to help you master the chapter's learning targets. They are designed to deepen your understanding of the chapter content, provide discussion topics for learning team meetings, and guide implementation of the practices taught in the chapter.

Forms for completing each activity can appear in editable Microsoft Word format in the Chapter 11 CD file. Documents on the CD are marked with this symbol:

Chapter 11 Learning Targets

At the end of Chapter 11, you will know how to do the following:

1. Select the kind of portfolio best suited to your context.
2. Determine the learning targets that will be the focus of the portfolio.
3. Engage students in selecting artifacts to include.
4. Prepare students to annotate entries and reflect on the portfolio contents.
5. Plan for sharing options.
6. Manage the process and minimize the mess.

Activity 11.1 Keep a Reflective Journal
Activity 11.2 Try a New Portfolio Option with Students
Activity 11.3 Revise an Existing Student Portfolio System
Activity 11.4 Start a Personal Portfolio
Activity 11.5 Review Your Own Classroom Assessment Portfolio
Activity 11.6 Reflect on Your Own Learning
Activity 11.7 Select Portfolio Artifacts
Activity 11.8 Reflect on Your Learning over Time

Activity 11.1

Keep a Reflective Journal

Keep a record of your thoughts, questions, and any implementation activities you tried while reading Chapter 11.

Reflective Journal Form

Activity 11.2

Try a New Portfolio Option with Students

Work independently, with a partner, or with your team to complete the following activity.

1. Review the section, "Kinds of Portfolios—Focus on *Purpose*." Decide on one kind of portfolio to establish in your classroom.
2. Decide the length of time students will keep the portfolio.
3. Determine what decisions students will make in creating the portfolio. Refer to Figure 11.4 for suggestions.
4. Review the section, "Portfolio Contents—Focus on *Learning Targets*." Determine the scope of learning targets to be represented in the portfolio, or determine learning targets in conjunction with students.
5. Identify the artifacts or types of artifacts that will go into the portfolio, either yourself or with students. Attend to the sampling considerations described in the section, "Portfolio Contents—Focus on *Learning Targets*."
6. Plan for individual work sample annotations. What kinds of comments will students make on each piece?
7. Consider making student goal setting a part of the portfolio process, either along the way or at the conclusion.
8. Plan an opportunity for students to review and reflect on the contents of the portfolio as a whole.
9. Determine what form students will use to reflect on the portfolio as a whole.
10. Decide how, with whom, and when students will share their portfolios.
11. Try the process out. Note strengths and areas needing revision.
12. Discuss with a partner or your team what you tried, how it worked, and what you noticed as a result.

Portfolio Planning Form

Activity 11.3

Revise an Existing Student Portfolio System

Conduct this activity independently, with a partner, or with your team if you have a portfolio system already in place.

1. Review the section, "Kinds of Portfolios—Focus on *Purpose*." Determine what type of portfolio you have assembled. If it includes a combination of purposes, determine whether it works well for you that way or if you want to narrow the focus or separate it into two or more different types of portfolios.
2. Examine the contents called for in your portfolio.
   - Is it clear what learning target or targets are the focus of the portfolio?
   - Do the artifacts called for all align with the purpose of the portfolio? Do they all work to tell the story the portfolio is designed to tell?
   - For growth, achievement, and competence portfolios, have all artifacts been assessed before or during selection?
   - Have sampling issues been adequately addressed?
   - Is there sufficient opportunity for student ownership of the contents?
   - Are individual work samples annotated with helpful information?
   - Are students provided an opportunity to reflect on the portfolio as a whole?
   - Has student goal setting been incorporated, if appropriate?
   - Does each student have a viable sharing opportunity to discuss their portfolio with someone?
3. Audit your portfolio process according to the four recommendations in the section, "Keys to Successful Use."
4. Make any changes suggested by your work in steps 1, 2, and 3. You may want to use the Portfolio Planning Form from Activity 11.2 if you are making extensive revisions.

Portfolio Auditing Form

Activity 11.4

Start a Personal Portfolio

Work independently to complete this activity.

1. Select an area of focus. It could be a part of your professional activities or something you do away from work.
2. Review the section, "Kinds of Portfolios—Focus on *Purpose*." Determine the purpose for your portfolio—the story you want your portfolio to tell.
3. Review the section, "Portfolio Contents—Focus on *Learning Targets*." Determine the scope of your own personal learning (your "learning targets") to be represented in the portfolio.
4. Identify the artifacts or types of artifacts that will go into the portfolio. Attend to the sampling considerations described in the section "Portfolio Contents—Focus on *Learning Targets*," as needed.
5. Plan individual artifact annotations. What kinds of comments will be most helpful on each piece?
6. Assemble your portfolio, either over time or from artifacts you have already created.
7. Review and reflect on the contents of your portfolio as a whole.
8. Decide how and with whom you might share your portfolio.
9. Consider discussing with a partner or your team what the process of keeping a portfolio has contributed to your learning.

Personal Portfolio Decision Form

Activity 11.5

Review Your Own Classroom Assessment Portfolio

Work independently or with a partner using your own growth portfolio to complete this activity.

1. Review the section, "Kinds of Portfolios—Focus on *Purpose*." Is the purpose for your portfolio clear? If not, what will you need to do to refine it?
2. Review the section, "Portfolio Contents—Focus on *Learning Targets*." Are the learning targets represented by each artifact clearly identified? If not, either identify the learning target each artifact illustrates or move the artifact into a different file for possible use for a different purpose.
3. Do the artifacts represent a sufficient sample size to fulfill the purpose of your portfolio? Do you have enough evidence to support the intended use of the portfolio? If not, consider adding more artifacts by completing additional activities associated with the learning target(s).
4. Is each individual artifact annotated with helpful information? If not, consider using the Portfolio Entry Cover Sheet (or a variation of it) to elaborate on how the artifact illustrates the learning target (see For Example 11.1).
5. Make any revisions suggested by these questions.
6. Review the section, "Student Self-reflection." Select (or create) a reflection option and reflect on the contents of your portfolio as a whole.
7. Discuss with a partner or your team what the process of keeping a portfolio has contributed to your learning.

Personal Portfolio Review Form

Activity 11.6

Reflect on Your Own Learning

Review the Chapter 11 learning targets and select one or more that represented new learning for you or struck you as most significant from this chapter. If you are working individually, write a short reflection that captures your current understanding. If you are working with a partner or a team, either discuss what you have written or use this as a discussion prompt for a team meeting.

Reflect on Chapter 11 Learning

Activity 11.7

Select Portfolio Artifacts

Any of the activities from this chapter can be used as portfolio entries. Select any activity you have completed or artifacts you have created that will illustrate your competence at the Chapter 11 learning targets:

1. Select the kind of portfolio best suited to your context.
2. Determine the learning targets that will be the focus of the portfolio.
3. Engage students in selecting artifacts to include.
4. Prepare students to annotate entries and reflect on the portfolio contents.
5. Plan for sharing options.
6. Manage the process and minimize the mess.

If you are keeping a reflective journal, you may want to include Chapter 11's entry in your portfolio.

 Chapter 11 Portfolio Entry Cover Sheet

Activity 11.8

Reflect on Your Learning over Time

Once you have a collection of artifacts representing your learning from your work throughout this book, select one or more of the following reflection options. You can use each relevant chapter's learning targets as the basis of self-reflection.

1. Use or adapt one of the suggestions for reflecting on growth given in this chapter to reflect on your own growth demonstrated by your collection of artifacts.
2. Use or adapt one of the suggestions for reflecting on growth given in this chapter to reflect on your students' growth as demonstrated by your collection of artifacts.
3. Use or adapt one of the suggestions for reflecting on a project given in this chapter to reflect on your own learning with this book.
4. Use or adapt any of the suggestions for self-reflection given in this chapter to reflect on any aspect of your work with this book.

 none

CHAPTER

12

Conferences About and with Students

Conferences with students as participants arise from and amplify assessment for learning practices. They provide the opportunity for students to understand their own learning needs and share their progress with others.

Conferences can be used to communicate in both assessment *for* and *of* learning contexts. All conferences involve sharing information; whether they are formative or summative in nature hinges on whether they occur during or after learning. Conferences are formative when the purpose is to give or receive feedback, to help students formulate goals, or to create with colleagues or parents an individualized program or other interventions for a student. Conferences are summative in nature when the purpose is to share the student's current status—information about learning that has already occurred—although these often lead to formulating a plan of action, so they also become formative. Summative *informs*, formative *takes action*.

To understand conference options, we can categorize them according to their purposes: offering feedback, setting goals, communicating progress, demonstrating competence, and planning an intervention. Figure 12.2 summarizes how topics, participants, and formats can be combined to create a variety of conference options to meet differing information and learning needs.

In this chapter we will describe each conference option and how to conduct it successfully to strengthen as well as report about learning.

Chapter 12 Learning Targets

At the conclusion of Chapter 12 you will know how to do the following:

- Select conference options suited to your students' and their parents' needs.
- Prepare for, conduct, and debrief each conference option.
- Organize conferences that don't require your participation.

FIGURE 12.1 Keys to Quality Classroom Assessment

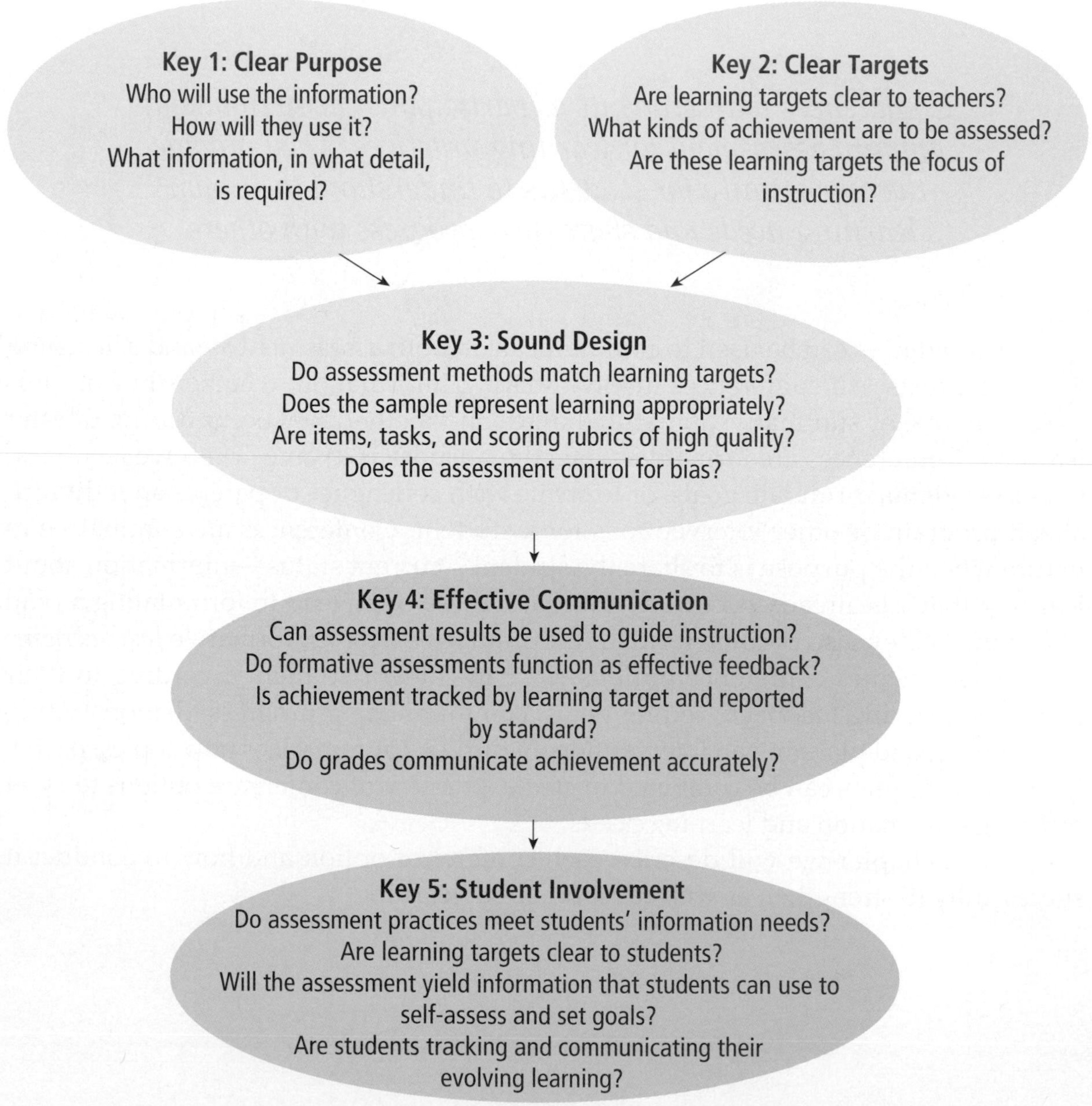

Key 1: Clear Purpose
Who will use the information?
How will they use it?
What information, in what detail, is required?

Key 2: Clear Targets
Are learning targets clear to teachers?
What kinds of achievement are to be assessed?
Are these learning targets the focus of instruction?

Key 3: Sound Design
Do assessment methods match learning targets?
Does the sample represent learning appropriately?
Are items, tasks, and scoring rubrics of high quality?
Does the assessment control for bias?

Key 4: Effective Communication
Can assessment results be used to guide instruction?
Do formative assessments function as effective feedback?
Is achievement tracked by learning target and reported by standard?
Do grades communicate achievement accurately?

Key 5: Student Involvement
Do assessment practices meet students' information needs?
Are learning targets clear to students?
Will the assessment yield information that students can use to self-assess and set goals?
Are students tracking and communicating their evolving learning?

FIGURE 12.2 Kinds of Conferences

Purpose	Topic	Focus	Participants	Location
Feedback	Strengths and areas for improvement	• Single work sample or small number of work samples	• Two students • Small group of students • Student and teacher • Student and parent	School or home
Goal setting	Long- or short-term achievement goals	• Single work sample or multiple work samples • Growth portfolio Achievement portfolio	• Student and parent • Two students • Student and teacher	School or home
Progress	Growth over time	• Two or more work samples ("before & after") • Growth portfolio • Project portfolio	• Student, teacher, and parent • Student and parent or significant adult • Student and teacher • Two or more students	School or home
	Level of achievement	• Achievement portfolio • Grade reports • Other teacher- or student-maintained records	• Student, teacher, and parent • Student and parent or significant adult • Teacher and parent	School or home
Showcase	Demonstrate competence or mastery of selected learning targets	• Competence portfolio • Project portfolio • Celebration portfolio	• Student, teacher, and parent • Student and parent or significant adult • Student, teacher, significant adults, community members	School
Intervention	Area of concern	• Body of evidence illustrating a problem or issue to resolve	• Teacher and parent • Teacher and student • Teacher, parent, and student • Teacher and other staff members • Teacher, other staff members, and parent • Teacher, other staff members, parent, and student	School

THE FEEDBACK CONFERENCE

In a *feedback* conference, students receive another's opinion about the strengths and weaknesses of their work. The purpose is to offer information that will provide them insight so they can continue to improve their work. A secondary purpose is to model the kind of thinking we want them to do when they self-assess. A feedback conference usually involves two people—student and responder. Although we most often think of teachers as the people giving the feedback, students who have had practice in discussing the quality of anonymous work can become quite good at offering useful insights into one another's work. For example, when students meet in writing groups, the purpose of the discussion is to offer formative feedback to each member. In any context, students can confer with a partner, or with a small group.

Feedback conferences are usually conducted at school, but students may also engage in a feedback conference with a parent at home. At school, these conferences can be scheduled so that all students are receiving or offering feedback at the same time, or students may be encouraged to schedule a conference with a partner whenever they need it or within a set time frame (as in the case of a project). Many teachers find it effective to allow students to choose whether they receive feedback from them or from a peer.

Keys to Success

First, remember the characteristics of effective feedback introduced in Chapter 2 (Chappuis, 2009):

1. Direct attention to the intended learning. Point out strengths and offer specific information to guide improvement.
2. Offer feedback during the learning.
3. Offer it only if student work demonstrates at least partial understanding.
4. Do not do all of the work for the student.
5. Limit corrective information to the amount of advice the student can act on in the given time.

Prior to the feedback conference, make sure students understand the learning targets at the focus of the discussion (Assessment *for* Learning Strategy 1) and give students practice with assessing work representing the learning targets they are to master (Assessment *for* Learning Strategy 2). You might also ask students to think about the strengths and weaknesses of their work in preparation for attending a feedback conference, which can make it take less time. Figure 12.3 shows a form that students can use to record their prior thinking and also make note of the feedback they receive from you or a peer.

FIGURE 12.3 Feedback Conference Form

Name: ______________________ Date: ______________

Assignment: ________________ Feedback Focus: ______________

MY OPINION

My strengths are ____________________________________

____

____

What I think I need to work on is _____________________

____

____

FEEDBACK

Strengths: ____

____

____

Work on: ____

____

____

MY PLAN

What I will do now: ___________________________________

____

____

____

____

____

____

ADDRESSING THE TIME ISSUE. Whether students are meeting in pairs, in groups, or with you, time will always be an issue. Obviously, it is a time saver for you whenever students offer useful feedback to each other. Your role then is to manage the time so everyone who needs or wants it has opportunity to receive feedback. Perhaps the most significant time problem arises in a student-teacher conference when the student needs extensive teaching in order to act on the feedback. The conference leaves the realm of feedback and enters the realm of private tutorial, which can cause it to take much more time than anticipated or practical. If you have limited time, make note of what feedback students don't understand or can't act on, rather than reteach extensively at each conference. Plan further large- or small-group instruction with those needs in mind. Another time saver is to schedule student-teacher conferences only with those who want or need one and allow other students to confer for feedback with each other.

HELPING PARENTS UNDERSTAND THE ROLE OF FEEDBACK. Have you ever received a student's homework and noticed signs of parents crossing the line between helping and coauthoring? Parents can benefit from understanding the characteristics of effective feedback. Encourage them to use feedback to support learning without doing the work for their child. Let them know that when their child can't do what is expected, they can explain it if they want to, but doing the work for the child only masks the problem and leads to an inaccurate conclusion about her level of understanding, which further ensures that she won't be offered another chance to learn it.

(For more about feedback and feedback conference options, see Chappuis, 2009, Chapter 3.)

THE GOAL-SETTING CONFERENCE

As we have seen throughout the book, students can set goals based on a single piece of work or on a collection of evidence. The purpose of a goal-setting conference generally is to guide them to the next steps in their learning within the framework of the content standards. The conference itself can be formal or informal; you can set aside a time when all students participate in a goal-setting conference; they can conduct one with a parent at home, at school with you or with a peer; it can be a part of an ongoing process that students engage in when they reach certain checkpoints in their learning; or it can be up to the student to select when it will occur. Students can set short-term or long-term goals. Goal setting is also often a part of other types of conferences—feedback, progress, and intervention conferences.

Not every student needs one-to-one guidance in setting specific and challenging goals. Once they are clear about the intended learning and know where they are now in relation to that learning, you can model the process and explain what they are to do at each step. Many students will be able to proceed on their own from here. Others will benefit from individual guidance. Students may be able to confer with each other or with their parents, or they may need you to help them, especially with their action plan.

Keys to Success

Prior to the conference, students (or the teacher, if needed) should select one or more pieces of work that clearly indicate present status in relation to desired status. That requires that the learning targets students are working toward are clear to them and they understand what level of achievement their work shows. Students may be examining a single piece of work or selecting several samples from a working file or a growth portfolio, as described in Chapter 11.

During the conference, the student and teacher (or other respondent) take the following steps:

1. Clarify the learning target.
2. Clarify current status.
3. State the learning target as a goal.
4. Make a plan.

For Example 12.1 shows an elementary and a secondary version of a frame that students can use to record their goals during the conference.

1. CLARIFY THE LEARNING TARGET. Ask the student to explain the learning target—what he is working toward, not in terms of a grade, but in terms of the learning accomplished. What will he know or be able to do at the conclusion of this plan? If the student struggles to do this, offer help in the form of questions or prompts as needed.

2. CLARIFY CURRENT STATUS. With the student, review the pieces of evidence, not just a list of scores or grades. Reviewing only a list of grades can lead to fuzzy or too-general statements, such as "I will get better at math." Ask the student to be specific in identifying strengths and areas needing improvement. Example 12.1 shows the level of specificity required. Offer help in the form of questions or prompts as needed.

3. STATE THE LEARNING TARGET AS A GOAL. Often it isn't the whole learning target that a student needs to work on, but only a part of it. So at this step, ask the student to identify what exactly she needs to learn or practice. Again, Example 12.1 shows the level of detail required.

4. MAKE A PLAN. The plan answers the question, "How will I accomplish my goal?" It specifies the action the student will take, which may involve reviewing material learned previously, reworking a product or performance until it meets a certain level of quality, or learning something the student missed in the course of instruction. It may also include a notation about what help the student will need, the time frame for accomplishment of the goal, and reference to the evidence students will use to document attainment of their goal.

For Example 12.1

Goal Frames

YOUNGER STUDENTS

Name: **Maria-Teresa Gonzales** *Date:* October 7

I will learn: multiplying when the numbers end in zero

My "before" picture—evidence I used to choose my goal: I got those ones wrong on the math check 10/6

My plan is to: practice some at home tonight, Monday night, and Tuesday night

I need these materials: practice problems

I will ask for help from: Miss Barton explain it + check my work. Mom if I get stuck

I will be ready to show my learning on this day: October 14

My "after" picture—I will show my learning by: doing the problems right on the test

OLDER STUDENTS

Name: *John Jurjevich* Date: *February 20*

Learning Target: *Explain how the immune system works*	
Current level of achievement: *don't understand how a neutrophil works to fight infection*	
Evidence: *quiz on communicable diseases 2/19*	
What I need to learn: *to explain what a neutrophil does at three stages: chemotaxis, phagocytosis, and apoptosis*	
Plan of action: *study the pages on pathogens and the immune system in the book and practice drawing the life cycle of a neutrophil, with all stages explained*	
Help needed—what and who: *book + me*	
Time frame: *before Feb. 26*	
Evidence of achieving my goal: *Test on Feb. 26*	

Selecting a Plan of Action. Even students who independently can identify what they need to work on sometimes need advice on how to go about getting better. For example, David may have reviewed his three previous lab reports and decided he needs to improve in writing hypotheses. He may have no idea how to do this, in which case his teacher can confer with him to explain what resources or opportunities are available.

Watch for students whose plan consists only of "Do my homework." Homework completion as a plan of action is tricky, because lots of learning problems *would* be solved if students would only do the practice work. All students *should* do their homework, and in all likelihood their achievement will improve when they attain this habit. However, a general action plan, "Do my homework," is not precise enough in most instances, and may not be the solution at all. Specific action beyond the regular work may be needed, and it may be accomplished in school or at home. When students create their action plans, they need to understand what role, if any, homework plays in attaining their specific goal.

Identifying Assistance. If every student needs assistance and they all need it from you, the teacher, this process will choke on its own rope. When Maria-Teresa (see For Example 12.1) knows what her goal is, but needs help learning the math procedure, she does need assistance. She may need it from you, or she may not. Could someone else in the room teach her the procedure for multiplying with zeroes? When you help students see their only resource is not always you, the line at your desk shortens and the process becomes more practical.

Determining Time Frame. Ask the student to set himself a time limit, or specify one. This helps him make a realistic plan and get motivated to start working. It also lets him decide or know when he will demonstrate his level of achievement of the goal.

Collecting "Before" and "After" Evidence. Goal setting is most satisfying when we see real progress toward the desired outcome. Part of the motivational hook for students and the key to re-engaging marginally interested students is tangible, hard evidence of progress. A system that lets students keep track of where they started and what they have accomplished increases accountability for follow through. Instituting a simple procedure for students to collect "before" and "after" evidence contributes to developing a sense that "I can set goals and carry them through to completion." If students do not have a folder or portfolio to keep track of their goals and evidence, you can set up a simple system, such as a "goals" folder or a manila envelope with the goal frame stapled to the outside and evidence such as the beginning point, progress toward the goal, and goal attainment tucked inside.

Ensuring Student Ownership. To make the process instructionally beneficial, let the student do as much of the talking and puzzling through the steps as possible. Remember, the student will need to understand three things: what the intended learning is, where she is now with respect to the intended learning, and what her options are for closing the gap. You can intervene as needed with questions or prompts, but try not to do the work for her. The person who sets the goals owns them, and if you own the goal, the student won't be doing much of the work.

THE PROGRESS CONFERENCE

A progress conference can focus on growth over time or on level of achievement. It can be conducted during school, after school, or at home. Students, parents, and teachers can all take part or students may conduct them without teacher participation. Several of the portfolios described in Chapter 11 can serve as the basis for the progress conference: project, growth, or achievement. You can also use the "Before" and "After" evidence and other artifacts from goal-setting conferences as a point of discussion in a progress conference.

Focusing on Growth over Time

This is a simple, narrowly focused conference topic, generally conducted between two people. Struggling learners especially benefit from noticing that they have been successful in achieving a short-term goal in a short period of time. The conference can take place with a parent or other adult at home, with another student at school, or with you or another staff member at school. You can specify the audience or you can let students choose who they wish to share with. Either the project or the growth portfolio work well to ground the discussion with evidence.

Focusing on Achievement Status

This type of progress conference focuses on a student's current level of learning. This is generally the type of parent-teacher conference scheduled at the end of a grading period to elaborate on information from the report card. When the student is present, these conferences are referred to as "student-involved" or "student-led" conferences. Because of their effectiveness in creating and sustaining student motivation, we believe that progress conferences focusing on achievement should involve students.

This type of conference is not limited to the end of a grading period: it can happen any time you or your students want or need to share information about their learning status. Any of the portfolios described in Chapter 11 can be used during these conferences. However, the growth, project, and/or achievement portfolios are the ones most frequently used to substantiate the discussion. If students have evidence of goal setting and attainment, you may want to include that, too.

Identifying Participants

Conference participants can vary to suit the topics and information needs. The structure generally takes one of two forms: a *two-way conference* or a *three-way conference*. In a two-way conference, the student meets with another student, the teacher, a parent, or another significant adult. In a three-way conference, participants are the student, the teacher, and a parent or significant adult. For many students and parents, it is a novel idea to have the student present during a conversation about the student's learning.

Some initial preparation is required to make two-way and three-way student-involved conferences run smoothly.

Preparing the Students

When the focus of the conference is to demonstrate growth over time, help students prepare by guiding their choice of artifacts to use as evidence of improvement. Portfolios and working folders come in handy here, as it can be quite powerful for students to assemble work samples showing a clear "before" and "after" picture of their learning. (Refer to Chapter 11 for more information on growth portfolios and working folders.) Students also should be prepared to explain the learning target or targets, talk briefly about what they did to improve, and summarize what they can do now that they couldn't do before.

Figure 12.4 shows a form that can be used both while preparing for and conducting a "Demonstration of Growth" conference.

When the focus of the conference is to provide an overview of the student's current achievement level, help students prepare by ensuring they have a clear understanding of the learning targets and work samples that show what they have learned. They must be able to discuss strengths, areas needing improvement or areas of challenge, and goals they have set for themselves. They will need time to rehearse the conference with others in the classroom.

Preparing the Parents or Other Adults

When the conference will involve parents or other significant adults, we recommend that you set a conference agenda together with students. Students, if they are able to,

FIGURE 12.4 Form for Demonstration of Growth Conference

Name:	Date:
Learning Target(s)	
Evidence of where I started	
Evidence of where I am now	
What I did to improve	
What I can do now that I couldn't do before	
What to notice about my work	

Date of conference:

Start and end times:

Participant(s):

Comments from participant(s):

can write the invitation to parents and/or other participants informing them of what to expect and what their role will be. Some teachers send work samples that will be the focus of the discussion home in advance for parents to think about in preparation for the conference.

When the format is a three-way conference, especially when it replaces the traditional parent-teacher conference, as a part of your explanation to parents, we recommend that you offer them the option of scheduling an additional meeting, without the student present, to discuss any concerns that they may not want to raise in the three-way setting.

Conducting a Two-Way Conference

You can schedule several two-way (student and parents) conferences at the same time throughout the day. Your role is to be available to clarify information as needed. Before the conference begins, each student introduces their parents to you. Then they all go to the conference area (for example, students' desks or tables set up for that purpose). Students begin by sharing the conference agenda with their parents. They then explain the learning targets and show samples of their work illustrating growth over time, level of achievement, or evidence of having met goals—whatever the topic of the conference is. Parents listen carefully, ask clarifying questions, and offer comments about students' work and learning. Students may have already set goals and created action plans for future work, which they can discuss at this time, or students and parents may do that together as a part of the conference.

Conducting a Three-Way Conference

The three-way conference is similar to the two-way conference, in that students introduce their parents to you and begin the conference by sharing the agenda. It differs in that, because you are a participant, you schedule only one at a time. Students explain the learning targets and proceed as described previously. The parents' role is also much the same. Your role as teacher is to help students clarify their comments, if needed, and to add to their descriptions of strengths and areas needing improvement, again if needed. We recommend that you end each conference with a summary of the student's strengths and positive contributions to the class.

Followup

It is important to find out how the experience went for all involved. Debriefing the conference can be as simple as asking students to complete a conference evaluation form, such as the one shown in Figure 12.5, reading the comments from participants, and discussing responses with the class as a whole.

You will also want to offer parents and other participants in the conference an opportunity to share their feedback on the experience. Have evaluation forms such as the

FIGURE 12.5 Conference Evaluation Form

Name:	Date:
What I learned from this conference	
What I liked about it	
What I would change about the conference	
Other comments	

one shown in Figure 12.5 available for them to complete. In rare instances, you may have to address a less-than-positive outcome for a student or a parent, in which case, you may want to schedule a followup conference.

THE SHOWCASE CONFERENCE

In this conference, the purpose is to demonstrate mastery of or competence on predetermined learning targets. Sometimes is it also used to share the celebration portfolio, as described in Chapter 11. Participants can include the student and one or more of the following: another student, parent, teacher, other significant adult, or another staff member at the school. Generally, these conferences take place at school. In a formal showcase conference focused on competence or mastery, the student meets with a group of any number of adults, from parents and significant adults to community members.

Preparing the Students

When the purpose is to demonstrate mastery or competence, help students prepare by ensuring they have a clear understanding of the learning targets and work samples that support the assertion of mastery or competence. Then guide them in preparing explanations of how their evidence supports their claim. The explanation should refer directly to the standards of quality you are using to define mastery or competence. They will need time to rehearse presenting their evidence and explanation with other students.

Conducting a Showcase Conference

The student's role in a showcase conference is to share the agenda with the participants, explain the learning targets that are the focus of the achievement, and present and discuss how the work samples presented illustrate competence on specified learning targets. The student also answers participants' questions. The participants in a showcase conference listen carefully, ask questions, and make comments about the work. Your role is to be prepared to facilitate, encourage, and clarify as needed.

Followup

As with previous conference formats, conducting followup is key to their success. We recommend that all participants, including students, complete a conference evaluation form (see Figure 12.5) so that you can obtain information about what worked well and what didn't (if anything), identify any problems you need to deal with, and gather ideas for what you might do next time. Summarize and share comments with students, parents, and any other participants. Also, give students the opportunity to debrief the experience as a group.

THE INTERVENTION CONFERENCE

Planning an intervention with others can occur any time a student is having difficulty. As a teacher, you meet with parents to discuss a problem with behavior, work habits, or achievement and make a plan for improvement. You meet with other teachers and specialists when a student's work is significantly above or below expectations to modify instruction or to recommend placement in a specialized program. Generally, the student is not present in these conferences, although in some cases, especially the parent-teacher discussion of a problem, the student's perspective and participation can help you craft a solution.

Central to the effectiveness of these conferences is the quality of records you keep. This context requires separate records for level of achievement, work habits, effort, attendance, and the like, as well as records that allow you to determine the student's strengths and weaknesses relative to the learning targets to be mastered. With such records, you are able to pinpoint problems and participate in recommending suitable solutions. Without them, you may lack credible data from which to draw conclusions about the best course of action.

Summary

In the majority of instances, conferences about students can include students to the benefit of all involved. They can participate in and even lead them, but only with the proper preparation throughout the year. To comment accurately and in detail about their work, students must have been involved all along in their learning and in assessment; they must be prepared to discuss what the intended learning is, where they are now with respect to it, and what they might do next to continue as learners.

In this chapter, we have looked at conferences that function in assessment *for* and *of* learning contexts: conferences whose purposes are to offer feedback, to set goals, to share improvement, to communicate about achievement, and to plan an intervention. We have suggested who to include in each type of conference, what preparation will maximize success for all involved, and what followup is needed. In addition, we have explained what happens in a two-way and three-way progress conference, and a showcase conference.

We encourage you to select carefully from the conference options available to meet your needs and the information needs of parents, but most especially to think about how students can be involved in conferences to take responsibility for their learning and to show what they have accomplished.

CHAPTER 12 ACTIVITIES

End-of-chapter activities are intended to help you master the chapter's learning targets. They are designed to deepen your understanding of the chapter content, provide discussion topics for learning team meetings, and guide implementation of the practices taught in the chapter.

Forms for completing each activity appear in editable Microsoft Word format in the Chapter 12 CD file. Documents on the CD are marked with this symbol:

Chapter 12 Learning Targets

At the conclusion of Chapter 12 you will know how to do the following:

1. Select conference options suited to your students' and their parents' needs.
2. Prepare for, conduct, and debrief each conference option.
3. Organize conferences that don't require your participation.

Activity 12.1 Keep a Reflective Journal
Activity 12.2 Conduct and Debrief a Feedback Conference
Activity 12.3 Conduct and Debrief a Goal-setting Conference
Activity 12.4 Organize a Student-led Conference
Activity 12.5 Reflect on Your Own Learning
Activity 12.6 Select Portfolio Artifacts
Activity 12.7 Stage a Share Fair

Activity 12.1

Keep a Reflective Journal

Keep a record of your thoughts, questions, and any implementation activities you tried while reading Chapter 12.

 Reflective Journal Form

Activity 12.2

Conduct and Debrief a Feedback Conference

After reading the section, "The Feedback Conference," work independently, with a partner, or with your team to complete this activity.

1. Select a learning target for which you have a descriptive rubric. (Refer to the Chapter 7 section, "Selecting, Revising, or Developing Rubrics" for more information on a suitable rubric.)
2. Narrow the focus of your feedback to a manageable number of criteria, should students' work need revision.
3. Make sure that students have had experience with the rubric and some version of Assessment *for* Learning Strategies 1 and 2. (Refer to the Chapter 7 section, "Seven Strategies for Using Rubrics as Instructional Tools in the Classroom" for more information on how to do this.)
4. Select two to three students whose work shows at least partial understanding or mastery to conference with. Copy a form such as the Feedback Conference Form in Figure 12.3 or the "Stars and Stairs" form for each student.
5. Prior to the feedback conference, ask the students to focus on one criterion and find rubric phrases that describe what they believe their strengths and areas needing improvement are. Have them write their thoughts on the form you have chosen.
6. Meet with students one at a time. Let them share their self-assessment first. Then share your feedback. If appropriate, point out a strength the student overlooked and add to or modify what the student said they need to work on. Let the student be the writer on the Feedback Conference Form. The student then completes the "My Plan" portion of the form taking into account their own thoughts and the feedback you have given. They can do this either under your guidance or on their own at your discretion. Many teachers find that when students think about their work first, these conferences can be successfully completed in three minutes or less.
7. Using the Conference Evaluation Form shown in Figure 12.5 as a guide, debrief the feedback conference a day or two later with each student.
8. If you are working with a partner or a team, share your experience with the feedback conference, using the Conference Evaluation Form in Figure 12.5 as a guide.

Source: Adapted from *Seven Strategies of Assessment* for *Learning* (pp. 82–83) by J. Chappuis, 2009, Upper Saddle River, NJ: Pearson Education. Adapted by permission.

Feedback Conference Form

Conference Evaluation Form

Stars and Stairs Form

Activity 12.3

Conduct and Debrief a Goal-setting Conference

After reading the section, "The Goal-setting Conference," work independently, with a partner, or with your team to complete this activity.

1. Select a learning target that students are in the midst of mastering.
2. Identify two or three students to engage in a goal-setting conference. These students should be partway through mastery of the learning target.
3. Select or have the students select one or more pieces of work that clearly indicate present status in relation to desired status.
4. Use, modify, or create a goal frame such as the ones illustrated in For Example 12.1. Make a copy for each student.
5. Conduct the conference with each student individually following the four steps discussed in the goal-setting subsection, "Keys to Success." Let the students be the writers on the form, unless they do not yet write, in which case you will need to write their goals for them.
6. Using the Conference Evaluation Form shown in Figure 12.5 as a guide, debrief the goal-setting conference a day or two later with each student.
7. If you are working with a partner or a team, share your experience with the goal-setting conference, using the Conference Evaluation Form in Figure 12.5 as a guide.

Activity 12.4

Organize a Student-led Conference

After reading the section, "The Progress Conference," work independently, with a partner, or with your team to complete this activity.

1. Decide whether you want to focus on growth over time or achievement status.
2. Identify who the participants will be and determine whether it will be a two-way conference or a three-way conference. Set a date or date range and time or time frame for the conferences.
3. Prepare the students following the instructions in the corresponding section of Chapter 12. Consider using a form such as the one illustrated in Figure 12.4.
4. Determine what preparation parents and/or other adults will need prior to participating in the conference. Prepare materials: set the agenda, have students write the invitations, and send out any other pertinent information as described in the section, "Preparing the Parents or Other Adults."
5. Let the students conduct the conferences.
6. Debrief the conference with students and with parents using the Conference Evaluation Form shown in Figure 12.5.
7. If you are working with a partner or a team, share your experience with student-led conferences, using the Conference Evaluation Form in Figure 12.5 as a guide.

Student-led Conference Planning Form

Conference Evaluation Form

Form for Demonstration of Growth Conference

Activity 12.5

Reflect on Your Own Learning

Review the Chapter 12 learning targets and select one or more that represented new learning for you or struck you as most significant from this chapter. If you are working individually, write a short reflection that captures your current understanding. If you are working with a partner or a team, either discuss what you have written or use this as a discussion prompt for a team meeting.

Reflect on Chapter 12 Learning

Activity 12.6

Select Portfolio Artifacts

Any of the activities from this chapter can be used as portfolio entries. Select any activity you have completed or artifacts you have created that will illustrate your competence at the Chapter 12 learning targets:

1. Select conference options suited to your students' and their parents' needs.
2. Prepare for, conduct, and debrief each conference option.
3. Organize conferences that don't require your participation.

If you are keeping a reflective journal, you may want to include Chapter 12's entry in your portfolio.

Chapter 12 Portfolio Entry Cover Sheet

Activity 12.7

Stage a Share Fair

Your learning team can plan a "share fair" to let others know what you have been doing in your classrooms and team meetings throughout the study of this book. The success of this activity depends on having kept a classroom assessment portfolio and having completed Activity 11.5, "Review Your Own Classroom Assessment Portfolio." Your audience can be other learning teams or colleagues who are not participating in this study. Both options are explained here.

Option 1: Sharing with Other Learning Teams

1. Meet with your own team to plan what you will share. Each learning team member brings their portfolio to the meeting and spends a few minutes explaining its artifacts and what they illustrate.
2. Your learning team selects from all team members' portfolios the artifacts to be shared with others and prepares a display that includes the key idea or ideas illustrated by each artifact, any brief explanatory information needed, the artifact itself, a reflection from Activity 11.5, and the name(s) and contact information of person(s) submitting the artifact. Often teams spend one meeting sharing and selecting artifacts and another preparing them for display.
3. Find a good place to stage your "Share Fair." Have each team set up around the room.
4. Assign one person to stay with the team's display to give a short explanation and/or to answer questions. The rest of the team circulates to other displays. You can rotate the responsibility of staying with the display so all have a chance to see what others have done.

Option 2: Sharing with Colleagues Who Are Not Part of a Learning Team

1. Meet with your team to plan what you will share. Each team member brings their portfolio to the meeting and spends a few minutes explaining its artifacts and what they illustrate.
2. Each of you then selects your own artifacts to share with others. Together, your team decides the method of sharing. Here are two options:
   - In a large group setting, such as a faculty meeting, you each can give a short description of the key idea your artifact illustrates and a brief explanation of how you used it and what you noticed happening with students as a result. You can involve the audience in a brief activity that simulates a part of what you had your students do, if appropriate.
   - You can follow the same procedure in a smaller group format, such a department meeting.

- You can each create a display similar to the one described in Option 1, and set the displays up in a room such as the cafeteria or library. You can each give a short explanation to small groups as they rotate through your team members' displays.

3. In each of the sharing options, be sure to include a description of the key idea or ideas illustrated and a reflection on its impact on students and learning.

Source: Adapted from *Seven Strategies of Assessment* for *Learning Study Guide* (p. 143) by J. Chappuis, 2009, Upper Saddle River, NJ: Pearson Education. Adapted by permission.

 none

APPENDIX

LEARNING TEAMS FACILITATION GUIDE

Part 1:

Introduction to the ATI Model of Collaborative Learning Teams
Article: "Supporting Teacher Learning Teams"
Discussion Questions - "Supporting Teacher Learning Teams"

Part 2:

Planning for Learning Team Implementation

Part 3:

Preparing to Lead Learning Team Study of *Classroom Assessment* for *Student Learning: Doing It Right—Using It Well*
Figure 1 Planning Decisions
Figure 2 Team Meeting Schedule
Figure 3 CASL Text Pacing Suggestions
Figure 4 Chapter Reading and Activity Assignments
Figure 5 Learning Team Meeting Agenda
Figure 6 Learning Team Meeting Log
Figure 7 Classroom Assessment Competencies

CHAPTER RESOURCES

Chapter 1

1. Activity 1.1 Reflective Journal Form
2. Activity 1.2 Connect Own Experiences to the Keys to Quality
3. Activity 1.3 Assessment Practices Inventory
4. Activity 1.4 Elementary Student Pre-survey
5. Activity 1.4 Elementary Student Post-survey
6. Activity 1.4 Secondary Student Pre-survey
7. Activity 1.4 Secondary Student Post-survey
8. Activity 1.6 Reflect on Chapter 1 Learning
9. Activity 1.7 Chapter 1 Portfolio Entry Cover Sheet

Chapter 2

1. Activity 2.1 Reflective Journal Form
2. Activity 2.2 Audit Your Assessments for Balance
3. Activity 2.3 Self-evaluation Survey
4. Activity 2.3 Survey Data Graphing Chart
5. Activity 2.4 My Feedback Practices
6. Activity 2.5 Prerequisites for Self-assessment and Goal Setting
7. Activity 2.6 Reflect on Chapter 2 Learning
8. Activity 2.7 Chapter 2 Portfolio Entry Cover Sheet

Chapter 3

1. Activity 3.1 Reflective Journal Form
2. Activity 3.3 Template for Classifying Learning Targets
3. Activity 3.4 Template for Identifying Clear Learning Targets
4. Activity 3.5 Template for Deconstructing a Content Standard
5. Activity 3.6 Template for Student-friendly Learning Targets
6. Activity 3.7 Reflect on Chapter 3 Learning
7. Activity 3.8 Chapter 3 Portfolio Entry Cover Sheet

Chapter 4

1. Activity 4.1 Reflective Journal Form
2. Activity 4.2 Target–Method Match Template
3. Activity 4.3 Audit an Assessment for Clear Purpose
4. Activity 4.4 Audit an Assessment for Clear Learning Targets
5. Activity 4.5 Test Blueprint Form A
6. Activity 4.5 Test Blueprint Form B
7. Activity 4.6 Debrief the AFL Application You Tried
8. Activity 4.7 Reflect on Chapter 4 Learning
9. Activity 4.8 Chapter 4 Portfolio Entry Cover Sheet

Chapter 5

1. Activity 5.1 Reflective Journal Form
2. Activity 5.2 Test of Franzipanics
3. Activity 5.2 Answers to Franzipanics Test
4. Activity 5.2 Test Blueprint Form A
5. Activity 5.2 Test Blueprint Form B
6. Activity 5.2 Selected Response Test Quality Checklist
7. Activity 5.3 Test Blueprint Form A
8. Activity 5.3 Test Blueprint Form B
9. Activity 5.3 Selected Response Test Quality Checklist
10. Activity 5.4 Debrief the AFL Activity You Tried
11. Activity 5.5 Reviewing and Analyzing My Results, Option A
12. Activity 5.5 Reviewing and Analyzing My Results, Option B
13. Activity 5.5 Goal Setting Form
14. Activity 5.6 Reflect on Chapter 5 Learning
15. Activity 5.7 Chapter 5 Portfolio Entry Cover Sheet

Chapter 6

1. Activity 6.1 Reflective Journal Form
2. Activity 6.2 Evaluate a Written Response Assessment for Quality
3. Activity 6.2 Checklist of Quality Guidelines for Written Response Assessments
4. Activity 6.3 Template for a Short-answer Item and Scoring Guide
5. Activity 6.3 Checklist of Quality Guidelines for Written Response Assessments
6. Activity 6.4 Templates for Extended Written Response Items and Scoring Guides
7. Activity 6.4 Checklist of Quality Guidelines for Written Response Assessments
8. Activity 6.5 Debrief the AFL Strategy You Tried
9. Activity 6.6 Reflect on Chapter 6 Learning
10. Activity 6.7 Chapter 6 Portfolio Entry Cover Sheet
11. Figure: Rubric for Inductive/Deductive Inference
12. Figure: Rubric for Comparison
13. Figure: Rubric for Classification
14. Figure: Rubric for Synthesis
15. Figure: Rubric for Evaluation

Chapter 7

1. Activity 7.1 Reflective Journal Form
2. Activity 7.2 Performance Task Evaluation Form
3. Activity 7.2 Rubric for Tasks
4. Activity 7.3 Task Development Template
5. Activity 7.3 Rubric for Tasks
6. Activity 7.4 RAFTS Format Template
7. Activity 7.4 Rubric for Tasks
8. Activity 7.5 Rubric Evaluation Form
9. Activity 7.5 Rubric for Rubrics
10. Activity 7.6 Rubric Development Template
11. Activity 7.6 Rubric Evaluation Form
12. Activity 7.6 Rubric for Rubrics
13. Activity 7.7 Create a Student-friendly Version of a Rubric
14. Activity 7.8 Debrief AFL Use of Rubrics
15. Activity 7.9 Debrief Structuring a Task for Formative Use
16. Activity 7.10 Reflect on Chapter 7 Learning
17. Activity 7.11 Chapter 7 Portfolio Entry Cover Sheet

Chapter 8

1. Activity 8.1 Reflective Journal Form
2. Activity 8.2 Frame Diagnostic Questions
3. Activity 8.3 Use Instructional Questions to Deepen Understanding

4. Activity 8.4 Seminar Discussion Rubric
5. Activity 8.4 Rubric Development Template
6. Activity 8.4 Rubric for Rubrics
7. Activity 8.4 Rubric Evaluation Form
8. Activity 8.4 Debrief Use of Class Discussion Rubric
9. Activity 8.5 Student Directions for Line-up
10. Activity 8.6 Test Blueprint Form A
11. Activity 8.6 Test Blueprint Form B
12. Activity 8.6 Template for Oral Examination Questions and Scoring Guidelines
13. Activity 8.6 Debrief the Oral Examination
14. Activity 8.7 Decisions about Using Journals or Logs
15. Activity 8.7 Debrief Use of Journals or Logs in the Classroom
16. Activity 8.8 Reflect on Chapter 8 Learning
17. Activity 8.9 Chapter 8 Portfolio Entry Cover Sheet

Chapter 9

1. Activity 9.1 Reflective Journal Form
2. Activity 9.2 Formative and Summative Assessment Plan
3. Activity 9.3 Organize Your Recording System
4. Activity 9.4 Track Work Habits and Social Skills
5. Activity 9.4 Debrief Tracking and Reporting Work Habits and Social Skills
6. Activity 9.5 Develop Student Record-keeping Forms
7. Activity 9.5 Student Feedback Form
8. Activity 9.6 Reflect on Chapter 9 Learning
9. Activity 9.7 Chapter 9 Portfolio Entry Cover Sheet

Chapter 10

1. Activity 10.1 Reflective Journal Form
2. Activity 10.2 Develop Solutions Other than Grades
3. Activity 10.3 Analyze Steps in Your Grading Process
4. Activity 10.3 Compare to Steps in Report Card Grading
5. Activity 10.4 Revisit How You Convert Rubric Scores to Grades
6. Activity 10.5 Rubric for Evaluating Grading Practices
7. Activity 10.5 Evaluate Your Grading Practices
8. Activity 10.5 Grading Practices Evaluation Form
9. Activity 10.5 Debrief Evaluating Your Grading Practices
10. Activity 10.6 Reflect on Chapter 10 Learning
11. Activity 10.7 Chapter 10 Portfolio Entry Cover Sheet

Chapter 11

1. Activity 11.1 Reflective Journal Form
2. Activity 11.2 Portfolio Planning Form
3. Activity 11.3 Portfolio Auditing Form
4. Activity 11.4 Personal Portfolio Decision Form
5. Activity 11.5 Personal Portfolio Review Form
6. Activity 11.6 Reflect on Chapter 11 Learning
7. Activity 11.7 Chapter 11 Portfolio Entry Cover Sheet

Chapter 12

1. Activity 12.1 Reflective Journal Form
2. Activity 12.2 Feedback Conference Form
3. Activity 12.2 Stars and Stairs Form
4. Activity 12.2 Conference Evaluation Form
5. Activity 12.3 Conduct and Debrief a Goal-setting Conference
6. Activity 12.3 Goal Frames
7. Activity 12.3 Conference Evaluation Form
8. Activity 12.4 Student-led Conference Planning Form
9. Activity 12.4 Form for Demonstration of Growth Conference
10. Activity 12.4 Conference Evaluation Form
11. Activity 12.5 Reflect on Chapter 12 Learning
12. Activity 12.6 Chapter 12 Portfolio Entry Cover Sheet

REFERENCES

Akron Global Polymer Academy. 2011. P–16 science education, best teaching practices: Wait time. Retrieved January 2011 from http://www.agpa.uakron.edu/p16/btp.php?id=wait-time

Ames, C. 1992. Classrooms: Goals, structures, and student motivation. *Journal of Educational Psychology, 84*(3), 261–271.

Arter, J. A., & K. U. Busick. 2001. *Practice with student-involved classroom assessment*. Portland, OR: Assessment Training Institute.

Arter, J. A., & J. Chappuis. 2006. *Creating and recognizing quality rubrics*. Upper Saddle River, NJ: Pearson Education.

Black, P., C. Harrison, C. Lee, B. Marshall, & D. Wiliam. 2002. *Working inside the black box: Assessment for learning in the classroom*. London: King's College Press.

Black, P., & D. Wiliam. 1998a. Assessment and classroom learning. *Assessment in Education, 5*(1), 7–74.

Black, P., & D. Wiliam. 1998b. Inside the black box: Raising standards through classroom assessment. *Phi Delta Kappan, 80*(2): 139–148.

Brookhart, S. M. 2004. *Grading*. Upper Saddle River, NJ: Pearson Education.

Butler, R. 1988. Enhancing and undermining intrinsic motivation: The effects of task-involving and ego-involving evaluation on interest and performance. *British Journal of Educational Psychology, 58*: 1–14.

Butler, R., & O. Neuman. 1995. Effects of task and ego-achieving goals on help-seeking behaviours and attitudes. *Journal of Educational Psychology, 87*(2), 261–271.

Chappuis, J. 2009. *Seven strategies of assessment for learning*. Upper Saddle River, NJ: Pearson Education.

Chappuis, J., & S. Chappuis. 2002. *Understanding school assessment: A parent and community guide to helping students learn*. Upper Saddle River, NJ: Pearson Education.

Chappuis, S., C. Commodore, & R. Stiggins. 2010. *Assessment balance and quality: An action guide for school leaders*, 3rd ed. Upper Saddle River, NJ: Pearson Education.

Chappuis, S., R. Stiggins, J. Arter, & J. Chappuis. 2004. *Assessment* for *learning: An action guide for school leaders*. Upper Saddle River, NJ: Pearson Education.

Cizek, G. J., R. E. Rachor, & S. F. Fitzgerald. 1996. Teachers' assessment practices: Preparation, isolation, and the kitchen sink. *Educational Assessment*, 3(2), 159–179.

Common Core State Standards Initiative. 2010a. *Common core state standards for English language arts & literacy in history/social studies, science, and technical subjects*. Washington, DC: Council of Chief State School Officers & National Governors Association. Retrieved January 2011 from http://www.corestandards.org/assets/CCSSI_ELA%20Standards.pdf

Common Core State Standards Initiative. 2010b. *Common core state standards for English language arts & literacy in history/social studies, science, and technical subjects. Appendix B: Text exemplars and sample performance tasks.* Washington, DC: Council of Chief State School Officers & National Governors Association. Retrieved January 2011 from http://www.corestandards.org/assets/Appendix_B.pdf

Common Core State Standards Initiative. 2010c. *Common core state standards for mathematics.* Washington, DC: Council of Chief State School Officers & National Governors Association. Retrieved January 2011 from http://www.corestandards.org/assets/CCSSI_Math%20Standards.pdf

Council for Economic Education. 2010. Voluntary national content standards in economics, 2nd ed. New York: Author. Retrieved January 2011 from http://www.councilforeconed.org/ea/standards/standards.pdf

Davies, A., & R. J. Stiggins. 1996. *Student-involved conferences: A professional development DVD.*

Upper Saddle River, NJ: Pearson Education. Copyright 2007 Pearson Education.

Dewey, J. 1933. Quoted in C. M. Wang & G. Ong. Questioning techniques for active learning. *Ideas on Teaching, 1* (Feb. 2003), n.p. Retrieved 25 February 2011 from http://www.cdtl.nus.edu.sg/Ideas/iot2.htm

Guskey, T. R. (ed.). 1996. *Communicating student learning*. Alexandria, VA: Association for Supervision and Curriculum Development.

Guskey, T. R. 2002. *How's my kid doing?: A parent's guide to grades, marks, and report cards*. San Francisco: Jossey-Bass.

Guskey, T. R., & J. Bailey. 2001. *Developing grading and reporting systems for student learning*. Thousand Oaks, CA: Corwin.

Harlen, W., & M. James. 1997. Assessment and learning: Differences and relationships between formative and summative assessment. *Assessment in Education: Principles, Policy, & Practice, 4*(3), 365–379.

Hattie, J., & H. Timperley. 2007. The power of feedback. *Review of Educational Research*. Retrieved October 9, 2007 from http://rer.sagepub.com/content/77/1/81.full.pdf+html

Johnston, P.H. 2004. *Choice words: How our language affects children's learning*. York, ME: Stenhouse.

Kendall, J., & R. Marzano. 1997. *Content knowledge: A compendium of standards and benchmarks for K–12 education*, 2nd ed. Aurora, CO: Mid-continent Regional Educational Laboratory.

Klauer, K. J., & G. D. Phye. 2008. Inductive reasoning: A training approach. *Review of Educational Research, 78*(1): 85–123.

Knight, J. E. 1990. Coding journal entries. *Journal of Reading, 34*(1): 42–47.

Marzano, R., D. Pickering, & J. McTighe. 1993. *Assessing student outcomes: Performance assessment using the dimensions of learning model*. Aurora, CO: Mid-continent Regional Educational Laboratory.

Munk, D. D., & W. D. Bursuck. 2003. Grading students with disabilities. *Educational Leadership, 61*(2): 38–43.

Murray, D. 2004. *A writer teaches writing*, 2nd ed., rev. Boston, MA: Thomson/Heinle.

NCS Pearson. 2007–2011. PowerTeacher 2.3 [computer software]. Minneapolis, MN: NCS Pearson.

New Oxford American Dictionary. 2001. Boston: Oxford University Press.

O'Connor, K. 2002. *How to grade for learning: Linking grades to standards*, 2nd ed. Arlington Heights, IL: Skylight.

O'Connor, K. 2011. *A repair kit for grading: 15 fixes for broken grades*, 2nd ed. Upper Saddle River, NJ: Pearson Education.

Rowe, M. B. 1972. Wait-time and rewards as instructional variables: Their influence on language, logic, and fate control. Paper presented at the annual meeting of the National Association for Research in Science Teaching, Chicago, April. ERIC ED-061103.

Rowe, M. B. 1987. Wait time: Slowing down may be a way of speeding up. *American Educator, 11*(1): 38–43, 47.

Sadler, D. R. 1989. Formative assessment and the design of instructional systems. *Instructional Science, 18*: 119–144.

Sadler, D. R. 1998. Formative assessment: Revisiting the territory. *Assessment in Education, 5*(1), 77–84.

Schmoker, M. 2002. The real causes of higher achievement. *SEDLetter, 14*(2). Retrieved 12 May 2004 from http://www.sedl.org/pubs/sedletter/v14n02/1.html

Schmoker, M., & R. Marzano. 1999. Realizing the promise of standards-based education. *Educational Leadership, 56*(6): 17–21. Retrieved 14 May 2004 from http://www.ascd.org/publications/ed_lead/199903/schmoker.html

Schunk, D. H. 1996. Goal and self-evaluative influences during children's cognitive skill learning. *American Educational Research Journal, 33*, 359–382.

Shepard, L. A. 2001. The role of classroom assessment in teaching and learning. In V. Richardson (ed.), *Handbook of research on teaching*, 4th ed. (pp. 1066–1101). Washington, DC: American Educational Research Association.

Shepard, L. A. 2008. Formative assessment: Caveat emptor. In C. Dwyer (ed.), *The future of assessment: Shaping teaching and learning* (pp. 279–303). New York: Lawrence Erlbaum Associates.

Shutes, R., & S. Peterson. 1994. Seven reasons why a textbook is not a curriculum. *NASSP Bulletin, 78*(565): 11–20.

Stiggins, R. J., & J. Chappuis. 2011. *Student-involved assessment* for *learning*, 6th ed. Upper Saddle River, NJ: Pearson Education.

White, B. Y., & J. R. Frederiksen. 1998. Inquiry, modeling, and metacognition: Making science accessible to all students. *Cognition and Instruction, 16*(1), 3–118.

Wiggins, G., & J. McTighe. 1998. *Understanding by design*. Alexandria, VA: Association for Supervision and Curriculum Development.

INDEX

A

Achievement
- clear purpose and, 26–27
- impact of formative assessment on, 22–27
- reflecting current level of, in academic grade, 341–342
- reporting in grading, 340–341

Achievement portfolios, 367
Activities
- planning instructional, 75
- using, in place of curriculum, 73–74

Affective goals, 44
Akron Global Polymer Academy, 269
Alignment, checking work for, 66
Ames, C., 28, 30
Analysis as reasoning pattern, 47, 48–49
Analytic rubric, 190, 226
Anderson, Laura, 143–144
Aptitude, 353
Arter, J. A., 154*n*, 230*n*, 233*n*, 250*n*, 251*n*
Artifacts
- assessment of individual, 370
- classification of, 93
- keeping track of, 376
- performance assessment and, 91
- as product target, 205
- project portfolios and, 367
- selection of, for portfolios, 369–371

Arts
- disposition targets in, 59
- knowledge targets in, 46
- product targets in, 58
- reasoning target in, 51
- skill targets in, 55

Assessment
- balanced, 20–21
- competencies in, 10–12
- critiquing overall, 192
- formative, 4, 5, 6, 19, 342
- interpreting and using results, 77
- involvement of students in, 8–9
- keys to quality, 3–10
- performance, 90–91, 95–100
- quality control criteria for, 2
- selected response, 89, 93–100
- soundness of design, in classroom, 7–8
- strategies of, for learning, 27–35
- summative, 5, 6, 342
- written response, 90, 95, 97, 99, 100

Assessment blueprints
- assessment *for* learning using, 115
- combining planning decisions into, 126–128, 173–174

Assessment development cycle, 102–104
- for performance assessment, 207–209
  - determining sample size, 208–209
  - determining users and uses, 207–208
  - identifying learning targets, 208
  - selecting methods, 208
- stages in
  - development stage, 103
  - planning stage, 103
  - usage stage, 103

Assessment literacy, 2–3
Assessment methods, 88–93
- in developing selected response assessment, 126
- matching, to learning targets, 93–102
- in performance assessment, 208
- selecting the appropriate, 107
- for written response assessment, 172

Audience
- in creating tasks to elicit good writing, 218
- for portfolio, 375

Authenticity in performance task, 211
Average ratings, 346–347

B

Balanced assessment system, 20–21
Barylski, Jessica, 29–30
Benchmarks. *See* Learning targets
Bias, sources of, that can distort results, 284–286
Black, Paul, 9, 22–23, 151, 246–247
Borderline cases, deciding, with extra evidence, 352
Braun, Shannon, 147–148
Brookhart, S. M., 341, 352
Buck, Michele, 194
Bursuck, W. D., 352
Butler, Neuman, 28, 30

C

Cameron, C., 153*n*
Cause and effect, identifying, 70
Celebration portfolios, 367–368
Chappuis, J., 25*n*, 27, 28*n*, 31*n*, 69, 94*n*, 151, 152*n*, 229*n*, 230*n*, 233*n*, 234*n*, 250*n*, 251*n*, 319*n*, 320*n*, 321*n*, 368*n*, 372, 375, 388
Chappuis, S., 21, 25*n*, 38*n*, 154*n*
Cheating, missing or late work and, 315–316
Children, helping, at home, 78
Cho, Sue, 79–80
Choices, offering, 180–181
Cizek, G. J., 353
Class discussions, 264, 275
- developing topics and questions, 276
- suggestions for effective use of, 276–277

Classification as reasoning pattern, 47, 49
Classrooms, strategies for using rubrics as instructional tools in, 245–250
Clear purpose, 87
- achievement and, 26–27

Clear targets, 42–81, 87
College and Career Readiness Anchor Standards, 275
Commodore, Carol, 21*n*, 38*n*, 52, 56*n*
Common Core State Standards, 60, 74. *See also* Learning targets
- deconstructing, 1

Common Core State Standards Initiative (CCSSI), 45, 51*n*, 55*n*, 57, 58*n*, 100, 101, 102, 275, 276
Common scale, converting entries to, 343
Communication. *See also* Personal communication
- effectiveness of, in classroom assessment, 8
- of learning targets to students, 68–72
- personal, 91–92
- using grades in, 336–340

Comparative reasoning, 47, 49, 70, 96
Competence in classroom assessment, 10–12
Competence portfolios, 367
Conceptual understanding, 45
Conclusions, drawing, 70
Conferences, 264, 279–280
- about and with students, 385–407
  - feedback conferences, 387, 388–390
  - goal-setting conference, 387, 390–393
  - intervention conference, 387, 398
  - progress conference, 387, 394–397
  - showcase conference, 387, 397–398
- developing questions and topics for, 279
- focusing discussion at, 80
- suggestions for effective use of, 279–280
- three-way, 394–395, 396
- two-way, 394–395, 396

Consistency of performance as sampling variable in performance assessment, 209
Content knowledge, mastering, 47
Content of rubric, 227, 229–230
Content standards. *See also* Learning targets
- deconstructing complex, 60–68

Content validity, 211
Contrast, 49
Coverage, avoiding, at expense of learning, 76–77
Criteria
- as categories of quality in analytic rubric, 227
- for rubric structure in performance assessment, 231

Curriculum
- need for good guides, 59–60
- using textbook in place of, 72–73
- written, as not taught, 72–74

Curriculum documents, 42
Cutoff mark, proximity to, in performance assessment, 209
Cynkar, Jessica, 67–68, 317–318

D

Davies, A., 153*n*, 280
Deconstruction
- of content standards, 60–68
  - in mathematics, 63
  - in reading, 64
  - in writing, 65
- Kentucky's flowchart for, 62
- process for, 61
- of product targets, 67

Deduction, 48, 51
Demonstrations, 91
Descriptors
- clustering, into traits, 237–238
- in rubrics, 232–235

Detail, kind of, in rubric for performance assessment, 232–233
Development stage for written response assessment, 174

Dewey, John, 264
Dialogue journals, 282, 283
Discussions, 264, 275
  developing topics and questions, 276
  focusing, at conferences, 80
  suggestions for effective use of, 276–277
Disposition targets, 44, 57–59
  examples of, 59
Dueck, Myron, 129–130
Dye, Kelly, 191–192

E

Eckert, Audrey, 29–30
Effort, reporting, in grading, 340–341
Eidam, Robyn, 29–30
English, target-method match and, 100–101
English language arts
  disposition targets in, 59
  knowledge targets in, 46
  product targets in, 58
  reasoning targets in, 51
  skill targets in, 55
Essential learnings. *See* Learning targets
Evaluation, 70
  as reasoning pattern, 47, 49
Exercises, developing or selecting, 128–144
Extended written response items, 90, 169
  devising, 177–180
  difference between performance assessment and, 210
Extra credit work, 315

F

Factual information, 45
Feedback
  characteristics of effective, 31
  offering regular descriptive, 30–31, 150–151, 246
  understanding and acting on, 78
Feedback conference, keys to success, 288–300
Fill-in-the-blank questions, 89, 133, 135–136
  guidelines for, 142
Final grades. *See also* Grades
  combining information into, 343–344
  combining rubric ratings with other assessment information to get, 348–350
  reporting, 350–354
Fitzgerald, S. F., 353
Focused revision, teaching students, 34, 157, 247–248
Folders, working, 368
Formative assessment
  communication of information, 8
  conditions for, 105–106
  distinguishing between summative assessment and, 24–25
  gathering of data about level of achievement during learning, 342
  impact of, on achievement, 19, 22–27
  for improving learning, 6
  purpose of, 5
  to support student learning, 4
  using, 1
Formative usefulness of rubric, 234–235
Frederiksen, J. R., 32

G

Generalization, 70, 96
  rubric for, 189–190
Gillespie, Kristen, 23–24
Glickman, Carl D., 77
Goals
  affective, 44
  setting, 78
    in performance assessment, 246–247
    for portfolios, 375
    teaching students in, 31–32, 151–153
Goal-setting conference, 387, 390–393
  keys to success, 391–393
Grade-level indicators. *See* Learning targets
Grades. *See also* Final grades
  combining information into final, 343–344
  converting rubric scores to, 345–349
  converting summative assessment information into, 332–363
  as gatekeepers, 332
  reflecting current level of achievement in academic, 341–342
Grading. *See also* Report card grading
  communication of student knowledge in, 1
  converting, to common scale, 343
  guidelines for, 336–342
  involving students in, 353
  norm-referenced, 344–345
  proficiency-based, 351–352
  reporting achievement in, 340–341
  rubric to evaluate practices in, 354–357
  zeroes in, 338–339
Graphs
  general rubric for interpreting, 185
  task-specific rubric for interpreting, 184–185
Gregory, K., 153*n*
Growth portfolios, 366
Guskey, Bailey, 337, 345

H

Harlen, James, 27
Harrison, C., 151
Hattie, Timperley, 30
Health/physical education
  disposition targets in, 59
  knowledge targets in, 46
  product targets in, 58
  reasoning targets in, 51
  skill targets in, 55
Heilman, Christine, 106–107
Herzog, Bruce, 249–250
Hiebert, J., 77
Holistic rubric, 226

I

Indicators, 227
Induction, 51
  Inductive inference, 48
Inference, 48, 70, 96, 97
  deductive, 48
  inductive, 48
  as reasoning pattern, 47
Inference questions, student-generated, 156
Information
  combining, into final grade, 343–344
  deciding where to keep, 306–310
  factual, 45
  summarizing, 342–345
  tracking and reporting, 77
  weighting, 343
Instructional questions and answers, 264, 270–275
  developing
    to assess knowledge and understanding, 270
    to assess reasoning, 270–271
  effective formative use of, 271–274
  summative use of, 275
Instructional tools, strategies for using rubrics as, in classroom, 245–250
Interference in performance task, 212
Interpretive exercises, 132
Interpretive items, devising, 179–180
Intervention conference, 387, 398
Interviews, 264, 279–280
  developing questions and topics for, 279
  suggestions for effective use of, 279–280
Items. *See also specific*
  assessing knowledge mastery, 177–178
  developing, for written response assessment, 174–181
  developing or selecting, 128–144
  formula for, 150
  writing, 134–136
    guidelines for quality, 136–142
Item types
  choosing, 133
  turning reading proposition into different, 136
  turning social studies proposition into different, 135

J

James, Amy, 104–105
Johnston, P. H., 273
Journals, 264, 281–284
  dialogue, 282, 283
  personal, 282, 283
  response, 282, 283
Judgment as basis for performance assessment, 204
Juxtaposition, 49

K

Kendall, J., 45, 46
Kentucky Department of Education, 62*n*, 63*n*, 64*n*
Klauer, K. J., 40, 50
Knight, Janice, 283
Knowing via reference, 45
Knowledge
  classifying targets as, 46–47
  developing instructional questions to assess, 270
  establishing base, in developing rubrics, 235–236
  identifying prerequisite or underlying, 61, 66
  procedural, 45, 53
Knowledge learning targets, 44–47
  assessing, 93–96
  converting, to student-friendly language, 69
  examples of, 46
Knowledge mastery
  items assessing, 177–178
  items combining, with reasoning, 178–179
Knowledge propositions, 131

L

Language arts, target-method match and, 100–101
Late work, cheating and, 315–316
Learning
  assessment for, using assessment blueprints, 115
  avoiding coverage at expense of, 76–77
  selected response assessment for, 148–157
  strategies of assessment for, 27–35

use of performance assessment to support, 205
using performance task as assessment for, 250–252
Learning intentions. *See* Learning targets
Learning logs, 282, 284
Learning outcomes. *See* Learning targets
Learning progressions. *See* Learning targets
Learning targets, 6
alignment of, in developing rubric for performance assessment, 227, 229
benefits of clear, 74–80
clarity of, 42–81
communicating, to students, 68–72
converting knowledge and reasoning, to student-friendly language, 69
coverage of, in performance assessment, 217
designing lessons to focus on, 32–33, 153–156, 247
in developing selected response assessment, 126
focusing on, in portfolios, 368–375
linking final grade to, 350–351
matching assessment methods to, 93–102
in performance assessment, 205, 208
portfolios and, 369
providing students with clear and understandable vision of, 28–29, 148–149, 245
specifying the intended, 106
types of, 44–59
disposition, 44, 57–59
knowledge, 44–47
product, 44, 55–57
reasoning, 44, 47–54
skill, 44, 54–55
for written response assessment, 172
Lee, C., 151
Lesson objectives. *See* Learning targets
Levels
content of, for rubric in performance assessment, 233
identifying samples that illustrate, in performance assessment, 238–239
on rubric, 227
Line-up, 277–278
Lists, 181–183
Lloyd, Jim, 6–7
Logs, 264, 281–284

M

Main idea, determining, 70
Marshall, B., 151
Marzano, R. D., 45, 49, 73
Matching items, 89, 133, 134–135
guidelines for, 141–142
Mathematics
deconstructing standard, 63
disposition targets in, 59
knowledge targets in, 46
problem solving, 50
product targets in, 58
reasoning target in, 51
skill targets in, 55
target-method match and, 101–102
Mattingly, Ken, 113–115
McKnight, C. C., 73
McTighe, J., 49, 76
Mean, 344
Measures of central tendency, 344
Median, 344
Missing work, cheating and, 315–316
Models of strong and weak work, using, 150
Motivation, grades and, 336–340
Mukai, Aaron, 79–80
Multiple-choice items, 89, 133, 134
guidelines for, 138–140
Multi-trait rubrics, 226
Munk, D. D., 352
Murray, D., 218

N

Norm-referenced grading, 344–345

O

Observation as basis for performance assessment, 204
O'Connor, Ken, 313*n*, 315, 338, 341, 344, 352
Online testing, 122
Oral examinations, 264, 280–281
developing questions for, 280–281
suggestions for effective use of, 281
Overbay, Jeff, 32–33, 75–76, 195–196

P

Parents, benefits of clear learning targets to, 78–80
Pattern of ratings, 347–348
Performance assessment, 204–253
assessment development cycle for, 207–209
determining sample size, 208–209
determining users and uses, 207–208
identifying learning targets, 208
selecting methods, 208
based on observation and judgment, 90–91
conditions influencing selection of, 206
defined, 204
difference between extended written response and, 210
for knowledge targets, 95–100
learning targets in, 205
parts of, 204
rubrics in, 204–205
selecting, revising, or developing rubrics in, 226–240
selecting, revising, or developing tasks in, 210–225
as subjective, 204
timing in using, 205–206
tools as opportunities for practice, 250
use stage in, 240
Performances, 93
Performance tasks
as assessment for learning, 250–252
content of, 211–212
evaluating, for quality in performance assessment, 221–225
sampling for, in performance assessment, 216–221
selecting, revising or developing task, 210–225
structure of, in performance assessment, 212–215
Personal communication
as classroom assessment, 264–296
classroom discussions, 275–278
developing topics and questions, 276
suggestions for effective use of, 276–277
conferences and interviews, 279–280
developing questions and topics for, 279
suggestions for effective use of, 279–280
instructional questions and answers, 270–275
journals and logs, 281–284
oral examinations, 280–281
developing questions for, 280–281
suggestions for effective use of, 281
sources of bias that can distort results, 284–286
timing in use of, 266–269
sampling, 267–269
wait time, 269
gathering of information about students through, 91–92
partial match for assessing skill targets, 99
poor match for assessing product targets, 100
strong match with knowlege targets, 96
Personal journals, 282, 283
Peterson, S., 73
Petry, Jody, 274*n*
Phye, G. D., 48, 50
Physical education. *See* Health/physical education
Pickering, D., 49
Planning decisions, combining into assessment blueprint, 110–111, 126–128, 173–174
Planning stage for written response assessment, 171–174
Poeppelman, Sara, 339–340
Points, counting rubric levels as, 346
Portfolios, 92, 364–384
achievement, 367
artifact selection for, 369–371
audience for, 375
celebration, 367–368
competence, 367
contents of, 368–375
creator of, 364
decision making and, 370–371
defined, 364
entry cover sheets, 373
goal setting for, 375
growth, 366
keys to successful use of, 376–377
learning targets and, 369
project, 367
sampling for, 370
sharing options for, 375–376
student self-reflection for, 372, 374
subject of, 364
work sample annotations for, 371–372
Predicting, 70
Procedural knowledge, 45, 53, 56
Products, classifying targets as, 56–57
Product targets, 54, 205
assessing, 100
deconstructing, 67
examples of, 91
focus of teaching and assessment, 55–57
in terms of artifacts, 44
Proficiency-based grading, 351–352
Progress, tracking, reflecting on, and sharing, 78
Progress conference, 387, 394–397
focusing on achievement status, 394
focusing on growth over time, 394
follow-up, 396–397
identifying participants, 394–395
preparing parents or other adults, 395–396
preparing students, 395
three-way, 394–395, 396
two-way, 394–395, 396
Project portfolios, 367

Projects, using, in place of curriculum, 73–74
Propositions, 149
defined, 130
knowledge, 131
reasoning, 131–132
writing, 130
Purpose, clarity of, 19
in classroom assessment, 4–6

Q

Quality
designing lessons to focus on, 32–33
evaluating performance task for, in performance assessment, 221–225
evaluating rubrics for, 240, 241–244
keys to classroom assessment, 20
sorting student work by, 236–237
Questions
developing
for conferences, 279
for interviews, 279
for oral examinations, 280–281
fill-in-the-blank, 89, 133, 135–136
guidelines for, 142
instructional, 264, 270–275
student-generated inference, 156

R

Rachor, R. E., 353
RAFTS writing task design, 218, 221
Raizen, S. A., 73
Ramaprasad, A., 27
Ratings
average, 346–347
pattern of, 347–348
Raw score, recording achievement information by, 316, 318
Reading proposition, turning, into different item types, 136
Reading standard, deconstructing, 64
Reasoning
classifying targets as, 52
comparative, 47, 49, 96
developing instructional questions and answers to assess, 270–271
evaluative, 49
identifying prerequisite or underlying, 61, 66
items combining knowledge mastery with, 178–179
patterns of, 47
propositions in, 131–132
relationships among patterns of, 50–51
Reasoning learning targets, 47–54
assessing, 96–98
converting, to student-friendly language, 69
specifying thought processes of students, 44
student-friendly definitions of, 70
Record keeping, 297–331
guidelines, 311
organize entries by learning represented, 311–314
recording achievement information by raw score, 316, 318
tracking information about work habits and social skills separately, 314–316
options for student, 318–323
preliminary decisions, 299
differentiating information for formative or summative use, 299–311
Reference, knowing via, 45
Report card grading. *See also* Grading
challenges of, 334–335
steps to accurate, fair, and defensible, 354
Response journals, 282
assessment for learning with, 283
Revision, teaching students focused, 34, 157, 247–248
Rowe, M. B., 269
Rubric levels, counting, as points, 346
Rubric ratings, combining, with other assessment information to get final grade, 348–350
Rubrics, 90, 183–192
analytic, 190, 226
characteristics of good, 231
content of, 227, 229–230
converting scores, to grades, 345–349
creating general, 189
creating task-specific, 186–188
descriptors in, 232–235
to evaluate grading practices, 354–357
evaluating, for quality, 240, 241–244
formative usefulness of, 234–235
general, for interpreting a graph, 185
for a generalization, 189–190
holistic, 226
length of, 230
levels on, 227
multi-trait, 226
in performance assessment, 204–205
process for developing, 235–240
selecting, revising, or developing, in performance assessment, 226–240
strategies for using, as instructional tools in classroom, 245–250
structure of, 228–229, 231–232
task-specific, for interpreting a graph, 184–185
task specific requirements in, 235
testing and revising as needed in performance assessment, 239–240

S

Sadler, Royce, 27
Samples
gathering, of student performances or products, 236
identifying that illustrate levels in performance assessment, 238–239
Sample size
determining
in performance assessment, 208–209
in selected response assessment, 126
in written response assessment, 172–173
determining appropriate, 107–108
Sampling, 108–110, 267–269
for performance tasks in performance assessment, 216–221
for portfolios, 370
Schmidt, W. H., 73
Schmoker, M., 73, 77
Schoo, Elizabeth, 71–72
Schroeder, Elizabeth, 301–302, 322–323
Schunk, D. H., 28
Science, 50
disposition targets in, 59
knowledge targets in, 46
product targets in, 58
reasoning target in, 51
skill targets in, 55
Scoring guides
defined, 181
preparing, 181–192
Scoring procedures, developing or selecting, 128–144
Selected response assessment, 122–158
developing, 125
for learning, 148–157
mastery of discrete elements of knowledge and, 93–94
misconceptions about, 124
planning steps in, 125–128
for reasoning targets, 96–97
for skill targets, 99
timing in using, 124–125
using steps in, 128–148
Self-assessment
being prepared for, 78
teaching students, 31–32, 151–153
in performance assessment, 246–247
Self-reflection, engaging students in, 34, 157, 248
Sharing options for portfolios, 375–376
Shepard, L. A., 27, 28, 30
Short answer items, 90, 169
devising, 175–177
Showcase conference, 387, 397–398
conducting, 397
follow-up, 398
preparing students, 397
Shutes, R., 73
Skills
classifying targets as, 54–55
identifying prerequisite or underlying, 61, 66
Skill targets, 44, 54–55
assessing, 99
Smith, E., 218*n*
Smith, Janna, 9–10
Social skills, tracking information about, 314–316
Social studies, 50
disposition targets in, 59
knowledge targets in, 46
product targets in, 58
reasoning targets in, 51
skill targets in, 55
turning proposition, into different item types, 135
Sound design, 87–115
Standards-driven environment, goal of grading in, 335
Standards for Mathematical Practice, 45
Stiggins, R. J., 21*n*, 38*n*, 57–58, 77–78, 94*n*, 146*n*, 154*n*, 314
Stigler, James W., 77
Strong work, using examples and models of, 245–246
Student-friendly language, converting knowledge and reasoning learning targets to, 69
Student performance or products, gathering sample of, 236
Students
benefits of clear learning targets to, 77–78
choices in performance task, 211–212
communicating learning targets to, 68–72
engaging, in self-reflection, 34, 157, 248
involving, in classroom assessment, 8–9
involving, in grading, 353
providing, with clear and understandable vision of learning target, 28–29, 148–149, 245
teaching focused revision, 34, 157, 247–248
teaching self-assessment and goal setting, 31–32, 151–153
Student self-reflection for portfolios, 372, 374
Student work, sorting, by level of quality, 236–237
Summarizing, 70
Summative assessment, 6, 322–323, 342
communication in, 8
converting, into grades, 332–363
distinguishing between formative assessment and, 24–25
purpose of, 5

Summative data, reviewing, for accuracy, 342
Swanson, Sierra, 303–304
Synthesis as reasoning pattern, 47, 50

T

Target alignment, 211
Target-method match, 98
  English and, 100–101
  language arts and, 100–101
  mathematics and, 101–102
Targets. *See also* Learning targets
  clarity of, in classroom assessment, 6–7
Tasks
  audience in creating, to elicit good writing, 218
  developing or selecting, 128–144
Task-specific rubrics
  creating, 186–188
  requirements in, 235
T-charts, 49
Teachers
  benefits of clear learning targets to, 74–77
  competencies of, 10–12
Testing time, determining, 144
Tests. *See also* Assessment
  assembling, 142
  combining planning decisions into blueprint for, 110–111
  steps in developing, 112–113
Textbook, using, in place of curriculum, 72–73
Three-way conference, 394–395, 396
Topics
  in creating tasks to elicit good writing, 219
  developing, for conferences and interviews, 279
Traits, clustering descriptors into, 237–238
True/false items, 89, 133, 134
  guidelines for, 140–141
Twenty Questions, 49
Two-way conference, 394–395, 396

U

Understanding, developing instructional questions to assess, 270
Units, using, in place of curriculum, 73–74
Urban, Kim, 155
Users
  in performance assessment, 207–208
  in selected response assessment, 125–126
  in written response assessment, 172
Uses
  in performance assessment, 207–208
  in selected response assessment, 125–126
  in written response assessment, 172
Use stage, 192–193

V

Validity, content, 211
Venn diagrams, 49

W

Wait time, 269
Weak work, using examples and models of, 245–246
White, B. Y., 32
Whiteboards, 269
Whole-class response systems, 269
Wiggins, G., 76
Wiliam, Dylan, 9, 22–23, 151, 246–247
Work
  tracking information about habits, 314–316
  using examples and models of strong and weak, 29–30
Working folders, 368
Work sample annotations for portfolios, 371–372
Writing, creating tasks to elicit good, 217–221
Writing items, 134–136
Writing standard, deconstructing, 65
Written response assessment, 169–197
  development stage for, 174
  for knowledge targets, 95
  for learning, 194–195
  planning stage for, 171–174
  for product targets, 100
  for reasoning targets, 97
  requiring student to construct answers, 90
  for skill targets, 99
timing in using, 171

Z

Zeroes in grading, 338–339